The Christian and His Decisions

The Christian and His Decisions

An Introduction to Christian Ethics

HARMON L. SMITH
LOUIS W. HODGES

ABINGDON PRESS
NASHVILLE AND NEW YORK

THE CHRISTIAN AND HIS DECISIONS

Standard Book Number: 687-06997-1
Library of Congress Catalog Card Number: 76-84714

SET UP, PRINTED AND BOUND BY THE PARTHENON PRESS, AT NASHVILLE, TENNESSEE, UNITED STATES OF AMERICA

To Bettye and Helen, good wives

Foreword

It is the custom these days to write a "foreword" in which one anticipates, and thereby cancels, the harsher critiques of reviewers and readers. One must never be direct in this matter, however. He is obliged by common practice to state his purpose, since everybody will then have to agree that his is the most apt method of securing that purpose! By building his case beforehand the author limits the less-than-kind critic to the opinion that he should have written another book, not this one. In this vein, therefore, here is what we have understood ourselves to be about.

We have written for the individual interested in being introduced to Christian ethics, whatever might be the basis of his interest. We seek to introduce the reader to a particular way of doing ethics, a way we have labeled "principled contextualism." It has been our intention not to provide a history of Christian ethics in the twentieth century but to show how some Christian ethicists seek to operate. That way of doing ethics is confessionally dependent on the theological insights of classical Protestant theology and avowedly indebted to the work of modern social scientists. We have sought to write within the broad framework of Protestant theology as it is being hammered out in our time. We have sought also to suggest the bearing of that theology on some of the chief problems of the modern world.

In the introductory chapter we aim not so much to do Christian ethics as to look at the doing of Christian ethics. The remainder of the book consists of three main sections. Part One deals with the theological foundations of Christian morality. Part Two develops the method and principles of Christian ethics which derive from the theological commitments delineated in Part One. Part Three focuses on a variety of particular moral problems of our time in light of the theological commitments and ethical principles in parts One and Two. In Part Three we have sought neither to deal with all the problems nor to give birth to *the* Christian resolution of any problem. We have written illustrative chapters in order to show the process by which the Christian might approach any moral situation.

In parts One and Two we have selected from among what we regard as the most important theological documents of the last few decades. Hopefully this method will make available under one cover a variety of writings by some of the most outstanding theologian-ethicists. We have not sought to include treatises by all the important molders of Christian theology. Our guiding principle in selection has been to find respected authors with concise treatments of the subjects we believe to be crucial to an ethic of principled contextualism. In Part Three we have written our own essays.

Throughout the preparation of the book we have continually been reminded of our indebtedness to people without whose help these pages could not have found their way into print. They include, especially, the librarians at Duke Divinity School and Washington and Lee University. Among them are our former teachers and our past and present students who have built in us the desire to write, as well as prompted us to refine our thinking to its present grain. Our wives, to whom we dedicate this effort, have encouraged and supported us in the act of writing. They, along with others less "close to home," have given critical appraisal (not always solicited!) of work in progress and sometimes not progressing. We acknowledge a special debt to Miss Florence Russell for her labors in preparing the index and to our secretaries, Mrs. Marjorie Poindexter and Mrs. Vivian Crumpler, for their patience as well as for their skill at the keyboard.

A special grant from the Ford Foundation to Washington and Lee University made possible a leave of absence for one of us in the fall of 1968. During that time portions of the manuscript were completed, and attention was given to details of publication. We gladly express gratitude to the Ford Foundation and to Washington and Lee University.

We are aware of our many dependencies, just as we remain acutely conscious that we alone stand responsible for whatever unrefined or erroneous words this volume contains.

LOUIS W. HODGES
The Department of Religion
Washington and Lee University
Lexington, Virginia

HARMON L. SMITH
The Divinity School
Duke University
Durham, North Carolina

Contents

Introduction

Christian Ethics: An Overview

I. THE NATURE OF ETHICS

The formal study of human behavior, whether in terms of empirical observation or philosophical investigation, is a very ancient and honored undertaking. Indeed, from the earliest periods of recorded history man has displayed an unerring sensitivity toward his conduct. He has developed elaborate regulatory schemes—sometimes highly ritualistic and symbolic, and sometimes very earthly and pragmatic—in order both to govern his actions and to account for them in some meaningful way. In the most primitive times, the concerns of ethics were closely interwoven with the entire social fabric. Prior to the time of Hippocrates (500 B.C.), for example, medicine and religion were virtually inseparable; and the shaman served as a tribal leader who represented in his individual person all the interests of the entire group. In fact, even after politics had become the special province of a designated tribal leader, the medicine man still united in himself the roles of physician and priest. But as we have come less and less to suppose any direct correspondence between natural occurrence and supernatural activity, the study of how human life ought to be conducted has become more and more specialized.

In consequence of this development it has become common in certain quarters of the modern world to question not only the fruitfulness of such an enterprise but even its very possibility. Nevertheless, systematic inquiry in the discipline proceeds apace with the establishment of courses in academic communities and through research and writing. It is the task of Christian ethics to bridge the gap between the concrete decisions which human beings must make and the theological framework in which Christians find meaning and purpose. Every man, of course, has his own way of spanning that gap. Every man has an ethic, either explicit or implicit, critical or uncritical. No one is wholly without some method, however systematic or chaotic, for formulating the answers to his own moral questions. People unavoidably make decisions and act. Why and how people decide and act is what ethics is all about. The purpose of this chapter, then, is to indicate the nature of ethical investigation in general and to note the characteristic ingredients of a distinctly Christian ethic.

A. ETHICS AND MORALS

In any description of ethics as a discipline it is helpful to distinguish at the outset between "ethics" and "morals." Though these terms have come to possess virtually synonymous meanings in current English usage, there are old and appropriate distinctions which employ these words to refer to different aspects of the total human activity of the regulation of conduct. We in fact have need for such a verbal distinction to mark the line of separation between the "moral" and the "ethical."

In the daily round of the sensitive person there is constantly raised the question, What must I do? or, What good shall I pursue? That is the moral question. The sum total of answers one gives to that question would constitute a set of morals. But the question, What must or shall I do? raises the logically prior question, Where do I turn to find out what I will or should do? That is the question of ethics. Morals has as its immediate end the matter of human action. Ethics has as its immediate end the reflection upon the various moral alternatives. Ethics is the science of moral value.

Morality and the desire to live a morally regulated life, then, serve as the basic motives behind the study of ethics and constitute at the same time a major part of the subject matter of ethics. As such, the formal study of ethics has as its practical end the informing of human conduct through a rational confrontation of oneself as a decision-making person in the context of the total moral environment. The larger subject matter is the entire process of decision-making. Ethics, generally defined, is man reflecting self-consciously on the act of being a moral being. It is the search for some kind of rational coherence in the regulation of conduct; it is the human actor "getting wise to himself." Ethics represents the attempt through the employment of reason to make conduct consistent with character.

So it is that all men are in some way ethicists. Some are more critically so, some less critically, but all have some means by which to deal with the probing question, Where shall I turn to find out what I ought? One may turn to a peer group, for example, thereby endowing that group with final authority. Or he may turn to some criterion like, Can I get away with doing this? He may turn instead to the traditional code of morals of some religious order. In practice most of us are not aware of our choice to turn here or there, but that choice is presupposed by and reflected in every decision we make. Ethics as a systematic discipline is born when we begin to reflect rationally and systematically upon characteristic ways of deciding moral questions.

The crucial implication of this for our purposes is that the truly penetrating study of ethics requires direct personal involvement of the ethicist, his looking at himself as a decision-making creature. Indeed, it is precisely this self-consciousness which distinguishes the discipline of ethics from the historical study of systems of morality, which is the study of history and not of ethics. Ethics as a discipline is thus inextricably tied up with morality. For that reason one who divorces morality from ethics invites irrationality in his deciding and leaves himself subject to the anarchic forces of individual whim and fancy or to whatever forces a social group may bring to bear on him.

B. ETHICAL SYSTEMS AS DERIVATIVE

Just as ethics as a discipline stands logically (though not normally chronologically) prior to morality it also logically follows another discipline—namely, metaphysics. The answer to the ethical question Where shall I turn to find out what I ought? cannot be provided by ethics itself. For that answer one must turn ultimately to some philosophical *a priori*, some judgment about reality or about value that in itself expresses finality. The answer given to the ethical question always reflects a basic commitment to something or someone which is taken to be ultimately real, ultimately true, ultimately good. The answer is thus in the final analysis a matter of faith or commitment; it consists of a judgment which can stand on nothing outside itself.

This can be readily illustrated in terms of Hedonist morality. The substance of Hedonism is "eat, drink, and be merry, for tomorrow you die." If you ask why one should regulate his conduct in terms of eating, drinking, and making merry the answer clearly is that death is the ultimate reality. All that matters in the present moment is human life and the maximization of personal pleasure. There is no transcendent purpose which endows human existence with meaning; there is no higher realm to which one might appeal for significance in human life. Man becomes the measure of all things, and he himself constitutes the only relevant consideration in the determination of his conduct. This conviction about ultimate reality is not an ethical conviction but a metaphysical one. Yet it determines the ethics and the morality of the practicing Hedonist. To be sure, contemporary Hedonist practice is rarely worked out in this systematic fashion; but it is now, as it was in ancient Greece, reflective of the loss of a sense of transcendent purpose or superhuman reality in the world.

The derivative character of ethics can be illustrated also in terms of two contemporary and competing economic theories: Marxism and *laissez-faire* capitalism. However curious it may seem, these two are at one in their basic assumptions about the meaning of human life. Marxist systems demand that the major portion of human effort be directed toward economic production. This demand is a moral judgment in that it presumes to declare what *ought* to be done. But behind this judgment is the presupposition that the final meaning of human life is to be found in the production and distribution of goods. This is a judgment about what is ultimately real, and therefore good, in the world. It is a metaphysical judgment, not an ethical one, and it is the assumption on which the morality of Marxism is based.

In much the same way *laissez-faire* (i.e., non-interference) capitalism derives its moral principles. Do whatever the unrestricted market will allow and permit trade to follow "natural" developments, capitalism preaches. Whatever produces wealth is a worthy enterprise, and it follows that the safety and well-being of the consumer and the producer may be largely ignored except when too severe neglect of the consumer threatens sales. The priests of this cult would therefore enthrone the sacred "law" of supply and demand. The purists, of whom few are left, assume that they are leaving the human economic enterprise at the disposal of some "unseen hand" which will work toward humane goals if left free of purposive human planning. If there is a demand for a product it is right to produce it and distribute it without interference from any agency, especially any government agency, regardless of its effect on those who produce it and consume it. This whole set of guidelines for behavior reflects the antecedent metaphysical assumption that material wealth is in itself the end most worthy of pursuit, an end of greater importance than the human beings involved. And that is the same basic assumption as the Marxist conviction! It is interesting to note that these two moralities which dominate the contemporary economic and political scene share with Hedonism the loss of a transcendent reference by which all systems of thought and action are to be judged. They represent the radically secular orientation of modern life.

The point, then, is that every moral judgment is rooted finally in some faith assumption, some *a priori,* some metaphysical judgment either expressed or implied. Ethics is concerned with the movement from these basic commitments to the realm of moral decisions.

For Christian ethics the ultimate reality, the *a priori,* is God whom Jesus revealed, the ground of human life and the proper referent of all human thought. The task of Christian ethics is to show the moral implications of the fact of God's transcendent reality, that is, in other words, to show the bearing and relevance of God's will for and judgment of human behavior. For this reason Christian ethics can never be divorced from Christian theology. In Christianity, as everywhere, ethics is a derivative discipline logically prior to morality but a discipline which reflects antecedent metaphysical assumptions and expresses *a priori* commitments.

II. ESSENTIALS OF CHRISTIAN ETHICS

Christian ethics has not seemed to some observers to be really distinctive. After all, Christians have been known to adopt first one and then another standard of behavior. In one moment Christians have been known to go docily to the wild beasts in Roman arenas and in another moment to be fierce soldiers of war. When the emperor Constantine adopted Christianity and found military success fighting under the sign of the Christian cross he had all his troops baptized, but with their sword-wielding arm held out of the water! Sometimes Christians seem to counsel distributive justice, and at other times they advocate justice tempered by mercy. Lack of agreement among Christians about moral matters has been a source of surprise to observers and the ground of not a few attacks upon Christianity. Christians, moreover, frequently act alongside people of quite different persuasion for some common goal, but for reasons very different from those which motivate non-Christians. The present movement in the field of civil rights, for example, has produced alliances, sometimes temporary and tenuous, between Christians and organizations like the Congress on Racial Equality. The action of Christians does not always appear to be different from the action of non-Christians.

Some observers are greatly puzzled,

therefore, when one mentions "Christian ethics." They do not understand what the phrase means. It seems that there is no such thing under the sun. The reason for this is that they cannot discern a common body of ethical teachings universally applicable for Christian behavior. Though Christians have taken some rather distinctive forms of action (like going to the beasts) the unique ingredient in the acts of Christians does not inhere in the nature of the thing done but rather in the reason for doing that thing. The distinctive ingredient is not the "what" of action but the "why." Christian morality is thus not a list of decisions already made and handed down by God but rather a way of deciding moral matters. *Christian ethics is not a study of codes of ethics but of ways Christians go about deciding.* In one sense, consequently, it would be proper to claim that there is no Christian ethics, only ethics as done by Christians. It is to some of the essentials which give Christian ethics its distinctive character that we now turn.

A. AN ACKNOWLEDGING ETHIC

One fundamental characteristic of Christian ethics is its responsive character. In brief the notion of response means that man is not, in the first place, the inventor of ethical content, just as he is not, in the second place, the initiator of moral action. Rather, man "acknowledges" the will of God and *responds* to it. The initiative and the authority lie in God's hands.

To claim that Christian ethics is responsive in content is to say that man is to discover what God wills and to consider that to be his duty. This stands in contrast to various attempts in human history to build or invent systems of morality. These attempts always presuppose some unquestionable criterion for the judgment of moral acts, most commonly the criterion being the utility of the act for achieving a preconceived end. Does it work? is the central question in such systems. More is to follow on utilitarian considerations in Christian morality, but for now the chief point is that Christian ethics is never the attempt to set up merely by human imagination and inventiveness a system of morality which will "work." Christian ethics is to be distinguished also from systems built on humanly defined goals. For the Christian it is God, not man, who finally establishes the justification of an act. There is a clear answer to the old question, Does God will it because it is good, or is it good because God wills it? For the Christian a thing or act is good because God wills it. To answer otherwise would be to presuppose that there is outside God some independently existing reality capable of establishing values to which God merely assents. This clearly would be nonsense in light of the very meaning of the word "God" for Christianity, i.e., the ground of all being.

So it is that the Christian claims that the content of the right and the good is already established and that it is man's task to respond to or acknowledge that antecedent reality. But this presupposes some means of discovering or coming to know the content of God's will. Knowledge of God's will is available, says the Christian, through the instrumentality of revelation. This term "revelation," smacking as it does of intuitionism, is a scorned word in the twentieth century, but it or some substitute with the same meaning is essential to Christian thought. By revelation the Christian does not properly mean (though some have so understood it) a kind of "bolt out of the blue" directive from God. Nor does it mean what Fundamentalists take it to mean—divine dictation of propositional truths, God's communication of *words* to man either audibly or inaudibly. Revelation does not have to do finally with the communication of truths, these being always human creations. Rather, revelation has to do with man's coming to perceive God as a living reality in human experience. Archbishop William Temple states it clearly: "What is offered to man's apprehension in any specific revelation is not truth concerning God but the living God Himself." "There is no such thing as revealed truth. There are truths of revelation; but they are not themselves directly revealed." [1]

The focal point of this revelation is Jesus of Nazareth whom Christians regard as the Christ, the "anointed one." The common claim of the early Christian church was that by seeing Jesus men gained insight into both God and man. His life, they claimed, showed what human life is authentically when bound up with God. Just how this impression was gained and just how these credentials were established is the province of systematic theology and need not concern us at this point. The critical issue is that Christians claim that the nature of man and of man's duty—i.e., the nature of God's will for man—is seen through the life and work of Jesus of Nazareth. He embodied God's will and thus is recognized as showing man the content of that will. It is precisely to that content that the Christian is to respond morally.

Thus Christian ethics rules out a subjectivist criterion of value, a criterion which is increasingly widespread in the contemporary world. Subjectivism assumes that a thing is valuable, good, or right merely *because a man values it.* How often it has been said in undergraduate classrooms that if a person values a thing it *is* valuable for him! The idea here is that his valuing it is what constitutes it a valuable thing, *for him.*

[1] *Nature, Man, and God* (New York: Macmillan, 1934), pp. 322, 316. On this subject the best contemporary treatment is John Baillie's *The Idea of Revelation in Recent Thought* (New York: Columbia University Press, 1956).

Somehow the circularity of this talk seems to escape subjectivists. The basic flaw is readily apparent, however, when one observes that food, for instance, is valuable not because man values it but because the value of food for human life is built into the very nature of human beings. The fact that one should eat is true not *because* man apprehends it. The value of food is established antecedently to man's valuing it. The psychic need for positive and mutual personal relationships in like manner makes love valuable independently of one's valuing it. The subjective state of valuing or disvaluing is quite irrelevant to the actual, the real, value of food or of love for a man.[2] It is in this fashion that value, right, and good are realities established in creation independently of the subjective appropriation of them by men. Without man's internalizing activity, of course, these real values do not control his behavior. In order for them to remake him he must acknowledge them—i.e., respond to their reality—and in this sense man is an active participant in establishing ethical duty. It remains, however, that the content of the right is not something which man can ordain but something which is ordained of God.

But there is a second sense in which Christian ethics is a response ethic. It has to do with the dynamic, the power, the initiative for action. In Christianity the initiative comes from God, an initiative to which men may only respond. Many religious ethics as well as nonreligious disciplines seek to aid men in the search for God and for the clue to the good life. Contemporary Unitarianism is one example of such a system in which the dynamic is self-contained in man. Other religious ethics would go so far as to picture man in the role of placating or controlling God through mysterious incantations or prayers seeking to have God do man's bidding. The Baalist cults of the ancient Hebrew world provide an example, as does the popular practice today in some Christian circles which presumes in prayer to advise God on how to run his universe.

Christian ethics is a response ethic in that it sees God as the primary actor, the initiator of relationships between himself and man. In the Christian view God seeks man before man seeks God. God comes to man and delivers to him the clue to the good life, reveals to him the way to authentic existence. God has found man, has spoken clearly to him, and thereby prompts as subsequent response man's moral action. The dynamic behind Christian ethics is thus God's prior action which evokes man's response.

In this connection it is to be noted not only that God has sought out man but that, in the Christian understanding, the divine initiative includes the establishment of a system of sanctions which encourages man to respond.

[2] Cf. H. Richard Niebuhr, "The Center of Value," reprinted below, pp. 161-73.

There is in the nature of things a necessity for man's obedience to God's will if man is to become a whole person. Note for instance that man is quite free to disobey the rules of the physical world (like jumping off a building) but he is not free to escape the consequences of his behavior (breaking himself on the ground below). Man must live, if he is to live at all, within the preestablished limits of his nature and his world. In like manner there is the necessity for obedience to the nonphysical world if man is to live effectively the life of a person, a *human* being. He is free not to love, of course, but he is not free to escape the consequences of failing to love. This latter fact stands as a ready witness to God's call to man to respond to his initiative. The presence of this inescapable set of consequences is referred to theologically as God's lordship over the created order.

It has been claimed against this view of things that natural science and modern technology are in the process of removing some of the limits formerly thought to bind man. In actual fact both science and technology have the role of showing where the limits are or of defining them in order that man may adjust more effectively to reality. Of all scholarship in our time science preeminently is preserving the sense of discovery of that which is given in the world, that which exists and to which man must adjust. Nor does technology remove the limits placed on human enterprise; rather it seeks to discover more satisfactory ways for man to adjust to the limits. For example, nuclear fission is a more effective adjustment to the necessity for power than is grain fed to a beast of burden.

It is in this fashion, then, that Christian ethics is a response ethic. It begins with God and God's action in human history as the antecedent reality. It does not understand man to be finally in charge of the universe, but rather sees God as the ground of all being, including human being. Christian ethics is theocentric, not anthropocentric. Man's task is not to establish the right but to respond to the right made known by God through Jesus of Nazareth.

B. A CORPORATE ETHIC

To talk about the Christian ethic in terms of a response to the will of God made known through Jesus of Nazareth, however, is not to talk primarily of some list of new rules or of divinely given discursive truths. It is rather to participate in a new way of life, to become part of a new reality, the reality of the Christian community, the church. Here we have a second essential characteristic of Christian ethics—namely, that it is always a corporate ethic. What this means chiefly is that the result of God's call to man, the consequence of his revelation of himself to man, is not new knowledge in the sense of propositional truth or moral directive, but rather a new community, a new organism, a new ethos, in which men come to participate in the new being. In short, the result of God's activity is not new rules but new men living in new community. The New Testament refers to this reality as the rebirth: the old man is passed away; behold, all has become new.

It cannot be our aim here to analyze the nature of the new being in depth nor to explore at length the notion of the church. More detailed analysis will be found among the selections in Part One. But because of the difficulty almost always encountered by Westerners in this century in understanding this corporate phenomenon it is necessary that a few observations be included at this point.

The major claim is that through participation in the new community, the church, the Christian is in the process of being remade, reconstituted as a radically changed entity. This change is possible as a result of the new realities with which the Christian community lives. God in Christ has demonstrated to the world that he accepts the world just as it is, unconditionally, with no strings attached. The church is constituted of those who take seriously that fact and who accept gratefully the fact of their acceptance by God. In the realization of being loved (accepted) by God the believer is freed from the necessity of pretending to be other than he really is. That is to say, the church is enabled to accept unconditionally those who come to it; it is able to love in a radically new and more complete way. The consequence is that those who participate in the community find their greatest longing fulfilled in their being unconditionally accepted by God and the church. The result is that they are freed from the necessity of pretending to be other than they are. In consequence of being loved they gain the basic psychic integrity or union with themselves which is the final inner need of man.[3] In this fashion the personality which has heretofore been divided against itself, being one thing for public view and quite another in private and in the recesses of the subconscious, begins to be reunited with itself. The result is the gradual loss of fear of one's neighbors. Since fear, in one form or another, is the root of most of man's exploitation of man the psychic ground is laid for new ways of relating to neighbor. Therefore, Christian morality as a new way of living is the direct expression of the new way of being, i.e., the new being constituted through participation in the community. The Christian ethic, then, is grounded not in a list of new and more complete rules for a new way of *doing;* it is rather a new way of *becoming,* in community. So it is that

[3] The psychological dynamics of this type of relationship are most effectively discussed by a non-Christian, Erich Fromm, in *The Art of Loving* (New York: Harper, 1956). Reference should be made to Fromm's excellent treatment of what he calls the "productive character orientation."

Christian ethics is a corporate ethic in the deepest possible sense of that word.

Not only is this a corporate ethic at the level of the dynamic of the human personality, but also as regards the content of Christian moral action. That is to say, the Christian is never left finally alone in his attempt to decide what to do in the daily round. These moral decisions are always made in the context of the whole body of the church. The experience of the church provides a vast storehouse of guidelines and principles which can be utilized, though not slavishly followed, by the Christian confronting moral decisions. He is never totally alone and without guidance and support. But at the same time his decisions are never made for him by the group. The corporate ethic is thus to be distinguished from both collectivism and individualism, two idolatries of the modern world, one of the Bolsheviks and the other of *laissez-faire* individualists.

Laissez-faire individualism, one of the idols of modern Western man, pictures man as not only the one who must decide moral issues but also as the source of the criterion by which moral questions are to be judged. This view sees society as a kind of contracted group of individuals who recognize that together they can more effectively meet their individual needs. Society consists of self-sufficient and autonomous units who voluntarily come together for mutual aid. This "social contract" is a convenience for individual, autonomous men. In contrast the Christian corporate view sees men as inescapably bound together, both physical and psychic survival being impossible apart from human relationships. To be sure, in the corporate view of things the individual remains the center of decision-making (only an individual can decide or choose), but he is never the sole source of the criterion by which decisions are to be judged.

Collectivism, on the other hand, subordinates the individual to the group in such a way as to make him important only for the sake of the group. One of the gravest difficulties encountered by early Bolshevism was precisely the threat to individuality posed by the collectivization of life. Just as doctrinaire individualism elevates the individual to the place of ultimate importance, so collectivism elevates the group. In the collective structure the individual man has no worth save that which derives from his usefulness to the group. A man *qua* man is nothing, whereas a man as a functioning part of the group is worth much *so long as* he plays his group role well.

In contrast to both these idolatries the Christian corporate view abandons the false dichotomy of the individual and the group in favor of an organismic understanding of human life. The individual relates to the group as one part of an organism relates to the other parts, each separate in function but inescapably interdependent, one part on the other. Moreover, just as a living organism is more than the sum of its parts, so a group of persons is more than the sum of the individuals who constitute it. Paul makes clear use of the organic image in Romans 12 where he talks about the church as the "body of Christ." The student of Christian ethics cannot hope to understand his subject unless he abandons the individual-group dichotomy which continues to plague Western thinking. Fortunately some sociologists are continuing to operate under organismic theories of human societies.

A final meaning of the claim that Christian ethics is always corporate is the fact that the goal of Christian ethics, as of Christian morality, is the increase of community among men. The content of the Christian's moral duty is none other than the furtherance of community among men, i.e., the establishment of love. The moral function of the community is to promote the reconciliation of divergent elements within human personality and among human beings. In this the church has the same task as the Christ was fulfilling, *viz.*, to reconcile the world to God. Paul states it: "God was in Christ reconciling the world to himself." (II Cor. 5:19 RSV) So it is that distinctly Christian ethics is aimed ultimately at producing community among men under God. Christian ethics is inescapably corporate. From this fact it follows that Christian ethics can never be static. Life in community is always in flux. In this dynamic situation new occasions must always present new duties. For that reason, among others, Christian ethics is never the study of a list of rules and regulations. It consists rather in a study of corporate life, man with God and man with man.

C. MAN: THE DECISION-MAKER

A third ingredient in the Christian's world view is that man is a deciding being. He is inescapably a moral creature. To say this is not merely to make the sociological observation that human societies everywhere create rules for the harmonious functioning of people and institutions. Nor is "moral" used here in contrast to "immoral," i.e., to claim that man is morally virtuous. It means rather that man is the creature whose distinguishing feature is his ability, indeed his necessity, for thinking "I ought. . . ." It means that man is essentially and inescapably constituted a moral being. It means that man may choose to be either moral (righteous) or immoral (unrighteous), but that he can never choose to be a-moral (without a moral dimension). Every decision is a moral decision, i.e., containing as one crucial dimension the ingredients of right or wrong, better or worse, ought or ought not. There are no universal codes of morals, to be sure, though there do exist in fact certain broad principles found in all societies, such as the prohibition of killing members of the ingroup. But everywhere you find man you find codes of morals. There is no universal morality, but man is universally moral.

It is precisely his ability to experience the "I ought" that, in the Christian estimate, sets man apart from other creatures. For the Christian man's distinctiveness lies not in his greater physico-neurological complexity, nor in his ability to reason (some of the other primates seem to reason in a rudimentary way). His distinctiveness is his power to feel obligation, to know guilt, to think "I ought." This capacity marks the fact of his participation in an order which transcends the natural sphere. It identifies him as a citizen of two worlds, called by Reinhold Niebuhr "spirit" and "nature." Man is thus a different kind of creature.

To be sure, there are other ways of interpreting the human capacity to experience the "ought" dimension of behavior. This capacity can be dealt with in naturalistic terms, i.e., in categories useful in analyzing subhuman life forms. A behavioristic approach to human being, for example, would claim that man is to be understood in terms of natural or organic (most often chemical and neurological) processes. The category "self" would be dismissed as useless by some behaviorists since it is not a measurable phenomenon. The experience of "I ought" is thought to be a holdover from, or outgrowth of, certain basic natural drives in the human organism.

Another form of naturalistic interpretation would seek to understand the ought dimension as being merely a function of man's natural capacity for self-awareness, i.e., the ability to be not merely conscious of an object but also to be conscious of the self as being conscious of that object. This capability would in turn be traced to the vast complexity of the human brain. In such a view the moral realm is regarded as nothing but a manifestation of the natural power of the mind to be aware of itself.

The major problem with such naturalistic interpretations is that they normally do not distinguish carefully between the methodological limitations of a mode of investigation and the philosophical conclusions about man drawn supposedly from the investigations. There is no problem with naturalistic investigation of man; indeed, this is a vital area of human knowledge. But there is a problem when the results of naturalistic study are confused with philosophical assertions about man. One can claim, for example, that something goes on in the brain when certain experiences are known to a person. Moreover, it is important that we find out just *what* goes on in the brain and how that relates to the conscious life of the person. On these relationships much psychiatric treatment is based, especially treatment with drugs. But it is quite another matter when the investigator begins to reduce the life of a conscious person to the natural, biological, neurological function of the human organism. It is quite acceptable to grant that man is an organism which can be studied naturalistically; it is not acceptable to assume, in consequence of this method, that man is *nothing but* an organism and that all factors in human experience, including the moral, can be accounted for in naturalistic terms.

The importance of the investigation of man as a chemical structure cannot be gainsaid, but that importance cannot be allowed to overshadow or obscure the personal dimension of human being. After all, man is not only an organism; he is also a person. He does use the pronoun "I" to refer to a living reality which he calls "self" or "person," or (earlier) "soul." Man not only has a brain; he is also "mind." While ideas have a neurological counterpart they can never be reduced to neurological impulses. Ideas have a kind of autonomy which, though connected to the operation of brain cells, are never merely cerebral. It is to this personal, as opposed to natural, sphere that ethics directs attention.

Naturalistic philosophies, of course, always carry their own ethical claims. A concrete example of this is present in what appears to be an increasingly popular way of thinking on college campuses. This simplistic view notes man's continuity with the animal world, concludes that man is merely or even chiefly animal, and decides that man ought therefore to regulate his behavior like other animals, "doing what comes naturally" and not "frustrating himself with the ridiculous conventions artificially imposed by society." What this kind of naturalism fails to note is that man, unlike other creatures, has to *choose* to regulate behavior in terms of "doing what comes naturally." It is to the necessity of this decision that we point when we say that man is inescapably a moral being.

So it is that Christian ethics is to be distinguished from all naturalisms. It is likewise to be separated from supernaturalism of a kind quite common in the Western world. This supernaturalism would deny to descriptive science a place in the study of man. The typical claim is that man is finally a stranger on earth, heaven being his true habitation, and any view which attaches significance to nature is to be rejected. The position is sometimes stated as a rhetorical question: What can science have to say about the realm of the spirit?

Supernaturalism, though it often is found masquerading as Christian and biblical, is fundamentally contrary to the biblical estimate of man. It reflects rather the medieval "faculty psychology," the view that man is made up of different and perhaps warring faculties of mind, body, and spirit. In such a view, of course, the functioning of the spirit is regarded as totally independent of the body, the physical, and the earthly. Supernaturalism of this kind, or "spiritualism," is largely rejected by both contemporary psychology and modern theology. Paul

Tillich, for example, has claimed that the Bible assumes that man is a multidimensional unity, not a composite entity.

The Christian claim, then, that man is a moral being, a deciding being, is neither a naturalistic nor a supernaturalistic claim. It recognizes rather both the natural content and the transcendent ground of the human "I ought." The Christian ethicist is most impressed with the fact that man is a being capable of feeling "I ought," and from that impression notes that man is inescapably a moral being. Decision among alternative courses of action, decision laden with possibilities of an imperative impinging from without, is universal among men. Human societies agree little on the details as to *what* one should do or what good one should seek, but *that* there is something which man should do, some good he should seek, is universally acknowledged.

One final and altogether crucial implication of this claim must be noted. The observation that man is a moral being carries with it the assumption of a real moral environment for man, an environment that transcends moral man just as the natural environment transcends natural man. In order to live as an organism, man must adjust to the natural environment, i.e., he must eat a certain quantity of food, get a certain amount of rest, avoid the absorption of too much radioactivity, and all the rest. This natural environment is a real environment, one which man does not imagine or create. In that same way man as a person must adjust to a real moral environment in order to continue to exist as a person: he must receive a certain degree of recognition from his fellows; he must enter a particular kind of accepting relationship which provides psychic security; he must come to positive self-acceptance and find fulfillment of other similar needs. It is ultimately this necessity to adjust to the moral environment that prompts man to build moral codes. This moral environment, claims the Christian, is established by the presence of the personal God, the creator of the universe. Thus the assertion that man is a moral being living in a moral environment is in actuality the claim that man is to be understood primarily in terms of his relationship to God.

D. LOVE: THE UNCONDITIONAL COMMAND

A fourth essential of Christian ethics concerns the nature of the good or the right, the form of one's duty. We have seen that "content" in the sense of moral codes is not prescribed by Christian ethics. But the absence of codified prescriptions does not mean that for the Christian there are no guides for the determination of behavior. While Christianity does not specify precisely what one is to do it does show unmistakably the way a Christian is to decide what to do. You are obliged always to do love, the one absolute to which all concrete decisions are relative. Herein lies the summary of all the law and the prophets: "Thou shalt love the Lord thy God with all thy heart, and with all thy soul, and with all thy mind, and with all thy strength; . . . thou shalt love thy neighbor as thyself." (Mark 12:28-34)

But what is love? Just what does it mean as the substantive principle of all Christian decision-making? The word love is plagued by its very fecundity of meaning. We speak of love of parents for children, of love of children for parents, of love of husband for wife, of love of football, or brotherly love. In each of these cases the term means something quite different from what it means in all the others. Perhaps it is out of this confusion that the steady evaporation of the Christian content of the word occurs. More likely, however, the root of the continual watering down of the meaning of Christian love comes from the very rigorous demands made by distinctly Christian love. In any case, Christian love has popularly been conceived primarily in the realm of feeling, of sentiment, a "warm heart" toward all humanity, a feeling approximating pity or sympathy. Only in this context could the claim be made "I love the Negro, but that does not mean that I have to give him the same opportunities for schooling that my children have. It does not mean that I have to go to school with him."

In contrast to love conceived as an inner feeling Christian love is active. It is not so much something you feel as something you do. When Jesus had told the parable we know as the story of the Good Samaritan he ended the discourse by saying, "Go and do likewise" (Luke 10:25-27 RSV). In sum, Christian love is none other than the very giving of the self in service to the neighbor. To love is to put oneself at the disposal of neighbor for the neighbor's good. Love of neighbor means to go actively about the business of seeing to it that the real needs of the neighbor are met. This of course is not something on which Christians have a monopoly. Many admirable humanist ethics counsel the same kind of service to others and with marvelous results in the upgrading of the humanity of men.

The distinctive character of Christian love lies not so much in what it demands that one do as in the reasons for making those demands. This can best be explained, perhaps, by reference to three Greek words, all translated "love." There is some question about how faithful the following treatment is to actual Greek usage, but the distinctions among these three forms of love have proved useful in distinguishing Christian love. It is to be stressed here that the differences among these forms of love inhere not in the nature of the object loved but in the motive-forces behind them.

Eros, the first of the three types, can be defined as the love of something because it is lovely or lovable. It is a possessive type of love, that which desires "to have and to hold." One has this kind of love for a person or a thing because of the effect of that person on him. One may "love" another person because that person is useful to him; she works tirelessly in his factory or satisfies his sexual desires.

It is to be noted that this kind of love in the final analysis is not really love of another person. It is rather the love of the effect that other person has on oneself, which is simply love of the self. The reason for a relationship between the two people in question is that one serves the needs of the other, usually in a mutually helpful way. Many of the sexual relationships of our time, both within and outside marriage, are of this type, but this motivation characterizes almost all relations of people to people and of people to things. It is love of something because it does something desirable to you. It is to love people as means to your own more important ends.

A second form of love is labeled *philia.* This type is essentially brotherly love or love of someone because of common interests. Two people who are drawn to a common pursuit participate in this kind of love relationship. But when *philia* is subjected to analysis it becomes apparent that, like *eros,* it is not the love of a person but the love of a quality that person possesses. The relationship is based on my love of the fact that he loves something which I also love. It is not so much love of a person as it is love of the fact that he loves something; it is love of a quality in the other person. Thus both *eros* and *philia* are conditional relationships. They are sustained only so long as the person in question has certain qualities which meet one's needs or complement one's interests.

The third type of love, *agape,* is love of someone for his own sake, i.e., a relationship based finally on the fact that the person needs to be loved. *Agape* is to give oneself to the other unreservedly, not counting the gain, without regard to qualities of the other, but solely because the other person has need of you. It is love of someone not because of who he is, nor because of what he is, but simply that he is. The epitome of this kind of relationship is demonstrated in the life and death of Jesus.

Now that for purposes of clarification the basic nature of Christian love has been set alongside other types of love, the various types must be reunified. It should be noted that *agape* always expresses itself through erotic and philial relationships. *Philia* and *agape* exist side by side in Christian friendships just as *agape* joins *eros* in such relations as those between employer and employee. After all, God also ordains *eros* and *philia!* But when *agape* is added to relationships basically characterized by *eros* and *philia* those relationships are transformed. There is added an unconditional element: "I give myself to you even when the qualities I admire in you are weakened or even lost."

The transforming character of *agape* can be illustrated in marriage. Some marriages are established on what are almost exclusively erotic motives; i.e., two people marry because they have mutual self-interests which may be served by marriage. With the passage of time the effect of one on the other, in terms of mutual interests, sexual desire, economic concerns, and the like, is modified and may even be reversed. Love may give way to repulsion. In such a relationship there is no ground for a new start and the establishment of regained harmony. But when marriages of this kind, conditional as they are, are grounded in *agape,* an unconditional love, the basis exists for new expressions of *eros* and *philia.*

The interplay of the conditional (*eros* and *philia*) and the unconditional (*agape*) can be seen also in relations between Yahweh and ancient Israel. The Hebrews used two words in characterizing their relation to their God. In his *ahabah* love Yahweh unconditionally and freely elected to give himself to Israel and bring her out of Egypt without regard to Israel's merit. But having done so he sought to bind Israel in a covenant relationship, thus manifesting his *chesed* love. The covenant based on conditional *chesed* love could be broken, and it was in fact broken by Israel. But behind the covenant always lay Yahweh's election (*ahabah*) love, the unconditional giving of himself to Israel and the ground for renewal of the covenant. Just as the unconditional *ahabah* expressed itself concretely in the conditional *chesed,* so *agape* expresses itself through *eros* and *philia.* Just as the covenant could be reestablished because of election, so can *eros* and *philia* be regained because of *agape.*[4]

So much, then, for the nature of Christian *agape.* We must look next to its dynamics. In Christian *agape* there is a reason for loving the person in an unconditional way. It is none other than the recognition that this person is one whom God loves. This person has worth, is worthy of my devotion, not because of some quality either inherent or acquired but simply because God regards that person as worthful. By valuing that person God confers value upon him in an absolute way. This kind of value in a person thus has nothing to do with that person's usefulness or with his merit. He is to be loved (i.e., served) not because he deserves it but simply because God wills it.

This kind of relationship, though similar at one point to the better humanisms, is to be sharply distinguished from all humanistic love. Humanism is rooted in the assumption that there is something inherently worthful about human beings. They are to be respected and served simply because human being is by its nature the highest form of being. Christian

[4] For a more complete exegesis of *ahabah* and *chesed* see Norman H. Snaith, ***The Distinctive Ideas of the Old Testament*** (London: Epworth Press, 1944), pp. 94-142.

agape goes one step further. Final worth lies in God alone, and ultimate duty is to him alone. Man, for the Christian, is not the final source of his own worth, man being finite just as are all other things and values on the planet. Man's worth is rooted rather in the infinite love (*agape*) of God for man. This places a higher valuation on human being than is possible in humanisms without a transcendental reference. Unfortunately the behavior of Christians has not always demonstrated the superiority of this ground of love.

So it is that Christian love is the active giving of the self in relationship to another *for God's sake*. *Agape* calls upon the Christian to serve the real needs of the neighbor. But what does it require me to do? *What* action does love demand? To that question, as we shall see in the next section, there can be no specific answer given in advance. To specify more concretely the "what" of love leads dangerously in the direction of the denial of love. This is the case in that love consists ultimately in concerned action for persons, not in concern for my right action toward them. When the focus of love is removed from people and turned to prescriptive rules, no matter how right those rules, the essence of *agape* is denied. One then easily moves from concern for others to the concern for cultivating the correct virtues in oneself, this being the most subtle and dangerous of sins because it seems always good to cultivate the virtuous life. The nurture of one's own righteousness, then, leads to preoccupation with oneself, not with the neighbor, with the consequent undermining of the fact of love itself. It is for this reason that love can never become one of the virtues to be sought after and nourished.

This leaves us with the crucial question as to how one comes to love by *agape*. If one cannot merely decide that he would like to love and then proceed to develop that facility, how is *agape* to come into being? And that question leads us to the heart and core of Christian theology, *viz.*, the acknowledgment of the fact of God's love, the reality ultimately at stake in the life and death of Jesus. In short, one comes to love by *agape* not through determined effort but by the simple acknowledgment of God's love for him. It is out of this overwhelming recognition of one's own worth in the eyes of God that the capacity and the motive for *agape* arise. *Agape* is spontaneously generated, not consciously cultivated, in the person who finds himself to be loved so deeply and without regard for his own merit. Here is the real burden of Paul's attempts in Galatians and Romans to reject the notion of justification by works (cultivation) in favor of justification by God's grace (love).

Thus at the very heart of Christian morality and ethics lies the fact of God's love (*agape*) for man, a fact the Christian sees demonstrated concretely in one figure in history, Jesus of Nazareth. It is because of his embodiment of God's love and the consequent regenerating effect on the believer that Jesus is known to the Christian as the Christ, the anointed one of God. If one asks what does love require, the Christian can point not to a commandment, nor to a code of laws, nor to a list of rules; he can point to the image of this Christ preserved in the pages of the New Testament and reflected, however dimly, in the church as the community of love. It is for this reason that the study of Christian ethics is never merely the study of the teachings of Jesus. The study of Christian ethics is the study of the implications for human conduct of the reality embodied in Jesus, the reality of God's love of man. To study Christian ethics is to ask what are the consequences for human behavior of the fact of God's love for man.

E. CASUISTRY: AN ETHIC OF PRINCIPLED CONTEXTUALISM

It is clear, then, that love provides the content of Christian moral duty. God requires of the Christian that he "do love." But how does one translate that absolute duty into concrete action in specific situations? How is one to know exactly *what* to do in love? The answers Christians have offered to that question can be understood in terms of their relation to two polar opposites, legalist and formal systems.

Legalist systems are those which seek to provide codes or lists of concrete rules directing action for this or that situation. The system of rules is spelled out in advance, thus enabling the decision-maker to consult the code for the command which applies in a given situation. His task as decision-maker is merely to decide which rule applies to the moral question of the moment. One example of this way of doing ethics is found in the practice of post-exilic Judaism. With the broad rules spelled out in the Mosaic code there remained the task of deriving more specific rules to fit an ever-increasing variety of situations. It was out of this need that the Talmudic law grew.

Protestant pietism or fundamentalism affords another example of legalist practice, though pietists do not pursue their task as thoroughly or rigorously as did the ancient Hebrews. The common practice in pietism is to offer a rather limited list of certain prohibitions—like cursing, drinking, smoking, dancing, and similar concerns of private personal purity. These rules are to be obeyed because the Bible commands it, so the argument goes, the assumption being that moral purity in obedience to commands is the overriding concern. In any case, the details of action are rigidly prescribed, and no deviation is allowed regardless of the consequences.

In contrast to code moralities "formal" systems avoid the building of lists of answers to specific questions. A formal system provides the actor with a general end or principle and leaves it entirely to him to design concrete lines of action for every specific situation. In the purely formal system no aid is given the decision-maker in determining appropriate concrete action. No guidelines or principles are suggested, thus leaving the actor to extemporize at the moment and do that which most urgently recommends itself. The practice of some modern "existentialists" approaches this method, as does that of some of the "situationist" ethicists within Christianity.

Just as is true of most heresies, the legalist and formalist heresies are exaggerations based on valid but partial truths. They characterize extremes in the recognition of the two poles between which all Christian decision-making must be done, those poles being the reality of God on the one hand and the concrete, contingent situation of the actor on the other. The ethical method which we are here calling "principled contextualism" represents an attempt to preserve a more creative tension between those poles of the moral life.

A Christian ethic of principled contextualism rejects legalist methods for three basic reasons. First, legalist systems too easily deteriorate into legalisms in which laws or rules or codes are taken to be more important than persons. In his self-conscious attempt to be virtuous through obedience to laws the attention of the actor is turned inward upon himself rather than toward the neighbor, the proper focal point of love. Obedience to rules becomes the dominant concern. Second, no list of rules can ever hope to be complete enough or sufficiently sensitive to cover the vast array of concrete situations, each with its own set of contingencies and alternative courses of action. The rules would have to be almost as numerous as there are specific decisions. Moreover, rules are always impersonal and consequently incapable of recognizing the needs of *this* particular neighbor in *this* peculiar situation. Third, legalist systems with their inevitable proliferation of rules and regulations short-circuit the decision-making process by which men grow into more complete human beings. The actor under a legal code must decide only which rule applies in a given case. He is left with the task of juggling regulations, not of entering creatively and responsibly into community with persons. The consequence is that he as a person does not increase his stature as a free and responsible creature made in the image of God.

Purely formal methods of deciding are rejected, in the first place, because they do not recognize the essentially corporate nature of the Christian life. The community of the Church simply does in fact articulate principles or guidelines based on past experience. To ignore these principles entirely is in effect to turn one's back on the community. In the second place, formal systems do not give men the support and direction they require as they confront the bewildering complexity of alternatives in most every concrete moral problem. Without some appeal to principles more specific than the general command to love his neighbor the Christian is baffled and inclined to follow some whim of the moment. A final failure of formal systems is their tendency to lapse into antinomianism—literally, "no law" or lawlessness. In dispensing with laws and codes one tends to dispense with principles as well. The result is that conduct is determined by individual fancy or simply by social convention. This normally means, as it did for one wing of second-century Christian Gnostics, a sophisticated licentiousness which surpasses anything found in pagan cultures—these cultures having some form of guilt not so easily rationalized as is possible for antinomians.

No complete list of guiding principles could be drawn up, of course, even if one were desirable, but a few examples might be offered here to clarify the method of principled contextualism. For example, in the area of race relations it can be declared that racial segregation is in principle wrong because it denies the equal worth of the minority and impedes the growth of full community between persons. Hence the Christian is obliged *in principle* to work toward desegregation. The pace of movement in that direction cannot be preestablished for every situation, and the exact course of action must be relative to the situation. Yet the direction in which love moves in this area is abundantly clear and may be articulated as a principle.

To take another example—this one in marital relations—it must be noted that divorce is wrong in principle because it represents the failure of love, the collapse of community. The Christian is obliged to work toward marital harmony. This does not mean that divorce is to be absolutely prohibited, as the legalist would do. There is but one absolute principle, and that is love. Though divorce is in principle wrong, the method of principled contextualism would recognize the realities of an impossible situation and counsel divorce as a relatively more fitting thing to do in special cases. Love may on occasion require the rejection of the guideline on divorce, but this in no way invalidates the principle.

One further example of the kind of principles which prove helpful in decision-making is taken from the world of economics. Economic systems which deprive some participants and enrich others are in principle wrong because they deny the equal worth of all human beings. The Christian must, therefore, work toward an appropriate balance in the distribution of goods in human society. It should be cautioned that this does not mean providing every person with the same amount of wealth. Nor does it forbid the accumulation of wealth and the control of vast wealth by a relative few, but such accumulation and control are justifiable only when the economic needs of the entire society can best be met in that way.

Principled contextualism, then, would seek never to lose sight of the radical command of love, or the ambiguities of concrete cases, or the "useful rules" contributed by the traditions and current reflections of the Christian community. In light of the tension between the demand of God and the contingencies of the world it would declare unmistakably that some things are wrong, however necessary they may be on occasion. To equate that which the contingencies of life make necessary with that which is right is in effect to deny the need for God's grace. If the action which seems relatively better is declared to be entirely right or good, then there is no place in the Christian for repentance or for the grace by which Christians find themselves reconstituted. The Reformation principle of *sola gratia* is lost, and man is to be regarded no longer as sinner but as righteous. In some contexts divorce, for example, may be the *fitting* thing to do, and he who decides for divorce may deserve moral credit for doing it. But divorce stands as wrong in principle and as an act over which man should feel remorse and for which he must acknowledge his need for God's grace. This is said in full recognition of the fact, let it be repeated, that on occasion divorce may be the more "loving" thing to do. But the basic thrust of love is always toward union, and divorce, as disunion, represents the failure of love. Given the failure to love, divorce may well be the fitting act; but at the deepest level it continues to betray the failure of man to love.

In this fashion principled contextualism would remain cognizant of the contingencies of human life and the ambiguities of moral choices, though at the same time acknowledging the main thrust of the final principle, God's radical demand for love. The essays in this volume will, hopefully, further illustrate and elaborate this theme.

Part One

The Theological Foundations of Christian Decision-Making

I. Revelation

The late Paul Johannes Tillich retired from the faculty of Union Theologic[illegible]inary, New York, in 1955. Prior to his death in 1965 he held chairs in theology at both Harvard and the University of Chicago.

The Reality of Revelation*

3. THE DYNAMICS OF REVELATION: ORIGINAL AND DEPENDENT REVELATION

The history of revelation indicates that there is a difference between original and dependent revelations. This is a consequence of the correlative character of revelation. An original revelation is a revelation which occurs in a constellation that did not exist before. This miracle and this ecstasy are joined for the first time. Both sides are original. In a dependent revelation the miracle and its original reception together form the giving side, while the receiving side changes as new individuals and groups enter the same correlation of revelation. Jesus is the Christ, both because he could become the Christ and because he was received as the Christ. Without both these sides he would not have been the Christ. Not only was this true of those who first received him, but it is true of all the following generations which have entered into a revelatory correlation with him. There is, however, a difference between original and dependent revelation through him. While Peter encountered the man Jesus whom he called the Christ in an original revelatory ecstasy, following generations met the Jesus who had been received as the Christ by Peter and the other apostles. There is continuous revelation in the history of the church, but it is dependent revelation. The original miracle, together with its original reception, is the permanent point of reference, while the Spiritual reception by following generations changes continuously. But if one side of a correlation is changed, the whole correlation is transformed. It is true

* Paul Tillich, *Systematic Theology,* I (Chicago: University of Chicago Press, 1951), 126-37. Used by permission.

that "Jesus Christ . . . the same yesterday, today, and forever" is the immovable point of reference in all periods of church history. But the act of referring is never the same, since new generations with new potentialities of reception enter the correlation and transform it. No ecclesiastical traditionalism and no orthodox biblicism can escape this situation of "dependent revelation." This answers the much-discussed question whether the history of the church has revelatory power. The history of the church is not a locus of original revelations in addition to the one on which it is based. . . . Rather, it is the locus of continuous dependent revelations which are one side of the work of the divine Spirit in the church. This side often is called "illumination," referring to the church as a whole as well as to its individual members. The term "illumination" points to the cognitive element in the process of actualizing the New Being. It is the cognitive side of ecstasy. While "inspiration" traditionally has been used to designate an original revelation, "illumination" has been used to express what we call "dependent revelation." The divine Spirit, illuminating believers individually and as a group, brings their cognitive reason into revelatory correlation with the event on which Christianity is based.

This leads to a broader view of revelation in the life of the Christian. A dependent revelatory situation exists in every moment in which the divine Spirit grasps, shapes, and moves the human spirit. Every prayer and meditation, if it fulfills its meaning, namely, to reunite the creature with its creative ground, is revelatory in this sense. The marks of revelation—mystery, miracle, and ecstasy—are present in every true prayer. Speaking to God and receiving an answer is an ecstatic and miraculous experience; it transcends all ordinary structures of subjective and objective reason. It is the presence of the mystery of being and an actualization of our ultimate concern. If it is brought down to the level of a conversation between two beings, it is blasphemous and ridiculous. If, however, it is understood as the "elevation of the heart," namely, the center of the personality, to God, it is a revelatory event.

This consideration radically excludes a nonexistential concept of revelation. Propositions about a past revelation give theoretical information; they have no revelatory power. Only through an autonomous use of the intellect or through a heteronomous subjection of the will could they be accepted as truth. Such acceptance would be a human work, a meritorious deed of the type against which the Reformation fought a life-and-death struggle. Revelation, whether it is original or dependent, has revelatory power only for those who participate in it, who enter into the revelatory correlation.

Original relevation is given to a group through an individual. Revelation can be received originally only in the depth of a personal life, in its struggles, decisions, and self-surrender. No individual receives revelation for himself. He receives it for his group, and implicitly for all groups, for mankind as a whole. This is obvious in prophetic revelation, which always is vocational. The prophet is the mediator of revelation for the group which follows him—often after it first has rejected him. Nor is this restricted to classical prophetism. We find the same situation in most religions, and even in mystical groups. A seer, a religious founder, a priest, a mystic—these are the individuals from whom original revelation is derived by groups which enter into the same correlation of revelation in a dependent way.

Since the correlation of revelation is transformed by every new group, and in an infinitesimal way by every new individual who enters it, the question must be asked whether this transformation can reach a point where the original revelation is exhausted and superceded. It is the question of the possible end of a revelatory correlation, either by a complete disappearance of the unchanging point of reference, or by a complete loss of its power to create new correlations. Both possibilities have been actualized innumerable times in the history of religion. Sectarian and Protestant movements in all the great religions have attacked given religious institutions as a complete betrayal of the meaning of the original revelation, although they still have kept it as their point of reference. On the other hand, most of the gods of the past have lost even this power; they have become poetic symbols and have ceased to create a revelatory situation. Apollo has no revelatory significance for Christians; the Virgin Mother Mary reveals nothing to Protestants. Revelation through these two figures has come to an end. Yet one might ask how a real revelation can come to an end. If it is God who stands behind every revelation, how can something divine come to an end? If it is not God who reveals himself, why should one use the term "revelation"? But this alternative does not exist! Every revelation is mediated by one or several of the mediums of revelation. None of these mediums possesses revelatory power in itself; but under the conditions of existence these mediums claim to have it. This claim makes them idols, and the breakdown of this claim deprives them of their power. The revelatory side is not lost if a revelation comes to an end; but its idolatrous side is destroyed. That which was revelatory in it is preserved as an element in more embracing and more purified revelations, and everything revelatory is potentially present in the final revelation, which cannot come to an end because the bearer of it does not claim anything for himself.

4. THE KNOWLEDGE OF REVELATION

Revelation is the manifestation of the mystery of being for the cognitive function of human reason. It mediates knowledge—a knowledge, however, which can be received only in a revelatory situation, through ecstasy and miracle. This correlation indicates the special character of the "knowledge of revelation."[1] Since the knowledge of revelation cannot be separated from the situation of revelation, it cannot be introduced into the context of ordinary knowledge as an addition, provided in a peculiar way, yet independent of this way once it has been received. Knowledge of revelation does not increase our knowledge about the structures of nature, history, and man. Whenever a claim to knowledge is made on this level, it must be subjected to the experimental tests through which truth is established. If such a claim is made in the name of revelation or of any other authority, it must be disregarded, and the ordinary methods of research and verification must be applied. For the physicist the revelatory knowledge of creation neither adds to nor subtracts from his scientific description of the natural structure of things. For the historian the revelatory interpretation of history as the history of revelation neither confirms nor negates any of his statements about documents, traditions, and the interdependence of historical events. For the psychologist no revelatory truth about the destiny of man can influence his analysis of the dynamics of the human soul. If revealed knowledge did interfere with ordinary knowledge, it would destroy scientific honesty and methodological humility. It would exhibit demonic possession, not divine revelation. Knowledge of revelation is knowledge about the revelation of the mystery of being to us, not information about the nature of beings and their relation to one another. Therefore, the knowledge of revelation can be received only in the situation of revelation, and it can be communicated—in contrast to ordinary knowledge—only to those who participate in this situation. For those outside this situation the same words have a different sound. A reader of the New Testament, for example, a philologist for whom its contents are not a matter of ultimate concern, may be able to interpret the text exactly and correctly; but he will miss the ecstatic-revelatory significance of the words and sentences. He may speak with scientific preciseness about them as reports concerning an assumed revelation, but he cannot speak of them as witnesses to an actual revelation. His knowledge of the documents of revelation is non-

[1] One should not speak of revealed knowledge because this term gives the impression that ordinary contents of knowledge are communicated in an extraordinary way, thus separating revealed knowledge from the revelatory situation. This is the basic fallacy in most of the popular and many of the theological interpretations of revelation and the knowledge mediated through it. The term "knowledge of revelation" (or revelatory knowledge) emphasizes the inseparable unity of knowledge and situation.

existential. As such it may contribute much to the historical-philosophical understanding of the documents. It cannot contribute anything to the knowledge of revelation mediated through the documents.

Knowledge of revelation cannot interfere with ordinary knowledge. Likewise, ordinary knowledge cannot interfere with knowledge of revelation. There is no scientific theory which is more favorable to the truth of revelation than any other theory. It is disastrous for theology if theologians prefer one scientific view to others on theological grounds. And it was humiliating for theology when theologians were afraid of new theories for religious reasons, trying to resist them as long as possible, and finally giving in when resistance had become impossible. This ill-conceived resistance of theologians from the time of Galileo to the time of Darwin was one of the causes of the split between religion and secular culture in the past centuries. . . .

There is, however, one limit to the indifference of the knowledge of revelation toward all forms of ordinary knowledge, namely, the presence of revelatory elements within assertions of ordinary knowledge. If, under the cover of ordinary knowledge, matters of ultimate concern are discussed, theology must protect the truth of revelation against attacks from distorted revelations, whether they appear as genuine religions or as metaphysically transformed ideas. This, however, is a religious struggle in the dimension of revelatory knowledge and not a conflict between knowledge of revelation and ordinary knowledge.

The truth of revelation is not dependent on criteria which are not themselves revelatory. Knowledge of revelation, like ordinary knowledge, must be judged by its own implicit criteria. It is the task of the doctrine of the final revelation to make these criteria explicit. . . .

The knowledge of revelation, directly or indirectly, is knowledge of God, and therefore it is analogous or symbolic. The nature of this kind of knowing is dependent on the nature of the relation between God and the world and can be discussed only in the context of the doctrine of God. But two possible misunderstandings must be mentioned and removed. If the knowledge of revelation is called "analogous," this certainly refers to the classical doctrine of the *analogia entis* between the finite and the infinite. Without such an analogy nothing could be said about God. But the *analogia entis* is in no way able to create a natural theology. It is not a method of discovering truth about God; it is the form in which every knowledge of revelation must be expressed. In this sense *analogia entis,* like "religious symbol," points to the necessity of using material taken from finite reality in order to give content to the cognitive function in revelation. This necessity, however, does not diminish the cognitive value of revelatory knowledge. The phrase "only a symbol" should be avoided, because nonanalogous or nonsymbolic knowledge of God has *less* truth than analogous or symbolic knowledge. The use of finite materials in their ordinary sense for the knowledge of revelation destroys the meaning of revelation and deprives God of his divinity.

B. ACTUAL REVELATION

5. ACTUAL AND FINAL REVELATION

We have described the meaning of revelation in the light of the criteria of what Christianity considers to be revelation. The description of the meaning of revelation was supposed to cover all possible and actual revelations, but the criterion of revelation has not yet been developed. We now turn to the Christian affirmation, no longer indirectly as in the preceding chapters, but directly and dogmatically, in the genuine sense of dogma as the doctrinal basis of a special philosophical school or religious community.

From the point of view of the theological circle, actual revelation is necessarily final revelation, for the person who is grasped by a revelatory experience believes it to be the truth concerning the mystery of being and his relation to it. If he is open for other original revelations, he already has left the revelatory situation and looks at it in a detached way. His point of reference has ceased to be the original revelation by means of which he had entered an original correlation, or, more frequently, a dependent correlation. There is also the possibility that a person may believe that no concrete revelation concerns him ultimately, that the real ultimate is beyond all concreteness. . . . For the Hindu the final revelation is the mystical experience, and for the humanist there is neither actual nor final revelation but only moral autonomy, supported by the impression of the synoptic Jesus.

Christianity claims to be based on the revelation in Jesus as the Christ as the final revelation. This claim establishes a Christian church, and, where this claim is absent, Christianity has ceased to exist—at least manifestly though not always latently. . . . The word "final" in the phrase "final revelation" means more than *last*. Christianity often has affirmed, and certainly should affirm, that there is continuous revelation in the history of the church. In this sense the final revelation is not the last. Only if *last* means the last *genuine* revelation can final revelation be interpreted as the last revelation. There can be no revelation in the history of the church whose point of reference is not Jesus as the Christ. If another point of reference is sought or accepted, the Christian church has lost its foundation. But final revelation means more than the last genuine revelation. It means the decisive, fulfilling, unsurpassable revelation, that which is the criterion of all the others. This is the Christian claim, and this is the basis of a Christian theology.

The question, however, is how such a claim can be justified, whether there are criteria within the revelation in Jesus as the Christ which make it final. Such criteria cannot be derived from anything outside the revelatory situation. But it is possible to discover them within this situation. And this is just what theology must do.

The first and basic answer theology must give to the question of the finality of the revelation in Jesus as the Christ is the following: a revelation is final if it has the power of negating itself without losing itself. This paradox is based on the fact that every revelation is conditioned by the medium in and through which it appears. The question of the final revelation is the question of a medium of revelation which overcomes its own finite conditions by sacrificing them, and itself with them. He who is the bearer of the final revelation must surrender his finitude—not only his life but also his finite power and knowledge and perfection. In doing so, he affirms that he is the bearer of final revelation (the "Son of God" in classical terms). He becomes completely transparent to the mystery he reveals. But, in order to be able to surrender himself completely, he must possess himself completely. And only he can possess—and therefore surrender—himself completely who is united with the ground of his being and meaning without separation and disruption. In the picture of Jesus as the Christ we have the picture of a man who possesses these qualities, a man who, therefore, can be called the medium of final revelation.

In the biblical records of Jesus as the Christ (there are no records besides the New Testament) Jesus became the Christ by conquering the demonic forces which tried to make him demonic by tempting him to claim ultimacy for his finite nature. These forces, often represented by his own disciples, tried to induce him to avoid sacrificing of himself as a medium of revelation. They wanted him to avoid the cross (cf. Matthew, chap. 16). They tried to make him an object of idolatry. Idolatry is the perversion of a genuine revelation; it is the elevation of the medium of revelation to the dignity of the revelation itself. The true prophets in Israel fought continuously against this idolatry, which was defended by the false prophets and their priestly supporters. This fight is the dynamic power in the history of revelation. Its classical document is the Old Testament, and it is just for this reason that the Old Testament is an inseparable part of the revelation of Jesus as the Christ. But the New Testament and the history of the church show the same conflict.

In the Reformation the prophetic spirit attacked a demonically perverted priestly system and produced the deepest split which has occurred in the development of Christianity.

According to Paul, the demonic-idolatrous powers which rule the world and distort religion have been conquered in the cross of Christ. In his cross Jesus sacrificed that medium of revelation which impressed itself on his followers as messianic in power and significance. For us this means that in following him we are liberated from the authority of everything finite in him, from his special traditions, from his individual piety, from his rather conditional world view, from any legalistic understanding of his ethics. Only as the crucified is he "grace and truth" and not law. Only as he who has sacrificed his flesh, that is, his historical existence, is he Spirit or New Creature. These are the *paradoxa* in which the criterion of final revelation becomes manifest. Even the Christ is Christ only because he did not insist on his equality with God but renounced it as a personal possession (Philippians, chap. 2). Christian theology can affirm the finality of the revelation in Jesus as the Christ only on this basis. . . .

Therefore, the final revelation is universal without being heteronomous. No finite being imposes itself in the name of God on other finite beings. The unconditional and universal claim of Christianity is not based on its own superiority over other religions. Christianity, without being final itself, witnesses to the final revelation. Christianity as Christianity is neither final nor universal. But that to which it witnesses is final and universal. This profound dialectics of Christianity must not be forgotten in favor of ecclesiastical or orthodox self-affirmations. Against them the so-called liberal theology is right in denying that one religion can claim finality, or even superiority. A Christianity which does not assert that Jesus of Nazareth is sacrificed to Jesus as the Christ is just one more religion among many others. It has no justifiable claim to finality.

6. THE FINAL REVELATION IN JESUS AS THE CHRIST

In accord with the circular character of systematic theology, the criterion of final revelation is derived from what Christianity considers to be the final revelation, the appearance of Jesus as the Christ. Theologians should not be afraid to admit this circle. It is not a shortcoming; rather it is the necessary expression of the existential character of theology. It provides a description of final revelation in two ways, first in terms of an abstract principle which is the criterion of every assumed or real revelation and, second, in terms of a concrete picture which mirrors the occurrence of the final revelation. . . .

All reports and interpretations of the New Testament concerning Jesus as the Christ possess two outstanding characteristics: his maintenance of unity with God and his sacrifice of everything he could have gained for himself from this unity.

The first point is clear in the Gospel reports about the unbreakable unity of his being with that of the ground of all being, in spite of his participation in the ambiguities of human life. The being of Jesus as the Christ is determined in every moment by God. In all his utterances, words, deeds, and sufferings, he is transparent to that which he represents as the Christ, the divine mystery. . . . According to the witness of the whole New Testament and, by anticipation, also of many passages of the Old Testament, it is the presence of God in him which makes him the Christ. His words, his deeds, and his sufferings are consequences of this presence; they are expressions of the New Being which is his being.

Jesus' maintenance of unity with God includes the second emphasis of the biblical writers, his victory over every temptation to exploit his unity with God as a means of advantage for himself. He does not give in to the temptation to which he is exposed as the designated Messiah, the success of which would have deprived him of his messianic function. The acceptance of the cross, both during his life and at the end of it, is the decisive test of his unity with God, of his complete transparency to the ground of being. . . . This sacrifice is the end of all attempts to impose him, as a finite being, on other finite beings. It is the end of Jesusology. Jesus of Nazareth is the medium of the final revelation because he sacrifices himself completely to Jesus as the Christ. He not only sacrifices his life, as many martyrs and many ordinary people have done, but he also sacrifices everything in him and of him which could bring people to him as an "overwhelming personality" instead of bringing them to that in him which is greater than he and they. This is the meaning of the symbol "Son of God."

The final revelation, like every revelation, occurs in a correlation of ecstasy and miracle. The revelatory event is Jesus as the Christ. He is the miracle of the final revelation, and his reception is the ecstasy of the final revelation. His appearance is the decisive constellation of historical (and by participation, natural) forces. It is the ecstatic moment of human history and, therefore, its center, giving meaning to all possible and actual history. The Kairos which was fulfilled in him is the constellation of final revelation. But it is this only for those who received him as the final revelation, namely, as the Messiah, the Christ, the Man-from-above, the Son of God, the Spirit, the Logos-who-became-flesh—the New Being. All these terms are symbolic variations of the theme first enunciated by Peter when he said to Jesus, "Thou art the Christ." In these words Peter accepted him as the medium of the final revelation. This acceptance, however, is a part of the revelation itself. . . . Jesus as the Christ, the miracle of the final revelation, and the church, receiving him as the Christ or the final revelation, belong to each other. The Christ is not the Christ without the church, and the church is not the church without the Christ. The final revelation, like every revelation, is correlative.

The final revelation, the revelation in Jesus as the Christ, is universally valid, because it includes the criterion of every revelation and is the *finis* or *telos* (intrinsic aim) of all of them. The final revelation is the criterion of every revelation which precedes or follows. It is the criterion of every religion and of every culture, not only of the culture and religion in and through which it has appeared. It is valid for the social existence of every human group and for the personal existence of every human individual. It is valid for mankind as such, and, in an indescribable way, it has meaning for the universe also. Nothing less than this should be asserted by Christian theology. If some element is cut off from the universal validity of the message of Jesus as the Christ, if he is put into the sphere of personal achievement only, or into the sphere of history only, he is less than the final revelation and is neither the Christ nor the New Being. But Christian theology affirms that he is all this because he stands the double test of finality: uninterrupted unity with the ground of his being and the continuous sacrifice of himself as Jesus to himself as the Christ.

The late Helmut Richard Niebuhr was at the time of his death in 1962 Sterling Professor of Theology and Christian Ethics, Yale University.

The Story of Our Life*

In external history value means valency or strength. The objective historian must measure the importance of an event or factor by the effect it

* Reprinted with permission of The Macmillan Company from *The Meaning of Revelation*, by H. Richard Niebuhr. Copyright 1941 by The Macmillan Company. Renewed 1969 by Florence Niebuhr, Cynthia M. Niebuhr and Richard R. Niebuhr. Pp. 67-90.

has on other events or factors in the series. Though he is also a self, living in community, having a destiny, and so unable wholly to escape a moral point of view, as scientific historian he is bound to suppress his own value-judgments as much as possible. Not what is noblest in his sight but what is most effective needs to be treated most fully. So Alexander may have a larger place in his account than Socrates, though as a self the historian may elect to follow right to martyrdom rather than might to victory. Economic motives in the framing of the American Constitution may require far more attention than moral ideals, though the historian be one who has abjured the ownership of property for himself and may live a semi-monastic life. Looking upon events in the manner of an impartial spectator, he seeks to suppress every response of love or repugnance and to apply a more or less quantitative measure of strength in determining the importance of persons or events.

In internal history, however, value means worth for selves; whatever cannot be so valued is unimportant and may be dropped from memory. Here the death of Socrates, the birth of Lincoln, Peter's martyrdom, Luther's reform, Wesley's conversion, the landing of the Pilgrims, the granting of Magna Charta are events to be celebrated; this history calls for joy and sorrow, for days of rededication and of shriving, for tragic participation and for jubilees. The valuable here is that which bears on the destiny of selves; not what is strongest is most important but what is most relevant to the lives of "I's" and "Thou's." Value here means quality, not power; but the quality of valued things is one which only selves can apprehend. In this context we do not measure the worth of even our own desires by their strength but by their relevance to the destiny of the self.

As with value so with time. In our internal history time has a different feel and quality from that of the external time with which we deal as exoteric historians. The latter time resembles that of physics. . . . Such time is always serial. In the series, past events are gone and future happenings are not yet. In internal history, on the other hand, our time is our duration. What is past is not gone; it abides in us as our memory; what is future is not non-existent but present in us as our potentiality. Time here is organic or it is social, so that past and future associate with each other in the present. Time in our history is not another dimension of the external space world in which we live, but a dimension of our life and of our community's being. We are not in this time but it is in us. It is not associated with space in a unity of space-time but it is inseparable from life in the continuity of life-time. We do not speak of it in precise numbers but say in poetic fashion with Lincoln, "fourscore and seven years ago," meaning not eighty-seven but our remembered past. In humbler fashion we correlate, as gossips do, the lives and deaths and wars of kings with shocks and joys in our own history. Such time is not a number but a living, a stream of consciousness, a flow of feeling, thought and will. It is not measurable by the hours and years of a planetary and solar rhythm; its ebb and flow, its pulsations and surges, its births and deaths and resurrections are incommensurable with lunar or atomic tides. If they are to be measured it must be done by a comparison with other inner alternations; in our history we do not correlate the death of the heart with the declining sun nor its rebirth with nature's spring but with a crucifixion of the son of God and with his rising to new life.

Human association also differs when regarded from the external or internal points of view. The external knower must see societies as made up of atomic individuals related to each other by external bonds. Yet even the human individuals are depersonalized, since they are understood as complexes of psychological and biological factors. Society, to his view, is a vast and intricate organization of interests, drives or instincts, beliefs, customs, laws, constitutions, inventions, geographic and climatic data, in which a critical and diligent inquiry can discover some intelligible structures and moving patterns of relation. In internal history, on the other hand, society is a community of selves. Here we do not only live among other selves but they live in us and we in them. Relations here are not external but internal so that we are our relations and cannot be selves save as we are members of each other. When there is strife in this community there is strife and pain in us and when it is at peace we have peace in ourselves. Here social memory is not what is written in books and preserved in libraries, but what—not without the mediation of books and monuments, to be sure—is our own past, living in every self. When we become members of such a community of selves we adopt its past as our own and thereby are changed in our present existence. So immigrants and their children do, for whom Pilgrims become true fathers and the men of the Revolution their own liberators; so we do in the Christian community when the prophets of the Hebrews become our prophets and the Lord of the early disciples is acknowledged as our Lord. Not what is after the flesh—that is what is externally seen—but what is after the spirit—what has become a part of our own lives as selves—is the important thing in this internal view. In our history association means community, the participation of each living self in a common memory and common hope no less than in a common world of nature. . . .

The relevance of this distinction between two histories to the subject of revelation must now have become apparent. When the evangelists of the New Testament and their successors pointed to history as the starting point of their faith and of their understanding of the world it was internal history that they indicated. They did not speak of events, as impersonally apprehended, but rather of what had happened to them in their community. They recalled the critical point in their own life-time when they became aware of themselves in a new way as they came to know the self on whom they were dependent. They turned to a past which was not gone but which endured in them as their memory, making them what they were. So for the later church, history was always the story of "our fathers," of "our Lord," and of the actions of "our God."

The inspiration of Christianity has been derived from history, it is true, but not from history as seen by a spectator; the constant reference is to subjective events, that is to events in the lives of subjects. What distinguishes such historic recall from the private histories of mystics is that it refers to communal events, remembered by a community and in a community. Subjectivity here is not equivalent to isolation, non-verifiability and ineffability; our history can be communicated and persons can refresh as well as criticize each other's memories of what has happened to them in the common life; on the basis of a common past they can think together about the common future.

Such history, to be sure, can only be confessed by the community, and in this sense it is esoteric. One cannot point to historic events in the lives of selves as though they were visible to any external point of view. Isaiah cannot say that in the year King Uzziah died God became visible in the temple nor Paul affirm that Jesus the Lord appears to travellers on the Damascus Road. Neither will any concentration of attention on Isaiah and Paul, any detailed understanding of their historical situation, enable the observer to see what they saw. One must look with them and not at them to verify their visions, participate in their history rather than regard it if one would apprehend what they apprehended. The history of the inner life can only be confessed by selves who speak of what happened to them in the community of other selves.

III. FAITH IN OUR HISTORY

The distinction between history as known by the pure and as apprehended by the practical reason, though it raises difficulties that must be met, does assist us to understand how it is possible for the word "revelation" to point to history and yet point to God also. It cannot point to God, as we have noted, if the history to which it directs attention is the chain of events that an impersonal eye or mind apprehends. For such history, abstracting from human selves, must also abstract events from the divine self and, furthermore, while it may furnish motives for belief in the occurrence of certain happenings it does not invite trust in a living God.

The error frequently made in the Christian community which has been the occasion for the rise of many difficulties in understanding and propagating the historical faith has been the location of revelation in external history or in history as known from the non-participating point of view. So revelation has been identified with some miracle, whether this was the single act of a person or his whole life or the life of a community, such as Israel or the church. In this way certain events in external history were set apart as sacred, or a sacred history of one community has been opposed to the secular histories of other societies. Sacred events were inserted into a context otherwise secular and the continuity between the two types of events denied. It was denied that the events of holy history were subject to the same type of explanation which might be offered for secular happenings; that so-called secular events might have a sacred meaning for those who participated in them as selves was not thought possible.

Much so-called orthodoxy identified revelation with Scriptures and regarded the latter as wholly miraculous, the product of an inspiration which suspended the ordinary processes of human thought and guaranteed inerrancy. But to validate the Scriptural miracle another needed to be inserted into history since that which stands completely alone is an impenetrable mystery, no matter how much astonishment it calls forth. So miraculous Scriptures were related to miracles in the realm of nature, to a sun that stood still, a virgin-born child, to water turned by a word into wine. Furthermore the psychological miracle of prophecy as a supernatural foretelling of events, as though by second-sight, was introduced to validate the wonder of the Bible. The consequence of this method of argument was that two systems of reality on the same plane—a natural, historical, rational system and a supernatural, super-historical and super-rational system—were set beside each other. They were on the same plane, perceived by the same organs of sense and apprehended by the same minds, yet there was no real relation between them. Revelation took place within the supernatural and super-historical system; reason operated in the natural series of events. The distinction between the history in which revelation occurred and that in which there was no revelation was transferred to persons and things having history; there were natural and unnatural events, persons and groups. It was assumed that the differences between nature and super-nature were due not to the beholder's situation but to the things viewed while the point of view remained constant. Hence arose the conflict between history and faith. For sacred events in a secular context must be secularly apprehended and to demand of men that they should exempt certain events in the chain of perceived happenings from the application of the laws or principles with which they apprehend the others is to ask the impossible or to make everything unintelligible. How much the tendency to self-defensiveness and self-glorification in Christianity contributed to this effort to exempt the faith and its history from the judgments applicable to ordinary events it is not possible to say. But it must be noted that the consequence of the attempt to isolate sacred from secular history led not only to fruitless quarrels with natural and social science but also to internal conflict and inconsistency since it tended to substitute belief in the occurrence of miraculous events for faith in God and invited dispute about the relative importance of many wonders.

If the distinction between history as seen from without by a pure reason and from within by a practical reason, and if the denial of the exclusive validity of either view be allowed, we are enabled to understand not only how faith and history may be associated but how in the nature of the case they must be allied. An inner history, life's flow as regarded from the point of view of living selves, is always an affair of faith. As long as a man lives he must believe in something for the sake of which he lives; without belief in something that makes life worth living man cannot exist. If, as Tolstoi points out in his *Confession,* man does not see the temporality and futility of the finite he will believe in the finite as worth living for; if he can no longer have faith in the value of the finite he will believe in the infinite or else die. Man as a practical, living being never exists without a god or gods; some things there are to which he must cling as the sources and goals of his activity, the centers of value. As a rule men are poly-theists, referring now to this and now to that valued being as the source of life's meaning. Sometimes they live for Jesus' God, sometimes for country and sometimes for Yale. For the most part they make gods out of themselves or out of the work of their own hands, living for their own glory as persons and as communities. In any case the faith that life is worth living and the definite reference of life's meaning to specific beings or values is as inescapable a part of human existence as the activity of reason. It is no less true that man is a believing animal in this sense than that he is a rational animal. Without such faith men might exist, but not as selves. Being selves they as surely have something for which to live as selves as being rational they have objects to understand.

Such faith in gods or in values for which men live is inseparable from internal history. It is the gods that give unity to the events of personal life. A nation has an internal history so far as its members have some common center of reference, some good for which they live together, whether that be an abstract value, such as equality or democracy which unites them in common devotion, or whether it be the personalized community itself, such as Athena, or Britannia, or Columbia. A man has one internal history so far as he is devoted to one value. For the most part persons and communities do not have a single internal history because their faiths are various and the events of life cannot be related to one continuing and abiding good. They have "too many selves to know the one," too many histories, too many gods; alongside their published and professed history there are suppressed but true stories of inner life concentrated about gods of whom they are ashamed. Without a single faith there is no real unity of the self or of a community, therefore no unified inner history but only a multiplicity of memories and destinies. Inner history and inner faith belong together, as the existence of self and an object of devotion for the sake of which the self lives are inseparable. . . .

IV. RELATIONS OF INTERNAL AND EXTERNAL HISTORY

. . . Though there be no metaphysical or meta-historical solution of the problem of historical dualism there is a practical solution. Though we cannot speak of the way in which the two aspects of historical events are ultimately related in the event-for-God we can describe their functional relationship for us. Such a description must once more be given confessionally, not as a statement of what all men ought to do but as statement of what we have found it necessary to do in the Christian community on the basis of the faith which is our starting point.

In the first place, beginning with internal knowledge of the destiny of self and community, we have found it necessary in the Christian church to accept the external views of ourselves which others have set forth and to make these external histories events of spiritual significance. To see ourselves as others see us, or to have others communicate to us what they see when they regard our lives from the outside is to have a moral experience. Every external history of ourselves, communicated to us, becomes an event in inner history. So the outside view of democracy offered by Marxists has become an event in the inner history of democracy. It has responded to that external view with defense but also with self-criticism and reformation. External histories of Christianity have become important events in its inner history. Celsus' description of the sources of Christian belief and his criticism of miraculous super-naturalism, Gibbon's, Feuerbach's and Kautsky's accounts of Christianity, other surveys made from the points of view of idealistic or positivistic philosophy, of Judaism or of the history of religion—these have all been events in the internal history of Christianity. The church has had to respond to them. Though it knew that such stories were not *the* truth about it, it willingly or unwillingly, sooner or later, recognized *a* truth about it in each one. In so far as it apprehended these events in its history, these descriptions and criticism of itself, with the aid of faith in the God of Jesus Christ it discerned God's judgment in them and made them occasions for active repentance. Such external histories have helped to keep the church from exalting itself as though its inner life rather than the God of that inner life were the center of its attention and the ground of its faith. They have reminded the church of the earthen nature of the vessel in which the treasure of faith existed. In this practical way external history has not been incompatible with inner life but directly contributory to it.

Secondly, just because the Christian community remembers the revelatory moment in its own history it is required to regard all events, even though it can see most of them only from an external point of view, as workings of the God who reveals himself and so to trace with piety and disinterestedness, so far as its own fate is concerned, the ways of God in the lives of men. It is necessary for the Christian community, living in faith, to look upon all the events of time and to try to find in them the workings of one mind and will. This is necessary because the God who is found in inner history, or rather who reveals himself there, is not the spiritual life but universal God, the creator not only of the events through which he discloses himself but also of all other happenings. The standpoint of the Christian community is limited, being in history, faith and sin. But what is seen from this standpoint is unlimited. Faith cannot get to God save through historic experience as reason cannot get to nature save through sense-experience. But as reason, having learned through limited experience an intelligible pattern of reality, can seek the evidence of a like pattern in all other experience, so faith having apprehended the divine self in its own history, can and must look for the manifestation of the same self in all other events. Thus prophets, for whom the revelation of God was connected with his mighty acts in the deliverance of Israel from bondage, found the marks of that God's working in the histories of all the nations. The Christian community must turn in like manner from the revelation of the universal God in a limited history to the recognition of his rule and providence in all events of all times and communities. Such histories must be regarded from the outside to be sure; in events so regarded the meeting of human and divine selves cannot be recorded, but all the secondary causes, all the factors of political and social life can be approached with the firm conviction of an underlying unity due to the pervasive presence of the one divine self. It is not possible to describe external history by reference to miraculous deeds but the revelation of the one God makes it possible and necessary to approach the multiplicity of events in all times with the confidence that unity may be found, however hard the quest for it. Where faith is directed to many gods only pluralistic and unconnected histories can be written, if indeed there is any impulsion to understand or write history. Where, through a particular set of historical experiences, the conviction has been established that all events have one source and goal it becomes possible to seek out the uniformities, the dependable patterns of process. That such history, though a product of piety, is not pious history, designed to exalt the inner life of the religious community or to emphasize the importance of religious factors in social life, must be evident. A faithful external history is not interested in faith but in the ways of God, and the more faithful it is the less it may need to mention his name or refer to the revelation in which he was first apprehended, or rather in which he first apprehended the believer. In this sense an external history finds its starting point or impulsion in an internal history.

Not only is the external history of other selves and communities a necessary and possible work of faith on the part of Christians but an external history of itself is its inescapable duty for two reasons. The revelation of God in history is, as we shall see, the revelation of a self. To know God is to be known of him, and therefore also to know the self as it is reflected in God. The church's external history of itself may be described as an effort to see itself with the eyes of God. The simultaneous, unified knowledge from within and from without that we may ascribe to God is indeed impossible to men, but what is simultaneous in his case can in a measure be successive for us. The church cannot attain an inclusive, universal point of view but it can attempt to see the reflection of itself in the eyes of God. What it sees in that reflection is finite, created, limited, corporeal being, alike in every respect to all the other beings of creations. To describe that vision in detail, to see the limited, human character of its founder, the connections between itself and a Judaism to which it often, in false pride, feels superior, between its sacraments and mystery faiths, between Catholicism and feudalism, Protestantism and capitalism, to know itself as the chief of sinners and the most mortal of societies—all this is required of it by a revelation that has come to it through its history.

Moreover, though there is no transition from external observation to internal participation save by decision and faith, yet it is also true that the internal life does not exist without external embodiment. The memory which we know within ourselves as pure activity must have some static aspect which an objective science, we may believe, will in time discover in the very structure of the neural system. What the neural system is to the memory of an individual self that books and monuments are to a common memory. Without the Bible and the rites of the institutional church the inner history of the Christian community could not continue, however impossible it is to identify the memory of that community with the documents. Though we cannot point to what we mean by revelation by directing attention to the historic facts as embodied and as regarded from without, we can have no continuing inner history through which to point without embodiment. "Words without thoughts never to heaven go" but thoughts without words never remain on earth. Moreover such is the alternation of our life that the thought which becomes a word can become thought again only through the mediation of the word; the word which becomes flesh can become word for us again only through the flesh. External history is the medium in which internal history exists and comes to life. Hence knowledge of its external history remains a duty of the church.

In all this we have only repeated the paradox of Chalcedonian Christology and of the two-world ethics of Christianity. But it is necessary to repeat it in our time, especially in view of the all too simple definitions of history and revelation that fail to take account of the duality in union which is the nature of Christian life and history.

The late John Baillie was at the time of his death in 1960 President of the University of Edinburgh Graduates Association.

The Divine Self-Disclosure*

DISCLOSURE FROM SUBJECT TO SUBJECT

Revelation literally means an unveiling, the lifting of an obscuring veil, so as to disclose something that was formerly hidden. To disclose

* From *The Idea of Revelation in Recent Thought,* by John Baillie (New York: Columbia University Press, 1956), pp. 19-40.

means to uncover, but in ordinary usage it does not mean to discover. I discover something for myself, but I disclose it to another. Or I say of one thing that I have discovered it, but of another that it has been disclosed to me; in the former case thinking of myself as primarily active, but in the latter as primarily passive.

There is a sense in which all valid knowledge, all apprehended truth may be regarded as revealed. Knowledge is indeed an activity of the human mind, yet not a creative activity but only a responsive one. There can be no valid knowledge except of what is already there, either waiting or striving to be known. The knowing mind is active in attending, selecting, and interpreting; but it must attend to, select from, and interpret what is presented to it; and therefore it must be passive as well as active. . . .

I see or hear aright when my seeing or hearing is determined, in every particular, by what is there to be seen or heard. The right answer to an arithmetical problem is the one which is wholly determined by the figures facing me. I think validly when my thought is completely controlled by the facts before me. If it be said that I manipulate these facts by means of the laws of thought, it must be answered that these laws of thought are not laws of mind in the sense that so-called natural laws are laws of nature. They do not tell us how the mind operates, but how it ought to operate. They are, therefore, laws *for* thought rather than *of* thought, laws to which mind is obliged to conform if it is to attain true knowledge. And the reason why mind is thus obliged to conform to them is that they are laws of the reality which mind is attempting to know. They are not descriptive of mind but only normative for it; what they are descriptive of is the most general relations subsisting between the objects with which mind is confronted. . . .

It is important to make this point because many theologians, in their anxiety to establish or conserve a clear distinction between divine revelation and what they have called rational knowledge, have made this task much too easy for themselves by speaking as if, while the former is something given to us, the latter is something we create for ourselves, as it were spun out of our own substance; as if the former must be explained by beginning from the realities apprehended, whereas the latter could be explained by beginning from the apprehending mind. They have thus . . . been guilty of an illicit lowering of the dignity of reason in order to exalt the dignity of revelation; and no good can come of such procedure. The fact is that no true knowledge, no valid act of perceiving or thinking, can be explained by beginning from the human end—whether it be my perception of the number of peas in a particular pod or my discovery of an argument for the existence of God. In either case my cognition is valid only so far as it is determined by the reality with which I am faced. In the latter case, of course, the reality facing me need not, so far as our present point is concerned, be God Himself. It may consist only of facts coercively pointing to Him; just as the reality directly confronting Adams and Leverrier, when they validly inferred the existence of Neptune, was not the planet itself but certain other phenomena which coercively pointed to its existence. . . .

But is then the revelation of which the Bible speaks only a special case of this? . . . The revelation of which the Bible speaks is always such as has place within a personal relationship. It is not the revelation of an object to a subject, but a revelation from subject to subject, a revelation of mind to mind. That is the first thing that differentiates the theological meaning of revelation, the revelation that is made to faith, from the sense in which all valid knowledge has been said to be revelation.

The theological usage is therefore not a special case of this general epistemological usage. Rather is it the other way about. The theological usage of the term is the primary one, and the other is weakened from this and is, in fact, only a metaphor. We have acknowledged the complete justification of the point the epistemologists were desirous of making, yet we cannot accept the phrase "The object of thought reveals itself to me" as anything but metaphorical. The object of thought itself undertakes no unveiling. When we thus speak of it we are personifying it; and this fact justifies the statement that, properly speaking, revelation has place only within the relationship of person to person.

But now a further qualification is necessary. Having differentiated the revelation of mind to mind from the revelation of object to mind, we must now further differentiate the revelation of divine to human mind from the revelation of one human mind to another. The former is much more deeply mysterious, but indeed the latter is mysterious enough. It defies precise analysis. I cannot possibly analyse for you, in any exhaustive way, how my friend revealed himself to me as what he is. Sometimes a man whom I have never met before reveals much of himself to me during a casual meeting of a few minutes; he "gives himself away," as we say. Sometimes we even think we know something about a man at a first glance. But we find it exceedingly difficult to say *how* we know. Our reflective analysis may carry us some way towards an explanation, but never all the way, or nearly all the way.

Moreover, this difficulty attaches not only to our way of knowing, but also to the content of the knowledge. When I try to tell you what I have found my friend to be, when I try to describe to you his personality or mind or character, it is impossible that I should do this exhaustively. My description will take the form either of cataloguing some of the qualities I have found in him, or of recounting a few revealing words or actions of his, or most probably it will be a combination of both. But no part of this description can be exhaustive. If I recount some of his words and actions, and choose my examples well, it may be that by means of them you will succeed in grasping something of the man himself; but that is only because you fill up what is lacking out of your own knowledge of other personalities to which you think my friend's personality must be in some degree analogous. And when I recount my friend's qualities, what I am doing is trying to fix certain aspects of my friend's personality in a number of abstract nouns. In other words I am *abstracting* something from the living tissue of his personality. But no number of such abstractions can exhaust the fullness of a living personality. . . . That is, each abstract noun I apply gives you a partly wrong impression of the man at the same time as it conducts you towards a right impression. I can correct this by making one abstraction modify another, as when I say that he is "brave without being foolhardy," or "humble without being cringing," but in all this I am but narrowing the type to which he belongs, rather than offering you the individual.

All these considerations apply with greatly increased force to the revelation of God to the human soul. It is doubly impossible that we should give exhaustive account either of the ways by which we know God or of the God whom we know. For God is not, like my friend, merely one being among others, but is the source of all being. While therefore my friend's relations with me can only be through the very limited medium of his own psychosomatic organisation, there is nothing through which God cannot reveal Himself to me.

Moreover, as to the God who is revealed, theology attempts to give an account of Him, a *logos* of *theos,* by an enumeration of "attributes" which are all expressed in abstract nouns. Yet no such enumeration of His attributes can be more than rough and ready; and none can be complete. In the deed of foundation of a well-known lectureship at Cambridge, each lecturer is instructed to deal with one or more of the attributes of God, but "when these are exhausted," he may go on to some other subject. But they can never be exhausted. The infinite riches of the divine Personality who is revealed to us in Christ cannot be exhaustively enclosed in any number of abstract nouns. In every such abstraction, in every such conceptualizing, we are also to some extent falsifying by regarding one aspect of a living whole in temporary isolation; and not all possible abstractions added together can make up the living whole itself.

DISCLOSURE OF SUBJECT TO SUBJECT

All revelation, then, is from subject to subject, and the revelation with which we are here concerned is from the divine Subject to the human. But there is a further distinction that must be drawn. We speak, as has been said, of a man's revealing himself, that is, his character and mind and will, to his fellow, but we also sometimes speak of a man's revealing to his fellow certain items of knowledge other than knowledge of himself. I may say, for instance, that a friend has "revealed" to me the proof of a geometrical theorem, the best way of roasting a partridge, or the number of apple trees in his orchard. This is, however, to use the term in a very much weakened sense, such as in many languages would appear a little precious. The Greek ἀποκαλύπτειν, the Latin *revelare,* the German *offenbaren,* are words too exalted to be used naturally in this way. Only if the information offered were something of a secret, as for instance the location of a rare wild flower, would such a word sometimes be called into service; or still more if what was in question was the "unveiling" of some "mystery."

In the Bible the word is always used in its proper and exalted sense. Not only is revelation always "the revelation of a mystery which was kept secret for long ages but is now disclosed,"[1] but the mystery thus disclosed is nothing less than God's own will and purpose. According to the Bible, what is revealed to us is not a body of information concerning various things of which we might otherwise be ignorant. If it is information at all, it is information concerning the nature and mind and purpose of God—that and nothing else. Yet in the last resort it is not information about God that is revealed, but very God Himself incarnate in Jesus Christ our Lord. If we consult Kittel's *Theological Dictionary of the New Testament,* which is as nearly impartial and as little tendentious a work of scholarship as is available, we shall be told that in the Old Testament

> revelation is *not* the communication of supranatural knowledge, and *not* the stimulation of numinous feelings. The revelation can indeed give rise to knowledge and is necessarily accompanied by numinous feelings; yet it does not itself consist in these things but is quite essentially the *action* of Yahweh, an unveiling of His essential hiddenness, His offering of Himself in fellowship.

While in the New Testament,

> revelation is likewise understood, not in the sense of a communication of supranatural knowledge, but in the sense of a self-disclosure of God. . . .[2]

[1] Rom. 16. 25 f.

[2] S.v. καλύπτω, pp. 575, 586. The article is by Professor Albrecht Oepke of Leipzig.

TRUTHS AND IMAGES

The present wide acceptance in this country of the view that revelation is not merely *from* Subject to subject, but also *of* Subject to subject, and that what God reveals to us is Himself and not merely a body of propositions about Himself, owes much to the teaching of Archbishop William Temple. . . . Passages like the following have been very widely quoted:

> What is offered to man's apprehension in any specific revelation is not truth concerning God but the living God Himself.[3]
>
> There is no such thing as revealed truth. There are truths of revelation; but they are not themselves directly revealed.[4]
>
> Under the influence of that exaggerated intellectualism which Christian Theology inherited from Greek Philosophy, a theory of revelation has usually been accepted in the Christian Church which fits very ill with the actual revelation treasured by the Church, . . . that through revelation we receive divinely guaranteed Truths.[5]

The same point had, however, been as clearly made by Wilhelm Herrmann of Marburg as early as 1887:

> The thoughts contained in Scripture are not themselves the content of revelation. . . . On the contrary, we must already be renewed and redeemed by revelation before we can enter into the thought-world of Scripture. What then is the content of revelation, if it is not the doctrines of Scripture? There should surely be no doubt among Christians about the answer. One must have practised much unfruitful theology and been subjected to much bad teaching if one hesitates at all. For the Christian, and indeed for devout men everywhere, who seek God alone, it goes without saying that *God* is the content of revelation. *All revelation* is the self-revelation of God.[6]

What this means is clear. The truths which Christians believe, the doctrines and dogmas which their Church teaches, are such as they could not be in possession of, if God had not first revealed Himself to His people—revealed His nature and mind and will and the purpose which, conformable to His will, He has in mind for their salvation. The propositions which the Bible contains, and likewise the propositions contained in the Church's creeds and dogmatic definitions and theological systems are all attempts, on however different levels, on the part of those who have received this revelation to express something of what it portends. They are far from being "unaided" attempts. The Biblical writers could not have written what they did, had the Holy Spirit of God

[3] Temple, *Nature, Man and God,* p. 322.
[4] *Ibid.,* p. 316.
[5] Baillie and Martin, eds., *Revelation,* p. 101.
[6] Herrmann, *Der Begriff der Offenbarung* (1887) ; reprinted in *Offenbarung und Wunder* (Giessen, 1908) , pp. 9 f.

not been with them and in them as they wrote. Nor could the later dogmatic labours of the Church have been carried through without ever-present divine assistance. Nevertheless the distinction must be kept clearly in mind between the divine and the human elements in the process, however inextricably these may be intermingled in the result. In what is given by God there can be no imperfection of any kind, but there is always imperfection in what we may be allowed to call the "receiving apparatus."

But let us now further hear Dr. Barth on this matter. Of the Bible he writes as follows:

> Why and wherein does the Biblical witness possess authority? Precisely in this, that it claims no authority at all for itself, that its witness consists in allowing that Other Thing to be itself and through itself the authority. Hence we do the Bible a misdirected honour, and one unwelcome to itself, if we directly identify it with this Other Thing, the revelation itself. This can happen . . . in the form of a doctrine of the general and uniform inspiration of the Bible.[7]

> Revelation has to do with the Jesus Christ who was to come and who finally, when the time was fulfilled, did come—and so with the actual, literal Word spoken now really and directly by God Himself. Whereas in the Bible we have to do in all cases with human attempts to repeat and reproduce this Word of God in human thoughts and words with reference to particular human situations, e.g. in regard to the complications of the political position of Israel midway between Egypt and Babylon, or to the errors and confusions of the Christian congregation in Corinth between A.D. 50 and 60. In the one case *Deus dixit,* but in the other *Paulus dixit;* and these are two different things.[8]

Of the later dogmatic definitions of the Church Dr. Barth writes further:

> Dogmas are not *veritates a Deo formaliter revelatae.* In dogmas it is the Church of the past that speaks—worthy of honour, worthy of respect, normative, *non sine Deo,* as befits her—but still the Church. She defines, that is she encloses in dogmas, the revealed truth, the Word of God. And thereby the Word of God becomes the word of man, not unworthy of attention, but rather supremely worthy of attention, but still the word of man.[9]

> Is *veritas revelata* the truth of a doctrinal proposition? Is the truth of revelation . . . like other truths in that one can lay it down as ἀλήθεια, that is, as the result of the unveiling of a hidden character by means of human ideas, concepts and judgments, and as being, so to say, preserved in this confined and defined form, even apart from the event of its becoming unveiled? Can one possess it in abstraction from the Person of Him who reveals it and from the revelatory act of that Person—the act in which that Per-

[7] Barth, *Die kirchliche Dogmatik,* p. 115. Where I have translated as "general and uniform," Barth has three adjectives, *"allegemeinen, gleichmässigen und dauernden";* but I am not sure what the third of these is intended to mean in this connection.

[8] *Ibid.,* p. 116.

[9] *Ibid.,* pp. 281 f.

son gives Himself to be perceived by another person? If the truth of revelation is the truth of a doctrinal proposition, then obviously we must answer, Yes.[10]

From Dr. Temple and Dr. Barth let us turn now to Dr. Austin Farrer, and to his Bampton Lectures of which mention has already been made. . . . Dr. Farrer's generalized conclusion is that "divine truth is supernaturally communicated to men in an act of inspired thinking which falls into the shape of certain images." [11] More fully, he writes as follows:

These tremendous images, and others like them are not the whole of Christ's teaching, but they set forth the supernatural mystery which is the heart of the teaching. Without them, the teaching would not be supernatural revelation, but instruction in piety and morals. It is because the spiritual instruction is related to the great images that it becomes revealed truth. . . .

The great images interpreted the events of Christ's ministry, death and resurrection, and the events interpreted the images; the interplay of the two is revelation. Certainly the events without the images would be no revelation at all, and the images without the events would remain shadows on the clouds. . . .

In the apostolic mind . . . the God-given images lived, not statically, but with an inexpressible creative force. . . . The stuff of inspiration is living images. . . .

We have to listen to the Spirit speaking divine things: and the way to appreciate his speech is to quicken our own minds with the life of inspired images. . . .

Theology tests and determines the sense of the images, it does not create it. The images, of themselves, signify and reveal.[12]

. . . At least part of Dr. Farrer's reason for speaking thus of the images seems to be that he hopes the position he now adopts will turn the edge of the objection to the idea of plenary inspiration. What cannot be affirmed of propositional truths will, he hopes, be conceded to images. This, however, can be only if it is believed that, whereas all propositional apprehension of truth contains a human element and therefore an element of possible error, the images are given directly by God and contain no such element. But what possible ground have we for such a discrimination? The human imagination is in itself just as fallible as the judgment-forming intellect, and it is difficult to find a reason for believing that revelation exercises a more coercive control over the one than over the other. . . .

To say that God directly injected into their [prophets and apostles] minds archetypal images or symbols which did not grow out of, and were not matched by, the living communion with God which had been granted to them, and by the love of

[10] *Ibid.*, p. 285.
[11] Farrer, *The Glass of Vision*, p. 57.
[12] *Ibid.*, pp. 42-44.

God shed abroad in their hearts by the Holy Spirit which was given to them,[13] would be a reversion to that mechanical idea of inspiration which is absent from the prophetic and apostolic writings themselves and from which, though it has been common enough in later Christian thought, most of us are anxious to depart.

II. Authority

Bernhard Word Anderson is Professor of Old Testament Theology at Princeton Theological Seminary.

The New World of the Bible*

The uniqueness of the Bible . . . cannot be understood adequately by treating it merely as a human book. The Bible was never designed to be read as great literature, sober history, naive philosophy, or primitive science. Men remembered stories, treasured traditions, and wrote in various forms of literature because of one inescapable conviction: they had been confronted by God in events which had taken place in their history. Though hidden from mortal sight in light unapproachable, the holy God had revealed himself to mankind. He had taken the initiative to establish a relationship with his people. He had spoken his Word of judgment and of mercy. "In many and various ways God spoke of old to our fathers by the prophets; but in these last days he has spoken to us by a Son." These opening words of the Letter to the Hebrews strike the keynote of the Bible. It is this central conviction which gives the Bible, both Old and New Testaments,

[13] Rom. 5.5.

* From *Rediscovering the Bible,* by Bernhard W. Anderson (New York: Association Press, 1951), pp. 9-22.

the status of sacred scripture in the Christian Church.

This faith is a stumbling block to the modern mind. It would be more honest, however, to reject the biblical claim outright than to insist that the message of God's revelation is peripheral and that these people actually meant to say something other than they seem to say. The Bible has suffered seriously from readers who, like the legendary highwayman of ancient Greece, have attempted to force its message into the Procrustean bed of modern ways of thinking. As a consequence, some people have dismissed the theology of the Bible as a poetic or mythical embellishment of men's maturing awareness of the distinction between right and wrong. Others have treated it as elementary philosophy, the first efforts of the Hebrews reflectively to understand Reality. These approaches to the meaning of human existence may be adequate outside the Bible. But the men of the Bible say something very different. It is their claim that God himself has spoken with a decisiveness, a once-for-all-ness. They do not tell us about searching for moral values, or attempting to reach a more satisfying philosophy by standing a bit taller on their intellectual tiptoes. Rather, they bear witness to their encounter with God in the midst of crucial events of history, their engagement with him in moments of historical crisis. And, above all, this revelation was not peripheral or incidental to their message; it was the vantage point from which they viewed everything else—politics, social injustice, and war; past, present, and future. They do not argue this faith; they proclaim it with confessional language: "Here I stand, I cannot do otherwise."

The subject matter of the Bible, then, is God's self-revelation to men. Because of this stupendous theme, traditional Christianity has described the Bible as the "Word of God" and has insisted upon the divine authorship of Scripture. Says a New Testament writer: "All Scripture is given by inspiration of God," that is, as the Greek word suggests, it is "God-breathed" or "filled with the breath of God" (II Timothy 3:16). However seriously one may take the human dimension of Scripture, he cannot easily disregard the central claim of the Bible itself to be the record and witness of revelatory events in which God has spoken. This is sacred scripture because the Holy Spirit breathes through the ancient words and reveals to men in every age the Word of truth.

THE INSPIRATION OF THE BIBLE

What does it mean to say that the Bible is inspired? This is the heart of our problem. It is no easy task to deal with the Bible in such a manner that one does justice both to its humanity and its divine authorship. Much confusion has been brought about by those who would oversimplify the matter, either by emphasizing the human element in Scripture to the point of stultifying its divine authorship, or by emphasizing the divine character of the Bible to the point of ignoring that it is a human book. The major cleavage in the Protestant churches in America is no longer denominational, geographical, or even doctrinal. The line is drawn at the point of the authority of the Bible, and in general Protestants can be divided according to which side they take in the debate over biblical inspiration.

Many Protestants have adopted a position which has been labeled "liberalism." Instead of hiding their heads, ostrich-like, in the barren sands of the past, these Christians sincerely and devoutly have attempted to make the Bible speak relevantly to the modern situation. A Christian cannot believe one set of ideas on Sunday and then live by another set of assumptions the rest of the week. Such religious "schizophrenia" is intolerable, for the Christian faith jealously demands the allegiance of the whole man. Therefore, liberals sought to adjust the inherited faith to the bewildering modern world whose outlook had been defined by the achievements of science. It was their intention to remain loyal to the biblical faith, but to make this faith relevant by translating its truths into the language of the modern age. This point of view was championed brilliantly by Harry Emerson Fosdick, who popularized the phrase, "abiding experiences in changing categories," and insisted that biblical truth could be lifted out of the biblical framework of expression and reinterpreted in the categories of modern thought.[1]

Specifically, this meant reinterpreting the Bible in terms of the concept of evolution, a scientific hypothesis which originally was applied in the field of biology but which soon was transferred to other fields of investigation until it became the dominant philosophical point of view on the American scene. This outlook found theological expression in the toning down or outright rejection of supernaturalism in favor of the idea of divine immanence, that is, God's indwelling in man and nature. For instance, creation by supernatural fiat was reinterpreted to mean God's continuing creation, his immanence in the long evolutionary upthrust. In "Each in His Own Tongue," William Carruth gave poetic expression to the new interpretation of creation:

A fire-mist and a planet,
  A crystal and a cell,
A jelly-fish and a saurian,
  And caves where the cave-men dwell;
Then a sense of law and beauty
  And a face turned from the clod,—

[1] See Fosdick's book, *The Modern Use of the Bible* (Macmillan, 1929), especially chap. 4.

Some call it Evolution,
  And others call it God.[2]

Applied to religious knowledge, the evolutionary interpretation found expression in the idea of "progressive revelation." That is to say, God works immanently within the historical process, revealing his timeless truths up to man's ability to understand; on man's side, this progressive illumination yields increasing "discovery" or expanding "insight." The Bible allegedly gives evidence of such progress. The religion of Moses is said to be comparatively primitive. But under the influence of the prophetic "genius," crude and barbarous elements were gradually removed, until Jesus finally came as the great discoverer of God and the teacher of the loftiest ethical principles. Since all humanity is involved in the evolutionary process, it is no more surprising that religions outside the biblical tradition should arrive at the same insights than it is that both Russia and America, working independently, should unlock the secret of the atom. According to this view, the greatness of Jesus is that he saw what many others had seen, or could have seen, but by his forceful teaching and sacrificial death he helped men to take truth seriously.

This modern view of the Bible enabled Christians to keep their heads erect in a world where only fools or fanatics would dare to challenge the assured results of science. Of course, liberals were also children of their time, and therefore fell into the temptation of revising the Bible in accordance with their own presuppositions. Nevertheless, liberalism at its best was governed by the spirit of evangelical Christianity.[3] This is noticeable, for example, in one of the characteristic elements of the liberal attitude: devotion to truth. A critical principle lies at the heart of the liberal attitude, the fearless application of which is akin to the spirit of ancient prophets who challenged all human securities. Just as the Protestant Reformation broke upon the world in protest against a Church which had identified itself with God's Kingdom on earth, so liberalism emerged as a prophetic challenge to a decadent Protestantism that had prematurely congealed Christian truth into a static system of belief. According to liberalism, all conclusions must be judged by truth itself. This attitude, when applied to biblical study, has aided in our rediscovery of the Bible by enabling us to read it in the light of the circumstances in which it was written.

Moreover, Protestant liberalism was a healthy relief from the one-sided emphasis upon the salvation of the individual soul. Liberalism flowered in the "social gospel" movement, as ably represented by men like Walter

---

[2] By William Herbert Carruth. Permission of Mrs. William Herbert Carruth.

[3] See H. P. Van Dusen's discussion of liberal theology in *The Vitality of the Christian Tradition*, ed. George Thomas (Harper, 1941), pp. 168-174.

Rauschenbusch. If the liberal's expectancy of building a Christian society on earth was too much under the influence of the faith of the Enlightenment, it was certainly akin to the this-worldly religion of the Bible according to which all of life must be brought under the sovereignty of God. Finally, liberalism at its best was motivated by a vivid and vital rediscovery of Christian experience. If, as Luther said, "every Christian must do his own believing, just as he must do his own dying," then likewise each age must make its own discovery of Christ and express its faith in its unique way. Liberalism did this for the late nineteenth and early twentieth centuries. Indeed, future historians undoubtedly will appraise liberalism as one of the most dynamic movements in the history of Christianity.

Although liberalism was swept along by a powerful current of evangelical Christianity, the theology of liberalism came too much under the influence of the modern world-view. It is one thing to attempt to translate the biblical faith into categories which modern man can understand; it is quite another thing to adopt modern categories as ruling principles of interpretation. In attempting to bring Christianity up to date, liberals virtually capitulated to the prevailing world-view of the day, so much so that the dividing line between liberal Protestantism and secularism became increasingly dim. Reaction was inevitable.

The reaction came in the form of a movement known as fundamentalism. Beginning during the period 1910-20 on an organized interdenominational basis, it was led by conservative Protestants who felt that "modernists" were "throwing out the baby with the bath" in their streamlining of the Christian faith. The historian will point out precedents for this movement in the sterile orthodoxy which set in shortly after the outburst of the Protestant Reformation, and in the decadent Calvinism which persisted in America, especially in rural areas, throughout the eighteenth and nineteenth centuries. Fundamentalism as such, however, is a distinctly twentieth-century phenomenon, and is properly regarded as essentially a reactionary protest against the excesses of the modernizing of the Bible. Precipitated by the crisis occasioned by the introduction of the theory of evolution, it was aimed at restoring and preserving the fundamentals of the Faith. The movement gained national and even international attention through the "heresy" investigation of Harry Emerson Fosdick in 1923, and the infamous Scopes "monkey" trial at Dayton, Tennessee, in 1925 where the anti-evolution case was championed eloquently by William Jennings Bryan. Even yet, fundamentalism is a powerful force in the American religious scene. Young people become familiar with crusading fundamentalism through the "Youth for Christ" movement or, on the college campus, through the "Inter-Varsity Fellowship."

The key "fundamental" of the faith, according to this group, is the inerrancy of Scripture. In the words of a representative statement, it is "an essential doctrine of the Word of God and our standards that the Holy Spirit did so inspire, guide, and move the writers of the Holy Scripture as to keep them from error." This means that the words of the Bible are the very words of God himself. The writers of the Bible were mere passive secretaries who mechanically transscribed the divine words, these words being the media for conveying the thoughts of the Infinite Intelligence who knows everything past, present, and future. Because God is literally the author of Holy Scripture, the whole Bible "from cover to cover" is held to be absolutely infallible. In popular practice fundamentalists have claimed infallibility for a particular version of the Bible: the King James Version of 1611! Apparent contradictions in Scripture, they say, are not real and are made to vanish by the magic of an interpretative method which weaves together texts from all over the Bible. It is supposedly a matter of faith for the Christian to take the Bible exactly for what it says. If the Bible says that the world was created in six days, that God made a woman out of Adam's rib, that Joshua commanded the sun to stand still, that Balaam's ass talked, or that Jesus turned water into wine, then these matters must be accepted as facts. Many young people have gone away to college burdened with the anxiety that it is a sin to question the literal accuracy of the biblical stories.

Fundamentalists argue that the doctrine of the inerrancy of Scripture is a Christian belief of long standing. It is quite true that both Protestantism and Roman Catholicism have spoken of the Bible in the highest terms. Calvin, for instance, referred to the Bible as the infallible Word of God, and described it by such phrases as "God's own voice," "dictated by the Holy Spirit," and so on. Moreover, a recent Vatican Council declared that the books of the Bible are sacred "not because, having been composed by human industry, they were afterward approved by her (the Church's) authority, nor merely because they contain revelation without error, but because having been written under the inspiration of the Holy Spirit, they have God for their author, and as such were handed down to the Church herself." But in neither case did insistence upon the divine authorship of Scripture carry with it a slavish devotion to the letter of the Scriptures or involve the belief that the Bible is the sole norm for everything under the sun.[4] It is a great mistake to identify fun-

[4] For a treatment of "The Reformer's Use of the Bible," see Paul Lehmann, *Theology Today*, October, 1946, pp. 328 ff. For a recent Catholic statement giving limited encouragement to biblical criticism, see the encyclical letter of Pope Pius XII, *Divino Afflante Spiritu* (1943).

damentalism with the thinking of men like Luther or Calvin. Unlike classical Christian orthodoxy, fundamentalism is slavishly bound to the literal text of the Bible, and manifests open hostility to anything which goes under the name of biblical criticism. The point bears repetition that fundamentalism is a twentieth-century reactionary movement.

To the credit of fundamentalism it should be said that these conservative Christians have been sincere and devout in their attempt to defend the fundamentals of Christianity behind a Maginot line of biblical literalism. As we have observed, liberalism tended to veer away from the main stream of evangelical Christianity and to become a "modernism" carried along by the current of secularism. Thus one may say that fundamentalists, in their dogmatic way, have been making a valid protest against a secularized Christianity which failed to remember Paul's advise: "Be not conformed to this world. . . ." The protest, however, has had little effect on the real frontiers of theological thinking. It is significant that the current theological revival, spoken of earlier, has not been led by fundamentalists but by liberal Protestants whose liberalism was deepened and chastened by involvement in the world crisis.[5]

The real strength of fundamentalism lies in its weaknesses. When the securities of life are threatened, men seek an authority which is visible and absolute. The Bible, therefore, came to be an Ark of salvation in which, like Noah and his family, the faithful could find refuge from the storms of agnosticism and change which were sweeping the world. Fundamentalism is really a form of bibliolatry, that is, it is a faith in the Bible itself, rather than faith in the God who speaks his Word through the Bible. Despite its high regard for the Bible, this movement offers men a false and—paradoxical though this may seem—an *unbiblical* authority.

Moreover, part of the appeal of fundamentalism lies in its reactionary social position. Too often the defense of the Bible has been allied curiously with a reactionary defense of the status quo. It is hardly accidental that frequently the fundamentalist leadership has been recruited from, and the financial support for the movement given by, successful businessmen who have been more concerned about "saving souls" for eternity than about redeeming society in the name of Jesus Christ. The biblical justification for this escape from social radicalism has been the "premillennial" hope, that is, the belief that Christ must come again before the millennium of justice and peace can be introduced; in the meantime, the evils of society must

[5] See the series of articles by Charles Clayton Morrison, "Neo-Orthodoxy's Liberalism," in *The Christian Century,* June 7, 14, and 21, 1950.

continue and even become worse.[6] The belief that "Jesus is coming soon"—as one reads on signs along our highways—produces evangelists, but does not inspire a "social gospel." If liberalism has capitulated to secularism, it is equally true that fundamentalism in its own way has made even more dangerous concessions to the status quo.

In summary, fundamentalism and liberalism are both partly right and partly wrong. Fundamentalists are right in insisting that the Bible on its own witness presents men with the Word of God. When liberals equate "progressive revelation" with "increasing discovery," the word revelation is virtually emptied of meaning. The reality has gone, leaving behind only the empty word, like the lingering grin after the disappearance of the Cheshire cat; for that which men can discover potentially—like the secret of the atom—is scarcely the traditional meaning of "revelation." If there is revelation, God must reveal to man what man in his blindness cannot or will not see. He must shed eternal light upon the mystery of life. He must offer a divine solution to an otherwise insoluble human problem. Fundamentalists are keen enough to see this. But unfortunately they make so much of the divine authorship of Scripture that the human element is virtually eliminated, the human secretary being only a mechanical or passive transmitter of God's revelation.

Liberalism, on the other hand, is right in emphasizing the humanity of Scripture—"the warp of human life on the loom of Scripture, across which the shuttle of the Spirit of God so constantly moved," as H. Wheeler Robinson has put it. Whatever the inspired content of the Bible is, "we have this treasure in a frail earthen vessel." If God speaks his Word, men must hear it and respond within the limitations of concrete historical situations. Since the men of the Bible were men and not God they inevitably used the language of their time to communicate their faith. These things liberalism emphasized and brilliantly verified by means of historical criticism. Unfortunately, however, the human element of Scripture was overemphasized, especially under the influence of the dominant evolutionary philosophy, with the result that "God" became little more than a force at work in the social process, leading men to the formulation of loftier ideas and sounder ethical insights. Thus the uniqueness of the biblical revelation was often discounted and the divine authorship of Scripture reduced to an empty figure of speech. As liberal scholars are now recognizing increasingly, the weakness of the liberalism of the past was not in the use of the method of historical criticism, but

[6] Fundamentalists base this belief on Revelation 20:2-3, which they interpret to mean that Christ must come to inaugurate the "thousand years" of peace.

rather the fault lay in the dubious presuppositions about the nature of man and history which governed the use of the method.[7]

THE WORD BEHIND THE WORDS

In the following chapters we shall attempt to take up the task of interpretation where liberalism left off, or at the point where liberalism went astray because it was too much influenced by the modern world-view. Unlike fundamentalism, we shall not take the Bible literally; like liberalism, we shall take the Bible seriously —more seriously than liberals of the past have been wont to do. Insofar as possible the approach to Scripture will be *inductive.* We shall attempt to let the Bible speak for itself rather than force it to uphold any theological dogma or preferred way of thinking. Our aim will be to view the Bible from the "inside out," rather than from the "outside in." Thus we shall hope to do justice to both the "deity" and the "humanity" of Scripture, that is, to both divine revelation and human response.

What do we mean when we speak of the Bible as the "Word of God"? Let us recognize at the outset that we are using the language of metaphor. When the prophets exclaimed "thus saith the Lord" they were not putting quotation marks around the actual words which had been spoken by God; and when they exhorted their countrymen to "hear the Word of the Lord" they did not refer to a Voice which was carried to them on the sound waves. Speaking and hearing are the ways in which persons become related to one another.[8] If my friend speaks to me and I hear his word, a bridge of communication is thrown out from his life to mine, with the result that a relationship exists between us. Analogously, the Word of God, when heard in a historical crisis, is the medium through which God enters into *relationship* with men. Thus it is proper to speak of God revealing himself by his Word—the word of the prophets of old, and Jesus Christ, "the Word made flesh."

According to the Bible, man encounters God in history. Sometimes we say that we are most aware of God as we behold the beauties of nature. So Wordsworth—that mystic lover of nature—has caught our poetic fancy:

And I have felt
A presence that disturbs me with the joy
Of elevated thoughts; a sense sublime

[7] See the essay by T. W. Manson, "The Failure of Liberalism to Interpret the Bible as the Word of God," in *The Interpretation of the Bible,* ed. C. W. Dugmore (London: Society for Promoting Christian Knowledge, 1944).

[8] C. H. Dodd has discussed this matter nicely in *The Bible Today* (Macmillan, 1947), pp. 104 ff. This book, based on a series of "open lectures" at the University of Cambridge, provides a readable and valuable introduction to the Bible.

Of something far more deeply interfused,
Whose dwelling is the light of setting suns,
And the round ocean, and the living air,
And the blue sky, and in the mind of men.

The men of the Bible testify that the heavens and earth declare the glory of God, but to them nature was not the *primary* sphere of God's revelation. They first heard God's Word in moments of historical crisis, in events which were experienced with a unique meaning. To be sure, the encounter with God often took place in a setting of nature. Moses heard the divine call in the severe grandeur and serene solitude of the desert of Sinai; Elijah was addressed by God in the silence which followed nature's tumultuous display of earthquake, wind, and fire; and Amos received the divine summons as he was tending his flocks in the rugged wilderness of Tekoa. But in each of these cases there was an acute awareness of the historical crisis in which Israel was involved at the moment. Thus the "Word of God" was essentially the interpretation of a historical crisis in which men were grasped by God's claim upon them. In order to communicate the discerned meaning of events, the writers of the Bible employed words, but words, of course, are only symbols for the conveyance of meaning. Therefore the biblical interpreter must go beyond the letter of Scripture to the meaning. He must seek "the Word behind the words," as someone has put it.

In the strict sense, then, it is inaccurate to speak of the Bible itself as the Word of God. Properly speaking, the Bible *contains* the Word of God. The subject matter of the Bible is God's approach to man in history, in particular the stream of Hebraic-Christian history which begins with the Exodus and culminates in the coming of Jesus Christ. Though this book is characterized by great diversity and variety, both in literary form and religious content, its internal unity is the drama of the working out of God's purpose in the events of Israel's history. As someone has said, this biblical history is His-Story, in which he reveals his judgment upon men's sin and his intention and power to recreate mankind. The plot has God's purpose at the beginning, God's ultimate triumph at the conclusion, and—at the tragic and victorious climax—a Cross, the sign of God's omnipotent love. Because the Bible is both the record of these unique events and the witness to their divine meaning, it may be called the Word of God.

If we are to hear God's Word spoken through the Bible to our situation today, our first task is to put ourselves within the world of the Bible. No casual or superficial reading of Scripture can accomplish this. We must avail ourselves of the results of historical criticism and biblical theology so that we may imaginatively relive the actual historical situation in which an Amos or a Paul heard the high calling of God. We must, as it were, sit where these ancient people sat and learn to look at the human scene from their unique point of view. We must live with the Bible until it becomes part of us, just as the actor identifies himself with the role that he plays. It is then, perhaps, that the Holy Spirit, breathing through the ancient words of the sacred page, will lead us to know that the "Word of the Lord" spoken by the prophets and embodied in Jesus Christ is actually the deepest interpretation of our own life situation and our world crisis in the twentieth century.

The late Peter Taylor Forsyth was at the time of his death in 1921 Principal of Hackney Theological College, Hamstead.

The Principle of Authority*

All turns on what makes authority authoritative there, on what legitimates it. Is it enough to say that the organ of authority is "the soul in communion with God"? That does not touch the question what it is in God that makes Him authoritative for the soul. The idea is too empirical, and too little ethical, as if the mere contact and impression were enough. But the effect of Christ was not mere impression; it was reconstruction; it was the new covenant with God, and the new creation of man. A tremendous impression does not necessarily give a legitimate authority. A true authority is an authority for action on the scale of all life; its assertion, therefore, must be in an act of the living God which has the *right* to control all possible action of man, to control history viewed as one colossal act. The question is not, therefore, How has God appeared? but, What has God done? God did not come to be seen but obeyed. The Christian answer is in the Cross of Christ. The nerve of Christianity is expressed in such a

* From *The Principle of Authority,* by P. T. Forsyth (London: Hodder & Stoughton, 1912), pp. 12-15, 21-24, 82-84, 354-56. Copyright by Jessie Caroline Andrews.

great and sweeping word as "Ye are not your own; ye are bought with a price." It means Christ's absolute property in us by a new creation. The sinlessness of Jesus, His ideal perfection, is not enough. It is too negative for authority. It really means the active holiness of Jesus, not merely as keeping Himself unspotted from the world, cherishing a pure experience, or going about doing good, but gathered to a universal, victorious, and creative head in the Cross. The whole range of right and demand opened by the holiness of God and its judgment must be surveyed. It is there that we have the absolute and its authority. It is there that the crucial issue of the Cross lies. It is in this nature and action of the Cross that the solution lies of the question of authority for Christianity, for history, for ever. It lies in the absolute holy right of the new Creator of Humanity. It does not lie in the consciousness of Christ, construed psychologically and acting aesthetically or by impression, but rather in His personality as effectuated in an act which changed the whole of human relation and destiny. That is to say, the work of Christ's person must be taken into prime account, His power not only to know and show His perfection, but to perfect His perfection in the new history of a sinful race. He had power not only to present His death-crowned life *before* us, but to present it *to* us as offered for us to God, and so to make it the life of His Church and of the new race. This was done only by His death. Jesus becomes for us historically both Christ and Lord (i.e. absolute authority) only through His death and resurrection (Romans i. 4). Authority does not lie in Christ as the Superlative of the conscience, but in Christ as the Redeemer of the conscience and its new life. The kingship of Jesus can only be established in the Cross, His universal and absolute kingship. It is not the authority of excellence, but of grace. He is not simply the soul supremely, sinlessly, in communion with God, the perfect saint, the saintly superman; He is God reconciling. The authority of Christ is not simply the pressure upon us of the divine obligation which He so perfectly embodies, but the action in us of the New Life founded for Humanity in His death taken as the crisis of His life and person. "The sinlessness of Christ," says one, "means His lordship of the human race in all the things of faith." I am afraid the meaning of this is not clear, till from sinlessness we rise to a holiness which was more than a supreme and unbroken communion with God; it became an act identical with that holy and Eternal act of God which secures His will always, and which sustains the universe, even to its Redemption.

The question of our authority is the question of our religion. It is a religious question first and last. We have no absolute authority over us except in our faith; and, without it, all relative authority becomes more and more relative, and less and less authoritative. There is no final answer to the question of any authority but the answer contained in our personal faith. And the first business of our religion is to provide us with an authority—an authority which shall be at once as intimate to active life as Mysticism is to the life contemplative, and more objective than the most Roman Church.

For life is as its religion. And religion can never now be less than Christian faith. And faith is in its nature an obedience; it is not primarily a sympathy. It is sympathetic obedience, truly, but obedience always. Eternal Life is absolute obedience, an attitude to One Who has a right over us high above all His response to us, One to be trusted and obeyed even amid any dereliction by Him and refusal of His response. He is our God, not because He loved and pitied, but because in His love and pity He redeemed us. God is for us and our release only that we may be for Him and His service. He is for us, to help, save and bless, only that we may be for Him, to worship Him in the communion of the Spirit and serve Him in the majesty of His purpose for ever. First we glorify Him, then we enjoy Him for ever.

The whole nature of authority is changed as soon as it ceases to be statutory and becomes thus personal and religious. It is no longer then what it is to most people—*a limit;* it becomes *a source of power.* It is not, in the first instance, regulative and depressive; it is expansive, it is creative. Like personality, it is not a delimiting circle, but an exuberant source. It makes the soul to be more than in its egoism it could ever be. It means increase, augmentation (*auctoritas*). By the true obedience we *are* more. It is the great culture, the great enrichment. Our great authority is what gives us most power to go forward; it is not what ties us up most to a formal past. It is of Grace and not of law. It cannot be a doctrine, nor a book, nor an institution; it must, for a person, be a person. And a person who is not an aesthetic ideal of perfection, but an active source of life, a person who is gathered up and consummated in a creative, redemptive act. There is no revolt when the authority is realized as the Lord and Giver of Life; for it is the passion for life and its largeness that is at the root of rebellion. . . .

What, then, does this involve in regard to authority? First, that the last authority is religious and not theological (in the current sense of that word), that it is an authority for the person for the soul, and not for the mind and its truth; and that the soul cannot live on an external authority as one merely traditional and liable to intellectual challenge. Of course, empirically, educationally, we do depend on external authority in the first part of our discipline. The order of time is not the order of reality. As children and youths (of whatever age) we must. It is a necessary stage of our growth. It is a mark of our minority. We depend on statements about religion made by other people who are in some historic position of religious authority over us—parents, teachers, churches, or apostles. That is to say, our most direct contact at that stage is not with the object of religion, but with people produced by that object. The authority for our faith is not yet the object of that faith; it is certain people who themselves have come to own, serve, and worship that object.

So it follows, secondly, that when by these stages we come to religious maturity *our only authority must be faith's object itself in some direct self-revelation of it.* Our authority is what takes the initiative with our faith. Only so is the authority really religious, only as creative. *Our only final religious authority is the creative object of our religion, to whom we owe ourselves.* Every statement about God is challengeable till God states Himself, in His own way, by His own Son, His own Spirit, His own Word, His own Church, to our soul, which He remakes in the process. And the challenge, coming at the right place (alas, for the heartlessness of those who force it!), is God's ordinance, to drive us onward and inward upon the soul's centre and King there. The present criticism of Church and Bible is, on the whole, providential. "He saith of Cyrus, he is My shepherd, My anointed, whose right hand He hath holden." It is meant to disengage crude religion from all temporary and paedagogic authority, however valuable, and to force us for our moral manhood upon the only authority truly religious, truly speaking the tongue, and meeting the need, of the adult soul.

In the last resort, therefore, the only religious authority must be some action of God's creative self-revelation, and not simply an outside witness to it. For instance, as to Christ's resurrection, if we had signed, sealed, and indubitable testimony from one of the soldiers at the tomb who saw Him emerge, it would have a certain value, of course; but it would not be a religious authority. It would not be equal in that respect to Peter's or Paul's, though they did not see Him rise. It would be more *historisch* and scientific but less *geschichtlich* and sacramental than theirs. It would not prove that the saviour rose in the triumphant power of his finished work over the world of nature as well as of man. It would only prove reanimation; so that He might, perhaps, get over His first failure as Saviour and try again. It would be no part of God's self-revelation through apostolic souls whom the risen and indwelling Christ taught with regenerative and final power. The soldier would be but a bystander of an event, not an agent of revelation, nor a subject of it. Men are an authority to us, to our conscience, not as they may be able to stand cross-examination by historical and critical research, but as they are made by the power of the God, the Christ, Who reveals Himself in His regeneration of their souls. The Apostles are authorities for Christ only in so far as Christ made them so, not as infallible chroniclers but as elect souls. And even these men fade into the rear when they have done their work; and they may crumble and dissolve, like the sacramental bread—so long as they have brought us to direct communion with God, with Christ, as His own voucher, and stirred the evidence of His Spirit's action and power in our soul's new life. The best documents are human sacraments. Holy men are the best argument of the Gospel, short of the Gospel itself, short, *i.e.*, of Christ's real presence with us in the Holy Ghost as our active Saviour. And when men have done their proper work, when they have introduced us personally to God and left us together, it is not fatal if we find flaws in their logic, character, or faith. There is so much spiritual truth as that in the Roman principle that defect in the priest does not destroy the effect of his sacrament. Defects in Church, Bible, or apostle, defects in the logic of creed, or inconstancies of conduct in Christian people, need not destroy the real religious witness they bear on the whole, their sacramental mediation of the Gospel to us. Secure in the God to Whom they led us, we turn at our ease and leisure to examine their flaws with a quiet and kindly mind, knowing that they do not cost us our soul's life. "A thousand difficulties do not make one doubt. . . ."

There is one danger which we incur in carrying out the modern transfer of faith's foundation from dogmatic inspiration to current experience. We run the risk of putting theology at the mercy of psychology. And this is no imaginary peril. In many quarters it has become an actual surrender. And the result has been not only to put belief at the mercy of the laws of thought but to develop an alarming subjectivity, and even debasement, in religion, its preoccupation with inner processes, problems, and sympathies, and its loss of contact with the reality behind these, or the authority over them. For psychology, like all science, can but co-ordinate experience or process; it is but descriptive; we must turn elsewhere, to a theory of knowledge, to a metaphysic, or to a faith of the will and conscience, for our grasp of reality, or its grasp of us.

It is unfortunate enough when in such a transfer the content of faith is handed over to the experience of the individual, and the tradition of experienced ages in the history of a church becomes of no account before the subjectivity of the spiritual amateur and his impressions. This is a special risk where the skilful preacher takes the idolised place in democracy which the theologian had in the seventeenth century, and his mixed crowds, royalist or rebel, claim to possess the arbitrament of belief. But even if we escape from the individual, even when we go beyond the experience of the hierophant, the crowd, and the age, even when we extend the area of the experience to the whole history of the devout Church, we do not evade the danger of a religion which is merely or mainly subjective in its tests and tone. Not that we need ignore the claim, which religious psychology now sets up, to be the final forum of Christian truth, and to move the venue to that court *ex foro Dei.* No harm but good is done if we mean by the claim only that the *court* is changed, or the language changed from external dicta to experience. The change of a court, or the change of the language used in a court, matters less. What does matter is the change of the judge, of the law, and of the authority they represent. What matters is the change from external authority to none. For the autonomy and finality of mere experience is an end to all authority. A real authority, we have seen, is indeed *within* experience, but it is not the authority *of* experience, it is an authority *for* experience, it is an authority experienced. All certainty is necessarily subjective so far as concerns the area where it emerges and the terms in which it comes home. The court is subjective, but the bench is not. Reality must, of course, be real for me. It must speak the language of my consciousness. But it makes much difference whether it have its *source* in my consciousness as well as its *sphere* —whether for instance the authority of reality is merely the total volume and weight of monistic substance (prolonged into an atom in me, and urging me so), or whether it be the moral action on me of another will. We may apprehend the movements of the reality only in the guise of subjective experience, and we may perceive that its immediate form is always that of psychological act or process, and not of voices in the air. But it is another thing to say that there is no more reality behind than that which is subliminal to the process, that the momentum is only the weight of the submerged part of the process, the unexplained residuum, *ejusdem generis et molis,* of the conscious experience, something which the progress of psychology may hope in due time by its own methods to explore and explain. Were psychology much farther advanced than it is for long likely to be, we should yet not have reached by it the objective reality which is the first condition of true religion. And we should not have acquired a standard whereby to test reality. For, I repeat, psychology after all is but a science; and science cannot go beyond method. It has no machinery with which to reach or test reality, and therefore it has no jurisdiction in the ultimates of religion. When it is a question of the reality of an object and its value, we are treating it in another dimension from that of science; for science but coordinates our impressions, and cannot gauge their ultimate weight or worth. The Judge of all the earth is not an object of knowledge, but of obedience and worship. He is to be met neither with an intuition nor an assent, but with a decision, a resolve. . . .

What we usually mean by authority is this. It is another's certainty taken as the *sufficient and final* reason for some certainty of ours, in thought or action. And that is what we are apt to ban hastily as external authority. But surely (as I have said) authority has no meaning at all unless it is external. No moral individual can be an authority to himself. Nor, collectively, can Humanity be its own authority without self-idolatry. If we are to retain either the word or the thing authority, it must be as something which does not depend but descend upon us, either to lead or to lift.

The sphere of authority is not in religion alone (though its final source is there). In all the affairs of life it has its action. Most people live under what they hold to be the authority of *all.* They do, or seek to do, what everybody else does. They are most secure in those things which are the universal fashion, in the primal unities, customs or instincts of society, in immemorial convention. In the religious sphere we are familiar with the principle as *"Quod semper, quod ubique, quod ab omnibus,"* or *"Securus judicat orbis terrarum,"* or the *"fides implicita."*

Some again are satisfied with the authority of *most.* They live as the politicians do—by majorities. They court and follow the multitude. Their ideal is the popular. Their standard is the general. What they dread most is "the heritage of a speckled bird," to make themselves singular or unpleasant to their side or party. They habitually obey its demands (and they have the *flair* for them), but they make none. They ride, like the strident seafowl, on the crest of the wave. They are never laden prophets to rebuke their own, they are only racy tribunes to champion them.

Others again follow the authority of the *few.* It may be a minority of experts, as in the case of science. Very many people accept without further question what their favourite paper tells them is the opinion of the scientific leaders, even about things where a mere scientific training does more to disqualify than to equip. And here we are growing "warm," as the children say. We seek more worthy shelter under another form of minority—that, for instance, of the Church as God's elect and militant minority on earth, or that of the Apostles, Fathers, and Bishops, as men specially commissioned and fitted forth for a special truth or task. As we have those whose authoritative minority is an *élite* of culture, so we have those for whom it is an elect of grace.

Narrowing the issue and growing "warmer" still, most Christian people would take Christ's certainty as a perfectly sufficient ground for any certainty of theirs. His word and teaching is for them the supreme authority in the world. And these pages are written in the belief that Christ is indeed the supreme authority: but it is Christ in His Gospel more even than in His precept; Christ as present, powerful, and absolute Redeemer rather than as past and precious teacher; Christ as breaking our moral ban by His new creation of Eternal Life, giving us to our forfeit selves by restoring us from perdition to God's communion, and leaving us with no rights but those so given, to rebuild faith, creed, and action from a new unitary centre and a monopolist throne. It is Christ as King in His Cross.

Wherever we have authoritative belief it stands or falls with the belief of the other, of the authority—whether that authority is single or collective, a man, a school or a church.

Robert McAfee Brown is Professor of Religion at Stanford University.

Authority: The Achilles' Heel*

THE COMMON DIFFICULTY WITH THE TRADITIONAL ANSWERS

All of these answers, whatever their strengths, share a common weakness: *instead of witnessing to Jesus Christ, they witness to themselves.* They should be means through which his authority is communicated; instead they are ends from which their own authority is radiated.

Whatever we call these authorities —church, Bible, or experience, Roman Catholicism, Protestantism or sectarianism, ecclesiasticism, Biblicism, or mysticism—their story is the same. Not content to be earthen vessels holding a treasure, they claim to be the treasure itself. They all displace the object of their witness.

We can see this tendency at work in each of the answers we have examined.

The church can witness to the

* From *The Spirit of Protestantism*, by Robert McAfee Brown, pp. 180-84. Copyright © 1961, 1965 by Oxford University Press, Inc. Reprinted by permission.

mighty deeds of God in Jesus Christ. But it has become an authority witnessing to itself. No longer does the gospel authenticate its claims within the church. Instead, the claims about the church authenticate the gospel. The gospel becomes what the church says it is, which means that men claim for the church an infallibility that can only belong to God. The object of faith becomes the church rather than the Lord who humbles himself to speak through the church.

The Bible can witness to the mighty deeds of God in Jesus Christ. But it, too, has become an authority witnessing to itself. No longer does the gospel authenticate its claim through the Bible. Instead, the claims about the Bible authenticate the gospel. The important thing is to hold correct views about the Bible, which means that men claim for the Bible an infallibility that can only belong to God. The object of faith becomes the Bible rather than the Lord who humbles himself to speak through the Bible.

Personal experience can witness to the mighty deeds of God in Jesus Christ. It, likewise, has become an authority witnessing to itself. No longer does the gospel authenticate its claim by transforming personal experience. Instead, the claims of personal experience transform the gospel. The gospel becomes whatever the experiencer says it is, which means that men claim for their own experience an infallibility that can only belong to God. The object of faith becomes the experience itself rather than the Lord who humbles himself to speak through personal experience.

These may seem overbold ways of making the point. But the point needs to be emphasized rather than underplayed. For *there are no resources within these alternatives to safeguard them from these conclusions.* That is the whole problem. Each of the traditional authorities, by becoming a witness to itself, forfeits the claim to be a faithful witness.

TOWARD A RESTATEMENT OF A PROTESTANT DOCTRINE OF AUTHORITY

To challenge these authorities is to run the risk that no authority can ever take their place. This is the Protestant risk. It involves a recognition that the final authority of Jesus Christ will overflow and even smash the vessels through which he comes to us. But this is also the glory of the Protestant risk. It is always the particular Protestant contribution to remind men that we have this treasure in earthen vessels, lest we claim the transcendent power for ourselves.

We stated at the outset that the problem was to find a way of asserting the final authority of Jesus Christ over human life. We have seen that in attempting to do this, Christians absolutize the vehicles through which they feel that his authority is channeled, and erect an infallible church, an infallible book, or an infallible experience. Is there a way to overcome this temptation? [1]

If such a way is to emerge, we can find it only by treading a precarious path—the path of using the earthen vessels, but using them in such a way that no one of them can claim to be the treasure. We must acknowledge the *relative* authority of each of the traditional answers, at the same time disavowing their claim to ultimate authority for themselves.

This will mean taking at least two steps:

1. We must recognize that *there is a convergence of testimony among the witnesses.*[2] If they cannot be permitted to point to themselves, we must discover in which direction they are pointing. And we discover that they are pointing in the same direction.

To what are they pointing?

In answering this question, we make a judgment, but it is a judgment which the convergence of the various witnesses increasingly substantiates. We discover that they are all witnessing to "the gracious God," and more specifically to "the grace of our Lord Jesus Christ," through whom God has acted authoritatively, and to whom our response must be submission in gratitude and joy, acknowledging that his authority extends over all human life.

How do we know that he is our authority? We know it because the testimony of the various witnesses converges on him.

We are confronted by, and involved in, a *community* that proclaims his grace, and tries, in its own stumbling fashion, to respond to it. The church through all its members, creeds, and deeds, witnesses to the gracious God who nevertheless remains greater than anything the church can be, or do, or say about him.

The community is confronted by a *book* containing the accounts of how this grace was actively released in human life—accounts that not only contain information but are themselves the channels through which the power they describe becomes available again. The Bible through all its pages witnesses to the God and Father of our Lord Jesus Christ, who nevertheless remains greater than anything the Bible can say about him.

---

[1] There has been surprisingly little full-scale attention given to the problem of authority. See P. T. Forsyth, *The Principle of Authority,* Independent Press, and Barth, *Church Dogmatics,* I, 2, especially Chapter 3. Johnson, *Authority in Protestant Theology,* Westminster, is a discussion of the problem from the Reformers to the present.

[2] The word "witness" is a key word in the rest of the discussion. A "witness" is one who calls attention to something other than himself, who gives testimony, who is called upon to give or to be evidence of something. The Greek word was *marturos,* from which we get the word "martyr." A martyr was a witness; he was not trying to draw attention to himself, but to witness to his trust in the power of God even over death.

These two things, community and book, become authoritative as the grace to which they witness confronts men in their own *experience,* and demands the response of joyful obedience. In personal experience we receive the grace of our Lord Jesus Christ, who nevertheless remains greater than anything our experience can encompass or exhaust.

Thus it is the converging testimony of all three witnesses—community and book and experience—that establishes Jesus Christ as the true authority. The witnesses derive their relative authority as they witness faithfully not to themselves but to him.

2. We must recognize that *there is a priority among the witnesses.* This is the second step, and it is a distinctively Protestant one. It is necessitated by the fact that we manipulate each of the relative authorities to serve our own ends.

It is notoriously easy to manipulate our personal experience and make it mean what we want it to mean. The history of the church bears record of the ease with which men twist the gospel and fashion a new message from it. The use men have made of the Bible shows that with a little ingenuity they can make its message serve their ends.

Even so, it is through the relative authority of the Bible that the corrective power of the gospel has the best chance to manifest itself. It is more difficult to manipulate the content of Scripture than to manipulate the content of our own experience, and it is more difficult to manipulate the printed page than to manipulate the traditions men introduce into the church, because the Bible has a *givenness* that does not change from generation to generation. Its given-ness does not depend upon our momentary mood or upon the currents of opinion prevalent within the church.

To be sure, we can interpret the Bible to suit our ends, as the history of Biblical interpretation makes all too clear. That history is full of instructive examples of men reading Scripture for what they want to find, rather than listening to Scripture for what they are afraid to hear. We will always face this temptation, and it will always be the peculiar Protestant temptation.

But we can never quite get away with it. The reason we cannot get away with it is that *the text is always there.* It retains its power to speak louder than the distortions we impose upon it. It speaks in accents we cannot succeed in stifling, no matter how hard we try or how momentarily successful we may appear to be. For just when men have succeeded in muffling its voice beyond all recognition, it breaks forth again with fresh and compelling power. No matter how hard we try to transform its message, the message will try harder to transform us. It was this impact of the Bible that made St. Augustine a Christian, that showed St. Francis an alternative to medieval pomp and circumstance, that gave direction to the life of Wycliffe, that empowered Martin Luther to be God's agent in the reformation of the church, that (in conjunction with some help from Brother Martin) "warmed" John Wesley's heart, that bound up the tattered fragments in the life of Blaise Pascal. The story has been told before and it will be told again. It is the clue to renewed vitality within the church.

If we are to give this relative priority to Scripture, we are under particular obligation to make sure that it does not lead to a new Biblicism. With Luther we must "urge the authority of Christ against the authority of the Bible."[3] With Luther also we must recall that the Bible is the cradle in which Christ lies. We must know something about the construction of the cradle, we must see how it fits together, we must be convinced of the integrity of those who built it. But we must not become so absorbed in its construction that we fail to notice the one who lies within it.

For the cradle is not empty. It holds Christ.

III. God

John Hick is Stuart Professor of Christian Philosophy at Princeton Theological Seminary.

The Judaic-Christian Conception of God*

MONOTHEISM

The terms used for the main ways of thinking about God are formed around either the Greek word for God, *theos,* or its Latin equivalent, *deus.*

Beginning at the negative end of

[3] Luther, Weimarer Ausgabe, Vol. 39, pp. 47, 19; cited in Pauck, *The Heritage of the Reformation,* Beacon, pp. 114, 304.

* From *Philosophy of Religion,* by John Hick, pp. 4-14. Copyright © 1963. Reprinted by permission of Prentice-Hall, Inc., Englewood Cliffs, N.J.

the scale, *atheism* (not-Godism) is the belief that there is no God of any kind; and *agnosticism,* which means literally "not-know-ism," is in this context the belief that we do not have sufficient reason either to affirm or to deny God's existence. *Scepticism* simply means doubting. *Naturalism* is the theory that every aspect of human experience, including man's moral and religious life, can be adequately described and accounted for in terms of his existence as a gregarious and intelligent animal whose life is organic to his material environment.

Moving to the positive side of the scale, *Deism* can refer either to the idea of an "absentee" god who long ago set the universe in motion and has thereafter left it alone or, as an historical term, to the position of the eighteenth-century English Deists, who taught that natural theology alone is religiously sufficient. *Theism* (often used as a synonym for monotheism) is strictly belief in a deity, but is generally used to mean belief in a personal deity. *Polytheism* (many-gods-ism) is the belief, common among primitive peoples and reaching its classic expression in ancient Greece and Rome, that there are a multitude of personal gods, each holding sway over a different department of life.[1] A person whose religion is a form of *Henotheism* believes that there are many gods but restricts his allegiance to one of them, generally the god of his own tribe or people. *Pantheism* (God-is-all-ism) is the belief, perhaps most impressively expounded by some of the poets, that God is identical with nature or with the world as a whole. *Monotheism* (one-God-ism) is the belief that there is but one supreme Being, who is personal and moral and who seeks a total and unqualified response from his human creatures. This idea first came to fully effective consciousness among men in the words, "Hear, O Israel: The Lord our God is one Lord; and you shall love the Lord your God with all your heart, and with all your soul, and with all your might." [2] As these historic words indicate, the Hebraic understanding of God, continued in Christianity, is emphatically monotheistic. . . .

INFINITE, SELF-EXISTENT

This monotheistic faith, finding its primary expressions in the commands and prayers, psalms and prophecies, parables and teachings of the Bible,

[1] For example, in the Greek pantheon, Poseidon (god of the sea), Ares (god of war) and Aphrodite (goddess of love).

[2] Deuteronomy 6:4-5. Earlier than this, in the fourteenth century B.C., the Egyptian pharaoh Ikhnaton had established the sole worship of the sun god, Aton; but immediately after Ikhnaton's death this early monotheism was overcome by the national polytheism.

has been philosophically elaborated and defined through the long history of Christian thought; and because Christianity is a more theologically articulated religion than Judaism, most of our material will be taken from this source.

A basic idea which recurs at innumerable points is that God is infinite or unlimited.

It is this insistence that God is unlimited being that has led Paul Tillich to hold that we should not say even that God *exists,* since this would be a limiting statement about him. "Thus the question of the existence of God can be neither asked nor answered. If asked, it is a question about that which by its very nature is above existence, and therefore the answer—whether negative or affirmative—implicitly denies the nature of God. It is as atheistic to affirm the existence of God as it is to deny it. God is being-itself, not *a* being."[3] This paradox, as it must sound in the mouth of a theologian, that "God does not exist" is not as startling as it may at first appear. It operates as a vivid repudiation of every form of belief in a finite deity. Tillich means not that the term "God" does not refer to any reality, but that the reality to which it refers is not merely one among others, not even the first or the highest, but rather the very source and ground of all being. Tillich is, in effect, urging a restriction of the term "exists" to the finite and created realm, thereby rendering it improper to ask of the infinite creator whether he exists or to affirm or deny his existence. But it is only on the basis of this restricted usage that Tillich repudiates the statement that God exists. He is emphasizing the point which was familiar to the medieval scholastics, that the creator and the created cannot be said to exist in precisely the same sense.

God then, according to Judaism and Christianity, is or has unlimited being; and the various divine "attributes" or characteristics are so many ways in which the infinite divine reality *is,* or exists, or has being.

First among these attributes we may place what the scholastics called *aseity* (from the Latin *a se esse,* being from oneself), usually translated as "self-existence." The concept of self-existence, as it occurs in the work of the great theologians, contains two elements.

1. God is not dependent either for his existence or for his characteristics upon any reality other than himself. He has not been created by any higher being. There is nothing outside him capable either of constituting or of destroying him. He just *is,* and is what he is, in infinite richness and plenitude of being as the ultimate, unconditioned, all-conditioning reality. In ab-

[3] Paul Tillich, *Systematic Theology* I (London: James Nisbet and Company, Ltd. and Chicago: The University of Chicago Press, 1951), p. 237. Copyright 1951 by the University of Chicago.

stract terms, God has absolute ontological independence.

2. It follows from this that God is eternal, without beginning or end. If he had a beginning, there would have to be a prior reality to bring him into being; and in order for his existence to be terminated, there would have to be some reality capable of effecting this. Each of these ideas is excluded by his absolute ontological independence.

The eternity of God means more, however, than simply that he exists without beginning or end, as is indicated in this passage from Anselm (1033-1109):

> Thus thou wast not yesterday, and thou shalt not be tomorrow, but yesterday and today and tomorrow thou art. Indeed, it is not even that thou art yesterday and today and tomorrow; rather, thou simply art, outside all time. For yesterday and today and tomorrow belong solely to time, but, though nothing exists without thee, thou art not in place or time, but all things are in thee. For nothing contains thee, but thou containest all things.[4]

CREATOR

God is conceived in the Judaic-Christian tradition as the infinite, self-existent Creator of everything that exists, other than himself. In this doctrine, creation means far more than fashioning new forms from an already given material (as a builder makes a house, or a sculptor a statue); it means creation out of nothing—*creatio ex nihilo*—the summoning of a universe into existence when otherwise there was only God. There are two important corollaries of this idea.

First, it entails an absolute distinction between God and his creation, such that it is logically impossible for a creature to become the Creator. That which has been created will forever remain the created. To all eternity the Creator is the Creator and the creature is creature. Any thought of man becoming God is thus ruled out as meaningless by the Judaic-Christian conception of creation.

A second corollary is that the created realm is absolutely dependent upon God as its Maker and as the source of its continued existence. Hence we find that this radical notion of creation *ex nihilo* expresses itself in prayer and liturgy as a sense of dependence upon God for man's being from moment to moment. We have a part in the universe not by some natural right, but by the grace of God; and each day is a gift to be received in thankfulness and responsibility toward the divine Giver.

What are the scientific implications of this idea? Does it entail that the

[4] *Proslogion,* chap. 19, tr. E. R. Fairweather in *A Scholastic Miscellany* (London: Student Christian Movement Press and Philadelphia: The Westminster Press, 1956), pp. 86-7.

creation of the physical universe took place at some specific moment in the far distant past?

Thomas Aquinas (1224/5-1274) held that the idea of creation does not necessarily rule out the possibility that the created universe may be eternal. It is, he thought, conceivable that God has been creative from all eternity, so that although his universe has a created and dependent status, it is nevertheless without a beginning. He also held, however, that although the concept of creation does not in itself imply a beginning, Christian revelation asserts a beginning; and on this ground he rejected the idea of an eternal creation.[5] A different and possibly more fruitful approach is suggested by Augustine's thought that the creation did not take place *in time* but that time is itself an aspect of the created world.[6] From this point of view the universe cannot be said to have had a beginning in time, and yet from our own vantage point within it the coming to be of the space-time continuum must, in theory though not necessarily in practice, be able to be located at a certain distance in the past. In this case it is also possible to speculate concerning the initial state of the universe. However, the theories developed by some of the physicists on these points are not to be identified with the religious faith that all things depend for their existence upon the creative act of God.[7] This faith does not entail the correctness of any particular cosmological theory although some, such as that of the "singular origin" of the universe, would lend the Judaic-Christian doctrine of creation a certain degree of external support.

Needless to say, the magnificent creation story in the first two chapters of the Book of Genesis is not regarded as a piece of scientific description by responsible religious thinkers today. It is seen rather as the classic mythological expression of the faith that the whole natural order is a divine creation. Indeed, this way of reading religious myths is very ancient, as the following passage, written by Origen in the third century, indicates.

> For who that has understanding will suppose that the first, and second, and third day, and the evening and the morning, existed without a sun, and moon, and stars? and that the first day was, as it were, also without a sky? And who is so foolish as to suppose that God, after the manner of a husbandman, planted a paradise in Eden, towards the east, and placed in it a tree of life, visible and palpable, so that one tasting of the fruit by the bodily teeth obtained life? and again, that one was a partaker of good and evil by masticating what was taken

[5] *Summa Theologica,* I, Q. 46, 2. There is a good discussion of Aquinas's doctrine of creation in F. C. Copleston, *Aquinas* (London: Penguin Books, 1955), pp. 136 f.

[6] *Confessions,* Book 11, chap. 13.

[7] Some of the current theories about the origin of the universe are discussed in Fred Hoyle, *Frontiers of Astronomy* (New York: Harper & Row, Publishers, Inc., 1955), chaps. 18-20.

from the tree? And if God is said to walk in the paradise in the evening, and Adam to hide himself under a tree, I do not suppose that any one doubts that these things figuratively indicate certain mysteries. . . .[8]

PERSONAL

The conviction that God is personal, *He* rather than *It,* has always been plainly implied both in the biblical writings and in later Jewish and Christian devotional and theological literature. In the Old Testament God speaks in personal terms (for example, "I am the God of your father, the God of Abraham, the God of Isaac, and the God of Jacob") [9] and the prophets and psalmists address him in personal terms (for example, "Hear my cry, O God, listen to my prayer.") [10] In the New Testament the same conviction as to the personal character of God is embodied in the figure of fatherhood which was constantly used by Jesus as the most adequate earthly image with which to think of God.

Although belief in the Thou-hood of God thus pervades the Judaic-Christian tradition, the explicit doctrine that God is personal is of comparatively recent date, being characteristic of the theology of the nineteenth and especially of the twentieth century. In our own time the Jewish religious thinker Martin Buber has pointed to the two radically different kinds of relationship, I-Thou and I-It;[11] and a number of Christian theologians have developed the implications of the insight that God is the divine Thou who has created us as persons in his own image and who always deals with us in ways which respect our personal freedom and responsibility. . . .[12]

Most theologians speak of God as "personal" rather than as "a Person." The latter phrase suggests the picture of a magnified human individual. (Thinking of the divine in this way is called anthropomorphism, from the Greek *anthropos,* man, and *morphe,* shape—"in the shape of man.") The statement that God is personal is intended to signify that God is "at least personal," that whatever God may be beyond our conceiving, he is not less than personal, not a mere It in relation to man, but always the higher and transcendent Thou. . . .

[8] *De Principiis,* IV, I, 16. *The Writings of the Ante-Nicene Fathers,* IV, 365.

[9] Exodus 3:6.

[10] Psalm 61:1.

[11] *I and Thou,* 1923, English translation, 2nd ed. (New York: Charles Scribner's Sons, 1958).

[12] Among them, John Oman, *Grace and Personality,* 1917 (London: Fontana Library, 1960 and New York: The Association Press, 1961); Emil Brunner, *God and Man* (London: The Student Christian Movement Press, 1936) and *The Divine Human Encounter* (Philadelphia: The Westminster Press, 1942 and London: The Student Christian Movement Press, 1944); H. H. Farmer, *The World and God* (London: Nisbet & Co., 1935) and *God and Men* (London: Nisbet & Co., 1948 and Nashville: Abingdon Press, 1961).

LOVING, GOOD

Goodness and love are generally treated as two further attributes of God. But in the New Testament God's goodness, love, and grace are all virtually synonymous, and the most characteristic of the three terms is love.

In order to understand what the New Testament means by the love of God it is necessary first to distinguish the two kinds of love signified by the Greek words *eros* and *agape*. *Eros* is "desiring love," love which is evoked by the desirable qualities of the beloved. This love is evoked by and depends upon the lovableness of its object. He loves her because she is pretty, charming, cute. She loves him because he is handsome, manly, clever. Parents love their children because they are their children. However, when the New Testament speaks of God's love for mankind it employs a different term, *agape*. This word already existed in the Greek language but was not generally used to convey any special meaning distinct from *eros* until New Testament writers, through their use of the word, imprinted upon it the meaning of "giving love." Unlike *eros, agape* is unconditional and universal in its range. It is given to someone, not because he has special characteristics, but simply because he *is,* because he is there as a person. The nature of *agape* is to value a person in such wise as actively to seek his or her deepest welfare and happiness. It is in this sense that the New Testament speaks of God's love for mankind. When it is said, for example, that "God is Love" [13] or that "God so loved the world . . . ," [14] the word used is *agape* and its cognates.

God's universal love for his human creatures, a love not rooted in their virtue or desert but in God's own nature as *agape,* is the basis for that side of religion which knows God as the final succour and security of man's life: "God is our refuge and strength, a very present help in trouble." [15] The ultimate of grace is believed to be also the ultimate of power, the sovereign love which guarantees man's final fulfillment and well-being.

The infinite divine love also gives rise to that side of religious experience in which God is known as claiming the total obedience of a man's life. God is thought to be our "Lord" and "King," as well as our "Father." The divine commands come with the accent of absolute and unconditional claim, a claim which may not be set in the balance with any other interest whatever, not even life itself. This element of demand can be viewed as an expression of the divine love, seeking the best that is within man. Even between human beings there is

[13] I John 4:8.
[14] John 3:16.
[15] Psalm 46:1.

nothing so inexorably demanding as a love that seeks our highest good and cannot be content that we be less than our potential best. Because it is infinite, the love of the Creator for the creatures made in his image implies a moral demand of this kind that is absolute and unqualified.

In this exposition we have subsumed the goodness of God under the love of God. But this idea does not avoid an important philosophical problem concerning the belief that God is good. Does this belief imply a moral standard external to God, in relation to which he can be said to be good? Or alternatively, does it mean that God is good by definition? Is the Creator offered as the final standard of goodness, so that his nature, whatever it may be, is the norm of goodness?

Either position involves difficulties. If God is good in relation to some independent standard by which he may be judged he is no longer the sole ultimate reality. He exists in a moral universe whose character is not of his own making. If, however, God is good by definition, and it is a tautology that whatever he commands is right, certain other implications arise which are hard to accept. Suppose that beginning tomorrow, God wills that human beings should do all the things which he has formerly willed they should not do. Now hatred, cruelty, selfishness, envy, and malice are virtues. God commands them; and since God is good, whatever he wills is right. This possibility is definitely entailed by the view we are considering; yet it conflicts with the assumption that our present moral principles and intuitions are generally sound, or at least they do not point us in a completely wrong direction.

Perhaps the most promising resolution of the dilemma is a frankly circular one. Good is a relational concept, referring to the fulfillment of a being's nature and basic desires. When humans call God good, they mean that his existence and activity constitute the condition of man's highest good. The presupposition of such a belief is that God has made human nature in such a way that man's highest good is to be found in relation to God. Ethics and value theory in general are independent of religion in that their principles can be formulated without any mention of God; yet they ultimately rest upon the character of God, who has endowed man with the nature whose fulfillment defines his good.

In connection with the goodness of God, reference should also be made to the divine "wrath," which has played so prominent a part in pharisaic and puritanical thought. "Flee from the wrath to come" has been the warning burden of much religious preaching. Much of this preaching has ironically embraced the very anthropomorphism which St. Paul, whose writings supply the standard texts concerning the Wrath of God, so carefully avoided. C. H. Dodd, in his study of St. Paul, pointed out that Paul never describes God as being wrathful, but always speaks of the Wrath of God in a curiously impersonal way to refer to the inevitable reaction of the divinely appointed moral order of the Universe upon wrong doing. The conditions of human life are such that for an individual or a group to infringe upon the structure of the personal order is to court disaster. "This disaster Paul calls, in traditional language, 'The Wrath,' or much more rarely, 'The Wrath of God.' . . . 'The Wrath,' then, is revealed before our eyes as the increasing horror of sin working out its hideous law of cause and effect." [16]

HOLY

Taken separately, each of these characteristics of God, as he is conceived in the Judaic-Christian tradition, presents itself as an abstract philosophical idea. But the religious person, conscious of standing in the unseen presence of God, is overwhelmingly aware of the divine reality as infinitely other and greater than he. This sense of the immensity and otherness of God was expressed with unforgettable vividness by Isaiah:

To whom then will you liken God,
  or what likeness compare with him?
The idol! a workman casts it,
  and a goldsmith overlays it with gold
  and casts for it silver chains.
He who is impoverished chooses for an offering
  wood that will not rot;
he seeks out a skilful craftsman
  to set up an image that will not move.
Have you not known? Have you not heard?
  Has it not been told you from the beginning?
  Have you not understood from the foundations of the earth?
It is he who sits above the circle of the earth,
  and its inhabitants are like grasshoppers;
  who stretches out the heavens like a curtain,
  and spreads them like a tent to dwell in;
who brings princes to nought,
  and makes the rulers of the earth as nothing. . . .
To whom then will you compare me
  that I should be like him? says the Holy One.
Lift up your eyes on high and see:
  who created these? [17]

Again, God is ". . . the high and lofty One who inhabits eternity, whose name is Holy," [18] whose ". . . thoughts are not your thoughts, neither are your ways my ways, says the Lord. For as the heavens are higher than the earth,

[16] C. H. Dodd, *The Meaning of Paul for Today*, 1920 (New York: Meredian Books, 1957), pp. 63-4.
[17] Isaiah 40:18-23, 25-26.
[18] Isaiah 57:15.

so are my ways higher than your ways and my thoughts than your thoughts." [19] The awareness of God as holy is the awareness of One who is terrifyingly mysterious, an intensity of being in relation to which men are virtually nothing, a perfection in whose eyes ". . . all our righteousnesses are as filthy rags," [20] a purpose and power before which we human beings can only bow down in silent awe.

We may now sum up the Judaic-Christian concept of God: God is conceived as the infinite, eternal, uncreated, personal reality, who has created all that exists other than himself, and who has revealed himself to his human creatures as holy and loving.

IV. Christ

At the time of his death in 1966 Emil Brunner was Professor of Theology at the University of Zurich.

The Person and the Work of Christ*

(I)

"God so loved the world that He gave His only begotten Son that whosoever believeth in Him should not perish, but have everlasting life." The coming of the Son of God is His work. His existence is the redeeming revelation. The work and the person of the Redeemer are an indissoluble unity. When we speak of the one we speak of the other; when we understand who He is we understand His work; it is impossible to understand who He is without comprehending His being as God's act for us. The Gospel actually consists in this very unity: in this unity of word and fact, of truth and reality,

[19] Isaiah 55:8-9.

[20] Isaiah 64:6 (King James Version).

* From *The Mediator,* by Emil Brunner, translated by Olive Wyon. The Westminster Press. Copyright 1947, by W. L. Jenkins. Used by permission of Westminster Press and Lutterworth Press. Pp. 399-415.

of person and cause, all of which are elements which outside this revelation are everywhere separate from each other. He *is* the Truth: but this "is" means life; vital, vigorous, effective. This truth is not "static," it is an event, a deed. Both these statements are equally important: that He is the Truth, and the fact that He is the Truth is itself an act.

Hence the contrast which modern theology has drawn between the "magico-natural" conception of salvation of the Eastern Church, and the "ethico-practical" conception of the Western Church constitutes a serious misunderstanding. We are not dealing with an absolute distinction at all; the difference is simply one of emphasis. The intention of both is the same; the apparent differences are due to the fact that different aspects of this truth are emphasized at different times. A real antithesis could only arise if the paradoxical unity which transcends the antithesis between nature and spirit were lost. If that were to take place, then all that would be left would be two forms of interpretation: the magical, material objective interpretation, and the rational, ethical subjective interpretation. What was said above about the doctrine of the Two Natures is also true in this connection: in principle the dogmatic definitions of the Early Church are right; but the doctrine has not been able to steer clear of certain malformations. These malformations, however, do not occur only in the direction of magico-natural sacramentalism; they appear just as frequently in the direction of rational subjective moralism.

In principle, however, the Early Church is absolutely right: the great miracle over which Christendom rejoices is the Christmas miracle of the Incarnation, the coming of the Son of God, the Incarnation of the Word; and this means the *Person* of the Mediator. That *He* is here, that the God-Man exists, this is salvation, this is revelation. If it is this "Being" that we mean, then we can confidently make our own the boldest statements of Indian or Greek philosophers, all that the speculative Idealists and mystics of all ages have said in their most exalted moments about the eternal Divine Being, about the "abiding ground" of Eternal Being contrasted with the ceaseless flux of earthly becoming. The false element in their views does not consist in their claim to find salvation and truth in the Divine Being. If there be any salvation at all, on what could it be based if not on the Being of God? If an ultimate redeeming truth does exist, could it be other than the eternal truth of God? Even the Bible itself knows no other: God is our refuge, God the Eternal and the Unchangeable. Revelation simply means the knowledge of this Eternal God. This is not where they go wrong; their error lies in the fact that they think that they already know and possess this God, the Eternal Truth.

The fact that Christ is the centre of the Christian message does not mean that the central element in this message is no longer the Eternal Truth and the Eternal Being of God. Nothing is more foolish than to try to play off "Theocentric" and "Christocentric" standpoints against one another. As if it were not this very "Christocentric" message of the Gospel in which God is absolutely central! If Christ means anything at all, it is simply and solely because through Him God is revealed, the eternal Unchangeable God, in His very Being. This is all that matters; nothing else counts at all. If we make a hole in a dark wall through which the heavens become visible and the sunlight streams in, we do not say that this window is opposed to the heavens and the sunshine. Jesus Christ is the window through which we can see God. When the Christian message says with emphasis, "Look to Christ," it does not mean "look away from God," but "look away to God where God really is," for if God is contemplated apart from Christ, if Christ is ignored, then God is not seen as He really is. Zeal for Christ is zeal for the true God; the exclusive element in the Christian creed: "in no other is there salvation . . ." is simply the exclusiveness of Divine Truth. Because the truth of God is one, and one only, and because in order to see this truth we must stand at a certain point, is the reason why we must make such exclusive claims for Christ.

But that which we are to see in Christ is absolutely nothing other than God, and indeed God's Eternal Being. ὃ ἦν ἀπ' ἀρχῆς, "that which was from the beginning . . ."; it is of this we speak, this is the whole meaning of the Gospel. Therefore the Gospel which is most evidently "Christocentric" begins with the words: "In the beginning was the Word." This is the point of view from which the writer intends all that follows to be read. His point is this, that the whole interest and significance centres in the Word which was from the beginning, the eternal truth, the truth of God. Fichte's saying, rightly understood—but certainly *not* in the sense in which the writer intended it—that it is only the metaphysical and not the historical element which saves us, is absolutely right, that is, if by the "metaphysical" we mean the real truth of God (which can only be known through Christ). Christ is really simply the window through which "the eternal Light streams in"; this is His significance, and His alone. Because in Him the Word which was from the beginning became flesh—for this reason, and for this alone, He is the Christ.

The Christian message therefore does not divert interest from the eternal to the historical sphere; on the contrary: through the "historical element"—and we now know what that may mean—our attention is directed towards the eternal; and indeed precisely towards this "static" truth of the eternal, unchangeable Being of

God. This truth is not a theory of creative evolution, or of divine development, or of a theogonic process, it is the message of the Word "which was from the beginning." If this were not the Word from the very beginning, then it could never be the divine, the redeeming Word. It is this which connects the Christian faith with religion and speculative philosophy of every kind: the fact that man seeks to take refuge in the Eternal, in the Unchangeable, the longing to escape from the stream of endless flux, which as such is fleeting, and therefore unblest. Wherever we hear this cry for the eternal, if it be a real cry, there we hear accents which are akin to the Gospel. The contrast between the temporal and the eternal is not weakened by the Christian Gospel; on the contrary, it is still more sharply accentuated than elsewhere. That redemption can be found only in the eternal cannot be expressed more clearly than in the central Christian doctrines of the Triune God, of His eternal purpose, and of eternal election.

(II)

Thus the difference between the message of Christ and the teaching of mysticism and of speculation does not lie here, but in the fact that in the Christian message this Eternal Word is not regarded as a truth which man, "at bottom," already possesses, but as a revelation, as something "given," as a Word which has "come." This Word *is* Christ. The ancient Fathers of the Church were not mistaken when they used to underline this word *"is."* He *is* the Word. "I *am* the Way, the Truth, and the Life." "I *am* the Door." "I *am* the Light of the world." His Being is itself redemption. To His Being we may and must point when we are speaking in a Christian way about salvation and the truth. This is not naturalism, a magical conception of salvation. If the Divine Being of God is the redeeming truth, then the Divine Being of Christ is also this truth. No human action is necessary. The activism of the West—I allude to the contrast between the Occident and the Orient—is not more spiritual than the quietism of the East. Both tendencies need rebirth; thus the Western theological definitions of the mystery of Christ are in no way more Christian or more spiritual than those of ancient Greek theology. In both there lies the danger of misunderstanding, but both also can be understood aright. Later theology, however, has certainly not understood the theology of the Eastern Church. That in itself would be enough to suggest that it has also deprived Western theology of some of its content.

The Incarnation is the fundamental Christian truth; not only the Greek

Fathers of the Church were conscious of this fact, but also our Protestant forefathers.[1] The best Protestant hymnology also bears witness to this fact. We need only remind ourselves of the Christmas hymns of our Church:—

"Gott wird Mensch, dir Mensch, zugute,
Gottes Kind, das verbindt
Sich mit unsrem Blute" [2]

The existence of the God-Man, as such, constitutes revelation and salvation. This is why He is called the Mediator, not primarily on account of His work, but because of what He is in Himself. He is the Mediator because in Him the eternal Word is present, in Him the eternal Light enters into our world, because in Him the eternal purpose of God, the mystery of God becomes known, because in Him we can see God. "He that hath seen Me hath seen the Father." Of course, this means he who sees Him as the eternal Son of God, who sees Him in the mystery of His Person, who recognizes Him in His unconditional divine authority, and this means, who knows Him as the One who is from above, not like ourselves, from below, One who has "come," the One "from the Other Side," the One whom we have not seen, if we only know the life of Jesus in the moral-religious historical sense, thus One whom we do not really "see" if by this we mean—however successful the attempt may be—merely an understanding of the inner life of Jesus. The "Self" in whom we see the Father is the "only One," the "only begotten," the Eternal Son, not the historical visible personality.

[1] It is one of the most astonishing things about the modern view of the history of the Reformation that the absolutely fundamental significance which this early Patristic central idea of the Incarnation possessed for the Reformers in general and for Luther in particular is overlooked; if the question is not overlooked altogether it is then assumed that the Reformers were in this respect "rather naïve," and limited by the outlook of their day; hence it seems quite a simple matter to eliminate this idea from the theology of the Reformers without altering the nature of their theology in any way. It is a good thing therefore that the edition of Luther which has at last been published by Theodosius Harnack leaves no further doubt on this question. It is unnecessary to prove this point in detail; here it will be sufficient to point to Luther's well-known exposition of the ladder to heaven in his Commentary on Genesis (indeed, this illustration is often used by Luther when he is speaking of the mystery of revelation as a whole) whose central idea is this: that "the secret of this descent down the ladder is that in Christ "God and Man are truly in one and the same Person." . . . "The ladder is therefore the marvellous union of the Godhead with our flesh. . . ." On this is based "the immense and indescribable dignity of the human race . . . because God has united Himself with human nature through this marvellous union," etc. That also for Calvin this idea had not lost the significance which it had in the Early Church, the twelfth chapter of the second book of the *Institutio* is sufficient evidence. At the same time we must admit that in general the theologians of the Reformation preferred to regard the Incarnation from the point of view of the doctrine of Satisfaction. But the indissoluble connection between these two "main articles" of the Christian Faith is also expressed by them with complete clearness and decision. It would be very valuable if the corresponding proof could be produced from the practical religious literature of the period of the Reformation. This ought not to be a very difficult matter.

[2] Lit.: "God becomes man, for thy sake, O man,
Child of God, who unites Himself
With our flesh and blood."—Tr.

That He has actually come to us, that He is given to us, that He is here, it is in this that Christendom should rejoice evermore. For this is what we lack: Himself. Not some status which God may graciously aid us to acquire, some kind of position in the world, or the possession of some kind of spiritual title to salvation, but *Himself:* God, in so far as He wills to impart Himself to us. The "Son" means God Himself as the Word. In Him we have been created. We have lost the Primal Word, and in Him the meaning of our existence, the Image of God, the fact that we belong to God, fellowship with God; the divine inheritance has been squandered. We have lost our home, we have left the Father's house, we are now homeless outcasts. That He Himself, He in whom we belong to God, He in whom we know God and ourselves according to the truth, He in whom is the meaning of our life, He in whom God names His own Name and thus our name also, is here once more among us, and that we can know Him, that He is in fellowship with us: what else could be desired as salvation? He is, of course, only present to faith and not to sight, He is here in hiddenness, not yet in glory and power. And yet "We beheld His glory." That this is possible, even though only with the eye of faith, that it can be seen in Him, is the grace which ought to suffice for the believer.

(III)

We may thus speak of the Being, of the "mere existence," of the divine-human "Nature" of the Mediator without falling back into a metaphysic of being, into speculation or mysticism, because this Being includes within itself the fact that He has come. Only as the One who has come is He the Son. The duality of His being, the "Two Natures," means simply that the Eternal Word has come. Therefore it is precisely this Being which stands in contrast to mysticism and to speculation: it is the Being of the Mediator. By the very fact that as the Mediator, as the God-Man, He stands before us, we are confronted by the fact that of ourselves we could not know God. If the Christian religion speaks of the Eternal Word, and the Eternal Son, it does not speak of Him like the Platonist Philo, nor like Hegel, nor like Meister Eckhart, for it is speaking of Jesus Christ. We differ from Platonism in this, that we know the Eternal Son and the Eternal Word only in Jesus, in this real historical fact: the life of Jesus. We differ from historical realism in this: that in this Jesus we know and confess in Him alone the Eternal Son, the Primal Word, the Christ after the Spirit.

The humanity of the Son of God

means that He has really come, it means the contingency, the uniqueness of the revelation. The divinity of the Son of Man means the eternity of the Word, the personal Presence of the Eternal God in Him. Therefore whoever speaks in a Christian manner about the Being, about the existence of the God-Man, is speaking at the same time of that which is revealed, of the divine self-movement, of the act of revelation. The incomprehensible co-existence of the predicates, God and Man, is simply the incomprehensible fact that the Eternal God comes, that the eternal truth is one which has become such for us, and that we only rightly understand it as that which has come and has become, thus that we cannot sever it from the fact that it has come without destroying it. There is no surer method of thoroughly damping the ardor of all speculative arrogance and metaphysical pretension than to look steadily at the message of the Being of the God-Man and at His dual Nature. In this monstrosity of a God-Man we know our own deformity, in this contradiction we see our contradiction, in this problem we see our own problem, the problem of humanity, evil, sin. For we need the Eternal Son as One who has come, as One who has come in time, and in human historical form, that is, in the form of a servant, just because we are sinners. The Incarnation is the divine and merciful answer to our falling away from God. The Mediator in His Person, by His very "constitution," is the mediation between the Creator and the fallen creature, in a double connection: as the Mediator of revelation and the Mediator of reconciliation.

Here therefore there can be no question of a metaphysic, because here we are dealing with the Word and with faith, with sin and reconciliation. We may also say, because we are here concerned with the whole personal relationship of faith between the personal God and our own decision. For faith alone can know the Mediator as the Mediator, the decisive act in which man is stripped bare of all pretensions by God, and in the presence of God; and this as one who of himself can neither know the truth nor live in it, nor can attain to a life in the truth, as one who is in a condition in which one expects deliverance alone through the act and speech of God. Recognition of the Mediator means the actual breaking down of our nature. This is why the natural man says "anything but this!" This too is what intellectual reason says. Everything within it revolts against this attack on its pride. The truth as something which has come into being, as something which is "given" through history! The Eternal Truth bound up with an accidental fact of history! And just as hotly does the moral will rebel against this also—and still more passionately because it is more personal: righteousness as something which is given to us as a free gift, what *I* ought to do done by another and reckoned to me as though I had done it, the right attitude to God won through that which another has done! Faith consists in conquering the "offence" and the "folly" constituted by the Mediator; for faith means allowing oneself to be humbled, and the boldness with which we accept the unspeakable mercy of God. This the Mediator is in His Person, because in His Person we meet the personal God. There is no other possibility of coming into contact with God. "No one cometh unto the Father save through Me." For the meeting must be real and personal; otherwise we remain by ourselves, carrying on a monologue with ourselves, with our own ideas. But God can be met only there where God personally and really comes towards us Himself. This is the Mediator. Only through the most grievous misunderstanding is it "possible" that the very faith in the Mediator can be perverted into a metaphysic, because by its very nature it desires to secure the existential, personal character of the meeting of the human soul with God.

(IV)

While we lay so much stress on the fact that the Person of the Mediator is in itself the revelation, at the same time we do not wish to suggest—as will be seen directly—that we either ignore the "Work" of the Mediator or even relegate it to a subordinate position. We do certainly mean, however, that we reject subordination of the opposite kind. Melanchthon, in his first edition of the *loci,* enunciated the following statement, which is not only well known, but we might almost say, from the theological point of view, epoch-making: *hoc est Christum cognoscere, beneficia ejus cognoscere.* Certainly the statement is right, and it is important in so far as it is directed against scholastic casuistries, against the metaphysical perversion of the doctrine of Christ. In this sense we might render it thus: it does not matter how the divine and the human Natures in Christ are united with each other, or how they can coexist, but what does matter is what we have in this Christ; how Christ speaks to us, not what we think about Him, is the problem for faith. This is evidently the real meaning of the statement of Melanchthon. His formula, however, has a shade of meaning which not only could easily lead one astray, but has actually done so. It contains the germ of the whole anthropocentric point of view of later Lutheranism, and this simply means of religious egoism. Man occupies the centre of the picture, with his need for salvation, not God and His glory, His revelation; thus God becomes the One who satisfies the needs of man. Not in vain has Ritschlian pragmatism so often appealed to these words. Christ is needful in order that men may be helped, God is the guarantee of the value of human life.

This is not the view of the Bible. God reveals Himself for His own sake, in order to create His Kingdom, in order to manifest His glory,[3] in order to restore His own order, His dominion. The Bible is the book in which the glory of God is the first concern, and the salvation of man comes second. In the self-manifestation of God, in the dominion of God, the salvation of man is also included, but it is not the other way round. This is salvation, that man should once more learn to set God at the centre, that he may once more be able to say with real conviction: whatever God does He does well. That God and His cause may be his first concern, and man and his salvation a secondary consideration, because he knows that God Himself, just in His unconditionedness, *is* the salvation of man. Not because Christ brings us *benficia* is He the Son of God, but because He reveals God to us do we know ourselves also as sheltered and healed in Him. Opposition to metaphysical speculation is indeed "practical" knowledge, and the Christian faith is—as Kaftan used to teach—"a practical concern." But the "practical" nature of faith ought not to be confused with a coarse or refined Eudaemonism. That God Himself really and personally meets with us, this is the practical, essential knowledge. This is the true antithesis, not religious pragmatism, which places man's self-end in the first rank and God, in the last resort, simply as the One who guarantees this end; which means that God becomes simply a means to an end.

Hence it is important that the doctrine of the Person of the Mediator should not be subordinated to that of His Work. The Mediator, in His Person, is not a means to an end, but a self-end. For He is the revelation of God. He is not merely—as, for instance, in the doctrine of Anselm—the instrument of the reconciliation. The doctrine of the Incarnation, the Christmas message, is as important as the doctrine of "satisfaction," the message of Good Friday. Neither can be separated from the other, for both mean this, that God comes. He comes to us Himself; and He really and actually comes to us, to us in our low estate.

(V)

The Being of the Mediator is the gift and the act of God. The New Testament bears witness to the Mediator as the great gift of God. God sent

[3] What can we say when a historian of dogma like Otto Ritschl thus explains to himself the fact that in the theology of Calvin the dominant idea is that of the Glory of God? "In this fact there is a transference of the vital idea of glory which means so much in the national life of the French to the concrete colouring of his Idea of God" (*Dogmengeschichte des Protestantismus,* III, p. 172). Then was Anselm of Canterbury a Frenchman, for the same idea is prominent in his teaching? And what about the Prophets of the Old Testament?

Him; He gave Him, He gave Him up. This refers not merely to the death of Christ, but to His whole existence, as indeed His whole existence is regarded from the point of view of "humiliation." The fundamental feature of the whole message of the Bible is this: that God is known through His action. But by this action is not meant His activity in the world in general, His preservation and rule over the world, the sphere of general revelation. In this sphere God appears to us in a sort of twilight, here God does His "strange work." Here He is not known as Himself, in His inner Being, as He is in Himself (*Ansichsein*). But by His action is meant His special action, His act of revelation. For this is the aim of this act of God: that He makes Himself known. His action means that He issues forth, He comes. The most important element in His action is always His own presence in this action, and the secret aim of this action is always this: that He may "dwell" among His people. This "dwelling," however, is not a physical but a spiritual state: "They shall all know Him." "The knowledge of the Lord shall cover the earth as the waters cover the sea." "His light shall break forth as the morning." The purpose of this action is the vision of God, the final revelation.

His Action is therefore the same as His Speech. The real gift of God is always His Word; but the message of prophecy does not fully express this intention. For it is still only a word about the Word. The real Word is the personal Word, which is identical with His personal Presence. This Word, as a personal Presence, is Christ, the Eternal Son, the Word which was from the beginning. Therefore He is the fulfillment of all the action and all the speech of God. As "Himself" He is the meaning, or rather the One who is meant, though here and now in faith and thus in the disjointed character of this earthly existence, but then in completion. If the prophetic revelation is already the work of God, the act in which He comes near to His people, then, far more, the revelation of Christ is the revelation which consists in the Person of Christ. To have Him means to have God. To have Him is the same as having Him given to us. His life is the divine effectual Word.

For in Him, in His existence, God has really found a firm footing within humanity. It is not as though humanity were not already in His Hands; even the heathen are His instruments whom He uses as He wills. But here we are speaking of a different kind of presence, of the Presence of God in revelation and in salvation. This Presence begins for us in Christ, through His "assumption" of human "nature." In Christ God takes the part of man in spite of the fact that man has fallen away from Him. This is not merely because Jesus *says* this, but by His very existence as the God-Man. For in Him God has entered into a new relation with man, He has united Himself with man.

It would not be difficult to slip into the magico-sacramental misinterpretation which turns redemption into a physical or hyper-physical event, and thus into an event which has no connection with the "Word," and thus presents no challenge to the human will. But this is not what is meant. Human nature—as we have seen—is not the physical nature of humanity; it is rather the world of history. By the fact that the eternal Logos became historical, became an event, an existing fact, within the reality of time and space, one historical personality among us historical personalities, by the fact that He became flesh, He has bridged the gulf which separates historical life from the eternal world. The fact that He has thus bridged the gulf is the whole point. How this happens, how it comes to pass that an historical man is the Eternal Son, who has "come," this is the secret of God. Those who know that this mystery, this marvel, is the Divine Intention will not feel inclined to try to probe into the mystery any further. But faith holds fast to the fact that it has happened, that in the Jesus of history we can behold the Eternal Son, that in Him God Himself can meet with us. Faith is not concerned with the Incarnation as a metaphysical problem. But the knowledge that in Jesus Christ the barrier which separates us from the Creator has been transcended, so that now God really meets us personally, constitutes the real knowledge of Christ.

God's act is the Incarnation of the Son of God. God sent Him, God gave Him. But this would not be the sending forth of the Eternal Son if this act were not also His own act. It is the act of the whole Trinity. The Son is not only the One who is sent, but also the One who willingly permits Himself to be sent. He is the One who has "emptied Himself." It is His act, both here and on the other side of the border-line between the two worlds of history and of eternity. He is here not simply as One who suffers and endures, but also as One who is active in the midst of His passive acceptance. He would not be a real person but merely a material instrument if His life were not also His own act. Therefore His whole life is His act, His Passion is revelation. As the personal act of Jesus Christ it is an act of revelation. But it is not only the act of God in so far as it is the life work of Jesus, as in the historical sense it is the personal act of Jesus. Neither the Birth nor the Crucifixion are in the historical sense acts of Jesus Christ, but they are indeed the act of God, and thus also the act of the Son, namely, precisely because they constitute His humiliation, His giving Himself to the flesh and to death. His historical life, and His action in the widest sense—thus, for example, also His teaching—is certainly a moment in the revelation, but it is not the revelation itself. The revelation, the *work* of the revelation, is the whole, which cannot be conceived in historical terms at all. Hence it is not the story of Jesus which is the object of the Christian faith, but the revelation of God in the Person and Work of the Mediator, as it is attested by the Church as a whole. Only he who sees this as a whole beholds the "Christ after the spirit." He who sees the historical only—just because he does not see it as a whole—does not see the Christ at all, but merely the life of Jesus, the "Christ after the flesh." He may indeed see the action and the Being of Jesus, but in this action and in this Being he does not see the revelation of God, even when he uses Christian terms to express what he sees.

This distinction is vital for the understanding of the historical activity of Jesus.

(VI)

Finally, there is still one more question to be discussed, which, if it is brought into the discussion at the wrong point, causes untold confusion: the question of the relation between special and general revelation. There is only one Logos. This Logos can only be known in Christ. But this Logos is the principle of all knowledge, and, above all, it is the central truth in all religion. Here everything depends on the order of the series: whether we say Christ is the truth of all philosophy and of all religion, or all that is true in philosophy and in religion is "Christ." In the latter instance the principle is superior to the illustration, and the revelation of Christ is merely an individual form of a general truth, a concrete instance of an idea. Thus from this point of view the idea triumphs over the revelation, the impersonal conquers personality. The truth of Christ becomes the special expression of the general revelation, alongside of other more or less equally justified forms; the historical illustration, the Person of Jesus as the bearer and discoverer of this idea, which is in principle detachable from His Person—this is the fundamental thesis of the modern view.

The Christian view, on the contrary, is that the revelation in Jesus Christ, this unique event, is the truth just because it is unique, by the very fact that it is connected with this time, this place, and this Person. But in asserting this we do not mean—as is so often laid to the charge of Christianity—that on this account we would claim that all philosophical, mystical, and general religious knowledge of God is not true. It is not absolutely untrue, but it is partial truth, half truth. Christ is here "divided." But that is an awkward comparison from the spatial and mechanical sphere. That which is divided can be brought together and formed into a whole. But this is not what is here meant. For when a living creature is divided it can never be put together again and formed into a whole. By the fact that it has been divided it has been killed. It is not merely in pieces, it is at the same time altered and spoiled; it has lost its original significance.

Thus the whole of the history of philosophy and of religion is a field which contains scattered elements of truth. It is the task of the Christian "philosophy of religion" to produce the proof for this general assertion. Philosophy recognizes Christ as the Eternal Logos, even though as an impersonal principle, yet still according to His absoluteness. Hence the Johannine conception of the Logos cannot be absolutely contrasted with the Platonic conception. Only the relation between them is the opposite of that which is usually claimed to be the case: Plato can only be understood in the light of John, not John from the point of view of Plato. For Platoism is a Christian truth which has been detached from the main body of truth. The historical relation between the two conceptions of "the Word" has nothing whatever to do with the matter. The subject with which the Gospel of John is dealing does not come from Plato—just as little as it has originated in the Mandaean Gnosis. John uses the Logos idea, which he reshapes from the very foundation, stamping it with the character of that which is personal and historical, in order that he may thus express the way in which he understands Christ. The old theory that Plato was a preparatory stage for Christianity, or that Plato drew his wisdom from Moses, is just as false historically as it is actually true to say that it is Christ, whom he, so to speak, perceived dimly from afar.

Likewise all living religion—which has not been watered down by rationalism and legalism—takes from the truth of Christ the moment of revelation in the sense of the contingent, "real," realistic means of the communication of knowledge and of life. But the more strongly this reality is present, the less it is watered down by speculative or mystical ideas, the more accidental does this revelation become, so far as its content is concerned: never quite without some elements of divine truth, but never without nonsense alongside of truth, the whole chaotic mass of polytheism, with its fantastic and frequently nonmoral mythology, and its equally weird and wild rites of worship—as well as so much that is great, which commands our genuine reverence.

Thus even outside the Christian revelation of the Bible man is not without God nor without truth. But in his search for truth the closer he approaches to the centre, the more his energies seem to fail, the more it becomes clear to him that even his search for God is always at the same time a flight from God, and that his service of God is always at the same time trivial and self-centred. The

Logos is also not outside His creation: for in the Logos it is created, and therefore it bears traces of its origin. But our collective knowledge of the world and our collective relations to the world are all interwoven, in the most complicated manner, with sinful illusion. Hence the knowledge of God in the world "outside," and in the relations of man to the world, only give us a confused picture of their divine origin; indeed, it does not yield a *theologia naturalis* which would be suitable as a basis for a Christian theology. The *analogia entis* might indeed have been the normal relation between God the Creator and His creature. But this normal relation no longer exists; it has been obscured and corrupted by the falling away of man from God. Confidence in a natural theology of this kind could only endure so long as the Christian consciousness was strong enough to oppose the destructive tendencies of a knowledge of the world based purely upon its own efforts. Since this support has been lost we can see how much there is in these "necessary truths of reason" so far as religion or theology is concerned.

Christ is the Truth and the Life. Hence He is the source of all knowledge. All truth is ultimately the truth of Christ. That which is true is true through the Logos who was in the beginning; the Logos, however, is not the One whom philosophy likes to read into the Johannine statements, the eternal principle, but the Eternal Son who reveals Himself to us in Jesus Christ.

V. Man

Reinhold Niebuhr is Professor of Applied Christianity, Emeritus, at Union Theological Seminary, New York.

Man as Sinner*

"In every religion," declared Albrecht Ritschl, the most authoritative exponent of modern liberal Christianity, "what is sought with the help

* Reprinted with the permission of Charles Scribner's Sons from *The Nature and Destiny of Man*, pp. 178-80, 181, 182-84, 185-89, 190, 191-202, by Reinhold Niebuhr. Copyright 1941 Charles Scribner's Sons.

of the superhuman power reverenced by man is a solution of the contradiction in which man finds himself as both a part of nature and a spiritual personality claiming to dominate nature."[1] It is perfectly true that this problem of finiteness and freedom underlies all religion. But Ritschl does not appreciate that the uniqueness of the Biblical approach to the human problem lies in its subordination of the problem of finiteness to the problem of sin. It is not the contradiction of finiteness and freedom from which Biblical religion seeks emancipation. It seeks redemption from sin; and the sin from which it seeks redemption is occasioned, though not caused, by this contradiction in which man stands. Sin is not caused by the contradiction because, according to Biblical faith, there is no absolute necessity that man should be betrayed into sin by the ambiguity of his position, as standing in and yet above nature. But it cannot be denied that this is the occasion for his sin.

Man is insecure and involved in natural contingency; he seeks to overcome his insecurity by a will-to-power which overreaches the limits of human creatureliness. Man is ignorant and involved in the limitations of a finite mind; but he pretends that he is not limited. He assumes that he can gradually transcend finite limitations until his mind becomes identical with universal mind. All of his intellectual and cultural pursuits, therefore, become infected with the sin of pride. Man's pride and will-to-power disturb the harmony of creation. The Bible defines sin in both religious and moral terms. The religious dimension of sin is man's rebellion against God, his effort to usurp the place of God. The moral and social dimension of sin is injustice. The ego which falsely makes itself the centre of existence in its pride and will-to-power inevitably subordinates other life to its will and thus does injustice to other life.

Sometimes man seeks to solve the problem of the contradiction of finiteness and freedom, not by seeking to hide his finiteness and comprehending the world into himself, but by seeking to hide his freedom and by losing himself in some aspect of the world's vitalities. In that case his sin may be defined as sensuality rather than pride. Sensuality is never the mere expression of natural impulse in man. It always betrays some aspect of his abortive effort to solve the problem of finiteness and freedom. Human passions are always characterized by unlimited and demonic potencies of which animal life is innocent. The intricate relation between pride and sensuality must be considered more fully presently. First we must analyse the relation of sin to the contradiction of finiteness and freedom.

[1] *Justification and Reconciliation,* p. 199.

II. TEMPTATION AND SIN

While the Bible consistently maintains that sin cannot be excused by, or inevitably derived from, any other element in the human situation it does admit that man was tempted. In the myth of the Fall the temptation arises from the serpent's analysis of the human situation. The serpent depicts God as jealously guarding his prerogatives against the possibility that man might have his eyes opened and become "as God, knowing good and evil." Man is tempted, in other words, to break and transcend the limits which God has set for him. The temptation thus lies in his situation of finiteness and freedom. . . .

. . . The situation of finiteness and freedom in which man stands becomes a source of temptation only when it is falsely interpreted. This false interpretation is not purely the product of the human imagination. It is suggested to man by a force of evil which precedes his own sin. Perhaps the best description or definition of this mystery is the statement that sin posits itself, that there is no situation in which it is possible to say that sin is either an inevitable consequence of the situation nor yet that it is an act of sheer and perverse individual defiance of God.

But what is the situation which is the occasion of temptation? Is it not the fact that man is a finite spirit, lacking identity with the whole, but yet a spirit capable in some sense of envisaging the whole, so that he easily commits the error of imagining himself the whole which he envisages? Let us note how quickly a mere analysis of the "situation" yields a definition of sin as error rather than as evil. Sin is not merely the error of overestimating human capacities. St. Paul rightly insists that "their foolish heart was darkened" and that "they became vain in their imagination." Neither the devil nor man is merely betrayed by his greatness to forget his weakness, or by his great knowledge to forget his ignorance. The fact is that man is never unconscious of his weakness, of the limited and dependent character of his existence and knowledge. The occasion for his temptation lies in the two facts, his greatness and his weakness, his unlimited and his limited knowledge, taken together. Man is both strong and weak, both free and bound, both blind and far-seeing. He stands at the juncture of nature and spirit; and is involved in both freedom and necessity. His sin is never the mere ignorance of his ignorance. It is always partly an effort to obscure his blindness by overestimating the degree of his sight and to obscure his insecurity by stretching his power beyond its limits. . . .

In short, man, being both free and bound, both limited and limitless, is anxious. Anxiety is the inevitable concomitant of the paradox of freedom and finiteness in which man is involved. Anxiety is the internal precondition of sin. It is the inevitable spiritual state of man, standing in the paradoxical situation of freedom and finiteness.[2] Anxiety is the internal description of the state of temptation. It must not be identified with sin because there is always the ideal possibility that faith would purge anxiety of the tendency toward sinful self-assertion. The ideal possibility is that faith in the ultimate security of God's love would overcome all immediate insecurities of nature and history. That is why Christian orthodoxy has consistently defined unbelief as the root of sin, or as the sin which precedes pride.[3] It is significant that Jesus justifies his injunction, "Be not anxious" with the observation, "For your heavenly Father knoweth that ye have need of these things." The freedom from anxiety which he enjoins is a possibility only if perfect trust in divine security has been achieved. Whether such freedom from anxiety and such perfect trust are an actual possibility of historic existence must be considered later. For the present it is enough to observe that no life, even the most saintly, perfectly conforms to the injunction not to be anxious.

Yet anxiety is not sin. It must be distinguished from sin partly because it is its precondition and not its actuality, and partly because it is the basis of all human creativity as well as the precondition of sin. Man is anxious not only because his life is limited and dependent and yet not so limited that he does not know of his limitations. He is also anxious because he does not know the limits of his possibilities. He can do nothing and regard it perfectly done, because higher possibilities are revealed in each achievement. All human actions stand under seemingly limitless possibilities. There are, of course, limits but it is difficult to gauge them from any immediate perspective. There is therefore no limit of achievement in any sphere of activity in which human history can rest with equanimity.[4]

---

[2] Kierkegaard says: "Anxiety is the psychological condition which precedes sin. It is so near, so fearfully near to sin, and yet it is not the explanation for sin." *Der Begriff der Angst,* p. 89. Kierkegaard's analysis of the relation of anxiety to sin is the profoundest in Christian thought.

[3] Martin Luther, in conformity with the general Christian tradition and quoting Sirach 10:14, writes in his *Treatise on Christian Liberty:* "The wise man has said: The beginning of all sin is to depart from God and not trust Him." Luther frequently defines the state of perfection before the Fall as being completely free of all anxiety. Here, as frequently in Luther's thought, he overstates the case. Ideally anxiety is overcome by faith but a life totally without anxiety would lack freedom and not require faith.

[4] Heidegger calls attention to the significant double connotation of the word "Care," *Sorge, cura,* that is a double connotation revealed in many languages. He writes: "The perfection of man, his becoming what in his freedom he can become according to his ultimate possibility, is a capacity of care or anxiety (*Sorge*). But just as basically care points to his being at the mercy of an anxious world, of his contingency (*Geworfenheit*). This double connotation of *cura* points to a basic structure in man of contingency and potentiality" (*geworfenen Entwurfs*). *Sein und Zeit,* p. 199.

This double connotation, according to Heidegger, is clearly revealed if *Sorgfalt* is juxtaposed to *Sorge,* that is care as carefulness to care as anxiety. Unfortunately the English language makes the distinction between *Angst* and *Sorge* impossible. Both of them must be translated as *anxiety.*

It is not possible to make a simple separation between the creative and destructive elements in anxiety; and for that reason it is not possible to purge moral achievement of sin as easily as moralists imagine. The same action may reveal a creative effort to transcend natural limitations, and a sinful effort to give an unconditioned value to contingent and limited factors in human existence. Man may, in the same moment, be anxious because he has not become what he ought to be; and also anxious lest he cease to be at all. . . .

Anxiety about perfection and about insecurity are thus inexorably bound together in human actions and the errors which are made in the search for perfection are never due merely to the ignorance of not knowing the limits of conditioned values. They always exhibit some tendency of the agent to hide his own limits, which he knows only too well. Obviously the basic source of temptation is, therefore, not the inertia of "matter" or "nature" against the larger and more inclusive ends which reason envisages. It resides in the inclination of man, either to deny the contingent character of his existence (in pride and self-love) or to escape from his freedom (in sensuality). Sensuality represents an effort to escape from the freedom and the infinite possibilities of spirit by becoming lost in the detailed processes, activities and interests of existence, an effort which results inevitably in unlimited devotion to limited values. Sensuality is man "turning inordinately to mutable good" (Aquinas).

Anxiety, as a permanent concomitant of freedom, is thus both the source of creativity and a temptation to sin. It is the condition of the sailor, climbing the mast (to use a simile), with the abyss of the waves beneath him and the "crow's nest" above him. He is anxious about both the end toward which he strives and the abyss of nothingness into which he may fall. The ambition of man to be something is always partly prompted by the fear of meaninglessness which threatens him by reason of the contingent character of his existence. His creativity is therefore always corrupted by some effort to overcome contingency by raising precisely what is contingent to absolute and unlimited dimensions. This effort, though universal, cannot be regarded as normative. It is always destructive. Yet obviously the destructive aspect of anxiety is so intimately involved in the creative aspects that there is no possibility of making a simple separation between them. The two are inextricably bound together by reason of man being anxious both to realize his unlimited possibilities and to overcome and to hide the dependent and contingent character of his existence.

When anxiety has conceived it brings forth both pride and sensuality. Man falls into pride, when he seeks to raise his contingent existence to unconditioned significance; he falls into sensuality, when he seeks to escape from his unlimited possibilities of freedom, from the perils and responsibilities of self-determination, by immersing himself into a "mutable good," by losing himself in some natural vitality.

III. THE SIN OF PRIDE

Biblical and Christian thought has maintained with a fair degree of consistency that pride is more basic than sensuality and that the latter is, in some way, derived from the former. We have previously considered the Biblical definition of basic sin as pride and have suggested that the Pauline exposition of man's self-glorification ("they changed the glory of the incorruptible God into an image made like unto corruptible man") is really an admirable summary of the whole Biblical doctrine of sin.[5]

[5] Again it cannot be claimed that Christian thought is absolutely consistent in regarding pride as the basic sin. Wherever the classical view of man predominates, whether in early Greek theology, or medieval or modern liberal thought, the tendency is to equate sin with sensuality. The definition of sin as pride is consistently maintained in the strain of theology generally known as Augustinian.

Augustine defines sin as follows: "What could begin this evil will but pride, that is the beginning of all sin? And what is pride but a perverse desire of height, in forsaking Him to whom the soul ought solely to cleave, as the beginning thereof, to make the self seem the beginning. This is when it likes itself too well. . . ." *De civ. Dei,* Book XII, Ch. 13.

Or again: "What is pride but undue exaltation? And this is undue exaltation, when the soul abandons Him to whom it ought to cleave as its end and becomes a kind of end in itself." *De civ. Dei,* Book XIV, Ch. 13.

Pascal's definition is: "This I is hateful. . . . In one word it has two qualities: It is essentially unjust in that it makes self the centre of everything and it is troublesome to others in that it seeks to make them subservient; for each I is the enemy and would be the tyrant of all others." Faugère, Vol. I, p. 197.

In Luther, pride and self-love are used synonymously (*Superbia et amor sui*). Original sin is sometimes defined as the lust of the soul in general (*Universa concupiscentia*) (Weimer edition III. 215), which expresses itself in the turning of the soul from God to the creature. Luther's definition of concupiscence is not in opposition to or sharp distinction from sin as pride. Both have their source in *caro,* which for Luther has the exact connotation of the Pauline σάρχ. It is not the "body" as symbol of man's finiteness but "flesh" as symbol of his sinfulness. Stomph defines Luther's conception as follows: "With 'self as flesh' Luther means that the sinner desires himself just as he is, though he does not see himself just as he is and does not expressly will himself as such." M. A. H. Stomph, *Die Anthropologie Martin Luthers,* p. 73.

Thomas Aquinas derives sensuality from a more basic self-love: "The proper and direct cause of sin is to be considered on the part of the adherence to a mutable good, in which respect every sinful act proceeds from inordinate desire for some temporal good. Now the fact that someone desires a temporal good inordinately is due to the fact that he loves himself inordinately." *Summa,* Part I, Third Number, Question 77, Art. 4.

Calvin consistently holds to the Pauline definition of sin given in Romans I. Sin is pride and not ignorance: "They worship not Him but figments of their own brains instead. This pravity Paul expressly remarks: 'Professing themselves wise they became fools.' He had before said 'they became vain in their imaginations.' But lest any should exculpate them, he adds that they were deservedly blinded, because, not content with the bounds of sobriety, but arrogating themselves more than was right they wilfully darkened and even infatuated themselves with pride, vanity and perverseness. Whence it follows that their folly is inexcusable, which originates not only in a vain curiosity but in false confidence and in immoderate desire to exceed the limits of human knowledge." *Institutes,* Book I, Ch. 4.

This Biblical definition is strictly adhered to in that strain of Christian theology which manages to maintain the Biblical viewpoint against the influence of the rationalist-classical view of man, in which sin tends to be identified with ignorance or the passions of the body. The Biblical view colours the definitions of Christian rationalists so that when they define sin primarily as sensuality, they recognize, at least, that this sensuality is not merely the expression of physical impulse but represents an inordinate quality made possible by the freedom of the spirit.[6] We are not at present concerned with the emphasis of Christian theology upon the inexcusable character of this pride and the insistence that sin is rooted in an evil will and not in some antecedent weakness of man.[7] Our present interest is to relate the Biblical and distinctively Christian conception of sin as pride and self-love to the observable behavior of men. It will be convenient in this analysis to distinguish between three types of pride, which are, however, never completely distinct in actual life: pride of power, pride of knowledge and pride of virtue.[8] The third type, the pride of self-righteousness, rises to a form of spiritual pride, which is at once a fourth type and yet not a specific form of pride at all but pride and self-glorification in its inclusive and quintessential form.

(a) "Of the infinite desires of man," declares Bertrand Russell, "the chief are the desires for power and glory. They are not identical though closely allied." [9] Mr. Russell is not quite clear about the relation of the two to each other, and the relation is, as a matter of fact, rather complex. There is pride of power in which the human ego assumes its self-sufficiency and self-mastery and imagines itself secure against all vicissitudes. It does not recognize the contingent and dependent character of its life and believes itself to be the author of its own existence, the judge of its own values and the master of its own destiny. This proud pretension is present in an inchoate form in all human life but it rises to greater heights among those individuals and classes who have a more than ordinary degree of social power.[10] Closely related to the pride which seems to rest upon the possession of either the ordinary or some

[6] Gregory of Nyssa for instance analyses anger as follows: "Thus the arising of anger in us is indeed akin to the impulses of brutes; but it grows by the alliance of thought." *On the Making of Man,* XVIII, 4.

[7] This aspect of the problem of sin will be considered in Ch. 9.

[8] This is a traditional distinction in Christian thought. *Cf.* Mueller, *On the Christian Doctrine of Sin,* Vol. I, p. 177.

[9] *Power, A New Social Analysis,* p. 11.

[10] "Every man would like to be God," declares Mr. Russell, "if it were possible; some few find it difficult to admit the impossibility." *Ibid.,* p. 11.

extraordinary measure of human freedom and self-mastery, is the lust for power which has pride as its end. The ego does not feel secure and therefore grasps for more power in order to make itself secure. It does not regard itself as sufficiently significant or respected or feared and therefore seeks to enhance its position in nature and in society.

In the one case the ego seems unconscious of the finite and determinate character of its existence. In the other case the lust for power is prompted by a darkly conscious realization of its insecurity.[11] The first form of the pride of power is particularly characteristic of individuals and groups whose position in society is, or seems to be, secure. In Biblical prophecy this security is declared to be bogus and those who rest in it are warned against an impending doom. . . .

The second form of the pride of power is more obviously prompted by the sense of insecurity. It is the sin of those, who knowing themselves to be insecure, seek sufficient power to guarantee their security, inevitably of course at the expense of other life. It is particularly the sin of the advancing forces of human society in distinction to the established forces. Among those who are less obviously secure, either in terms of social recognition, or economic stability or even physical health, the temptation arises to overcome or to obscure insecurity by arrogating a greater degree of power to the self. . . .

Since man's insecurity arises not merely from the vicissitudes of nature but from the uncertainties of society and history, it is natural that the ego should seek to overcome social as well as natural insecurity and should express the impulse of "power over men" as well as "power over matter." The peril of a competing human will is overcome by subordinating that will to the ego and by using the power of many subordinated wills to ward off the enmity which such subordination creates. The will-to-power is thus inevitably involved in the vicious circle of accentuating the insecurity which it intends to eliminate. "Woe to thee," declares the prophet Isaiah, "that spoilest, and thou wast not spoiled; and dealest treacherously, and they dealt not treacherously with thee! when thou shalt cease to spoil, thou shalt be spoiled" (Is. 33:1). The will-to-power in short involves the ego in

[11] In modern international life Great Britain with its too strong a sense of security, which prevented it from taking proper measures of defense in time, and Germany with its maniacal will-to-power, are perfect symbols of the different forms which pride takes among the established and the advancing social forces. The inner stability and external security of Great Britain has been of such long duration that she may be said to have committed the sin of Babylon and declared, "I shall be no widow and I shall never know sorrow." Germany on the other hand suffered from an accentuated form of inferiority long before her defeat in the World War. Her boundless contemporary self-assertion which literally transgresses all bounds previously known in religion, culture and law is a very accentuated form of the power impulse which betrays a marked inner insecurity.

injustice. It seeks a security beyond the limits of human finiteness and this inordinate ambition arouses fears and enmities which the world of pure nature, with its competing impulses of survival, does not know. . . .

We have provisionally distinguished between the pride which does not recognize human weakness and the pride which seeks power in order to overcome or obscure a recognized weakness; and we have sought to attribute the former to the more established and traditionally respected individuals and groups, while attributing the latter to the less secure, that is, to the advancing rather than established groups in society. This distinction is justified only if regarded as strictly provisional. The fact is that the proudest monarch and the most secure oligarch is driven to assert himself beyond measure partly by a sense of insecurity. This is partly due to the fact that the greater his power and glory, the more the common mortality of humankind appears to him in the guise of an incongruous fate. Thus the greatest monarchs of the ancient world, the Pharaohs of Egypt, exhausted the resources of their realm to build pyramids, which were intended to establish or to prove their immortality. A common mortal's fear of death is thus one prompting motive of the pretensions and ambitions of the greatest lords.[12]

. . . Life's basic securities are involved in the secondary securities of power and glory. The tyrant fears not only the loss of his power but the possible loss of his life. The powerful nation, secure against its individual foes, must fear the possibility that its power may challenge its various foes to make common cause against it. The person accustomed to luxury and ease actually meets a greater danger to life and mere existence in the hardships of poverty than those who have been hardened by its rigours. The will-to-power is thus an expression of insecurity even when it has achieved ends which, from the perspective of an ordinary mortal, would seem to guarantee complete security. The fact that human ambitions know no limits must therefore be attributed not merely to

[12] Bertrand Russell doubts whether fear or anxiety could be regarded as the root of the will-to-power among the great leaders of mankind. He is inclined to believe that a "hereditary position of command" is a more plausible basis for it. He would, in other words, sharply separate the pride which does not know its own weakness and the pride which compensates for a recognized weakness. He cites Queen Elizabeth as one whose will-to-power was prompted by an hereditary position rather than by fear (*op. cit.*, p. 20). Yet a modern historian makes this interesting observation upon the fears which harassed Elizabeth: "Strong as was her sense of public duty, it failed her here [in dealing with the problem of her succession]. Her egotism blinded her to the dangers to which her failure to discuss the subject was likely to expose the state. The thought that her dignities must, by the efflux of time, pass to another seems only to have suggested to her the insecurity of her own tenure of them and the coming extinction of her own authority. Such a prospect she could not nerve herself to face." J. K. Laughton in *The Cambridge Modern History,* Vol. III, p. 359.

the infinite capacities of the human imagination but to an uneasy recognition of man's finiteness, weakness and dependence, which become the more apparent the more we seek to obscure them, and which generate ultimate perils, the more immediate insecurities are eliminated. Thus man seeks to make himself God because he is betrayed by both his greatness and his weakness; and there is no level of greatness and power in which the lash of fear is not at least one strand in the whip of ambition.

(b) The intellectual pride of man is of course a more spiritual sublimation of his pride of power. Sometimes it is so deeply involved in the more brutal and obvious pride of power that the two cannot be distinguished. Every ruling oligarchy of history has found ideological pretensions as important a bulwark of authority as its police power. But intellectual pride is confined neither to the political oligarchs nor to the savants of society. All human knowledge is tainted with an "ideological" taint. It pretends to be more true than it is. It is finite knowledge, gained from a particular perspective; but it pretends to be final and ultimate knowledge. Exactly analogous to the cruder pride of power, the pride of intellect is derived on the one hand from ignorance of the finiteness of the human mind and on the other hand from an attempt to obscure the known conditioned character of human knowledge and the taint of self-interest in human truth. . . .

Intellectual pride is thus the pride of reason which forgets that it is involved in a temporal process and imagines itself in complete transcendence over history. "It is this appearance of independent history of state constitutions, systems of law, of ideologies in every special field which above all has blinded so many people," declares Friederich Engels.[13] Yet intellectual pride is something more than the mere ignorance of ignorance. It always involves, besides, a conscious or subconscious effort to obscure a known or partly known taint of interest. Despite the tremendous contribution of Marxist thought in the discovery of the ideological taint in all culture, it is precisely the element of pretense which it fails to understand. Its too simple theory of human consciousness betrays it here. Thus Engels declares: "The real driving force which moves it [ideology] remains unconscious otherwise it would not be an ideological process." [14] But the real fact is that all pretensions of final knowledge and ultimate truth are partly prompted by the uneasy feeling that the truth is not final and also by

[13] From a letter to F. Mehring, quoted by Sidney Hook, *Toward an Understanding of Karl Marx*, p. 341.

[14] *Ibid.*, p. 341.

an uneasy conscience which realizes that the interests of the ego are compounded with this truth. . . .

There is in short no manifestation of intellectual pride in which the temptations of both human freedom and human insecurity are not apparent. If man were not a free spirit who transcends every situation in which he is involved he would have no concern for unconditioned truth and he would not be tempted to claim absolute validity for his partial perspectives. If he were completely immersed in the contingencies and necessities of nature he would have only his own truth and would not be tempted to confuse his truth with *the* truth. But in that case he would have no truth at all, for no particular event or value could be related meaningfully to the whole. If on the other hand man were wholly transcendent he would not be tempted to insinuate the necessities of the moment and the vagaries of the hour into the truth and thus corrupt it. Nor would he be prompted to deny the finiteness of his knowledge in order to escape the despair of scepticism which threatens him upon the admission of such ignorance. Yet the ignorance of ignorance which underlies every attempt at knowledge can never be described as a mere ignorance. The ignorance presupposes pride, for there is always an ideal possibility that man should recognize his own limits. This implicit pride becomes explicit in the conscious efforts to obscure the partiality of the perspective from which the truth is apprehended. The explicit character of this pride is fully revealed in all cases in which the universalistic note in human knowledge becomes the basis of an imperial desire for domination over life which does not conform to it. The modern religious nationalist thus declares in one moment that his culture is not an export article but is valid for his nation alone. In the next moment he declares that he will save the world by destroying inferior forms of culture.

The insecurity which hides behind this pride is not quite as patent as the pride, yet it is also apparent. In the relations of majority and minority racial groups for instance, for which the negro-white relation is a convenient example, the majority group justifies the disabilities which it imposes upon the minority group on the ground that the subject group is not capable of enjoying or profiting from the privileges of culture or civilization. Yet it can never completely hide, and it sometimes frankly expresses the fear that the grant of such privileges would eliminate the inequalities of endowment which supposedly justify the inequalities of privilege.[15] The pretension of pride is thus a weapon against a feared competitor.

[15] *Cf.* Paul Levinson, *Race, Class and Party,* for striking examples of this sense of insecurity in the dominant group.

Sometimes it is intended to save the self from the abyss of self-contempt which always yawns before it.[16]

(c) All elements of moral pride are involved in the intellectual pride which we have sought to analyse. In all but the most abstract philosophical debates the pretension of possessing an unconditioned truth is meant primarily to establish "my good" as unconditioned moral value. Moral pride is revealed in all "self-righteous" judgments in which the other is condemned because he fails to conform to the highly arbitrary standards of the self. Since the self judges itself by its own standards it finds itself good. It judges others by its own standards and finds them evil, when their standards fail to conform to its own. This is the secret of the relationship between cruelty and self-righteousness. When the self mistakes its standards for God's standards it is naturally inclined to attribute the very essence of evil to non-conformists. The character of moral pride is perfectly described in the words of St. Paul: "For I bear them record that they have the zeal of God, but not according to knowledge. For they, being ignorant of God's righteousness and going about to establish their own righteousness, have not submitted themselves unto the righteousness of God" (Romans 10:2-3). Moral pride is the pretension of finite man that his highly conditioned virtue is the final righteousness and that his very relative moral standards are absolute. Moral pride thus makes virtue the very vehicle of sin, a fact which explains why the New Testament is so critical of the righteous in comparison with "publicans and sinners." This note in the Bible distinguishes Biblical moral theory from all simple moralism, including Christian moralism. It is the meaning of Jesus' struggle with the pharisees, of St. Paul's insistence that man is saved "not by works lest any man should boast," in fact of the whole Pauline polemic against the "righteousness of works"; and it is the primary issue in the Protestant Reformation. Luther rightly insisted that the unwillingness of the sinner to be regarded as a sinner was the final form of sin.[17] The final proof that man no longer knows God is that he does not know his own

[16] An interesting example of pride as defense against self-contempt is offered by an historian of the French Directory. He writes: "These profiteers were also doctrinaires and they clung to their doctrines with the greater tenacity because only thus could they escape the self-contempt which otherwise they would have felt in their secret hearts. They were under no illusion as to the life they were leading, the system of government they had established or the persons they employed to maintain it. But sunk though they were in foulness they cling to the shadow of an ideal aim. . . . They asked nothing better than to be stigmatized as sectaries, illuminati and fanatics, for in that case people would forget to call them 'rotten.'" Pierre Gaxotte, *The French Revolution,* p. 390.

[17] *Superbus primo est excusator sui ac defensor, justificator,* Weimar ed. of *Works,* Vol. 3, p. 288.

sin.[18] The sinner who justifies himself does not know God as judge and does not need God as Saviour. One might add that the sin of self-righteousness is not only the final sin in the subjective sense but also in the objective sense. It involves us in the greatest guilt. It is responsible for our most serious cruelties, injustices and defamations against our fellowmen. The whole history of racial, national, religious and other social struggles is a commentary on the objective wickedness and social miseries which result from self-righteousness.

(d) The sin of moral pride, when it has conceived, brings forth spiritual pride. The ultimate sin is the religious sin of making the self-deification implied in moral pride explicit. This is done when our partial standards and relative attainments are explicitly related to the unconditioned good, and claim divine sanction. For this reason religion is not simply as is generally supposed an inherently virtuous human quest for God. It is merely a final battleground between God and man's self-esteem. In that battle even the most pious practices may be instruments of human pride. The same man may in one moment regard Christ as his judge and in the next moment seek to prove that the figure, the standards and the righteousness of Christ bear a greater similarity to his own righteousness than to that of his enemy. The worst form of class domination is religious class domination in which, as for instance in the Indian caste system, a dominant priestly class not only subjects subordinate classes to social disabilities but finally excludes them from participation in any universe of meaning. The worst form of intolerance is religious intolerance, in which the particular interests of the contestants hide behind religious absolutes.[19] The worst form of self-assertion is religious self-assertion in which under the guise of contrition before God, He is claimed as the exclusive ally of our contingent self. "What goes by the name of 'religion' in the modern world," declares a modern missionary, "is to a great extent unbridled human self-assertion in religious disguise." [20]

Christianity rightly regards itself as a religion, not so much of man's search

---

[18] *Nescimus, quid Deus, quid justitia, denique quid ipsum peccatum sit. ibid.*, Vol. 2, p. 106.

[19] One example is worth quoting, the manifesto of Philip of Spain against William of Nassau: "Philip by the grace of God, King of Castile . . . whereas William of Nassau, a foreigner in our realm once honoured and promoted by the late emperor and ourselves, has by sinister practices and arts gained over malcontents, lawless men, insolvents, innovators, and especially those whose religion was suspected, and has instigated these heretics to rebel, to destroy sacred images and churches and to profane the sacraments of God . . . with a view of exterminating by impieties our Holy Catholic faith . . . whereas the country can have no peace with this wretched hypocrite . . . we empower all and every to seize the person and property of this William of Nassau as an enemy of the human race and hereby on the word of a king and minister of God promise any one . . . who will deliver him dead or alive . . . the sum of 25,000 crowns in gold . . . and we will pardon him of any crime if he has been guilty and give him a patent of nobility."

[20] Henrik Kraemer, *The Christian Message in the Non-Christian World*, p. 212.

for God, in the process of which he may make himself God; but as a religion of revelation in which a holy and loving God is revealed to man as the source and end of all finite existence against whom the self-will of man is shattered and his pride abased. But as soon as the Christian assumes that he is, by virtue of possessing this revelation, more righteous, because more contrite, than other men, he increases the sin of self-righteousness and makes the forms of a religion of contrition the tool of his pride.

Protestantism is right in insisting that Catholicism identifies the church too simply with the Kingdom of God. This identification, which allows a religious institution, involved in all the relativities of history, to claim unconditioned truth for its doctrines and unconditioned moral authority for its standards, makes it just another tool of human pride. For this reason Luther's insistence that the pope is Anti-Christ was religiously correct. A vicar of Christ on earth is bound to be, in a sense, Anti-Christ. The whole contemporary political situation yields evidence of the perils of the Catholic doctrine of the church. Everywhere the church claims to be fighting the enemies of God without realizing to what degree these enemies are merely the rebels against a corrupt feudal civilization.

But as soon as the Protestant assumes that his more prophetic statement and interpretation of the Christian gospel guarantees him a superior virtue, he is also lost in the sin of self-righteousness. The fact is that the Protestant doctrine of the priesthood of all believers may result in an individual self-deification against which Catholic doctrine has more adequate checks. The modern revival of Reformation theology may be right in regarding the simple moralism of Christian liberalism as just another form of pharisaism. But the final mystery of human sin cannot be understood if it is not recognized that the greatest teachers of this Reformation doctrine of the sinfulness of all men used it on occasion as the instrument of an arrogant will-to-power against theological opponents.[21] There is no final guarantee against the spiritual pride of man. Even the recognition in the sight of God that he is a sinner can be used as a vehicle of that very sin.[22] If that final mystery of the sin of pride is not recognized the meaning of the Christian gospel cannot be understood. . . .

[21] Luther's attitude toward Schwenkfeld for instance and Calvin's against Castellio and Servetus. It may not be amiss to call attention to the fact that Karl Barth engaged in theological controversy with Emil Brunner some years ago on the theological issues raised in this chapter. He feared that Brunner's pamphlet on "Nature and Grace" conceded too much to the natural goodness of men. His own answer, entitled *Nein,* is informed by a peculiar quality of personal arrogance and disrespect for the opponent.

[22] "Discourses on humility are a source of pride to the vain," declares Pascal, "and of humility in the humble." *Pensées,* 377.

Emil Brunner

The New Man*

6. The New Birth is not a magical process[1]; it is the same thing as the act of faith; it is that state in which man no longer strains after God but receives his life and strength from God; it means living on the powers which flow from "justification by grace alone." Through the New Birth the new person, the being whose life is derived from God, the self which has its home in God, in Christ, and not in the Self, is established. From the subjective point of view the centre of this process is the fact that the soul is at peace, is reconciled to God in the conscience. The hounds of hell are chained. The conscience is no longer allowed to accuse us. Our refuge is in God, and there, too, is our new personality, the new man, "in Christ." As soon as this takes place—and in so far as we believe—both our false unity and our false isolation from our fellow-creatures are removed: in faith each of us is wholly and entirely "the individual," in the sense in which Kierkegaard uses this expression; and in faith all isolation ceases; for in faith each one—so far as he really is an individual of this kind—is at the same time a member of the "Body of Christ," a member of the Christian community, of the Church. And finally, in this process the false bondage to ourselves and our false dominion over the world is removed: in faith the desire for the world ceases to exist—"dead to the world" is the forceful expression used to describe this fact—and at the same time, and only now, there begins a life "directed towards the world," in service; the new man is free *from* the world *for* the world.

7. It is both allowable and necessary to inquire also into the subjective sphere in which this process takes place. Faith, by the emergence of which the bad conscience is silenced by the word of justification, is the work and the gift of God. But just as the Incarnation of the Word of God

---

* From *The Divine Imperative*, by Emil Brunner, translated by Olive Wyon. The Westminster Press. Copyright 1947, by W. L. Jenkins. Used by permission of Westminster Press and Lutterworth Press. Pp. 159-62.

[1] It is incontestable that the Lutherans of last century—here even v. Oettingen is no exception—had a magical conception of the New Birth. To presuppose the germ of faith in the baptized infant means emptying the concept of faith of all meaning. On the other hand, it is a mistake to suppose that to deny this magical effect is to deny "baptismal grace" altogether; only the historical interpretation has replaced the magical one: as soon as faith exists we know that we are one with the person who was baptized at a particular time; we know that the convenant word which was then spoken was the prevenient word of Divine Grace, which preceded our present situation.

in Jesus Christ takes place not alongside of but within historical existence—although concealed and only visible to faith—so also faith, in spite of the fact that it is the work of God, is a personal act. Indeed, it is the only "fully personal act." For in it alone, in its achievement, does it come to pass that the person who outside of faith is disintegrated, is again directed towards the centre and thus "integrated." Faith is not only knowing God and the Self, it is not only an assent and a resolve—the resolve to live no longer in self-dependence, but in dependence on God—but it is also feeling: the certainty and joyfulness of belonging to God which lifts us above the abyss of absolute terror.

Indeed, only in the fact that faith is also determined by feeling does this knowledge and this assent become wholly "my" faith, or to use the language of the Bible: faith of the heart.[2] The heart does not *know,* nor does it *will,* but the heart can *believe,* and such faith alone is genuine. To use the expression of Kierkegaard faith is *passion,*[3] a passionate interest, the strongest and most subjective appropriation of the Word which can possibly be imagined. This integration of all functions takes place neither in an act of reason, nor in an act of sensuousness, nor yet in the aesthetic consciousness which unites them both, but in the personality as a whole. Faith is in the highest sense objective, it is the redress of all ills by the Word of truth alone; and it is in the highest degree subjective: as "existential thinking," as decision, a new self-consciousness, even feeling of oneself. In faith that deep fear of existence is overcome—although it is still present as something which has been overcome—through the joyful certainty of trust; but it is this subjective element itself which reposes on and consists in the Word which has been perceived, in Christ. Faith means leaving oneself behind—"Christ is my righteousness"—and in that very fact it means being wholly oneself, the removal of division within the personality. For the personality is only truly "itself" when it is with God. Indeed, the power of this integration extends not only to feeling but through feeling and the unconscious right down into the organic sphere, even though this may only be experienced in a very imperfect manner. For even in faith we live "in the body of sin," in "this body of death." [4]

8. Thus, since faith is still very partial and imperfect, since we still harbour a great deal of unbelief, we are constantly forced to renew our decision. The process which, in its divine aspect, we know as "the New

[2] On this point cf. the excellent remarks on the "heart" in the language of the Bible by Delitzsch: *Biblische Psychologie,* pp. 203 ff.

[3] On this see my lecture: *Die Botschaft Sören Kierkegaards* in the *Neue Schweizer Rundschau,* 1930.

[4] Rom. vii. 24.

Birth," becomes "conversion," when viewed from the human standpoint. That faith only has reality *in actu*—and not otherwise—means that it is only able to direct the Self because it is itself controlled from without, it can only achieve self-knowledge because it is known by God. What we "possess" in faith is not a quality or a possession, the mystery of the divine action and the divine giving is fulfilled—beyond our understanding—in the very fact of our acceptance and our passive yielding to God.[5] The new man, the new person, is not simply "present" like a newly planted life-germ, as something which is present to be thought of in biological terms; but the new man exists and continues to exist only in the obedience of faith. This is his reality. Therefore immediately behind the indicative: "Thou art the new man," stands the imperative: "*Be* the new man!" "Put on the new man!" [6] Thus the new man, like faith itself, is both God's gift and God's demand.

It is this very "personality"—which is the only true personality—which must not be conceived in any categories of substance;[7] faith, or the "new man," can only be understood in a personal sense *in actu* of God, and thus *in actu* of man. But to be a person means responsible existence. Thus faith, or the new way of life, means a responsible existence, an existence which complies with moral demands, which perceives that it is being addressed from without; it means a self-knowledge, a self-determination which springs from the deliberate acceptance of one's life from the Hand of God. We have no right to attempt to remove this final paradox. To attempt to resolve it into something which we could conceive with our minds would mean turning the personal into the impersonal. The reality of existence, however, can only be experienced in faith in the Word which lies beyond all experience. And this faith, and it alone, is, as actual obedience towards God, required of us. All the commandments are included in the First Commandment. There is nothing in the whole wide world which we are bound to do save this: to glorify God, and this means: to believe. "Whatsoever is not of faith is sin." [8] Thus we have now returned to the point at which we started; only in the realm of

[5] Naturally, by this I do not mean anything in the nature of "synergism"; synergism doubtless intends to stress the personal character of the act of appropriation, but it does not understand the comprehensive character of grace. It does not understand that it is due to grace that we can thus respond to God. On the other hand, a doctrine of grace which obscures this personal element by the use of naturalistic images of appropriation for the sake of the objectivity of grace is just as incorrect; this has often been done by modern Lutherans, but not by Luther himself. Luther, indeed, also uses naturalistic images, as also does the New Testament, but he uses personal expressions at the same time; above all, in Luther's teaching there is no idea of a New Birth which precedes faith.

[6] Eph. iv. 24.

[7] Cf. Bonhöffer: *Akt und Sein,* 1931.

[8] Rom. xiv. 23.

faith man does not see himself in the light of theory; here alone does he cease to regard himself in an abstract and general way; here alone does his "understanding" of himself involve an *act*. It is for this reason that the question of the "agent" must be a primary one in all ethical studies; indeed, it is this discussion which will decide all the other problems. For before the Good can be done the agent must be good. But the only Doer of good deeds is God. Man, therefore, can only do good deeds in so far as God does them in him, in so far as our action is obedience to the will of God, wrought in us by God Himself.

VI. Church

The Rt. Rev. John A. T. Robinson, Bishop of the Church of England, is Dean of Trinity College, Cambridge.

The Christian Society and This World*

There are many other religions which say, 'Do not love the world': there is no other which says at the same time, 'God so loved the world that he gave,' and whose central affirmation is of the Word made flesh. And it is this paradox which governs the distinctive style of the life of the Christian society in this world, which we must now go on to try and define.

For such a definition there is still no better place from which to begin than the famous passage in the anonymous Epistle to Diognetus, penned perhaps within fifty years of the New Testament period. Let me recall some sentences from it:

> Christians are not distinguished from the rest of mankind either in locality or

* From *On Being the Church in the World*, by John A. T. Robinson. Published in the U.S.A. by The Westminster Press, 1962. Copyright © J. A. T. Robinson, 1960. Used by permission of Westminster Press and the British publishers, SCM Press. Pp. 17-22.

in speech or in customs. For they dwell not somewhere in cities of their own, neither do they use some different language, nor practice an extraordinary kind of life. . . . But while they dwell in cities of Greeks and barbarians as the lot of each is cast, and follow the native customs in dress and food and the other arrangements of life, yet the constitution of their own citizenship, which they set forth, is marvelous, and confessedly contradicts expectation. They dwell in their own countries, but only as sojourners; they bear their share in all things as citizens, and they endure all hardships as strangers. Every foreign country is a fatherland to them and every fatherland is foreign. . . . Their existence is on earth, but their citizenship is in heaven. They obey the established laws, and they surpass the laws in their own lives. . . . In a word, what the soul is in a body, this the Christians are in the world. . . . The soul is enclosed in the body, and yet itself holdeth the body together; so Christians are kept in the world as in a prison-house, and yet they themselves hold the world together. . . . So great is the office for which God hath appointed them, and which it is not lawful for them to decline.[1]

Such a style of life is certainly not other-worldliness in the usual sense of that word: 'they bear their share in all things as citizens.' In fact, it is marked by the awareness of living, and living to the full, in two worlds at once. Yet it is equally far from what is meant by having the best of both worlds. The phrase which perhaps describes it better than any other is one coined by Dr. Alec Vidler. He has defined the characteristically Christian way of life as 'holy worldliness.' [2] Let me try to draw out what I take that to mean.

First, the Christian style of life is marked by an extraordinary combination of detachment and concern. The Christian will care less for the world and at the same time care more for it than the man who is not a Christian. He will not lose his heart to it, but he may well lose his life for it. This, paradoxical as it sounds, is not, I believe, difficult to recognize for the authentic Christian attitude when we see it. The trouble is that we so seldom do see it. The Christian community is neither sufficiently detached nor sufficiently concerned. The Church's perennial failing is to be so identified with the world that it cannot speak to it and to be so remote from it that, again, it cannot speak to it. These would appear to be opposite and mercifully incompatible sins; but it is remarkable how easy it is for the Christian society and for the Christian individual to commit both of them at once.

Holy worldliness involves constantly walking on a knife-edge:[3] it is only too simple to slide off into becoming too

[1] Epistle to Diognetus, 5 and 6. Trans. J. B. Lightfoot, *The Apostolic Fathers,* pp. 503-5.
[2] The title of a lecture reprinted in his *Essays in Liberality,* pp. 95-112.
[3] Cf. the striking chapter on Christian prayer written from this point of view in G. F. Macleod's *Only One Way Left,* pp. 146-63.

worldly or too other-worldly—and neither is holy, though the latter has often been hailed as sanctity. To be concerned but not involved is just as great a temptation for the Church as to be involved but not concerned.

A second mark of the Christian style of life is an equally paradoxical commitment to what Dr. Vidler has elsewhere called 'evangelization' and 'civilization' at the same time.[4] There has been a perennial tension within the Christian tradition between saving men's souls and ministering to their bodies, between offering them the pure milk of the Gospel and proffering the cup of cold water. There are Christians who quite sincerely believe that the Church has more important things to do than to become involved in the latter concern, a concern which may lead very rapidly these days into the provision of water-mains and sewerage, hydro-electric schemes and Aswan dams, and so into the time-consuming, divisive and dirty business of politics. No, the Christian must give himself to spreading the Gospel and not allow himself to be diverted into filling bellies or filling forms.

But the dilemma is a false one, and comes once again from an unbiblical attitude. For preaching the Gospel in the categories in which Jesus himself preached it is preaching the gospel of *the Kingdom,* of the sovereign rule of God over the whole range of human life. And it is this kingdom, or commonwealth, of which Christians are the citizens and ambassadors within 'this world.' There is no department of the world's life into which they are not commissioned to go. They find themselves concerned with evangelization *and* with civilization, because in the long run (though not always in the short run) the two are the same—the bringing to men and society of the *civitas dei,* that divine commonwealth which must ultimately transform the kingdoms of this world till they become the kingdom of God and of his Christ. And the Christian style of life is the expression of the *total* design of God for his world, and not of one side of it alone or of the other. 'Only let your manner of life,' says St. Paul in Phil. 1.27, 'be worthy of the gospel of Christ'; and for 'manner of life' it is significant that he uses the same word, *politeuesthe,* which later in the Epistle he is to use of the Christians' *politeia,* or citizenship, in heaven, and which we use for 'politics.' Being worthy of the Gospel, evangelization, *includes* the concern for civilization. No definition of 'the spiritual life,' of the individual or the community, which leaves out political engagement in the broadest sense of that term can claim to be true to the whole counsel of God.

This leads me, finally, to some closing observations on the *place* of the Christian society in 'this world.' I have just indicated that the Christian

[4] *Christian Belief and This World,* pp. 44-6.

society, the Church, is the instrument of *the Kingdom.* And it is vital to keep this relationship clear. For the perennial temptation of the Church is to equate itself with the kingdom of God on earth, and so to regard itself as the only agent of God in this world.

Properly defined,[5] the Church is the society in which the universal kingship of God in Christ is *acknowledged.* It is the society, therefore, in which that kingship is embodied, or should be embodied, more fully than in any other section of humanity: it exists, in St. James' words (Jas. 1.18), as 'a kind of first fruits' of God's redemptive purpose; it is the instrument by which the rest of creation is to be restored and conformed to the image of his Son.

But it is easy from this high doctrine of the Church to go on to regard it also as the instrument of God's *creative* purpose, to assume that what God is doing in this world he must be doing through the Church, that the space to watch, as it were, if one really wants to see what God is up to, is the Church papers. Now no non-Christian, it is safe to say, would ever imagine this. Nor—which is more important—would anyone reach this conclusion from reading the Bible.

In the Old Testament, the people of God is certainly not the rudder by which the course of history is steered. It is much more like a cork bobbing on the ocean borne this way and that, at times almost submerged, by the swirl and current of events. True, the biblical writers insist that it provides the clue to the *understanding,* and even more to the *redemption,* of this process. It is 'the saints of the Most High' rather than the secular world-empires which provide the pattern and the pledge of God's victory. But the answer to the question 'What is God doing?' is at any moment just as likely to be given in the operations of Pharaoh, or the king of Assyria, or Cyrus King of Persia, as in any activity which today would be regarded as the work of the Church.

And in the New Testament, this is still true. It is most obviously true in the Book of the Revelation, the only New Testament book to deal specifically with the theology of the secular world. In it, though God is indeed acting *for* the Church, he is never contemplated as bringing about the consummation of history *through* the Church. What *is* to be done 'through the Church' is, as St. Paul says in Ephesians, for the plan of God's redemptive mystery to be made known to the principalities and powers of this world (Eph. 3. 9f.). The Church alone holds the clue to God's purpose; and holding that clue it has to be in the world, to 'redeem the time' (Eph. 5.16). It is the instrument of God's *reconciling* work (Col. 1. 18-20). But

[5] For a fuller statement of the relation between the Church and the kingdom of God, see O. Cullmann, 'The Kingship of Christ and the Church in the New Testament,' *The Early Church,* pp. 101-37.

though *creation,* the continuous creation of God's advancing purpose, is firmly declared in the New Testament to be 'in Christ' (John 1.3f.; Col. (1.15-17), it is never thought of as set forward specifically or primarily through the Church.

Obviously it is possible to press this distinction too far, for there is no final distinction in God between creation and redemption. But it is equally perilous to ignore it. The Church's task is to be wherever God is at work, in the van of his process, baptizing and transforming it in Christ. But, contrary to what is sometimes assumed, the Church cannot claim advance knowledge of God's plan of campaign, except in so far as it is given to the Christian prophet to see deeper and further into the mind of God *as he is actually about* his creative purpose. The Church can never say in advance what instrument, what channel, God will use or refuse. And any schema which implies that it can, that it has an inside knowledge of the pattern of history, is an idol. And this is true even, or especially, when that schema centres in the missionary work of the Church, as though this were the clue to the dialectic of events. The missionary work of the Church bears, indeed, a vital relation to the End (cf. Matt. 24.14): it is that through which the old is to be made *new.* But it is nowhere claimed in the Bible as the mainspring of God's action in history. The Christian society must always be expecting God to be acting decisively outside its ranks.

The purpose of these seemingly rather negative remarks is to urge that Christians be found in the right place in 'this world.' Let me end by putting the matter in terms of a parable. Last Good Friday two processions met, or rather were diverted from meeting, in the streets of Reading. The one was that of the Campaign for Nuclear Disarmament, on its march of protest from Aldermaston to London. The other was a Good Friday procession of witness by the local Christian Churches. What was the relation between these two processions in the purpose of God, and where should Christians have been? Clearly, they had a responsibility to the second, bearing their distinctive witness to the redemptive act of God in Christ. But may it not have been equally, if not more important, that some at least should have been in the first—as, of course, they were? If the concern for which that secular pilgrimage stood represents in any way a word of God to our generation, then the Christian's place is to be at the point which God has reached in his creative purpose, to be there to inform it with the mind of Christ, to redeem it from the 'powers of this present age'—and, last but not least, himself to be addressed and humbled by God through it.

The power to do all this will be given to him only through his membership of the Christian society. It is this alone (unless it lose its own savour) which, as the salt of the earth, will prevent 'this world' from going bad. It is the leaven of the new creation. But the leaven must always be in the lump. Christians may often be tempted to think how much purer it would be if it were kept out of it. For their involvement in 'this world,' to be the soul in what St. Paul has no hesitation in describing as 'this body of death' (Rom. 7.24), is always a call to share, not only in the sovereignty, but in the suffering and the endurance, which are ours in Jesus (Rev. 1.9). 'Christians are kept in the world as in a prison-house.' 'Yet they themselves hold the world together. . . . So great is the office for which God hath appointed them, and which it is not lawful for them to decline.'

VII. Eschatology

Amos Niven Wilder is Hollins Professor of Divinity, Emeritus, at The Harvard Divinity School.

Ethics in the Time of Salvation*

Our first part has dealt with the sanction aspect of the relation of eschatology to ethics. We have to turn now to an even more significant aspect. How did the eschatological conception affect the content and nature of the ethics, if at all? Does Jesus call for a different righteousness, and if so, how is it related to the conception of the end?

In the first section we have assumed that eschatology meant an event still in the future. As long as we thus confine ourselves to the thought of the

* Abridged from pp. 145-48, 151-53, 159-62 in *Eschatology and Ethics in the Teaching of Jesus*, rev. ed., by Amos N. Wilder. Copyright 1939, 1950 by Harper & Brothers. Reprinted by permission of Harper & Row, Publishers.

coming Judgment with its rewards and penalties, our problem is comparatively simple. The coming event is, then, motive for repentance and for urgency in doing righteousness, and the particular demands are looked on as conditions of entrance to the future Kingdom. If this were all, the problem would be much simplified. Then the Baptist and Jesus would be prophetic exponents of the law in its inner meaning, calling the nation to prepare itself by righteousness for the coming day of Jehovah.

But in our analysis of the eschatology taught by Jesus we have seen that it includes elements anterior to the parousia and Judgment. The eschatological period begins with the proclamation of the Baptist and the work of Jesus, and goes on through the death and resurrection of the latter to the coming of the Son of Man. This interpretation by Jesus of the events of his own lifetime and of the days immediately to follow it is evidenced throughout, as we have seen, especially by such words as those designating the Baptist as Elias who should come and by the significance assigned to his own work. This whole reading of events is based upon the Scriptures. Logically, we would suppose that a clear distinction would be made between the present age and the age to come, with all evidences of God's work of salvation strictly confined to the latter. It was not so in fact. Lake and Jackson point out that there was no fixed doctrine of the future, and that the "Good Time Coming" at times included both the Days of the Messiah as well as the Age to Come proper.[1] That is, the Scriptures warranted the expectation of various aspects of the time of salvation before the decisive catastrophe itself. We can understand this when we recall the history of Jewish eschatology. The earlier Davidic messianism envisaged a redeemed people living in the world in conditions not greatly changed. When the apocalyptic ideas came in with their picture of a regeneration and a transcendental Kingdom, it was not easy to submit the older earthly ideals to the new, and the older were not therefore abandoned or subsumed under the new entirely. Thus many details in the Scriptures there losely assigned to the coming time of salvation, could be legitimately interpreted as fulfilled in the days of John the Baptist and Jesus. The return of Elijah and the preaching of a Last Repentance were of course most naturally assigned to the last days before the new age. But there was hardly less difficulty in seeing a present fulfilment of the prophecies of the washing away of the sins of the people, the purifying of the priests and the Temple, the outpouring of the Spirit, the giving of a new heart of flesh to Israel, the overthrow of Satan and the demons, the forgiveness of sins and other features of the messianic days. Thus

[1] *The Beginnings of Christianity,* I, Part I, chap. vi.

Jesus found abundant warrant for his interpretation of the phenomena of his day as evidence of the expected time of salvation, as part of the eschatological program in the larger sense. Many prophets and wise men had desired to see these days. "Today hath this scripture been fulfilled in your ears."

This fact presents us with a new aspect of the relation of eschatology to ethics and opens up an essentially different problem. The eschatological period is already present. It is now not the sanction of the ethical teaching that is in question, but its very content. How is the ethic affected by the fact of the present eschatological situation? This new situation is constituted by the presence of the Kingdom in its first and humbler manifestation, with its accompanying benefits and powers, and by the activity of Jesus, whose humble role was none the less closely related to the coming of the Son of Man in power. In these circumstances it is not surprising to find that a correspondently modified ethic is taught.

1. *A new situation has arisen with the presence of the Baptist and Jesus which has a significant relation to ethics.*

Some students would have us believe that Jesus taught no other righteousness than that of the law. But Jesus speaks as though the *present* Kingdom of God presupposes a different relation between man and man, and man and God, and therefore a different ethic. We have noted that on occasion Jesus speaks of the Kingdom as present. The overthrow of Satan is another aspect of the present Kingdom. And in so far as the Kingdom is already come a new order of relationships and responsibilities is offered.

Jesus' reference to a new covenant (Mark 14:24 and parallels; cf. I Cor. 11:25 and Lk. 22:29, 30) is questioned by many scholars advisedly. Yet it is clear that he thought of his generation as living in a time like that foreshadowed in such passages as Jer. 31:31 ff., Ezek. 24:8, Zech. 9:11. "Jesus nowhere refers to these promises," says Windisch of the Jeremiah and Ezekiel passages, "yet he assumes that the inner condition of his hearers is such that they can 'live according to God's statutes' or that he himself it is who by his word has put the command of God 'in their inward parts' and written it 'in their hearts.' "[2] It is notable that a feature of Jeremiah's picture of the new covenant has to do with God's "law."

> But this is the covenant that I will make with the house of Israel after those days, saith Jehovah: I will put my law in their inward parts, and in their heart will I write it. 31:33.

Similar promises, in terms of future

[2] Windisch, *Bergpredigt,* p. 73.

sonship, are found in Hos. 1:10, Is. 43:6, Ps. Sol. 17:27, Jub. 1:23-25. Jesus looks on his followers as heirs of these promises. The new situation is there for those who respond.

The new condition of things is evidenced also by Jesus' power in exorcism. By the spirit of God he casts out devils and the presence of the Kingdom is manifest. The strong man, Satan, is bound, as is evidenced by the overthrow of his agents. The passage (Mt. 12:28-29) [3] and context connect all this closely with Jesus himself. The reduction of Satan to impotence has significance for ethics.

Again, of the parables of the Kingdom, at least those of the mustard seed, the seed growing of itself and the leaven, show us Jesus' thought that the Kingdom is present in anticipatory form already before the parousia. In these three the relation of the outcome to the initial action is so essential as to call attention to the intervening phase. . . .

In effect, the new situation, with the present preaching of the Kingdom, has new ethical aspects. The same truth is reflected, finally, in the parable of a certain man, who made a great supper.[4] By the Baptist and by Jesus, God is represented as extending his general invitation to the imminent supper or marriage feast of the Kingdom. But this is evidently, then, a new and extraordinary situation and one involving corresponding special responsibilities.

2. *Jesus out of his unique sense of mission has authority to rule freely on ethical issues.*

We have seen that Jesus looked upon his day as one in which the conditions of the ethical life were changed. The law and prophets were until John. Now the Kingdom comes. Now Satan is bound. God is evidently drawing near to soften the hearts of publicans and sinners. These were the days that many wise men and prophets had longed to see.

Can we say more than this? Can we go on and say that not only is the situation as regards ethics changed but that Jesus gives a new content to the will of God? Not merely over against the prevailing ethics of the scribes, but over against the law itself, the written law? We believe that this can be claimed. Jesus out of his fuller and deeper understanding of God and man and their relation by word and action fulfilled and corrected the law. With sovereign originality and insight he gave a new expression to the will of God and related it in a new way to the religious life.

The evidence for this is apt to be obscured if we turn only to the well-known passages where Jesus deals with the law, the Sabbath, ablutions, etc., and the debate here is endless. The more conclusive evidence is drawn

[3] Cf. the temptation account, also Lk. 10:18-19 and 13:10-17, cf. Bultmann, *Jesus,* pp. 29-30; *Jesus and the Word,* p. 28.

[4] Lk. 14:16-24 (Mt. 22:1-10).

from the total picture, from Jesus' sense of vocation, from what we have seen of his ultimate appeal to moral discernment rather than to authority, from his approach to the "sinners," his declaration of the forgiveness of sins, and some of his great statements, the implications of which were revolutionary.

Let us, however, consider the evidence in the gospels for his attitude to the law at the debated points. Examination of Mt. is of special value, here. What, according to Mt., is Jesus' relation to the law, written and oral? A simple answer cannot be given to this question. There are contradictions in Jesus' words and actions bearing on this subject. He is represented in some instances as ascribing great authority to the law in all its details. "For verily I say unto you, Till heaven and earth pass away, one jot or one tittle shall in no wise pass away from the law, till all things be accomplished" (5:18). "The scribes and Pharisees sit on Moses' seat: all things therefore whatsoever they bid you, these do and observe. . ." (23:2-3). But in other instances Jesus is represented as overriding or directly contradicting the law, and as transgressing it in action. Any interpretation of his attitude as Mt. gives it which tries to reduce it to a simple principle will be unsatisfactory.

The fact is that the evangelist has included in his gospel sayings from different traditions and from different points of view. Students often conceive of the editorial role in the gospels in a mistaken way. The compiler did not pursue a deliberate dogmatic and tendentious aim in such matters, nor did he have the highly perspicacious attention we attribute to him in these issues. He was assembling materials and ordering them in a given situation, indeed. But the "tendencies" natural to that situation would be rather unconscious than deliberate. And the shaping process would lack much of our modern logical preoccupation.

At the bottom of the discrepancies, moreover, we may reasonably assume a genuine variety of expression in the case of Jesus himself. Recognition of the place of overstatement in his pedagogical method, and of the diversity of situation to which he spoke, would sufficiently account for considerable variation in reports of his attitudes and actions.

However, it still remains possible to generalize as to Jesus' relation to the law and to reach a conclusion as to the sayings which should be deemed most indicative. We hold that amidst the diversity of representations of Mt.'s Jesus, those that show him ruling and overruling freely and authoritatively on matters concerning the law are most significant, and best fit the total picture of the gospel. . . .

Jesus' sense of authority over against the law comes out further in his attitude to the sinners of his time. It is true that the scribes and Pharisees were peculiarly censorious as regards this group. But more than that, in view of the character of the law itself, the publicans and sinners were debtors and offenders. For though grace lay behind the Torah yet the will of God for ethical and ceremonial practice was set forth in the law in the form of a commandment. Restoration to the favor of God and pardon depended therefore emphatically on the initial repentance of the sinner. In the period with which we are concerned the prevailing attitude to the law reinforced this expectation. But Jesus breaks with this situation by not waiting for the repentance of the unrighteous. In his parable of the two debtors this understanding of the matter is illustrated by the words: "And when they had not wherewith to pay, he forgave them both." [5]

Jesus approaches ethical issues, then, with a sovereign independence arising out of his own prophetic insights, but also in immediate relation to the dawning of the new age. . . .

We know that Jesus spoke with great authority and independence in the matter of ethics. We know that he looked upon his day as the expected time of salvation. We know that he spoke and acted out of a sense of vocation whose messianic character he could not, perhaps, finally deny. We conclude that we have evidence here then, which indicates how the differentia of his ethics is determined by an eschatological factor: the presence of the Kingdom.

3. *The ethics determined by the new situation can best be characterized not as interim ethics but as ethics of the time of salvation or new-covenant ethics.*

We have said that the new situation determines a new ethic. We have said that Jesus rules freely on ethics and the law. What characterizes the new ethic that results?

We take it that it is not an interim ethic. The new situation is not *essentially* characterized by the fact that it is a respite before the terrors of the Judgment. The new situation is rather the anticipated time of salvation in which men are no longer hard-hearted, in which they become God's sons in a full sense, receive forgiveness on the occasion of the Great Repentance, know the Spirit, and recognize the overthrow of Satan and the demons. It is the time in which God is enacting his great deliverance, and in which he is drawing near to men in a way he had not done since the time of Moses, and is making a new covenant with them, not as the covenant which he made with them in the time of Moses, which they had broken. The feature that Jesus is present as herald of this gospel, and as central evidence of this new situation, is subsidiary to the main fact of God's action.

Thus the ethic is not an interim ethic. It is not even a repentance ethic in the sense of an extreme renunciation or asceticism as penance for the

[5] Lk. 7:42.

emergency. It *is* a repentance ethic in the sense that it calls for "fruits worthy of repentance," i.e., conduct evidencing the changed disposition. Rather, it can be best designated as an ethic of the present Kingdom of God or a new-covenant ethic. It is not primarily an ethic for the relations and conduct of the future transcendental Kingdom. Nor is it a Kingdom ethic in the sense that its practice would admit to the Kingdom nor that it would "build" the Kingdom. It is a Kingdom ethic in the sense that it represents the righteousness of those living in the days of the new covenant and empowered and qualified by the reconciliation and redemption of that age.[6]

But what of the transcendental Kingdom? It is true that Jesus taught that the new era is to have its all-important manifestation in a supernatural way: advent of the Son of Man, Judgment and the miraculously instituted Kingdom. And it is true that Jesus cast his ethic, with the repentance it involves, in the form of entrance conditions to that Kingdom. The point is, *the conception of that eschatological culmination so partook of the nature of myth or poetry that it did not other than formally determine the ethic.* The conception of the Judgment and the supernatural rewards, including the Kingdom, stand to Jesus and to the community as *representations,* with full validity and credibility, indeed, of the unprophesiable, unimaginable but certain, God-determined future. This future and God's action in it lend immense weight and urgency to their present moral responsibility. Yet this temporal imminence of God is but a function of his spiritual imminence, and it is this latter which really determines conduct. It is not a dualistic other-worldliness that meets us in Jesus' inattention to property, family ties and citizenship, but a selective valuation and a particular focus of concern consequent upon immediate confrontation with God. The sense of the divinely determined future, however apocalyptically it may be formulated, does not in actual fact put an end to the this-worldly concern of Jesus and the church. Reserves may be made for the evidences of true interim phenomena of the early church, but these are not typical. The radical character of Jesus' ethics does not spring from the shortness of the time but from the new relation to God in the time of salvation. The sanction for it is not the sanction of imminent supernatural retributions—except formally—but the appeal to the God-enlightened moral discernment recognizing the nature and will of God and inferring consequences (thence eschatologically dramatized).

[6] We can see how easily and naturally the ethics so understood would be taken over by the church of the time of the evangelist as basic guide for its code, both in relation to the law and in relation to the conduct of life generally. Thus the church was thought of more and more as itself the Kingdom of God.

What these ethics were we can only suggest. Jesus virtually supersedes the law by the lengths he goes in appealing to its deeper principles. We can see that the dispute as to whether he did or did not overthrow the law is ambiguous. Many scribes exercised their judgment in discriminating the weightier or more central demands of the law; and it can well be said that Jesus upheld by saying and act the word of God in the law. But we are satisfied to rest the case for his *virtual setting aside of the law on the degree of independent interpretation he exercises. He goes so far beyond such scribes in matters of emphasis and spirit that the difference in degree becomes a difference in kind,* and confirmation of this is found in the attitude to him of the scribes and Pharisees.

Going on we note further as to the ethics that Jesus goes back to the great principles of the prophets, judgment, mercy and truth, but he sees these in a religious background different from that of the prophets, namely, his new portrayal of the nature of God. The ethics are conceived as responses to the nature of God, along emphatically positive lines. God's generosity, his forgiveness become determinative. Purity, sincerity and unreserved devotion answer all to another main aspect of his religious conception, the fact of such full sonship as implies immediate relation of obedience and response. The full personal will of the individual is therefore in play. This is a point that Bultmann makes much of. Ethics is now unqualifiedly the relation of the heart to God, person to Person, and this is ever present and controlling in the relation of man to man.

Part Two

The Principles of Christian Decision-Making

I. Gospel and Law

At the time of his death in 1968 Karl Barth was Professor of Theology, Emeritus, the University of Basle.

Reconciliation*

V. 12 [Romans 5] has usually been taken as an anacoluthon. More probably it should be taken as a kind of heading to what follows. *For this reason* (*dia touto*) are we such as vv. 1-11 described us, *for this reason* shall we be saved by sharing in the risen life of Jesus Christ, *for this reason* do we glory in our hope through Him—namely, that already as weak, sinners, godless, and enemies, already as children and heirs of Adam, and so in the past from which we came, we were not completely beyond the reach of the truth of Jesus Christ, but stood in a definite (even if negative) relationship to His saving power. V. 12 sets out this negative relationship. "As through one man sin has broken into the world, and through sin death, and as death has spread to all men, for that all men have sinned"—in other words, the relationship between Adam and all of us *then,* in the past, corresponds to the relationship between Christ and all of us *now,* in the present. Because of that correspondence it is true, as Paul has already emphasized in vv. 6, 8, 10, that Christ died for us while we were still living in the unredeemed past with Adam. Because of it, even in that past we were not completely forsaken and lost. Because of it, we can now look back at that past with good cheer—and can therefore "so much the more" glory in our present, and in the future that opens out from it. We were not, even then, in an entirely different world. Even then, we existed in an order whose significance was of course just the opposite of that of the Kingdom of Christ, but which had the same structure.

When we look back we must and we may recognize the ordering principle of the Kingdom of Christ even in the ordering principle of the world of Adam. Even when we were weak, sinners, godless, enemies, though we were traveling in a very different direction, the rule of the road strikingly resembled—was indeed the same

* Abridged from pp. 26-30, 34, 46-48, 51-54, 89-91, 92-94 in *Christ and Adam,* by Karl Barth; translated by T. A. Smail. Copyright © 1956, 1957 by Harper & Brothers. Reprinted by permission of Harper & Row, Publishers.

as—the one we know now. Between our former existence outside Christ and our present existence in Him there is a natural connection. Our former existence outside Christ is, rightly understood, already a still hidden but real existence in Him. Because of that, we dare to confess that we have peace with God, we dare to glory in our future salvation—we who still have that past, we who today are still the same men who were once weak, sinners, godless, and enemies. Our past cannot frighten us: in spite of it, and even taking it fully into account, we are still allowed and required to confess our reconciliation and glory in our salvation, just because our past as such—namely, the relationship between Adam and all of us—was already ordered so as to correspond to our present and future—namely, the relationship between Christ and all of us. That is what is made clear in the heading in v. 12.

The meaning of the famous parallel (so called) between "Adam and Christ," which now follows, is not that the relationship between Adam and us is the expression of our true and original nature, so that we would have to recognize in Adam the fundamental truth of anthropology to which the subsequent relationship between Christ and us would have to fit and adapt itself. The relationship between Adam and us reveals not the primary but only the secondary anthropological truth and ordering principle. The primary anthropological truth and ordering principle, which only mirrors itself in that relationship, is made clear only through the relationship between Christ and us. Adam is, as is said in v. 14, *typos tou mellontos,* the type of Him who was to come. Man's essential and original nature is to be found, therefore, not in Adam but in Christ. In Adam we can only find it prefigured. Adam can therefore be interpreted only in the light of Christ and not the other way round.

This then is our past—Adam and all of us, Adam in his relationship to us, we in our relationship to Adam. This is the history of man and of humanity outside Christ: the sin and death of a single man, of Adam, the man who in his own person is and represents the whole of humanity, the man in whose decision and destiny the decisions and destinies, the sins and the death of all the other men who come after him, are anticipated. It is also true that each of these others has lived his own life, has sinned his own sins, and has had to die his own death. Even so, the lives of all other men after Adam have only been the repetition and variation of his life, of his beginning and his end, of his sin and his death. That is our past. So were we weak, sinners, godless, and enemies, always Adam in us and ourselves in Adam, the one and the many, in the irremovable distinctness of the one over and against the others, in the irremovable unity of the others with the one. But now our past existence without Christ has no independent status or importance. Because it was constituted by this double relationship between the one and the others, it is now only the type, the likeness, the preliminary shadow of our present existence, which is itself constituted by the relationship between the One Christ and the many others and by the grace of God and His promise of life to men. Now the way in which our past was related to Adam can be understood only as a reflection and witness of the way in which our present is related to Christ. Human existence, as constituted by our relationship with Adam in our unhappy past as weak, sinners, godless, enemies, has no independent reality, status, or importance of its own. It is only an indirect witness to the reality of Jesus Christ and to the original and essential human existence that He inaugurates and reveals. The righteous decision of God has fallen upon men not in Adam but in Christ. But in Christ it has also fallen upon Adam, upon our relationship to him and so upon our unhappy past. When we know Christ, we also know Adam as the one who belongs to Him. The relationship that existed between Adam and us is, according to v. 12, the relationship that exists originally and essentially between Christ and us. . . .

The status of Adam is lower than the status of Christ, the sin of Adam counts for less than the righteousness of Christ. So also the relationship of the many to Adam is less significant than their other relationship to Christ. The only thing that is *common* to both relationships is that in two different contexts true human nature is revealed, and that in two different ways it is shown to be subject to the ordering of God its Creator. But to discover this common factor that connects the two sides, we have to take into account the decisive difference between them. And this difference is that our relationship to Adam is only the type, the likeness, the preliminary shadow of our relationship to Christ. The same human nature appears in both but the humanity of Adam is only real and genuine in so far as it reflects and corresponds to the humanity of Christ. . . .

The death and the resurrection of Jesus Christ, our reconciliation through His blood on the one hand, and our hope in the power of His life on the other, are two aspects—two very different aspects, it is true—of one single action. For that reason, in vv. 15-17 also, it is not enough merely to distinguish the truth in Adam from the truth in Christ. Because there is a valid and recognizable connection between Christ's death for sinners and His rising to bring life to men, there must also be a valid and recognizable connection between Adam in whom men sin and die and Christ in whom they are pardoned and made alive. The only connection between Christ and Adam is that for Adam Christ died and rose again. From the sin of Adam, as such, no way leads to the grace of Christ, no way from *krima* (judgment) to *dikaiōma* (righteousness), no way from *katakrima* (condemnation) to *sōtēria* (salvation), no way from death to life. If we looked from left to right, we would find every attempt to move in that direction frustrated, every door closed. If we could regard Adam and our participation in his sin and condemnation as an isolated and self-centered whole, then it would be impossible to find there any connection with Christ and our participation in His grace and life.

But so to regard Adam is impossible. Paul does not go to Adam to see how he is connected with Christ; he goes to Christ to see how *He* is connected with Adam. Already in vv. 9-10 he has looked *back* at our unhappy past, and in so doing has brought it into positive relation with our present and future, which at first sight seemed to have nothing in common with it at all. The present and future belong to Christ and in belonging to Christ they are connected with the past, because the past contains not only Adam's sin and Adam's death, not only our weakness, sin, godlessness, and enmity, it contains also the crucifixion of Jesus Christ, and through it our reconciliation to God. It is because Christ has thus invaded the world of Adam and claimed it for Himself, that Paul can find a connection between the two, a way that leads from Adam to Christ for himself and all believers, *prosagōgē eis tēn charin tautēn, en hē hestēkamen* (an access to this grace in which we in fact stand [v. 2]). Thus in vv. 15-17 Paul cannot treat the truth in Adam as though it were independent and self-contained. The truth in Christ will not allow it to be that, for Christ has challenged the right of sin and death to rule over Adam's world, by invading that world and making it His own. Only by overlooking or forgetting the truth in Christ which has broken into the world of Adam, could we judge the truth in Adam to be absolutely without light. It has, of course, no light of its own. But it is drawn into the light by the fact that Jesus Christ is risen from the dead. And when that light shines, it shows us the cross on which the same Jesus Christ suffered and died for the sin of Adam and the sin of all men, and by which Adam and all men are reconciled and pardoned and can find again the now reopened way to life with God. . . .

. . . To that we might reply that it is by no means sure or certain that Christ's death has brought reconciliation to men; the world is still as ignorant as ever of what Christ did for men. Men are still sinners, who do not know that Christ died for them and that they are therefore reconciled sinners; sinners, who make no thankful response to God's grace, but still go on rejecting it; sinners who still cry "Crucify Him!" and commit all over again the very sins that Christ bore away, sinners who all over again make themselves liable to the death that He suffered for them, and from which they have already been rescued by His death on the cross. That is the real dark mystery that surrounds our reconciliation, which Christ claims to have accomplished once and for all. And the heart of the mystery is that we are thus left in our ignorance, because here amidst the sin of the world even Christ Himself seems to win no triumph, but is present in His complete humiliation. This is the place where sinful man, where Church and State, where we in our ingratitude, successfully stand out against Him. There is nothing there to stop us. Nothing happens to open our eyes, to rescue us from our ignorance. Sin takes its course. The *krima* (judgment) is pronounced and not revoked, the *katakrima* (condemnation) follows with a relentless logic that is only too easy to understand. Christ suffers, dies, and is buried. . . .

But we have forgotten the very thing that we ought not to forget—namely, that it was at the very moment when this happened that we were reconciled, and that our reconciliation is no less real or valid because that was how it came about. On the contrary, unless we had been reconciled amidst the darkness of the mystery of sin, we could not have been reconciled at all. Is Christ less Christ because He is present only in His humiliation? How else can He be completely Christ except in His complete humiliation? And is He not completely Christ here, because here in His utter loneliness He is abandoned by all? How else could He be the Christ who is for all? Could He be exalted, were He not also thus humiliated? Must not He always be acknowledged, even in His exaltation, as the Christ who was humiliated by all, and also by us, and so as the Christ who was humiliated for all and also for us? Is it surprising that here our relation to Him is terrible ignorance? Would we be the sinners for whom He had to die and did die, if it were otherwise? No, this is the only way in which our reconciliation can be valid and real. This is the only way in which there can break in upon the dark world of sin the light of Easter Day. In that darkness our reconciliation has taken place, God's righteous decision has been carried out, Adam's pardon and ours has been pronounced in spite of his sin and the *paraptōmata tōn pollōn* (transgressions of the many). God's decision for us has here been made completely and entirely in opposition to us. "All we like sheep have gone astray; we have turned every one to his own way, but the Lord hath laid on Him the iniquity of us all" (Is. 53:6). The place where He bore our iniquity must be a dark place. But into that darkness there shines the bright light of Easter, because there He bore our iniquity for our salvation and to the glory of God. And if, when it is seen in that light, even our unhappy past is made bright, "how much more" bright is our present over which the light of Easter shines without any darkness at all. For its brightness shines also on our past, so that indirectly and subsequently we have to acknowledge that here in the darkness (where all was done without us and in spite of us and so, in reality, for us) Christ's decisive work, which has absolute superiority over Adam's work and all its results for ever, has been performed. That happened in the humiliation of Christ, in which He is to all eternity our Saviour and King. It happened in His blood in the power of which He intercedes for us as the Risen and Exalted Lord. And so, if the light of Easter, falling indirectly on our past, makes it clear that in that past our salvation and hope have their eternally unshakable foundation, "how much more" sure and certain are that salvation and hope when we see them in the same light's direct and unreflected blaze! . . .

What is said in vv. 1-11 is not just "religious" truth that only applies to specially talented, specially qualified, or specially guided men; it is truth for *all* men, whether they know it or not, as surely as they are all Adam's children and heirs. The assurance of Christians, as it is described in vv. 1-11, has as its basis the fact that the Christian sphere is not limited to the "religious" sphere. What is *Christian* is secretly but fundamentally identical with what is *universally human.* Nothing in true human nature can ever be alien or irrelevant to the Christian; nothing in true human nature can ever attack or surpass or annul the objective reality of the Christian's union with Christ. Much in true human nature is unrelated to "religion," but nothing in true human nature is unrelated to the Christian faith. That means that we can understand true human nature only in the light of the Christian gospel that we believe. For Christ stands above and is first, and Adam stands below and is second. So it is Christ that reveals the true nature of man. Man's nature in Adam is not, as is usually assumed, his true and original nature; it is only truly human at all in so far as it reflects and corresponds to essential human nature as it is found in Christ. True human nature, therefore, can only be understood by Christians who look to Christ to discover the essential nature of man. Vv. 12-21 are revolutionary in their insistence that what is true of Christians must also be true of all men. That is a principle that has an incalculable significance for all our action and thought. To reject this passage as empty speculation is tantamount to denying that the human nature of Christ is the final revelation of the true nature of man.

What Rom. 5:12-21 is specially concerned to make clear is that man as we know him, man in Adam who sins and dies, has his life so ordered that he is both a distinct individual and, at the same time, the responsible representative of humanity and of all other men. In the same way there are no other responsible representatives of humanity than individual men. We are what Adam was and so are all our fellow men. And the one Adam is what we and all men are. Man is at once an individual and only an individual, and, at the same time, without in any way losing his individuality, he is the responsible representative of all men. He is always for himself and always for all men. That being so, can we build on this foundation? Is it true that essential human nature must always be the existence of the man in humanity and of humanity in the man? We recognize that, first, only in relation to Adam and the many who are like him, and so only in relation to sinful and dying men like ourselves. But have we understood man correctly when we understand him in that way? Could not all that be quite wrong? Might not humanity be a corporate personality of which individuals are only insignificant manifestations or fragmentary parts? Or might not the whole notion of humanity be a fiction, and the reality consist only of a collection of individuals each essentially unrelated to the others and each responsible only for himself? Rom. 5:12-21 points in neither of these directions. If we base our thinking on this passage, we can have nothing to do with either collectivism on the one hand or individualism on the other. It understands the true man in neither of these ways. . . .

The answer is in vv. 13-14 and 20, where it is shown that the formal correspondence and identity between Adam and Christ is based upon their material disparity. In the encounter between them Christ has more right and power, and Adam less. It is only in this disparity of status and in this disproportion that they can be compared. Adam is subordinate to Christ, and not Christ to Adam. And if Adam is subordinate to Christ, then Adam represents true and genuine human nature in so far as he shows us the man in humanity and humanity in the man. Whatever else in his representation of human nature may have to be accounted for by its later corruption and ruin, this ordering principle at least belongs to its condition and character as created and untouched by sin. For the subordinate representation of human nature in Adam here corresponds to its primary representation in Christ. In Christ also, the man is in humanity and humanity is in the man. With one important difference: Adam is not God's Son become man, and so he cannot, like Him, be man, and at the same time be *over* all men. Adam, as the one, can represent the many; he as man can represent humanity—but only as one among others. Thus he can represent all the others only in the same way that each of them can represent him. Adam has no essential priority of status over other men. He cannot be their lord and head; he cannot determine their life and their destiny. He can anticipate their life and destiny in himself, only in so far as he is the first man among many others, only in so far as he is *primus inter pares*. The *pollō mallon* (much more) of vv. 15-17 marks this difference. Where it is taken into account, what remains of the identity between Adam and Christ is the unity of the one and the many on both sides, of his deeds and their deeds, of his condition and theirs. In this unity Christ is, like Adam, man. In this unity of the one and the many Adam is the type and likeness of Christ, although formally he differs from Christ because he is not lord and head in this unity, and materially he differs from Him, because his nature is perverted by sin. But this unity, as such, belongs not to the perversion of his nature but to its original constitution. And so Paul makes no arbitrary assertion, and he is not deceiving himself when he presupposes this unity as simply given even in Adam. He does so because he has found it given first and primarily in Christ.

Christ is not only God's Son; He is also a man who is not a sinner like Adam and all of us. He is true man in an absolute sense, and it is in His humanity that we have to recognize true human nature in the condition and character in which it was willed and created by God. To it there certainly belongs this unity of man and humanity. When we inquire about the true nature of man and seek and answer in terms of this unity, we are on firm ground, in so far as even sinful man, whom alone we know, reflects back, as far as this unity is concerned, the human nature of Christ and so has not ceased to be true man and has not ceased to show man's true nature to us.

Alexander Miller was at the time of his death in 1960 Professor of Religion, Special Program in the Humanities, Stanford University.

The Ethics of Justification*

Historically and philosophically there are, very broadly speaking, two possible approaches to the problems of conduct. They correspond to the two religious options which, as we have seen, biblical religion characteristically avoids. Koestler's *Yogi* and *Commissar* symbols not only correspond to two types of world outlook, but they also stand representative of the two peren-

* From *The Renewal of Man*, by Alexander Miller, pp. 85-98. Copyright © 1955 by Alexander Miller. Reprinted by permission of Doubleday & Company, Inc., and Victor Gollancz, Ltd.

nial options in ethical thinking. The *Commissar* represents an ethic of pure calculation, the *Yogi* that of pure compassion. They correspond, as we noticed, to the two perennial options in the sphere of religion: the deification of the vitalities of nature and history, or the attempted transcendence of these dynamisms in sheer abstraction from the world. Koestler's problem is that pure compassion cannot implement itself in action and so passes into contemplative withdrawal; while the ethic of calculation which is designed to maximize the human good by efficient social engineering degenerates, without the restraint of compassion, into sheer nihilistic ruthlessness.

Historically speaking, of course, neither of these options is ever found pure. Natural religion and world-renouncing spirituality tend as we have seen to pass into each other according as men look *at* nature or look *through* it, find it fascinating or revolting: and since as Koestler sees it the final consequences of either course tend to be humanly intolerable, in life and in fact men's moral behavior is less tidy than any simple theory can account for. It is notorious for example that Kant's absolute ethic of conscience can connect itself with the real world of decision and action only by importing the most blatant element of calculation ("Act only on that maxim which you can will to become a Universal Law of Nature"), and the Marxists, who attempt an ethic of pure calculation of the greatest good of the greatest number, end by sacrificing indefinite numbers to a purely formal historical and social dogma.

Just as the Bible avoids both natural religion and world-renunciation, so it surefootedly avoids both the purely prudential and the purely rational, abstract types of ethical thinking. It knows nothing of idealism *or* of pragmatism. But before we attempt to set out the biblical faith in its relation to conduct, it is worth noticing that in point of fact both the rational and pragmatic views of ethics stand far removed from the etymological meaning of the word. For *ethics* relates to *ethos,* just as *morals* are tied to *mores,* and these etymological connections suggest a social origin and a social character for moral standards which are too little taken account of either by the rationalists or the pragmatists, and might seem at first to give comfort to the ethical relativists, who emphasize the socially conditioned and provisional character of all "values."

There is an increasing volume of Christian writing on the problems of conduct which is not only content but concerned that the ethics derived from biblical faith should be discriminated once and for all from rational idealism (with its correlative *natural law*) and would argue that they can be so separated without falling into pure relativism. Here, for example, is Professor Paul Lehmann of Princeton on

The Foundation and Pattern of Christian Behaviour.[1]

Christian ethics, as a theological discipline, has to do with the "ethos" of Christians. The word "ethos" is derived from a Greek verb *eiotha* meaning "to be accustomed to." The idea is that what one is accustomed to gives stability to the human situation and thus makes conduct possible and meaningful. By some such correspondence between language and reality, "ethos," as a noun, meant "dwelling" or "stall." What was originally referred to animals as giving stability and security to their existence came also to be applied to human relations. So, the ethos of a society denotes that which gives stability and security to human behavior. Ethos is, so to say, the cement of human society. . . .

"The cement of society" . . . but of what society? For every type of human society tends to generate its own ethics—the family, the fraternity, the nation, each attempts to impose its own standards, and that is precisely where the problem lies. Let's take one representative out of my undergraduate constituency. This girl, a charmer and much in demand, was tormented about a conflict in sex standards between her home training and the campus mores. The boys, she said, expected heavy petting as a normal part of campus dating, and from this she revolted. But her concern was that as a rational modern she could give no rational reason for this revulsion, either to herself or to others. And again the assumption was that there must *be* some rational reason, and that it was the business of the Christian moralist to provide it. So I asked her to tell me, off the top of her head, what seemed to her to be the real ground of her resistance. "It's too silly," said she, "but I suppose it's because my mother told me not to!" Now it seems to me that my first business was to point out that this reason is by no means as silly as, to a rational modern, it sounds: for what she really meant was that in the community of her first loyalty she had learnt standards of restraint and self-possession, to deny which would be to loosen her loyalty to that primal community, and to break confidence. That is clearly not the end of the matter, since on this and more important issues she must find some stance from which she could evaluate and correct the provisional standards of the home. But would this new stance be a self-validating rational standard?

In point of fact, from the viewpoint of biblical faith, No. For biblical ethics are not rational ethics, just as biblical faith is not a variety of rational idealism. And what the Christian moralist can offer is not a self-validating rational standard, but a community of loyalty which transcends and holds in some sort of proportion and relation the loyalty to home and to peer-group and to nation, and whatever other

[1] In *Christian Faith and Social Action,* John A. Hutchison, Editor (Scribners, 1953).

communities of loyalty lay demands upon us.

Let us be more precise about this. "Christian ethics, as a theological discipline, has to do with the *ethos* of Christians." Which is another way of saying that biblical ethics are covenant ethics, just as biblical religion is covenant religion. The revelatory events which were crucial for Israel's history, which brought the community of faith into being, by the same token created a community *ethos,* a set of community *mores.* We have seen this illustrated at two points: in the first place the *Law* of the Hebrews is a transcript of the community's understanding of its own life in relation to the God who claimed the community for his own in the Sinai-event; and the *Prophetic Witness,* as we have noticed, appeals not to a private and personal, mystical or rational, disclosure, but to the loyalty which is involved in being a member of the community at all, as it lives its life in relation to the God of love and righteousness. Biblical ethics, that is to say, are neither rational nor experimental, neither idealist nor pragmatic: they are community ethics. In New Testament terms they are *koinonia* (fellowship) ethics, as the essay of Paul Lehmann's already referred to makes emphatically clear. He quotes *The Letter to the Ephesians:*

> . . . we are meant to hold firmly to the truth in love, and to grow up in everything into Christ the Head. For it is from the Head that the whole Body, as an harmonious structure knit together by the joints with which it is provided, grows by the proper functioning of individual parts to its full maturity in love. . . . Live life, then, with a due sense of responsibility, not as men who do not know the meaning and purpose of life but as those who do. . . ." [2]

And that is always the sequence of the New Testament argument. "If God so loved us, we ought also to love one another." There is not, to put it baldly, a trace of rationalism or experimentalism in it. It is ethics (*ethos*) in the strict and forgotten sense. It calls a community to a "style" of life consonant with its origin and nature. The Christians are summoned to live as the sons of God they are, to behave like members of that *koinonia* which is the costly fruit of God's self-offering in Christ, the reconstituted family of mankind.

This means in practical fact that in the face of the confusion of standards, the conflict of mores, which torments the undergraduate and the modern world, what the Christian faith has to offer is not a set of rational standards rationally perceived, but *another set of mores,* the mores of the Church (*koinonia*) or better, the mores of the Kingdom of God. The Christian faith need not at all be taken aback by the assertion that ethical standards are social products, that all ethics are *rela-*

[2] Ephesians 4-5. As in J. B. Phillips, *Letters to Young Churches* (Macmillan, New York, 1950).

tional ethics.[3] From the biblical and Christian point of view the question, of course, is, in what context of relations is the discussion carried on? Does it have an authentic center and sufficient scope, or is it distorted and idolatrous, or distorted because it is idolatrous?

The concern of biblical faith is not the sanctification of the world or any part of it, or the transcendence of the world, but the organization of the world around its true and authentic center, which is God the Creator and Redeemer, the God of love and righteousness, who is the God of Abraham, Isaac and Jacob, the God and Father of our Lord Jesus Christ. And this God as we have seen is not a rational principle, but the Creator of community and that community's living focus of love and loyalty. It is within this community of faith that there are generated the mores which transcend and correct all provisional and local standards. Since, however, this community is constituted not by rational agreement but by living and personal loyalty to the One God, its *ethics* constitute not a set of rational and formal principles, but a mesh of obligations determined by the relation of one member of the Community to another, and of all to the community's Head.

Christian ethics in this sense are inseparable from the peculiar biblical understanding of salvation and justification. To be justified is to have life *rectified,* so that it is not organized around the false and idolatrous center of the self (nor around any enlarged or expanded idolatrous self such as family or nation) but moves upon its true and authentic fulcrum. The other side of the transaction is justification, wherein the citadel of self is ravaged and Christ reigns where self was, all that is done is done, as Luther says, "simply to please God thereby." And what pleases God most, as the New Testament makes abundantly clear, is the simple and selfless service of the neighbor, in the most practical fashion and the most down-to-earth way. This is that "Faith active in Love," which is the slogan form of Reformation ethics, and whose content has to be rediscovered and relived in every generation and in every situation.

The difficulty is to put content into it without falling again into the legalism of rationalism, or into pure pragmatism. The most massive and influential attempt at it in our generation is probably Emil Brunner's *The*

[3] H. Richard Niebuhr of Yale in an important essay *The Center of Value* (in *Moral Principles of Action,* Ruth Nanda Anshen, Editor, Harper, 1952) argues that in practice all ethics are relational ethics, and that the frank recognition that this is so is not only entirely congenial to Christianity, which has too long been confused with idealism, but would open a fruitful debate between Christianity and the naturalists. The importance of this is clear, for example, as it affects our attitude to a frankly relational value theory like that of Ralph Barton Perry, in which values are "objects of interest." [The Niebuhr essay is reproduced herein, pp. 161-73. Ed.]

Divine Imperative.[4] Brunner begins by affirming the authentic starting point of Christian ethics, in comment on Kant: "There is no good will save that which is rooted in justification by faith," and goes on to discuss in the most detailed and illuminating fashion how such good will will implement itself in the natural communities of family, labor, economics, politics and culture. But he runs into difficulty; and instead of holding to the question how in all these relationships the human good may be maximized, he falls back upon rational and "natural" criteria of what that good must be. He rests his case for monogamy, for example, in part upon the alleged fact that it is primitive (and therefore "natural") or alternatively that it is late, historically and sociologically speaking, and has the tendency to assert itself over alternative forms of sexual organization. Now these facts, in so far as they are facts, may have their importance as illustrating the necessities of the human case, but they do not make a "Law." For from the Christian point of view the good is defined neither by what is early nor by what is late, by what is rational or by what is natural, but by what is good for man. There is an element of thoroughgoing pragmatism in Christian ethics, which is more fully taken account of in the work of Reinhold Niebuhr, in particular in *An Interpretation of Ethics*,[5] in which the Christian life of faith and obedience is set explicitly between the love-commandment which is the quintessence of the divine Law and defines the life of the community of the justified, and the necessities of the practical case.

If we use that starting point ourselves, what do we find?

We might begin here by noticing certain points of comparison and contrast with extra-biblical ethics both rational and experimental, both philosophic and scientific.

Broadly speaking it is clear that any form of absolute ethics, either of the rational sort or in the form of Kant's ethic of conscience, tends to care more for motives than for consequences; while a pragmatic ethic (e.g., Marxism) manifestly cares more for consequences than for motives. The point of view on motives and consequences which stems from biblical faith is somewhat more complex than either of these. The biblical concern about the divine righteousness is a concern not only that the wills of men be rightly oriented, but that the affairs of the world be rightly ordered. This involves a preoccupation both with motives *and* with consequences. Now it may be argued that over motives we have some sort of control, but that consequences are frequently incalculable and therefore such a calculation cannot be decisive at the point of ethical decision. Modern psychology would teach us to be wary of any cer-

[4] The Westminster Press, Philadelphia, 1947.
[5] Harper and Brothers, New York, 1935.

tainty about motives, either our own or those of other people. They are regularly as undiscoverable as consequences are incalculable. The fact is that we can neither pinpoint motives nor calculate consequences with any precision (cf. Peter Slavek in Koestler's *Arrival and Departure*), so that while we are bound to try to clarify motives and estimate consequences, at both the internal and external boundary of ethical action we are thrown upon the mercy of God, without whom "nothing is true, nothing is perfect." We shall be concerned more precisely with this matter in later discussion of political choice; but we might mark here a saying of Dietrich Bonhoeffer[6] in his *Letters from Prison:*

> To say that we are justified by faith and not by success is a very different thing from saying that we can be indifferent to success or failure.

There is in Christian ethics both an absolute element *and* an element of calculation: but Christian ethics differ from idealist ethics in that the absolute is an absolute loyalty and not an absolute principle, while the Christian calculation differs from typical pragmatism in that, while there is always a hidden absolute in pragmatism, an unadmitted presupposition about what is good for man, in the Christian scheme the calculation is grounded in a very precise understanding of what is good for man, determined by the revelation of God in Christ: "Live life, then," says St. Paul, "not as men who do not know the meaning and purpose of life but as those who do."

It is possible now to set out the elements which enter into a Christian ethical decision, which is not made on the basis of a deduction from rational principle, as in the characteristic "natural law" fashion, nor on the basis of "pure expediency."

A valid Christian decision is compound always of both *faith* and *facts.* It is likely to be valid in the degree to which the faith is rightly apprehended and the facts are rightly measured. It is the product, that is to say, of an absolute loyalty related to a pragmatic choice. Its precondition is a prayerful conformity in thought and life to "the truth as it is in Jesus," with all that this involves of profound submission to the mind of Christ in the Gospel, and the will of Christ to create for himself a community of brethren out of the separated individuals and the sundered communities of mankind: that first of all. But this does not provide the necessary ingredients of decision. It is to be noted that none of the "ethical sayings of Jesus" are actually prescriptive of conduct: rather they define the character of the new community into which men are brought by submission to the truth of

[6] Bonhoeffer, whom we have referred to earlier, was a Protestant theologian of great devotion and penetration who spent two years in Hitler's prisons, had a part in the plot on Hitler's life, and was hanged on the eve of possible rescue by the Americans.

the Gospel. But to be told to love our neighbor as ourselves, salutary and exacting as it is, does not resolve the question whether to go into Korea or to stay out, or define the precise degree of compromise necessary for political participation. For such daily decisions the faith must be conjoined to the facts, and what the faith does is not to alter the shape of the facts, but to tutor us to estimate them with disinterested precision, so that we may manipulate them to the maximum human and social good. This is, I take it, what Karl Barth means when he urges Christians to "sleep neither over their Bibles nor over their newspapers." For while the Bible is the source from which our faith is nurtured, in which the *ethos* of the kingdom of God is best communicated, the newspapers represent our access to hard and secular fact, the kind of fact which determines the form of our contemporary decision, the raw material for the sanctification of life.[7]

It should be added here that while the faith does not alter the facts, it does alter the dimension in which they are seen, and the depth with which they are comprehended. Statistics about living standards, for example, while they do not change in Christian hands, do become the bearers of a human content and a weight of anguish, so that it may be that caloric content, if it means starvation, represents for the Christian not simply an arithmetical symbol for intellectual comprehension, but a profound demand for costly identification with the brethren for whom Christ died. One should say then that a valid Christian ethical decision is compound not only of faith and facts, but involves a real process of *identification,* which welds faith to facts in the same movement which unites us to our brother men. "And this I pray," wrote Paul to the Philippians, "that your *love* may abound more and more in *knowledge* and in all *judgment.*" [8] Love in this context is a synonym for faith: the knowledge which arms faith for action includes knowledge of the relevant facts; but the judgment or the insight which Paul craves for the Christians is generated when the facts are brought into relation to the faith, and so yield their full human meaning.

Does all this mean, as it seems to mean, that every ethical decision must be approached *de novo,* without the guidance of any general principles at all? In a sense it does mean that. But it does not mean that we are left without the kind of resources which rational and general ethical principles are supposed to provide. We are delivered from legalism, but we are not surrendered to individualism. We may have to live life without general principles, but we do have the resources of

[7] Barth's reference to the newspapers I take to be symbolic and not naïve. He is as well aware as the next man that it is necessary not only to read them, but to notice who owns them!

[8] Philippians 1:9. Italics ours.

a cumulative inheritance. The community to whose *ethos* or *mores* we are concerned to conform, which has its life from Christ and its charter from the Scriptures, is a living community of faith, in whose corporate experience most of the problems we confront have been up for decision either in the precise form in which we meet them, or in forms not unrelated to our contemporary dilemma. Communities not only generate mores, they form habits. And just as any wholesome family inculcates habits of restraint and consideration which condition conduct, so the ongoing life of the Christian *koinonia* fosters a life of such a style and shape that it predetermines conduct in many a representative situation. This does not mean that all Church habits are good ones, but it does mean that when bad habits are formed within the Church, as they regularly are, the best resource for their correction is within the tradition of the Church itself, in the recollection of its primal origin and of its original charter.

Another question of real importance immediately arises. Does not this determination of Christian conduct in terms of a community *ethos* set the Christian too far apart from other men of good will and destroy the basis for co-operation with such men on matters of common ethical concern? And does it not discount the extent to which the life and conviction of such men of good will parallels and even excels the record of Christian men both in clarity of ethical conviction and integrity of ethical life?

The traditional view has been that the agreement on matters of conduct between Christians and non-Christians, for example their common convictions about the urgencies of social justice, presupposes some rational or natural law, known to all rational men, and independent of the specific nurture of the Christian community. Now the agreement is there and to be cherished. But what does it really imply? Does the fact that Christians and non-Christians commend the costly sacrifice of the four chaplains means that either Christians or non-Christians can give rational grounds for it? Or does it mean simply that our revulsion against cruelty and selfishness, and the lifting up of our heart in the face of heroic compassion, are part of our human constitution, reinforced by our recognition that the human community is impoverished by the one and enriched by the other? It seems to me that most of what is traditionally attributed to rational natural law can be accounted for by the recognition of the necessities of human society on the one hand, and on the other by an innate compassion (sometimes hard put to it to find rational justification) which may wage an uneasy and uncertain war against our latent egoism, yet is powerful enough to put its impress upon our common mind, upon our tradition and upon our institutions. In this sense, as Paul says, men without the Law do by nature the things contained in the Law: but the Law as Paul knows it is not the law of reason but the law of Moses, the mores of the believing community: and the "nature" which holds men to compassion and to justice is not rational nature as the Greeks thought, but human nature which carries compassion at times beyond the bounds of reason. The residual image of God? Maybe. In any event it is ground for rejoicing from the Christian camp, and sufficient ground for a working ethical agreement along most of the road where Christians walk with others.

H. Richard Niebuhr

The Meaning of Responsibility*

In summary of the foregoing argument we may say that purposiveness seeks to answer the question: "What shall I do?" by raising as prior the question: "What is my goal, ideal, or telos?" Deontology tries to answer the moral query by asking, first of all: "What is the law and what is the first law of my life?" Responsibility, however, proceeds in every moment of decision and choice to inquire: "What is going on?" If we use value terms then the differences among the three approaches may be indicated by the terms, the *good,* the *right,* and the *fitting;* for teleology is concerned always with the highest good to which it subordinates the right; consistent deontology is concerned with the right, no matter what may happen to our goods; but for the ethics of responsibility the *fitting* action, the one that fits into a total interaction as response and as anticipation of further response, is alone conducive to the good and alone is right.

The idea of responsibility, if it is to be made useful for the understanding of our self-action, needs to be brought into mind more clearly than has been done by these preliminary references to its uses in past theory and in common experience. Our definition should not only be as clear as we can make it;

* From pp. 60-68 in *The Responsible Self,* by H. Richard Niebuhr. Copyright © 1963 by Florence M. Niebuhr. Reprinted by permission of Harper & Row, Publishers.

it should, if possible, be framed without the use of symbols referring to the other great ideas with which men have tried to understand their acts and agency. Only so will it be possible for us to develop a relatively precise instrument for self-understanding and also come to an understanding of the instruments' possibilities and limitations.

The first element in the theory of responsibility is the idea of *response.* All action, we now say, including what we rather indeterminately call moral action, is response to action upon us. We do not, however, call it the action of a self or moral action unless it is response to *interpreted* action upon us. All actions that go on within the sphere of our bodies, from heartbeats to knee jerks, are doubtless also reactions, but they do not fall within the domain of self-actions if they are not accompanied and infused, as it were, with interpretation. Whatever else we may need to say about ourselves in defining ourselves, we shall need, apparently, always to say that we are characterized by awareness and that this awareness is more or less that of an intelligence which identifies, compares, analyzes, and relates events so that they come to us not as brute actions, but as understood and as having meaning. Hence though our eyelids may react to the light with pure reflex, the self responds to it as *light,* as something interpreted, understood, related. But, more complexly, we interpret the things that force themselves upon us as parts of wholes, as related and as symbolic of larger meanings. And these large patterns of interpretation we employ seem to determine—though in no mechanical way—our responses to action upon us. We cannot understand international events, nor can we act upon each other as nations, without constantly interpreting the meaning of each other's actions. Russia and the United States confront each other not as those who are reflexively reacting to the manufacture of bombs and missiles, the granting of loans, and the making of speeches; but rather as two communities that are interpreting each other's actions and doing so with the aid of ideas about what is in the other's mind. So Americans try to understand Russia's immediate actions as expressions of the Communist or the Russian mind, which is the hidden part of the overt action, and we make our responses to the alien action in accordance with our interpretation of it as symbolic of a larger, an historic whole. The process of interpretation and response can be followed in all the public encounters of groups with each other. When we think of the relations of managers and employees we do not simply ask about the ends each group is consciously pursuing nor about the self-legislated laws they are obeying but about the way they are responding to each other's actions in accordance with their interpretations. Thus actions of labor unions may be understood better when we inquire less about what ends they are seeking and more about what ends they believe the managers to be seeking in all managerial actions. One must not deny the element of purposiveness in labor and in management, yet in their reactions to each other it is the interpretation each side has of the other's goals that may be more important than its definition of its own ends. Similarly in all the interactions of large groups with each other, law and duty seem to have a larger place in the interpretation of the other's conduct to which response is being made than they have in the immediate guidance of the agent's response. We use the idea of law less as a guide to our own conduct than as a way of predicting what the one will do to whom we are reacting or who will react to us. When lawyers try to discover under what law the judge will make his decisions, they are doing something akin to what we do in all our group relations; as Catholics or Protestants, also, we act less with an eye to our own law than to the other's action under his law, as we understand that law.

The point so illustrated by reference to groups applies to us as individuals. We respond as we interpret the meaning of actions upon us. The child's character may be formed less, the psychologists lead us to believe, by the injunctions and commandments of parents than by the child's interpretation of the attitudes such commandments are taken to express. The inferiority and superiority feelings, the aggressions, guilt feelings, and fears with which men encounter each other, and which do not easily yield to the commandment of neighbor-love, are dependent on their interpretations of each other's attitudes and valuations. We live as responsive beings not only in the social but also in the natural world where we interpret the natural events that affect us—heat and cold, storm and fair weather, earthquake and tidal wave, health and sickness, animal and plant—as living-giving and death-dealing. We respond to these events in accordance with our interpretation. Such interpretation, it need scarcely be added, is not simply an affair of our conscious, and rational, mind but also of the deep memories that are buried within us, of feelings and intuitions that are only partly under our immediate control.

This, then, is the second element in responsibility, that it is not only responsive action but responsive in accordance with our *interpretation* of the question to which answer is being given. In our responsibility we attempt to answer the question: "What shall I do?" by raising as the prior question: "What is going on?" or "What is being done to me?" rather than "What is my end?" or "What is my ultimate law?" A third element is *accountability*—a word that is frequently defined by recourse to legal thinking but that has a more definite meaning, when we understand it as referring to part of the response pattern of our self-conduct. Our actions are responsible not only insofar as they are reactions to interpreted actions upon us but also insofar as they are made in anticipation of answers to our answers. An agent's action is like a statement in a dialogue. Such a statement not only seeks to meet, as it were, or to fit into, the previous statement to which it is an answer, but is made in anticipation of reply. It looks forward as well as backward; it anticipates objections, confirmations, and corrections. It is made as part of a total conversation that leads forward and is to have meaning as a whole. Thus a political action, in this sense, is responsible not only when it is responsive to a prior deed but when it is so made that the agent anticipates the reactions to his action. So considered, no action taken as an atomic unit is responsible. Responsibility lies in the agent who stays with his action, who accepts the consequences in the form of reactions and looks forward in a present deed to the continued interaction. From this point of view we may try to illuminate the question much debated in modern times of the extent to which a person is to be held socially accountable for his acts. In terms of responsibility the question is simply this: "To whom and in what way ought a society through its courts and other agencies respond?" If a homicide has taken place, is the only one to whom there is to be reaction the killer himself, or is there to be response also to the society in which he acted as a reactor? Further, is the reaction to the individual criminal agent to be reaction guided by purely legal thinking, which interprets him solely as an unobedient and perhaps a self-legislating being, or is it to be informed by a larger interpretation of his conduct—one which takes into account other dimensions of his existence as a self? Is the criminal to be dealt with as a self who can anticipate reactions to his actions and so be acted upon as a potentially responsive person, or is the social reaction to him to be confined to his antisocial physical body only and he be regarded as a being that cannot learn to respond with interpretation and anticipation? Is education, psychiatry, or only incarceration the fitting response?

This third element in responsibility —the anticipation of reaction to our reaction—has brought us within view of what at least for the present seems to be its fourth and final significant component, namely *social solidarity*. Our action is responsible, it appears, when it is response to action upon us in a continuing discourse or interaction among beings forming a continuing society. A series of responses to disconnected actions guided by disconnected interpretations would scarcely be the action of a self but only of a series of states of mind somehow connected with the same body—though the sameness of the body would be apparent only to an external point of view. Personal responsibility implies the continuity of a self with a relatively consistent scheme of interpretations of what it is reacting to. By the same token it implies continuity in the community of agents to which response is being made. There could be no responsible self in an interaction in which the reaction to one's response comes from a source wholly different from that whence the original action issued. This theme we shall need to develop more fully in the second lecture.

The idea or pattern of responsibility, then, may summarily and abstractly be defined as the idea of an agent's action as response to an action upon him in accordance with his interpretation of the latter action and with his expectation of response to his response; and all of this is in a continuing community of agents.

The idea of the moral life as the responsible life in this sense not only has affinities with much modern thinking but it also offers us, I believe, a key—not *the* key—to the understanding of that Biblical ethos which represents the historic norm of the Christian life. In the past many efforts have been made to understand the ethos of the Old and New Testaments with the aid of the teleological theory and its image of man-the-maker. Thus the thinking of the lawgivers and prophets, of Jesus Christ and the apostles, has been set before us in the terms of a great idealism. Sometimes the ideal has been described as that of the vision of God, sometimes as perfection, sometimes as eternal happiness, sometimes as a harmony of all beings, or at least of all men, in a kingdom of God. Each of these interpretations has been buttressed by collections of proof texts, and doubtless much that is valid about the Bible and about the Christian life which continues the Scriptural ethos has been said within the limits of this interpretation. But much that is in Scriptures has been omitted by the interpreters who followed this method, and much material of another sort—the eschatological, for instance—has had to be rather violently wrenched out of its context or laid aside as irrelevant in order to make the Scriptures speak in this fashion about the self. At all times, moreover, but particularly among the German interpreters in whom the Kantian symbolism holds sway, the deontological interpretation of man the obedient legislator has been used not only as the key to Biblical interpretation but for the definition of the true Christian life. For Barth and Bultmann alike in our times, not to speak of most interpreters of the Old Testament, the ethics of the Bible, and Christian ethics too, is the ethics of obedience. How to interpret Christian freedom and what to make of eschatology within this framework has taxed the ingenuity of the interpreters severely. Bultmann has transformed eschatology into existentialism in order to maintain an ethics of radical obedience; Barth has had to transform the law into a form of the gospel and the commandment into permission in order to reconcile the peculiarity of gospel ethos with deontological thinking. There is doubtless much about law, commandment, and obedience in the Scriptures. But the use of this pattern of interpretation does violence to what we find there.

If now we approach the Scriptures with the idea of responsibility we shall find, I think, that the particular character of this ethics can be more fully if not wholly adequately interpreted. At the critical junctures in the history of Israel and of the early Christian community the decisive question men raised was not "What is the goal?" nor yet "What is the law?" but "What is happening?" and then "What is the fitting response to what is happening?" When an Isaiah counsels his people, he does not remind them of the law they are required to obey nor yet of the goal toward which they are directed but calls to their attention the intentions of God present in hiddenness in the actions of Israel's enemies. The question he and his peers raise in every critical moment is about the interpretation of what is going on, whether what is happening be, immediately considered, a drought or the invasion of a foreign army, or the fall of a great empire. Israel is the people that is to see and understand the action of God in everything that happens and to make a fitting reply. So it is in the New Testament also. The God to whom Jesus points is not the commander who gives laws but the doer of small and of mighty deeds, the creator of sparrows and clother of lilies, the ultimate giver of blindness and of sight, the ruler whose rule is hidden in the manifold activities of plural agencies but is yet in a way visible to those who know how to interpret the signs of the times.

It will not do to say that the analysis of all our moral life in general and of Biblical ethics in particular by means of the idea of responsibility offers us an absolutely new way of understanding man's ethical life or of constructing a system of Christian ethics. Actuality always extends beyond the patterns of ideas into which we want to force it. But the approach to our moral existence as selves, and to our existence as Christians in particular, with the aid of this idea makes some aspects of our life as agents intelligible in a way that the teleology and deontology of traditional thought cannot do.

Some special aspects of life in responsibility are to occupy us in the succeeding lectures. In none of them shall I take the deontological stance, saying, "We *ought* to be responsible"; nor yet the ideal, saying, "The *goal* is responsibility"; but I shall simply ask that we consider our life of response to action upon us with the question in mind, "To whom or what am I responsible and in what community of interaction am I myself?"

II. Value and Virtue

H. Richard Niebuhr

The Center of Value*

Whatever may be the general reflections of value theorists on the meaning and nature of "good," when they deal with more concrete ethical problems they usually employ a relational theory of value which defines good by reference to a being for which other beings are good. Insofar as Plato's *Republic* is concerned with the good-for-man, man's psychical structure is the starting point for the determination of what is good. Nikolai Hartmann, having defined value abstractly as essence, as that which ought-to-be without dependence on the existent, turns in his ethics to the question of the good-for-man, confining his analysis of values to the virtues—the kinds of excellence appropriate to man—and insisting that the freedom of man must always be considered so that his question really is, "What is good for free man?" G. E. Moore, after attempting to indicate the meaning of value in abstraction from every relation, assumes the standpoint of conscious, social man as soon as he undertakes to answer the question, "What things, then, are good?" He answers, "By far the most valuable things, which we can know or can imagine, are certain states of consciousness, which may be roughly described as the pleasures of human intercourse and the enjoyment of beautiful objects." It is not possible for Moore to read out of the picture the being for whom these things are good, however much he may speak of the intrinsically good. He employs a relational theory of value though he asserts that "personal affection and the appreciation of what is beautiful in Art or Nature, are good in themselves." He has posited a being with consciousness and sociality as that for which these things are good, not as desired but as desirable, as necessarily complementary to its existence.

As intuitionists and rationalists move from their objective theories of value to relational views when they

* "The Center of Value," by H. Richard Niebuhr, from *Moral Principles of Action,* edited by Ruth Nanda Anshen.

turn to ethics, so the empiricists also seem to abandon their subjectivist views when they deal with concrete questions. Hume has greater awareness of what he is doing than is the case with many of his followers, for though he seems to regard value as a function of feeling, yet he considers that judgments about moral values have a rational character, not only in the sense that they abstract from personal feelings and consider virtues and vices in relation to social feeling expressed in approval or disapproval, but in the more objective sense that they are directed toward what is useful to society. His discussions, to be sure, are so confined to the consideration of "moral" values, i.e., to virtues and vices, that the larger pattern of his relational theory does not come to complete expression. Yet it is clear that he not only employs but argues for the validity of an ethical theory which makes society its starting point and inquires into the comparative goodness for society of self-love, benevolence, fidelity, and so forth, in its citizens. Though he mates agreeableness with usefulness to society the latter relation is always in his view, and in his context it is not a narrow means-end idea. The shift from subjectivism to relational theory is accomplished with apparent unawareness of the change by Bentham as he moves from explicit hedonism with its desire theory of the good to utilitarianism with its question about what is good for society as represented by the greatest number of its individual members.

Similar movements of thought from subjective relativism to relationism may be noted in Westermarck, Schlick, and A. J. Ayer. For Westermarck as for Hume the assertion that good depends on emotion soon makes place for the idea of *disinterested* moral emotion which observes the relation of a moral quality to the emotions of a society, and this understanding is then supplemented by a theory of usefulness. For it is assumed that the disinterested moral emotion is itself good for social life, that specific institutions or customs were originally approved because of their utility, and that "correct utilitarian considerations" can and should be employed in criticizing mores which are maintained by feelings only. In this case as in Hume's, *usefulness* means far more than simple means-to-an-end. Schlick thinks that "the question whether something is desirable for its own sake is no question at all, but mere empty words. On the other hand, the question of what actually is desired for its own sake is of course quite sensible, and ethics is actually concerned only with answering this question." Again, " 'value' is nothing but a name for the dormant pleasure possibilities of the valuable object." Yet when he turns to the question, "What then is good?" he posits the social human being with capacity for happiness and designates kindness as the good which corresponds to that capacity, not because it pleases all men but because it is in conformity with human nature. The value of kindness is not relative to actual feelings of pleasure but stands in such relation to the capacity for happiness that it is possible to make the judgment that kindness is good for man with his social impulses and his capacity for happiness. Though Ayer dismisses the term "value" or "good" as nothing but the expression of an emotion, he employs relational value theory in his contention that the scientific method is of great importance to man. Evidently he does not regard this statement as an emotional ejaculation but argues that science is good for man because it is the useful instrument by means of which he is enabled to survive and to meet his needs, even the simplest.

The relational value theory which is implicit in the ethical reflections of such objective or subjective value theorists is objective in the sense that value relations are understood to be independent of the feelings of an observer but not in the sense that value is itself an objective kind of reality. The statement that "justice is good" or that "justice ought to be" may be regarded by some as an emotional outburst equivalent to the statement, "I like justice." By others it may be defended as a verbal formulation of a direct intuition of objective value, but it is difficult to see what difference there is between such subjectivism and such objectivism so far as the consequences of the opposing positions are concerned. The indefinable cannot be used in communication or analysis. Yet the statement that justice is good for a society with many parts, in the sense that a just-right relationship between such parts must be sought in order that the society may live and realize its potentialities, is an objective statement which an observer can make quite apart from his intuitions or his desires. Furthermore, the meaning of the term "justice" in this situation is subject to specific analysis on the basis of prior inquiry into the constitution of the society. Relational value theory agrees with objectivism on this further point, that what is good-for-man, or for society or for any other being which represents the starting point of inquiry, is not determined by the desire of that being. Whether food or poison is good for animal existence has little to do with the desires in such existence; whether error or truth is good for mind has little connection with the desire of an intellectual being for one or the other. What is fitting, useful, and complementary to an existence can be determined only if disinteredness, or abstraction from desire, is practiced and the nature and tendency of the being in question are studied. Yet relational value theory does not pretend that value has existence in itself, that independence from desire is equivalent to independence from the being for which the valuable has worth. It agrees with the subjective value theory insofar as the latter regards value as relative to being, disagreeing, however, with the relativism which makes the good relative to desire rather than to need, or which makes it relative to man as absolute center of value.

In view of the manner in which relational value-thinking has been intertwined with the *motifs* of objectivism and subjectivism it is desirable that its main points should be set forth as clearly as possible without reference to these complicating strains of thought. Its fundamental observation is this: that value is present wherever one existent being with capacities and potentialities confronts another existence that limits or completes or complements it. Thus, first of all, value is present objectively for an observer in the fittingness or unfittingness of being to being. In the one case it is present as positive, in the other case as negative value; it is present as good or as evil. Whether the starting point be a biological existence in the presence of a fitting or an unfitting environment, or a society in the presence of another society as friend or enemy, or mind confronting patterns, ideas, chaos, or brute power in the data given to it—in every case there is good or evil in this situation. Good is a term which not only can be but which—at least in the form of one of its equivalents—must be applied to that which meets the needs, which fits the capacity, which corresponds to the potentialities of an existent being. It is, in this sense, that which is "useful." Evil, on the other hand, is that which thwarts, destroys, or starves a being in its activities.

Yet the situation in which good and evil occur is, it is apparent, not only one of reciprocity among existent beings. It is also one in which such existences are in a state of becoming, in which they are not yet what they "ought" to be—not in any legal sense of the word "ought" but in the sense that they have not yet achieved their own internal possibilities of becoming good for others, or of supplying to others in the community of being what they "owe" them. Medicine is good for the sick in view of their movement toward health, which is good for the self in relation to other selves and other beings in general; education is good for the child in its movement toward the realization of its capacities for activities beneficial to human society, other selves, and other beings in general; science is good for the intellectual life in its development and in its service to the needs of being.

In this situation of being, in process of becoming itself (always as social self) and among others becoming themselves (also as social), value appears in many relations of which two may be particularly distinguished. On the one hand, that is good for a being which, separate from itself, assists it in its realization of its potentialities. On the other hand, the state of realization (the excellent or virtuous state) is good. This latter good is also a "good-for-ness," not primarily as a good for the becoming self but as a good for other beings in its whole community, and then secondarily, in the endless interactions of self and others, a good-for-the-self. The former of these is often called the instrumental good, the latter the intrinsic or end good; but these designations are misleading. For existent being does not seek the complementary good necessarily for the sake of achieving its own state of perfection; it may well seek and serve the complementary good as a kind of end and thereby grow toward its internal good, the realization of its essence, without direct concern for the latter. The mind grows toward the realization of its possibilities by seeking truths about nature and history, but these truths are its ends and its growth may come as by-product. It is not evident that in seeking food the animal uses as instrumental the good which is the object of its direct quest; this is its end-good in the situation while life, health, and physical growth are consequents. On the other hand physical, moral, intellectual, and spiritual excellence is less an end value for the self than a good for other beings. Relational value theory cannot be utilitarian in the sense that it posits a being with its own survival or self-realization in view as its end, a being which thereupon uses as means to the end the complementary goods of environing beings. It must do justice to the fact that value is not dependent on a conscious finalism for which some goods may be designated as intrinsic goods, others as instrumental. There are good states of the self and there are goods-for-the-self which are not self-states. Self-states are goods first of all for other selves, or other beings, and only by indirection goods-for-self. Yet value exists in the reciprocal relations which beings realizing potentiality have to other beings. In this situation every good is an end and every good a means.[1]

The Aristotelian form of relational value theory seems to be inadequate

[1] In an excellent critique of this essay as originally published, Prof. George Schrader seems to have missed the point I am trying to make here and so to have been misled elsewhere in interpreting my thought. (Cf. George Schrader, "Value and Valuation," in *Faith and Ethics,* 1957, pp. 173-204.) Doubtless my statement was inadequate; hence I have revised it somewhat in the hope of clarifying the idea. Since others also may encounter difficulties in understanding what I am trying to say I shall point out I do not wish to maintain that there is value in the self's relation to itself (or to its potential self) apart from its relation to others. The self's growth in intelligence, kindness, integrity, etc. is doubtless good or these are goods, i.e., virtues; but their goodness is primarily their goodness for other selves; secondarily, they are good-for-the-self as social being dependent not only on approval but on service of others. It is highly questionable for me whether we can call the virtues good in the self apart from their goodness for other selves or for the community of selves. The theory of value I am seeking to present is through and through social; I know of no self-relatedness apart from other-relatedness or self-alienation apart from alienation from the other. Potentiality in the whole realm of being is an important component in the situation in which there is value but the basis of this relational value theory is not the relation of existence to essence, it is that of self to other. Philosophically, it is more indebted to G. H. Mead than to Aristotle; theologically, it is closer, I believe, to Jonathan Edwards ("consent of being to being") than to Thomas Aquinas.

at this point since it attaches greater value to the state of the being which realizes its potentialities than to the being in the presence of which such potentiality is realized. Only in his final discussion of the happy life of the contemplator does Aristotle, greatest of relational value theorists, indicate the duality of the good—that it is to be found not only in the activity of the contemplative being but also in that object toward which such contemplation is directed and which corresponds to the excellent activity. Objective good, or the value to a subject of that reality other than itself which is necessary to its activity, and subjective good, or the value of increased and perfected activity directed toward good objects, are inseparable from each other. Is Schlick's ethics of kindness concerned with the kindness of fellow men, a kindness which is good for the man with a capacity for happiness, or is it concerned with the kindness of this ethical subject, good to his fellow men? He gives us no adequate answer, but seems to be concerned with both; yet the two are evidently distinct goods. Consistent relational value theory will keep in mind that value in the sense of that which is *good-for* a subject always includes two kinds of worth which may be conveniently designated as external goods and internal goods and that these cannot be separated from each other in activity though they can and must be recognized in their distinctness.

Relational value theory, to be complete, holds together, while it distinguishes, these three relations: first, the relation of an existent being to other existent beings which are its objective or external or complementary goods; second, the relation of the existent being to its own essence, its internal or subjective good; and third, the relation of the movement of the being toward the former good to its movement toward the latter. Even so the situation in which good appears and can be analyzed has not been completely described, for the existent being which is becoming what it is potentially and which meets such complementary good in its environment, is itself good-for the other beings (if not bad-for them) and it forms a part of larger complexes of being, as when men live in society, or animals participate in the evolutionary process of life. These also are on their way to becoming what they are in essence. Thus relational value theory is concerned with a great multi-dimensionality of value, which is not the multidimensionality of an abstract realm of essential values but rather the multidimensionality of beings in their relations to each other.

Such relational value theory is then relativistic, not in the sense that value is relative to emotion, hence private and irrational, but in the sense in which physical science is relativistic without loss of objectivity. Though this relativism raises great problems of its own, it offers intelligible answers to many of the questions which vex absolute and subjective value theories. The problem of the relation of value to being does not need to be answered in the paradoxical fashion in which intuitionists and emotionalists leave it. The former having defined value as *sui generis,* distinct from existence, tend almost inevitably, it seems, to confuse it then with a certain kind of being, that of the ideas for instance, and at the same time to deny value to nonideal existence. They quickly confuse good with the idea of good and the latter with the goodness of ideas. The bifurcation between being and value becomes identified with the bifurcation of being into essence and existence, or of idea and power. The prejudice in such value theories for the goodness of the spiritual as opposed to the material, and for the goodness of the nonexistent as opposed to the existent, involves them in many consequent difficulties to which the history of ethics bears ample witness.

On the other hand, the equally or more extreme disjunction between value and being which appears in the subjectivisms that regard good as a function of desire, relating value to only one sort of power and that an ultimately unintelligible one, results in the irrationality of separating value judgments from fact judgments. It is an irrational result since it leaves value judgments beyond the range of rational criticism and ignores the presence of value judgments in all fact judgments. Those who demand the substitution of scientific method in ethics for the emotional value judgments which are said to prevail are actually operating with a prior value judgment which they do not acknowledge or criticize, namely, the assertion that knowledge is the greatest good for man. Moreover, they ignore and leave uncriticized the presence of value judgments in every factual judgment which asserts that some factors in a given situation are more important or significant than others.

Relational value theory understands that being and value are inseparably connected but that value cannot be identified with a certain mode of being or any being considered in isolation, whether it be ideal or actual. Value is present wherever being confronts being, wherever there is becoming in the midst of plural, interdependent, and interacting existences. It is not a function of being as such but of being in relation to being. It is therefore universal, co-extensive with the realm of being, and yet not identifiable with any being, even universal being. For if anything existed simply in itself and by itself, value would not be present. Value is the *good-for-ness* of being for being in their reciprocity, their animosity, and their mutual aid. Value cannot be defined or intuited in itself for it has no existence in itself; and nothing is valuable in itself, but everything has value, positive or negative, in its relations. Thus value is not a relation but arises in the relations of being to being.

On the basis of relational value

theory the problem of the knowledge of the good receives a new solution. It is understood that there is an objective element in all such knowledge insofar as an observer stands apart from the being for which another or some future state of its own existence is good. Medical and political judgments about what is good for a physical being or a society can be objective enough, though, of course, they may be mistaken. Yet no being, no self at least, realizes the goodness of the good-for-it without desire. So long as a self does not desire a state of being for itself—such as health—and the external goods which are necessary for that state of being; or so long as it does not desire the presence of a being external to itself as its good—such as a true science or a friend—and that state of its own being which is necessary for the apprehension of that external good; so long it fails to *recognize* the good as its good. It is as blind to its good as without visual perception it would be blind to objects. Yet desire uncriticized by a rational nonparticipating, disinterested view of the relations of being to being is as subject to error as is sensation without rational interpretation. The "blooming and buzzing confusion" of sensation unorganized by rational pattern is no greater than the vagueness, confusion, and indeterminacy of desire reaching out for it knows not what. A version of the Kantian observation seems applicable in connection with the knowledge of value: "Desire without reason is blind; reason without desire is impotent." There is no rational knowledge of value without rational empirical knowledge of the beings for which others and states of itself are valuable; but the rational knowledge of value is inadequate to move a being toward its own goods. Beliefs about the good-for-me may be true; they do not become effective until the good-for-me becomes the object of desire.

Again relational value theory can distinguish between the good and the right without reducing the one to the other or setting up two independent principles. "Right" means that relation between beings, good-for-each-other, in which their potentiality of being good for each other is realized. It is that relation in which beings that are actually bound together in their interdependent existence consent to each other, actually further each other, in the realization of their potentialities. It indeed becomes a part of the good as when the right relation of citizens to each other in a society becomes component to the goodness of that society for other societies or as when the right relations between emotion and reason in an individual become component to his goodness for his fellow men.

But, in the interaction of being with being, right is not merely a means to the good; it is the goodness of relatedness in action. It is never definable in the abstract but only by reference to the nature and the relations of beings in interaction. The "ought" in which the sense of right comes to expression is a statement of what is owed to another being. It has significance in such a sentence as "A man ought to pay his debts to his creditors," since he is bound to his creditors in an actual community of interdependent life. What significance it has in such a sentence as "Justice ought to be," is hard to discern. Even truth carries obligation with it because it is a relation between beings, specifically between persons, who are bound to each other in communication and who owe each other the truth because they are values and disvalues to each other. Apart from the interrelation of beings having value and disvalue for each other, "right" and "ought" are probably meaningless terms. Yet to confine the term "right" to that situation in which a being seeks a state of itself as its end and uses various external goods as means to the achievement of this end is to ignore the multiplicity of value relations. The "right" is coextensive with the realm of interdependent values, that is, of interdependent beings.

Though relational value theory is actually widely employed even where it is not acknowledged and though it offers solutions to problems which remain insoluble by means of other hypotheses about the nature of the good, yet it is regarded with understandable suspicion by men who are profoundly concerned not only about truth in human society but also about other kinds of right relations between human beings and between these and the nonhuman environment. Though relational value theory is not psychologically relativistic it is evidently dogmatically relativistic since it is necessary to take one's standpoint with or in some being accepted as the *center of value* if one is to construct anything like a consistent system of value judgments and determinations of what is right. The difficulty becomes apparent in the essentially relationist, though apparently psychological, theories of English empiricism. The continuing concern of this empiricism was the substitution of a "realistic" for traditional ethics. It sought to move legislators and citizens to answer the questions, "What is really good for man?" and "What is really good for society?" on the basis of an understanding of human needs and potentialities rather than by reference to established maxims. Its frequent definition of man as fundamentally a pleasure-seeking creature or as economic man interested in and in need of material goods was evidently too narrow for its own use, since, at least implicitly, it recognized his social nature, his need for other men as good-for-him and his reflective nature, his recognition of his good-for-ness in relation to others and his society.

Its real problem, however, seemed to center in its recognition that there were two dogmatic starting points for its inquiry. On the one hand it was individualistic, making the individual person the center of value and inquiring what was good for him. From this point of view it required of society that it make all its judgments about good and right by reference to the needs of individuals in their process of becoming. Its hedonistic subjectivism was translated, as in utilitarianism, into objective relationism. The legislator was not expected to ask, "What is good for me?" but rather, "What is good for the individual citizens?" On the other hand, this empiricism was aware of another value-center, the society. Here was a continuing existence, the English community, and the question from this point of view was, "What is good for this society?" Between these two objective but relativistic value systems English ethics sought to find some kind of reconciliation but never with complete success.

Another dogmatic relativism appeared when life itself was made the value-center by evolutionary ethics and it appeared that questions could be significantly raised about the good-for-life. Further, the dogmatic nature of every starting point came to consciousness in the questions easily brushed aside but not easily forgotten about the kind of value system which fish or ants might construct if they could consciously make themselves, as individuals or as communities, the centers of value. So it seems that on the basis of an objective but relativistic value theory there can be as many theoretical value systems as there are beings in existence. Yet none of these relative systems is relativistic in the sense of being dependent on feeling or desire; each can be objective in the sense that it may be a system dealing with actual value relations and in the sense that the value judgments made within that frame of reference are subject to critical inquiry into their truth or falsity.

In view of this necessity of beginning with a value-center it seems evident that every theory of value, so far as it is relational, is religious in character. Every such theory adopts as its explicit or implicit starting point some being or beings in relation to which good is judged to be good and evil evil, in relation to which also the rightness or wrongness of its relations to other beings is examined. The question of the goodness of this central being for other beings is usually not considered, as when in the relational value-thinking of an Aristotle the question about man's goodness for other beings is not raised; the beginning and the end of his ethics is man.

Thus also vitalistic or evolutionary value systems beginning with life or the community of living beings can make rational judgments about what is good for life—the fitness of an environment, the mutual limitation of living beings in right relations of the struggle for existence—but it cannot or does not raise the question what the community of the living is good for. Sometimes a single value, such as knowledge, is deified as the value-center about the goodness of which for other valuable beings no one inquires, though more often duality of deity seems to be posited here as when science is regarded as the great good for man and man is thought of as the servant of knowledge, whose meaning lies in his service to science. More frequently the relational value theories, implicit or explicit in purportedly objective or subjective theories, are caught up in a polytheism which posits two or more centers of values. So on the one hand Hartmann presents us with a kind of Epicurean faith in which the center of value is the realm of ideal essences which have their being above the world of existences in self-sufficiency, yet so that only in relation to them anything else has value. On the other hand man is his center of value, in relation to whom even the ideas of value alone have actual worth. Or the polytheism is that of human society and the human individual and the community of living beings as centers of value which must somehow be reconciled.

Although Christian and Jewish theologies have often identified themselves in their value-thinking with objective and spiritualistic theories of value, relational value theory is much more compatible with their fundamental outlook and much more in line with the realism of their reverence for being. Its relativism, when recognized, agrees with their concern that relative things should be kept relative and never confused with the transcendent absolute. Its realism, that is, its solid founding of value on the nature of being, agrees with their conviction that the starting point of all inquiry lies in the recognition of *that which is.* The objections which they raise to relational value-thinking are not directed toward its rational relativism but against its tendency to fall into a psychological relativism for which "there is nothing either good or bad but thinking makes it so," and against the unconquerable tendency to absolutize some relative starting point such as man, or society, or ideas, or life. Dogma, doubtless, there must be, since the analysis even of value cannot begin in the void but must start with an act of decision for some being as value-center. But the dogmatism of a relativism which assumes the privileged position of one finite reality, such as man, is so narrow that it cuts off inquiry into great realms of value, and tends to confine the discussion of the good to an arbitrarily chosen field, for instance to that of the human good.

For the polytheistic theologies of value, usually called philosophical, which confine themselves to two or three of these relative systems, and then become involved in questions about their interrelations, monotheistic faith substitutes, first, a central value theory and then the recognition of an infinite number of possible, relative value systems. Its starting point, its dogmatic beginning, is with the transcendent One for whom alone there is an ultimate good and for whom, as the source and end of all things, whatever is, is good. It may indeed use a sort of psychological relativism at this point, since it cannot say that God has need of any being external to himself; hence it may be able only to say that whatever is exists because it pleases God. But whether the relation is to need or to desire, in any case the starting point is that transcendent absolute for whom, or for which, whatever is, is good. Such faith no more begins by asking what God is good for than humanistic or vitalistic ethics begins with the inquiry what man or life is good for. But it has the great advantage over humanism and vitalism that it does not offer an evident abstraction of one sort of finite being from the rest of existence with the consequent appearance of arbitrariness in the selection of finite centers of value that from any disinterested point of view have no greater claim to centrality than any others.

With this beginning the value theory of monotheistic theology is enabled to proceed to the construction of many relative value systems, each of them tentative, experimental, and objective, as it considers the interaction of beings on beings, now from the point of view of man, now from the point of view of society, now from the point of view of life. But it is restrained from erecting any one of these into an absolute, or even from ordering it above the others, as when the human-centered value system is regarded as superior to a life-centered system. A monotheistically centered value theory is not only compatible with such objective relativism in value analysis but requires it in view of its fundamental dogma that none is absolute save God and that the absolutizing of anything finite is ruinous to the finite itself.

There is room within the objective relativism of monotheistic faith for the recognition of the value of ideal essences for minds, and of minds for ideal essences, but none for the absolutizing of such essences or such minds as good in themselves. There is room here for the recognition of the value of man for the ongoing community of life and vice versa, but none for the dogmatic choice of life or man as the absolute centers of value. When it turns to human ethics theocentric value theory inevitably will become relatively man-centered, yet tentatively so and never with forgetfulness of the question of what man is good for in his relations not only to the transcendent One but also to the other existent beings.

Hence it is not monotheistic faith that is uncritically dogmatic in its construction of value theories. Uncritical dogmatism is the practice of those explicit or disguised relational systems of thought about the good which arbitrarily choose some limited starting point for their inquiries and either end with the confession that value is an irrational concept which must nevertheless be rationally employed because nature requires this, or otherwise rule out of consideration great realms of value relations as irrelevant. Critical thought based on theocentric faith has no quarrel with the *method* of objective relativism in value theory and ethics. It objects only but strongly to the religious foundations of these relativisms.

Emil Brunner

Goodness and the "Virtues"*

PROPOSITION: *The Command of God, so far as the subject is concerned, requires one thing only: existence in love, but this implies the existence of every "virtue."*

1. Good, in the radical sense, does not mean "doing good" but "being good." God wants to have me—myself —for His own, and not merely my actions. In the strict sense of the word no action can be "good"; only the agent of the action can be "good." The aristocratic ethic of the "noble," "well-born" man (Scheler), in contradistinction to the democratic ethic of the "good will," is not wholly wrong; it indicates the weak point in the ethic which deals with man's "disposition"; the ethic of the "good will" does not sound the depths of man's being; it remains in the air, concentrated on moral effort, on the isolated act of the will. It does not perceive that the true Good can never flow from this feverish intensity of effort from all this labour and pain, from all this painstaking endeavour to attain the Good, but simply and solely from the central source of goodness as a state of existence. The "Good" which issues from effort is, for that very reason, not really good; the Good must descend from above, not be striven for from below, otherwise it lacks genuineness and depth.

On the other hand, the ethic of the good will, when compared with the naturalistic ethic of the "well-born" man, is so far right in that it insists that the Good can never be a natural fact. To have a good disposition does

* From *The Divine Imperative,* by Emil Brunner, translated by Olive Wyon. The Westminster Press. Copyright 1947, by W. L. Jenkins. Used by permission of Westminster Press and Lutterworth Press. Pp. 163-69.

not mean being good. To be good is a personal determination, not a natural tendency. The secret of being good therefore lies neither in the act of the will, nor in the fact of natural birth, but in the new birth, which takes place on the further side of this contradiction—the paradox of the newborn—personal will, or rather: of the person who has become good. The subject of a Christian ethic is neither birth nor race, nor a habit which has become a custom ("inherited nobility") nor is it even "the Christian character," but it is the new person, which, as such, is always something given and demanded, a divine and human "central act," an event which affects life as a whole, the whole being of the self in question.

2. But in so far as this new being is, paradoxically, one which is demanded, what kind of life then is it that is demanded? As a state of obedience? But that is simply tautology. Then, as a life of faith? But that is not the question. For (on the basis of that which was laid down in the last chapter) we are asking a further question about the moral nature of the life lived in faith. What sort of man is the man who in faith is obedient? This very natural question, however, is the point at which so many Christian moralists, and, indeed, whole centuries of ethical thinking, have been led astray into the false path of a doctrine of the virtues which is contrary to Christian thought. The true being of a man can never be indicated by a human quality, but only—as is implied in the expression "to be in faith"—by the actual state of his relation with God. We ought rather to ask: *Where* is man when he is in the right place? and answer: "True being" means being "in Christ"; for "Christ is my righteousness." God's Being in Christ, however—once again not as a quality but as act—is His being in love. The true being of man therefore can mean nothing else than standing in the love of God, being drawn into His love of man. Or, to put it differently: it means living a life which from its source in God is directed towards man, towards the interests of others.

3. Love in the sense in which the New Testament uses the word, is not a human possibility at all, but it is exclusively possible to God. Love is an "ultimate" eschatological possibility; for it will be the last thing when everything else, even faith, has vanished. Hence the state of "living in love" is not something which man can achieve by his own efforts and in his own strength, but it is something which happens to man in faith, from God. The decisive element in this life in love is therefore always to allow ourselves to be loved by God.[1] Once more it becomes clear how it is that the Good can only be understood from the point of view of justification. As we see from the expression that "man

[1] See particularly the First Epistle of John.

is created in the image of God," we are not in any sense fixed stars: God alone shines in His own light, He alone possesses aseity. We are planets which can only shine in a borrowed light, that is, in His light. "Let your light so shine before men that . . . they may glorify your Father in heaven." [2] To be good in the right way is only possible when we desire to be nothing.

4. Love is not merely an isolated act. Even in ourselves natural love, erotic love, for instance, is not genuine if it does not develop from "being in love" into real love. Only when a person is truly "in love" is it possible to love. Love is a personal form of existence. Love is not an abstract form of loving, but it is the flowing forth of love. The Divine love is the possibility of human loving; it is the river whence the tiny rivulets of human love can pour themselves into life.

Therefore God only demands one thing: that we should live in His love. In His prophetic message Jesus summons men to "Love!" The apostolic exhortation, which points back to the gift of God in Christ, summons us to "Live in love." [3] Or, still more plainly: to *"Remain* in love." For the apostolic exhortation is addressed to believers, that is, to those who are already in the love of God. This commandment transcends the contrast between mysticism and morality. It is the summons to remain within the giving of God, to return to Him again and again as the origin of all power to be good, or to do good. There are no "other virtues" alongside of the life of love.

Even love is not a "virtue," because it is not a quality which can be assigned to man as such—it is not the light of a fixed star—but it is the state in which man stands in the light of God. The ancient conception of virtue can only spoil the Christian statements about being good. Today we are rightly very suspicious of all talk of "virtues," indeed we are tired of all such language. For the ancient conception of virtue, which also dominates the whole medieval system of morality,[4] turns a quality which de-

[2] Matt. v. 16.

[3] The *phrases* are distinctly "Johannine," but the subject is equally "Pauline." Cf. Rom. xii. 1; 2 Cor. v. 15; Phil. ii. 5.

[4] This individualistic and at the same time naturalistic conception of virtue prevails absolutely in the Thomist ethic, so far as natural virtues are concerned; it only partially prevails where the infused supernatural or theological virtues are concerned; it is at this point that St. Thomas's dependence upon Aristotle and his anthropology comes out most clearly. The Aristotelian ethic is the ethic of the active, creative human being, of the man therefore who can be perfect "in himself," in so far as "material" is given to him which he is "capable" of moulding. In accordance with this point of view St. Thomas also defines virtue as *habitus* and *bona qualitas,* and indeed as self-acquired (in contra-distinction from the "infused" supernatural virtues), as *acquisita,* gained by activity as the habit of being active (St. Thomas, II, I, *qu.* 55 and 63). The Augustinian conception of virtue as God-given, by being limited to the theological virtues, is explicitly rejected, whereby the theological virtues do not make natural virtue really good, but only fit for the attainment of the supernatural goal (*qu.* 62). This Aristotelian-Thomistic conception of virtue then became that of the Enlightenment.

pends for its very existence upon the reality of the Divine action into a human acquisition. Behind this present-day revulsion from the "virtuous man"—often decorated with all kinds of "orders" for his virtuous conduct—lies the feeling that there is something wrong in this virtue which man has so to speak "created," that all this talk of "possessing virtues" and of "being virtuous," indeed even the striving after such virtues, and even the mere ideal of virtue, is presumptuous. The idea of virtue leads man to justify himself—and this is the very opposite of all genuine goodness.

There is, however, a second point which is connected with this ancient idea of virtue as a quality which belongs to man as he is in himself, namely, that of the plurality of virtues.[5] Once the perversion has taken place which conceives "being good" as a human quality, then inevitably the second point follows, that there are a number of such virtues. The result is the atomization of the Good. For then man does not possess one quality, but many.[6] Thus he has not merely one virtue but—if he is "perfect"—many virtues. The Good, which is one, is divided into little pieces, goodness is severed from the person as a whole, and qualities are turned into independent entities as "virtues." There then exists a whole system of virtues. The conception of the Good has become wholly externalized.

5. Thus if, in spite of this, the New Testament has adopted the conception of virtue, this can only be understood in one sense, namely, that it wishes to exhibit in the individual virtues the various forms of the one life in love. It is an ancient saying that love is "the mother of all the virtues." This saying suggests that there is no other Good at all save that which consists in living in love, but that this one life appears in a great variety of ways in connexion with the life of others. For as goodness is not something which belongs to man inherently, but only to his existence in relation to God, so the practical manifestation of this life with God is a life in relation with others, determined according to each particular relationship. Thus even in

[5] I have already pointed out the contradiction which exists within the Thomist Ethic between the system of the natural virtues and the three "theological" virtues. On the one hand, St. Thomas maintains that, in the last resort, love alone makes an action really good, while on the other hand a system of individual virtues—based on the Aristotelian cardinal virtues—is developed, which do not become real "virtues" through love alone, but which have an independent existence; if this were not so, the whole of this sub-structure would be rendered insecure; or, to put it more exactly, it would become, what it is in the teaching of the Reformers, merely the doctrine of the *justitia civilis*. But the Catholic Church may not teach this. Therefore she is obliged to assert the existence of a number of independent, real virtues, of which it is possible to possess some and not others.

[6] The theory of "qualities" plays as disastrous a part in our view of ethics as the theory of "faculty" or "capacity" (German: Vermögen) does in psychology; for instance, in pedagogy there is nothing so disastrous as to hold a person responsible for his "qualities." We only have "qualities" in so far as we are not personal. To regard a person in the light of his "qualities" means that we do not take him seriously as a person.

respect of others "virtue" is not *my* quality, something which can be thought of as belonging to the individual, but it is always a *"co*-existence," a way of being related to others.

Even where we speak of a plurality of virtues, the ancient conception of virtue has been fundamentally altered, in so far as virtue is never an individual mode of existence, but is always characterized as *co*-existence. There are no "individual" virtues, like those orders and decorations adorned with which the individual struts about among his fellows; but virtues only exist in life lived in relation with others.[7] Thus as the Self only achieves "goodness" in personal relation to God, so also "virtue" can only be attained in our relations with our fellowmen. And further: as life in love is a life which flows from the love of God, so also the individual virtue, as a particular manifestation of the one goodness, is always something which flows from another dimension, namely, from the fact of life as determined by the existence of our neighbour. For to live in love means concretely to allow one's life to be determined by the existence of others, by being "subject" to their needs and demands. Each virtue is a way of "entering into contact" with another person, of knowing that one "belongs" to him. Thus the variety of the virtues comes not from the self but from the other as the definite way in which through his particular situation or peculiarity my existence is determined by his. If it is impossible to conceive of any individual virtue as a quality of the Self, then also there are no virtues which can be individually conceived. Each virtue, one might say, is a particular way in which the person who lives in love takes the other into account, and "realizes" him as "Thou."

6. Only thus is the variety of the virtues to be understood aright. Truthfulness, for instance, is the special way of living in love, or of living in relation with others, which perceives or realizes the claim of the other man on my knowledge of the truth. Peaceableness is a particular way of living in relation with others in which I perceive the claim of the "Thou" for undisturbed fellowship with me. All these virtues are only really conceived in a personally actual, non-substantial manner, when they are conceived in terms of awareness of the claims of others, as a readiness to re-act, to respond to a definite call. Thus they are all *negative,* not positive, in character. They consist in having one's mind and heart open in a certain direction, but this does not imply that they possess positive content. All the virtues consist in "being

[7] Or, more literally: "As the 'I' can only 'be good' in relation to the Divine 'Thou,' so the 'I' can only 'be virtuous' in relation to the 'Thou' of another human being."—Tr.

ready." In this respect, too, the virtues cannot be defined in reply to the question *How?* but in reply to the question *Where?* The very fact that I—because I am living in love—am not self-centred and isolated but am in touch with others, constitutes virtue in its varying forms.

There is no need here to deduce and describe the individual virtues. Traditional ethics has gone into this subject already in quite sufficient detail. What we need is to regain the right fundamental understanding of the principle which governs the conception of virtue, which has been so badly distorted both by the ancient tradition, and by the medieval scholastic tradition; we need to break away from the individualistic and anthropocentric conception of virtue. It is, indeed, no wonder that Luther hated Aristotle with such a passionate hatred! For the Aristotelian conception of virtue, which governed his own ethic and through this the ethic of Scholasticism, is the purely individualistic conception, which is dominated by the idea of the individual's self-improvement, till he achieves perfection. One of the most important tasks of a Christian ethic is to break away from this idea as completely as possible.

7. But, once this has been said, a second observation must be made as a secondary consideration. Man does not only consist of distinct acts; his life is also characterized by what one may describe as "settled conditions" or a "state of being." Just as we must not forget the fact of the physical existence of man in considering his power to act in a personal way, so also we must not forget the fact that his life falls into a certain "state" of being in a broader sense of the word. We do not live merely in acts of decision, but in our life there is also a region of the habitual, of that which has come to be in the empirical sense of the word. A detailed doctrine of the New Birth would have to take note of the fact that the act of faith has a reflex influence upon the condition of the person in question, with great caution it is true, but still quite clearly. There does exist what we call *character,* which can be described in empirical terms, the permanent element, the element which goes on working yesterday, today, and tomorrow. There is a relative constancy, an attitude, a certain stamp, whose external sign is the fact that we are in the body. And faith extends its influence into this region of the factual, habitual state just as much as sin does. There does exist something which can be described as a "Christian character"—different as this character is from faith, and in spite of the fact that faith is not to be understood from this standpoint. Faith may be "materialized" in a certain state of believing, a habitual state of faith. Hence faith exists as something which has grown thus, and there-

fore also as something which is growing, increasing or decreasing. The *person* can never be conceived in terms of qualities, but the *character* may be.

And just as this element of habit is one aspect of faith, so it is with love. There is therefore an "exercise in love," a process of growth in love, a more or a less, a "treasure," a power at the disposal of the moment of action, which distinguishes the mature soul from the beginner, there is a really present "excellence" and even a virtuosity of loving. In brief: there does exist what Aristotle and the Catholic moralists mean when they speak of virtue.

In this region virtues do exist as qualities in the person. Here, indeed, there really are individual virtues of which one may have more of one and less of another, just as also in technical excellence one may be "stronger" at one point and "weaker" at another. This point of view should and must also have its place in a Christian ethic, even though this place may be a secondary one; this subject will be treated in connexion with the discussion of the *justitia civilis*. The error of the usual doctrine of virtue does not consist in the fact that it points to these virtues—which really are present in individual persons as such—but in the fact that it makes them the fundamental and the main thing, that it interprets man as a being who strives upwards from "below," rather than as a being who depends on something which is granted to him from "above," that it regards continuity as an ascending rather than a descending scale, that it does not perceive that this order of progression is completely reversed by repentance and faith, that *gratia* is not *superponit naturam*, but that it consists in a "dying" and "becoming new"; that even the "virtue" which proceeds from faith only comes into being when the gaze of the soul is directed, not towards the "I," and that which is present, but towards Christ and His word of justification. We can only speak of this virtue as a "state" without doing harm if we are quite clear that it is nothing natural, nothing constructed by man, if we realize that its growth proceeds from the actuality of faith; otherwise we shall fall into a hopeless morass of Naturalism or Substantialism, which knows grace only as Supernature, and in so doing falsifies its nature from the very root.

But to deal with these virtues is not so much the task of ethics as of pedagogy. The place of pedagogy is the habitual, as its essential categories are practice and custom, although certainly a right pedagogy can only be produced when it looks at that which lies beyond its own sphere. Here, therefore, all that concerns us is to give an indication of this connexion between ethics and the empirical considerations and practice of pedagogy.

III. Love and Justice

Reinhold Niebuhr

The Spirit of Justice*

In the Christian faith the final law in which all other law is fulfilled is the law of love. But this law does not abrogate the laws of justice, except as love rises above justice to exceed its demands. The ordinary affairs of the community, the structures of politics and economics, must be governed by the spirit of justice and by specific and detailed definitions of rights and duties.

American Christianity tends to be irrelevant to the problems of justice because it persists in presenting the law of love as a simple solution for every communal problem. It is significant that the "social gospel," which sought to overcome the excessive individualism of the Christian faith in America, never escaped this sentimentality and irrelevance because it also preached the same ethic that it pretended to criticize. It insisted that Christians should practice the law of love not only in personal relations but in the collective relations of mankind. In these relations love as an ecstatic impulse of self-giving is practically impossible. Nations, classes, and races do not love one another. They may have a high sense of obligation to one another. They must express this sense of obligation in the desire to give each one his due.

The effort to substitute the law of love for the spirit of justice instead of recognizing love as the fulfillment and highest form of the spirit of justice, is derived from the failure to measure the power and persistence of self-interest. It is because self-interest is not easily overcome in even the life of the "redeemed" that most of the harmonies of life are not the perfect harmonies of fully co-ordinated wills but the tolerable harmonies of balanced interests and mutually recognized claims. Even in the family, in which the spirit of love may prevail more than in any other human institution, the careful calculation of rights is an important element in the harmony of the whole, though it must be observed that rights are so complexly intertwined in intimate relations that the calculations of justice

* This essay by Reinhold Niebuhr is from *Christianity and Society*, Summer, 1950.

lead to friction if love is not constantly infused into them.

Christians pride themselves upon an ethic that exceeds the requirements of law. But it is significant that Jews, schooled in their legalistic tradition and also the inheritors of the prophetic spirit, are on the whole more adept in the field of justice than Christians. They might well say to Christians what Cosimo de' Medici said to Catholics in the Renaissance: "You have built your ladders into the heavens. We will not seek so high nor sink so low." Christian businessmen are more frequently characterized by a spirit of philanthropy than by a spirit of justice in assessing the claims and counterclaims of economic groups. Love in the form of philanthropy is, in fact, on a lower level than a high form of justice. For philanthropy is given to those who make no claims against us, who do not challenge our goodness or disinterestedness. An act of philanthropy may thus be an expression of both power and moral complacency. An act of justice on the other hand requires the humble recognition that the claim that another makes against us may be legitimate.

The pronouncements of church bodies and the preachments of the pulpit still tend to smell of sentimentality in our day because the law of love is presented without reference to the power of the law of self-love. "All coercion," wrote a Christian businessman recently, "is foreign to the Christian life because we Christians know that only uncoerced goodness is real goodness." This does not take into account that we need a great deal of second-rate goodness to get along with one another. We have to have a taxation system that demands more of us than we are inclined to give voluntarily; and we must maintain a social security system that holds us responsible for the security of other families than our own beyond our natural inclination. We cannot preserve the health of the free world without American aid to other nations that must go far beyond the utmost limits of voluntary philanthropy.

Reinhold Niebuhr

Justice and Love*

"A Christian," declared an eager young participant in a symposium on Christianity and politics, "always considers the common welfare before his

* This essay by Reinhold Niebuhr is from *Christianity and Society*, Fall, 1950.

own interest." This simple statement reveals a few of the weaknesses of moralistic Christianity in dealing with problems of justice. The statement contains at least two errors, or perhaps one error and one omission.

The first error consists in defining a Christian in terms which assume that consistent selflessness is possible. No Christian, even the most perfect, is able "always" to consider the common interest before his own. At least he is not able to do it without looking at the common interest with eyes colored by his own ambitions. If complete selflessness were a simple possibility, political justice could be quickly transmuted into perfect love; and all the frictions, tensions, partial co-operations, and overt and covert conflicts could be eliminated. If complete selflessness without an admixture of egoism were possible, many now irrelevant sermons and church resolutions would become relevant. Unfortunately there is no such possibility for individual men; and perfect disinterestedness for groups and nations is even more impossible.

The other error is one of omission. To set self-interest and the general welfare in simple opposition is to ignore nine tenths of the ethical issues that confront the consciences of men. For these are concerned not so much with the problem of the self against the whole as with problems of the self in its relation to various types of "general welfare." "What do you mean by common interest?" retorted a shrewd businessman in the symposium referred to. Does it mean the family or the nation? If I have to choose between "my family" and "my nation," is the Christian choice inevitably weighted in favor of the nation since it is the larger community? And if the choice is between "my" nation and another nation, must the preference always be for the other nation on the ground that concern for my own nation represents collective self-interest? Was the young pacifist idealist right who insisted that if we had less "selfish concern for our own civilization" we could resolve the tension between ourselves and Russia, presumably by giving moral preference to a communist civilization over our own?

Such questions as these reveal why Christian moralism has made such meager contributions to the issues of justice in modern society. Justice requires discriminate judgments between conflicting claims. A Christian justice will be particularly critical of the claims of the self as against the claims of the other, but it will not dismiss them out of hand. Without this criticism all justice becomes corrupted into a refined form of self-seeking. But if the claims of the self (whether individual or collective) are not entertained, there is no justice at all. There is an ecstatic form of agape which defines the ultimate heroic possibilities of human existence (involving, of course, martyrdom) but not the common possibilities of tolerable harmony of life with life.

In so far as justice admits the claims of the self, it is something less than love. Yet it cannot exist without love and remain justice. For without the "grace" of love, justice always degenerates into something less than justice.

But if justice requires that the interests of the self be entertained, it also requires that they be resisted. Every realistic system of justice must assume the continued power of self-interest, particularly of collective self-interest. It must furthermore assume that this power will express itself illegitimately as well as legitimately. It must therefore be prepared to resist illegitimate self-interest, even among the best men and the most just nations. A simple Christian moralism counsels men to be unselfish. A profounder Christian faith must encourage men to create systems of justice which will save society and themselves from their own selfishness.

But justice arbitrates not merely between the self and the other, but between the competing claims upon the self by various "others." Justice seeks to determine what I owe my family as compared with my nation; or what I owe this segment as against that segment of a community. One of the strange moral anomalies of our times is that there are businessmen and men of affairs who have a more precise sense of justice in feeling their way through the endless relativities of human relations than professional teachers of morals. Practical experience has made them sensitive to the complex web of values and interests in which human decisions are reached, while the professional teachers of religion and morals deal with simple counters of black and white. This certainly is one of the reasons why the pulpit frequently seems so boring and irrelevant to the pew. At his worst the practical man of affairs is morally heedless and considers only his own interest, mistaking collective self-interest for selfless virtue. At his best he has been schooled in justice, while his teacher confuses the issue by moral distinctions which do not fit the complexities of life.

The realm of justice is also a realm of tragic choices, which are seldom envisaged in a type of idealism in which all choices are regarded as simple. Sometimes we must prefer a larger good to a smaller one, without the hope that the smaller one will be preserved in the larger one. Sometimes we must risk a terrible evil (such as an atomic war) in the hope of avoiding an imminent peril (such as subjugation to tyranny). Subsequent events may prove the risk to have been futile and the choice to have been wrong. If there is enough of a world left after such a wrong choice we will be taxed by the idealists for having made the wrong choice; and they will not know that they escaped an intolerable evil by our choice. Even now we are taxed with the decision to resist nazism, on the ground that the war against nazism has left us in a sad plight. The present peril of communism seems to justify an earlier capitulation to nazism. But since we are men and not God, we could neither anticipate all the evils that would flow from our decision to resist nazism, nor yet could we have capitulated to the immediate evil because another evil was foreshadowed.

The tragic character of our moral choices, the contradiction between various equal values of our devotion, and the incompleteness in all our moral striving, prove that "if in this life only we had hoped in Christ, we are of all men most miserable." No possible historic justice is sufferable without the Christian hope. But any illusion of a world of perfect love without these imperfect harmonies of justice must ultimately turn the dream of love into a nightmare of tyranny and injustice.

Paul Ramsey is Harrington Spear Paine Professor of Religion and Chairman of the Department of Religion, Princeton University.

Christian Love in Search of a Social Policy*

This, then, is the situation: On the one hand, stands Christianity, which is a religion seeking a social policy; and, on the other, there are a multitude of social policies generating religions, or seeking to attach themselves to the Christian religion. Christian love is always in search of a social policy. Our preceding study has made clear that it is improper to speak of a Christian economic order or Christian politics, or for that matter Christian rules for personal behavior absolutely binding as laws. "The liberty of the Christian man" means that he *may* get along without any of these things and is subject to none. Nevertheless, he cannot get along without seeking to find the best possible social ethic in which Christian love may incarnate itself. Because of its very nature, Christian love must take on the flesh of

* Reprinted with the permission of Charles Scribner's Sons from *Basic Christian Ethics,* pp. 326-27 and 337-51, by Paul Ramsey. Copyright 1950 Charles Scribner's Sons.

some specific social order. What more can be said concerning what Christian love seeks to do in actual life? This question the present chapter undertakes to answer. We shall consider first certain basic principles for social policy already contained within Christian ethics itself, and then go on to ask what Christian love, in search of a social policy, may learn from other sources. Christian ethics already possesses certain definite implications for social policy, and an adequate social ethic can in large measure be drawn from within its own nature alone. To the extent that this is true it would be misleading for us only to speak of Christian love in search of a social policy. We should first see how far a Christian social ethic may be stated primarily in terms of Christian notions alone. . . .

II. IS CHRISTIAN "OBEDIENT LOVE" ITSELF A SOCIAL POLICY?

The next question to be raised is this: Does the norm of Christian love in itself contain positive and definite enough social requirements for us to draw a Christian social policy directly out of this norm alone without need of searching elsewhere? We have spoken of the negative policy of restraining sin. The issue raised in this section concerns a more positive Christian social ethics. Does Christian "obedient love" tell us what positively should be done in the common life? to what extent or in what way does Christian love contain a positive social policy and to what extent or in what way does such love still seek to determine a proper social ethic?

In contrast to any form of intuition-ethics, the ethics of love shows abundant content. In contrast to any form of legalism, however, the ethics of love appears to be without determinate content, always in search of a social policy yet never completely identifiable with any current program with which it happens to make common cause.

Acting from immediate feelings of right and wrong has always had large place among ordinary Christian folk. Even the most sophisticated person makes many decisions on the basis of what he would describe as intuitive moral knowledge. Pacifist Christians who have given up attempting to rationalize their position by appealing to "the *power* of non-violence" frequently defend their pacifist witness on the basis of an immediate call of duty for them. Moreover, in certain so-called Barthian circles today there is a good deal of talk about "responding moment by moment to the absolute demands of God." These "demands" from one moment of decision to another have in common only some sense of "the absolute." There is no universal truth in them, no quality characterizing what God may demand, and therefore no ground for ethics except the particular command present at one moment, quite another command at another moment in which the absolute impinges upon us. This view may be called theological intuitionism—intuitionism on stilts!

In *Fear and Trembling* Kierkegaard asks the question, "Can there be a teleological suspension of ethics?" and answers affirmatively. Abraham, he says, became the Father of Faith because he was willing to abide in his "absolute relationship to the absolute," even when this involved a religious suspension of his ethical duty toward his son, Isaac.[1] Such theological intuitionism may be objected to on two counts: In the first place, no content immediately presented through the relation of absolute faith in God can countermand human conscience or, in this instance, the dawning ethical insight that it is wrong to offer children as blood sacrifices. Religious faith proves important for the growth of natural morality, not first of all because it counters the conclusions of natural reason, but because faith speaks to the problem of saving man from the sinful employment of whatever standards moral reason leads him to accept. Faith doubtless renders more impartial and sensitive the employment of reason in actually making moral judgments, but reason itself assesses the worth of any ethical truth disclosed to it. The first mistake of such theological intuitionism lies in deriving some ethical content to supplement, if not actually to contradict, moral reason simply from an asserted immediate impression of the "absolute demands" of God.

In the second place, if Christian love defines perfect obedience to God, then no felt ethical demands should be allowed to contradict or run counter to it, no matter if these intuitions are accompanied by a high degree of felt-absoluteness. An ethic of Christian love, in contrast to an ethic of immediate moral impressions, shows abundant content for determining what should be done. This provides a principle for discriminating not only among normal ethical intuitions on the part of the common man, but also among the intuitions glorified by religion into "absolute demands" calling for "radical decision" in "the moment." We must try every spirit to see if it be of God. We must test every intuition, no matter how powerful, to see if it be a manifestation of the holy Spirit of God which is the spirit of Christ. No intuited moral demand speaking to us in this spirit can call Christ cursed; none can call Christ lord except by the spirit. Hereby we know what God demands, and can discriminate among intuitions by their specific quality and not simply respond to them as felt power or powerful feeling. "God shows his love for us in that while we were yet sinners [help-

[1] Soren Kierkegaard, *Fear and Trembling*, Princeton University Press, p. 49.

less, ungodly, unrighteous, his enemies] Christ died for us" (Rom. 5:6-10). This norm in itself carries us far in the direction of specific decisions in the problems of actual life. *Non tantus vile pro quo Christus mortus est.* Call no man vile for whom Christ died. The ethic of Christian love may fall far short of a complete social policy, yet clearly Christian love contains more positive implications for formulating a social ethic than certain forms of theological ethics which rest everything on "decision" or the momentary response of faith.

Nevertheless, Christian love takes on the aspect of a quite indeterminate norm when compared with any and all forms of legalistic social ethic. The Christian man is lord of all and subject to none of the rule-morality. Set free on account of his so great responsibility, he must therefore be constantly engaged in "building up" an adequate social ethic realistically adjusted, not to precedents in law or existing conventions of society, but to concrete and changing neighbor need. Searching for a social policy Christian love may make *use* of, say, the ethical insights summed up in the so-called "natural law," but its *base* of operations never shifts over onto the ground of the rational moral law. Precisely what the connection is between the two when there occurs a Christian *employment* of the theory of natural law or the principles of some other social policy our next section attempts to elucidate.

It is difficult to tell whether the theory of natural law should be criticized because it is a new form of legalism or because it is an ethic of intuition. On either count, natural law cannot occupy the ground floor of Christian ethics. On the one hand, Jacques Maritain remarks that the metaphor of a law written in the heart of man "has been responsible for a great deal of damage, causing natural law to be represented as a ready-made code rolled up within the conscience of each of us, which each one of us has only to unroll, and of which all men should naturally have an equal knowledge." [2] If this is not what the "first principles" of natural morality mean, then it would seem that some sort of intuition constitutes the beginning of moral reasoning. The law in the heart, as Maritain says, is "hidden from us as our own heart." Interpreting "natural law" as not even a rudimentary code of law or set of first principles but as some primary intuition, it should then be said that all such intuitions need to be schooled by Christ before they become an accredited part of Christian ethics.

On the other hand, Maritain defines *jus naturale* as law which follows "in *necessary* fashion, and *from the simple fact that man is man,* nothing else being taken into account." [3] He admits,

[2] *The Rights of Man and Natural Law,* Scribners, 1943, p. 62.
[3] *Ibid.,* p. 63.

it is true, that *jus naturale* has no definite content except in the form of *jus gentium,* or law which follows "from the first principle in a *necessary* manner, but this time supposing certain conditions of fact, as for instance the state of civil society or the relationships between people." [4] This is either meaningless or self-contradictory. How can a natural law *without definite content* follow in such *necessary* fashion simply from reflecting on man as man or for that matter from anything? And how can anything else follow in such *necessary* fashion from a natural law which itself has no specific content, even supposing any number of conditions of fact? Maritain wants a natural law which both does and yet does not follow from first principles in necessary fashion. Either the natural law has specific content and may be "unrolled" according to these stages, or else by natural law is meant only a form of intuition ethics, possibly quite variable intuitions. Neither of these provides a distinctively Christian social policy. Rather such a policy follows from reflecting on man as man or on certain conditions of fact in the light of Christian love. Christian love formulates social policy by taking into account every concrete element in the situation which determines how in fact some actual good may be done for the neighbor in the state of civil society and the relationships among people existing at present. Catholic absolutism, *e.g.,* in sex ethics, would be finally corrected if once and for all it were admitted that in this area right should be determined by *Christian love* reflecting upon man as man in relation to certain conditions of fact. Instead, Catholic ethics continues to say, while trying hard not to say, that "natural law" may simply be unrolled from natural moral reason alone; and consequently such ethics remains in bondage to a law which teaches a number of unlovely things.

Early in the development of the theory of natural law the extreme demands of "absolute natural law" (no war, no slavery, no property) were modified into a "relative natural law" ("just" war, justice to slaves, common "use" of private property). This accommodation was partly an adjustment to the fact that what ought to be done in specific moral decisions cannot be fully anticipated by any legal code, partly an adjustment to the fact that sin prevents man from achieving the absolute law of nature. For both of these reasons the "relative natural law" tends to lose its legalistic character. Emil Brunner points out quite correctly that the "relative Law of Nature is not a law at all, but only a *regulative principle,* from which no definite demands can be deduced," that it "simply expresses the necessity (which cannot be expressed in legal terms) of adapting the absolute Law of Nature to sinful reality," and that therefore, it really means "absence

[4] *Ibid.,* p. 70.

of principle."[5] No one can actually draw up a statement of the precepts of natural law for the workaday world. Social policy has to be formulated in any case in realistic adjustment to the concrete factors in any given situation; it cannot be derived through step by step deduction from a revealed or an intuitively grasped absolute natural law. "Relative natural law" may therefore be defined as intuition in search of a social policy. Moreover, there takes place no impartial apprehension of an absolute natural law (from which specific decision *might* be derived), since "in a sinful humanity" it is questionable whether "there are any 'impartial' people at all."[6]

Christian social ethics consists neither of intuition in search of a social policy nor of natural law possessed of a social policy. Christian love itself contains more definite or determinate directions for social policy than natural law interpreted as an intuition; in terms of these intuition should be guided. On the other hand, the ethics of love approaches the task of finding a social policy with an indefinite, indeterminate and liberating norm when this is contrasted with any legalistic understanding of the law of nature.

III. THE RELATION BETWEEN CHRISTIAN LOVE AND SOCIAL POLICIES

If Christianity may be spoken of as a religion in some measure seeking a social ethic, then what is the nature of the relationships which come to exist between Christian love and any of its adopted social policies? In attempting to answer this question it should first be pointed out that throughout this book frequent reference has been made to the connection between the ethics of love and specific types of regulation which Christian love sometimes accepts. The main point has been that, while Christian love cannot get along without seeking to find from any source the best possible social ethic, such love remains *dominant* and *free* in any partnership it enters.

For example, the distinction was made between the "strategy" of Christian love, which remains unaltered, and what such love sometimes does as a matter of "tactics." The latter may be variable and indeed should vary directly and promptly with the neighbors' needs and with the actual conditions for being of some real benefit to them. This may not be in every respect an apt analogy, but our reference to strategy and tactics suggests at least this much of truth: Christian love ought never to be identified with

[5] *The Divine Imperative,* Westminster Press, 1937. Note 8 to p. 269, Notes and Appendices, pp. 629-630.

[6] *Ibid.,* p. 631.

or permanently bound to any particular program or stipulation for action, however important. Yet no one ever did a Christian deed from Christian love alone without some reasonable, realistic decision about what specifically should be done. Very few wars have been won by those whose tactics were not subject to constant reexamination and readjustment; none have been won by strategy alone.

It has been pointed out that Christian love always occupies the "groundfloor"; no next-of-kin ethical viewpoints are allowed to move into residence there. Although much needs to be added from many sources to complete the whole edifice of Christian social ethics, no other foundation can be laid than that which has been laid. Frequently in the preceding pages criticism has also been made of "coalition" ethics. This too may be an inexact expression; but in context our meaning has been clear enough. By rejecting coalition ethics, we have rejected the idea that there need be any *necessarily permanent* coalition between Christian ethics and any other school of ethics founded on philosophical insight or the findings of social science. Of course, Christian ethics makes permanent coalition with "the truth" wherever it may be found; but as truth varies or advances, or is believed to be different from the suppositions of some other school of philosophy or science, so vary Christian ethical theory and practice. A Christian need not defend to the death either Platonism, Aristotelianism, Idealism or Naturalism; the course of Christian thought should make this quite evident.

By rejecting coalition ethics, we have also rejected the idea of allowing Christian love to become merely an equal or sleeping partner in the business of determining the full meaning of obligation. For Christian love to be the senior or controlling partner would be an entirely different sort of coalition. Perhaps the position set forth in this volume may be made clearer by saying that while Christian love makes alliance or coalition with any available sources of insight or information about what should be done, it makes *concordat* with none of these. Christian love must, indeed, enter into such alliances; it must go in search of some social policy. Yet in the relationship between Christian love and the principles of an acceptable social ethic, Christian love remains what it is, dominant and free. It does not transform itself into the coin of any realm, though it enters every realm and becomes debtor both to the Greek and to the barbarians.

It cannot be too often said or too strongly emphasized that biblical "justice," which enters into alliance with ancillary conceptions of justice formulated by Aristotle, natural-law theory, Rousseau, or any one else, can perfectly well get along without them if such reasonably accredited notions of justice be not forthcoming. Man may be not *Homo sapiens* but *Homo faber;* human reason "technical reason." If this be so, then in making law and fabricating systems of justice man must build his little systems and establish orders of life without the guidance of "first principles" or any sort of natural justice, but not without biblical Justice; for ultimately laws are not right simply because they are spontaneous or natural or rational rather than pragmatically devised according to the positive theory of law;[7] they are just to the degree in which they accord with the justice of God made known through covenant, old and new. From this even the technical, legislating reason of *Homo faber* may know "what is good" and the meaning of "doing justice." Man, that "most religious of animals," [8] should construct his systems of law having in mind the righteousness of God, whether he also has capacity for "first principles" or not. Then all will go well with him. This is not said in order to prompt cynicism, agnosticism or relativism regarding rational moral norms (in the author's opinion, these views are far from true). Moral relativism need not be encouraged to prepare the way for "revealed ethics." This is said simply to show that the Christian has whereon to stand even were he forced to distrust moral judgments made by reason alone. He does not cease to stand on this same ground when Christian love enters into combination with moral principles believed to be universally valid and available to all reasonable men.

Christian love must seek to find out whatever may be known concerning the just ordering of human life. It cannot be too often said or too strongly emphasized that biblical "justice," when it begins to establish some order, can make use of any of the ideas or norms for determining "worldly justice" which happen to be convincing. At the same time, it must be said with equal emphasis that a Christian, impelled by love whose nature is to incarnate itself wherever there is need, cannot remain aloof but must enter fully into the problem of determining right action under the particular, concrete circumstances which surround him and his neighbor. Christian love lives always in quest of a social ethic adequate to any given situation. If philosophy fails to uncover permanently valid norms, the Christian continues the search and determines or posits his action in terms of the best knowledge available to him through the social or psychological sciences. Biblical justice demands: "To each according to the measure of his real need, because this alone is the measure of God's righteousness toward him." *Non tantus vile pro quo Christus mortus est.* This in turn poses the problem: How shall the

[7] Jacques Ellul, *Le fondement théologique du droit* (Neuchâtel and Paris: Delachaux & Niestlé, 1946), chap. iii, sec. 1.

[8] Plato, *Timaeus,* 41.

neighbor's real need be determined, and what adjustment should be made among the competing needs and claims of many neighbors? Impelled by its own concern for more than one neighbor to find *some* answer to this question, biblical justice makes coalition with various rational norms of justice or natural law, but concordats it makes with none. The fact that biblical justice never admits any other conception of justice or definition of obligation into an equal partnership appears even in Brunner; for, before changing love into the small coin of Aristotelian justice, Brunner in fact baptizes Aristotle and to a great extent Christianizes his justice. We saw other examples of the independent influence Christian love exerts in making use of themes drawn from outstanding philosophical theories of ethics in the revision and reconstruction Platonism underwent in the mind of St. Augustine and Aristotelianism in the mind of St. Thomas Aquinas; and our suggestion was then that this process simply needs to be renewed and made more thoroughgoing by constant reference to New Testament ethics.

The reason Brunner has such difficulty in relating love to "the world of systems" is that in purging love of *selfish* concern for one's own rights he tends to eliminate from it also all enlightened concern for *the neighbor's* right. Like Tolstoy, he seems to think that a love which by nature has no *selfish* partiality can find no reason for ever preferring the cause of one neighbor to that of another but must serve them all at random or as they happen to come. Consequently, Brunner concludes, "Love in itself establishes no order, on the contrary when it is about its business it transcends all orders, all laws. It inquires neither into its own right *nor into those of others,* for to all it gives itself, whole and undivided and beyond all limits." [9] But love which is unselfish need not *therefore* be unreasoning or unenlightened or accept no distinctions in its vocational obligations. It is true that love which does not inquire into its rights need not wait on determining the just rights of another *against one's self.* But such love, itself whole and undivided and limitless, will need to know all that can be known about "the others," since in actual life not all of them *can* be served effectively. Love which seeks not its own may very well seek *the neighbor's own.* It must establish some order, and to do so may employ all available ways of determining what may be the neighbor's own in comparison with another. Once this is allowed, then nothing in the nature of biblical "justice" prevents it from becoming "worldly justice." Such justice may be defined as what Christian love does when confronted by two or more neighbors. Justice perhaps means treating similar cases similarly (Aristotle's corrective justice) when a Christian judges, not between himself and his neighbor, but between two or

[9] Emil Brunner, *Justice and the Social Order,* Harpers, 1945, p. 50 (italics mine).

more neighbors; or it may even mean treating them dissimilarly, taking into account essential inequalities between them (Aristotle's distributive justice), preferring some to others especially on account of their manifest good will and potential neighbor-regarding service.

The present writer happens to be convinced that, more than Aristotle or natural-law theory, Rousseau's notion of the general will gives a clue to the nature of minimal justice in the ordering of human relationships. The least that justice should do is to establish orders having "objective generality" and enact laws applying equally to all, so that "the conditions are the same for all; and, this being so, no one has an interest in making them burdensome to others." [10] This is that justice of which it may be said, "Love can only do more, it can never do less, than justice requires." [11] Biblical "justice," itself concerned to treat similar cases (my own and my neighbor's) *dissimilarly,* can never do less than treat a number of neighbors *similarly* when comparing their needs (not with my own but) with one another and when arranging some stable order of life in which they all may live. A will to make the burdens lighter upon those in need of help certainly excludes any selfish propensity for making the conditions more burdensome on some than on others. Willingness to give must surely first renounce special claims for the self and conquer the interest we all have in making the conditions lighter for ourselves and by comparison more burdensome for others. When this has been accomplished, biblical justice goes on to do more than Rousseau's justice; or rather, biblical justice accomplishes at least this in the course of doing more.

These two parts of justice find support in the religious man's personal existence before God. With whatever judgment you judge, you shall be judged; with what measure you mete, it shall be measured to you again! At the crucial point where selfishness tempts us to make an exception of ourselves, God stands as a threatening witness of our existence. His judgment insures that we do no less than bear our equal burden, that we at least do not make exceptions of ourselves. Since whatever measure we apply rebounds on us again, no one has an interest in making law or institutions more burdensome on others. The religious man's understanding of his own personal existence "before" God guarantees widespread and persistent acceptance of a "this-applies-to-me" attitude which must undergird every effective effort to establish justice. It has frequently been affirmed that the main individualistic elements of secular democratic theory, natural rights, the dignity of man, etc., historically may be traced to their source in the

[10] J. J. Rousseau, *The Social Contract,* Book I, chap. vi, p. 15.
[11] Emil Brunner, *op. cit.,* p. 129.

religious tradition of the west. Equally likely (and equally difficult to demonstrate) is the connection between the "objective generality" of law and a religious sense of the inescapable and universal judgment of God, between "equality of application" and equality before God, between willingness to be no more than equal to another before the law and acknowledgment that we are no more than equal before God. This demands minimal justice on earth, but only *minimal* justice however far such justice exceeds our actual performance.

God's righteous judgment (*tsedeq*) places the stress elsewhere, as in Jesus' parable of the servant whom a merciful king released from debt to the fantastic amount of ten million dollars who nevertheless insisted that his fellow-servant pay in full a debt of twenty dollars. "Then his master called him in and said to him, 'You wicked slave! I canceled all that debt of yours when you entreated me. Ought you not to have taken pity on your fellow-slave, as I did on you?'" (Matt. 18:32, 33). From this story it is evident that righteousness which for itself claims nothing may yet for the sake of another claim everything, that any one who unhesitatingly and times without number renounces "what is due" when he himself alone bears the brunt of such a decision may nevertheless turn full circle and insist with utter severity that the neighbor receive what is due him in terms of righteousness, in terms of *mishpat* which pronounces judgment on men and institutions and social policies that are not slanted toward love.

The relation between Christian love and existing social institutions therefore may be summed up as the constant criticism and reshaping of the institutions of society in the course of using them. And the relationship between Christian love and *other theories of social ethics* may be summed up as the constant criticism and bending of these social policies in the course of using them.

The expression "middle axiom" has been used in recent years to refer to elements of a social policy which a large number of Protestant Christians judge to be imperative in the present day. The word "axiom" is misleading, suggesting as it does the "first principles" of a natural morality on which there can be no disagreement among reasonable people. "Middle axioms" are intended rather as attempts "to define the directions in which, in a particular state of society, Christian faith must express itself. They are not binding for all time, but are provisional definitions of the type of behavior required of Christians at a given period and in given circumstances." [12] Thus, John Bennett remarks, "a 'middle axiom' is more concrete that a universal ethical principle and less specific

[12] W. A. Visser 't Hooft and J. H. Oldham, *The Church and Its Function in Society*, Willett, Clark, 1937, p. 210.

than a program that includes legislation and political strategy." [13] Assuming that in Christian love we have the "universal ethical principle" of Christian ethics, undoubtedly there are these aspects or stages or degrees of particularity in determining the specific recommendations of Christian love. Going into action and in search of a social policy, Christian love undoubtedly passes through a number of "mid" points before arriving at concrete decision: there may be axiomatic first principles of moral reason, general but provisional and non-axiomatic directions for social practice, and concrete proposals for immediate adoption through legislation or other means. Granting all this, there was need for further analysis of the connection which holds these stages of policy determination together. What stands between a "universal ethical principle" and a "middle axiom" or between one of these and specific plans for action? Surely not another "middle axiom"! The purpose of this section has been to suggest that "the controlling love of Christ," as both standard for action and impulse toward action, in its quest for a social policy gives the unity to Christian theory and practice and itself always remains dominant and free. In finding out what to do, "middle axioms" are uncovered and appropriated, alien ground becomes adopted ground, and in fact no ground and no source of understanding are alien to love whose nature is to incarnate itself in the flesh and blood of actual life. The impact of Christian love should be felt ideally throughout the whole range of formulated social policy by its being bent in the direction such love requires. To some degree this actually happens, unless Christian love suffers fundamental alteration through bondage to the social ethics it began by using.

No matter how strongly we have insisted that Christian love cannot get along without searching for a social policy, the final word must place the accent again on freedom, freedom even from the social policies Christian love may have found in times past. The Christian criticism of life means also the Christian criticism of every known, or yet to be discovered, social policy. Christian love works as a ferment underneath every social institution and conventional code of conduct in Christendom. Whether conforming to the old or helping to create a new mode of conduct, a Christian man subjects everything to this imperial test: let every man *now* consult his neighbor's need. This may call for respecting the tried and tested ways of doing things. When however we observe how these have failed in so many ways to keep pace with the world in which we and our neighbors live, who can doubt that Christian love today requires of us willingness to take some new departure? Even the humblest

[13] *Christian Ethics and Social Policy*, Scribners, 1946, p. 77.

Christian man must rapidly become willing to have the structures and customs of his world otherwise than they now are. These will not stand long in any case. Why not bend them more to love's desiring? Even the most unlearned (or the most schooled) must be willing to sit loose within truth as he now sees it and willingly accept the best from the words of the latest prophet or the newest discoveries of science. Nay, he must go in search of new truth, loving his previous "findings" with the moderation of an employer and not with the ardor of a lover, since only the neighbor should be loved with infinite compassion. The Christian pilgrim, therefore, should pass from one age to another with the ease and serenity of freedom, assisting the new which is always struggling to be born, because in every age he loves not the times or some abstract truth but the neighbor.

IV. Freedom and Authority

John A. T. Robinson

The New Morality*

THE REVOLUTION IN ETHICS

Prayer and ethics are simply the inside and outside of the same thing. Indeed, they could both be defined, from the Christian point of view, as meeting the unconditional in the conditioned in unconditional personal relationship. And it is impossible to reassess one's doctrine of God, of how one understands the transcendent, without bringing one's view of morality into the same melting-pot. Indeed, the two are inseparable. For assertions about God are in the last analysis assertions about Love—about the ultimate ground and meaning of personal relationships. As John Wren-Lewis puts it, interpreting the teaching of the Prophets and the New Testament,

* From *Honest to God*, by John A. T. Robinson. Published in the U.S.A. by The Westminster Press, 1963. © SCM Press Limited, 1963. Pp. 105-21. Used by permission.

Moral assertions about human interrelationship are not derived 'at second hand' from the fact that the Being called 'God' just happens to be interested in justice—they are directly and integrally bound up with assertions about God's Being *in itself*.[1]

But there is no need to prove that a revolution is required in morals. It has long since broken out; and it is no 'reluctant revolution.' The wind of change here is a gale. Our only task is to relate it correctly to the previous revolution we have described and to try to discern what should be the Christian attitude to it.

There are plenty of voices within the Church greeting it with vociferous dismay. The religious sanctions are losing their strength, the moral landmarks are disappearing beneath the flood, the nation is in danger. This is the end-term of the apostasy from Christianity: the fathers rejected the doctrine, the children have abandoned the morals. Indeed, we could use almost unaltered the words quoted earlier from Bonhoeffer about the process of secularization: 'Catholic and Protestant . . . are agreed that it is in this development that the great defection from God, from Christ, is to be discerned, *and the more they bring in and make use of God and Christ in opposition to this trend, the more the trend itself considers itself to be anti-Christian.*'[2] And therein, of course, lies the danger. Christianity is identified *tout court* with the old, traditional morality. That would not matter if this morality were Christian. But in fact it is the equivalent in the ethical field of the supranaturalist way of thinking. And though this undoubtedly served the Church in its day, and still seems perfectly adequate—and indeed vitally necessary—to the religious, it would be calamitous if we allowed Christianity to be dismissed with it. And precisely that is what we are encouraging.

To this way of thinking right and wrong *are* derived 'at second hand' from God. They are the commandments which God gives, the laws which he lays down. According to the classic mythological statement of this position, they are delivered to Moses on the mountain top, graven on tablets. They come down direct from heaven, and are eternally valid for human conduct. But in morals as in metaphysics, the transition from the God 'up there' to the God 'out there' has long since been made, and these 'absolute standards' are normally now presented for our obedience stripped of their mythological garb. They may as a result be thought of more in terms of 'natural law' than of 'positive law,' but they are still written into the universe, they are still 'given,' objectively and immutably. Certain things are always 'wrong' and 'nothing can make them right,' and certain things are always 'sins,' whether or not they are judged

[1] *They Became Anglicans*, pp. 170 f.

[2] Bonhoeffer, *Letters and Papers from Prison*, p. 146. Italics mine.

by differing human societies to be 'crimes.' The supreme example of this way of thinking is, of course, the corpus of Roman Catholic moral theology, and it is magnificent in its monolithic consistency. But it is a way of thinking that pervades, even if in more muddled form, the whole of the Church's ethical teaching, Catholic and Protestant, official and unofficial.

A conspicuous example of this is the traditional thinking on one of the most hotly debated of moral issues, that of marriage and divorce. There are, of course, widely divergent views within the Church on this question, even within what might be called the supranaturalist camp. There is, for instance, a deep division on the interpretation of the 'indissolubility' of marriage. There are those who say that 'indissoluble' means 'ought not to be dissolved,' ought *never* to be dissolved. There are others who take it to mean 'cannot be dissolved': a physical or metaphysical union is created by wedlock which cannot be abrogated any more than two persons can cease to be brother and sister. This latter view is in fact an interesting example of a way of thinking that has characterized the whole supranaturalistic view of the world and which Dr. Wren-Lewis has analysed in his essay 'The Decline of Magic in Art and Politics.' [3] This is the supposition that the network of empirical relationships is but a veil for a world of occult realities which lie behind the outward order of things and constitute the truth about man or society or nature, however much the empirical facts may appear to dispute it. 'The divine right of kings' is an example, or the medieval doctrine of 'signatures,' or of 'degree'—the mystical hierarchy based on 'primogeniture and due of birth.' Behind the empirical relationships there are invisible realities, essences, structures, whose validity, grounded in the eternal order of things, is independent of anything that can be inferred or questioned from the phenomena. To this same category belongs the notion that the essence of marriage is a metaphysical or quasi-physical reality, constituted by the sacrament, which endures quite independently of the actual quality of the personal relationship or any indication that it may for all practical purposes be non-existent. The reality cannot be affected by any empirical facts or undone by any legal fiction. According to this version of the supranaturalist view, divorce is quite literally, and not merely morally, impossible. It is not a question of 'Those whom God hath joined together *let* no man put asunder': no man could if he tried. For marriage is not merely indissoluble: it is indelible.

There are those who are ready enough to borrow arguments—and apparently invincible arguments—from this way of thinking to uphold 'the sanctity of marriage,' but it is questionable how many today really believe this form of the doctrine that

[3] *The Critical Quarterly,* Spring 1960, pp. 7-23.

'marriages are made in heaven.' It is certain at any rate that their chances of commending it are small indeed to a world in full retreat on every front—scientific, political, artistic and religious—from such an occult view of life. Moreover, and more important, it is far from obvious that it has any basis in the teaching of Jesus or the New Testament. There is nothing specifically Christian about it, any more than there is about the mythological world-view. It is simply the metaphysic of a pre-scientific age. To tie Christianity to it is simply to ask for the one to be discredited with the other.

But there is another version of the supranaturalist ethic of marriage which is much more widespread, especially among Protestants. This bases marriage, like all else in life, upon the absolute command or law of God, or upon the teaching of Christ interpreted in the same legalistic manner. According to this view, God has laid down 'laws which never shall be broken.' Divorce is always and absolutely wrong. If any accommodation is made to it, it is 'for the hardness of men's hearts.' But in any case they must be made to realize from what they are falling short. For the 'absolute moral standard' is written and engraven for all to see. The supranaturalist ethic has behind it the sanction of Sinai and 'the clear teaching of our Lord.' There can be no doubt about Christian standards in this or any other matter. In any change they are unchangeable: the only question is whether men live up to them. The task of the Church is to recall men to them, and to the religion on which they are based.

This position has a far wider popular appeal. It is indeed what men expect the Church to stand for—and for anyone, especially a bishop, to appear to contradict it is regarded as profoundly shocking. But equally obviously it is a position that men honour much more in the breach than the observance. The sanctions of Sinai have lost their terrors, and people no longer accept the authority of Jesus even as a great moral teacher. Robbed of its supranatural supports, men find it difficult to take seriously a code of living that confessedly depended on them. 'Why shouldn't I?' or 'What's wrong with it?' are questions which in our generation press for an answer. And supranaturalist reasons—that God or Christ has pronounced it 'a sin'—have force, and even meaning, for none but a diminishing religious remnant.

But is it not perhaps for such a remnant that the Christian ethic is intended? There is, indeed, no sanction in the Gospels for believing that the gate is anything but narrow, 'and few there be that find it.' [4] But equally there is no suggestion in the Gospels that the Christian ethic is for 'the religious' only. It is for all men: it is

[4] Matt. 7:14.

based upon the nature of man, and for the foundation of his teaching on marriage Jesus specifically went behind Moses and the Law to creation.[5] It is for all men universally: it is not for *homo religiosus.*

THE TEACHING OF JESUS

A much more fundamental criticism of this supranaturalistic ethic than that it now restricts its relevance to those who can accept its foundation is that it seriously distorts the teaching of Jesus. 'The clear teaching of our Lord' is taken to mean that Jesus laid down certain precepts which were universally binding. Certain things were always right, other things were always wrong—for all men everywhere.

But this is to treat the Sermon on the Mount as the new Law, and, even if Matthew may have interpreted Jesus that way, there would hardly be a New Testament scholar today who would not say that it was a misinterpretation. The moral precepts of Jesus are not intended to be understood legalistically, as prescribing what all Christians must do, whatever the circumstances, and pronouncing certain courses of action universally right and others universally wrong. They are not legislation laying down what love always demands of every one: they are illustrations of what love may at any moment require of anyone.[6] They are, as it were, parables of the Kingdom in its moral claims—flashlight pictures of the uncompromising demand which the Kingdom must make upon any who would respond to it. The word to the rich young man, 'Go and sell all that you have,' [7] is not a universal principle of the ethical life, but as it were a translation into the imperative of the parable of the rich merchant, who went and did just this for the pearl of great price.[8] This transition to the imperative—'Go and do likewise' [9]—is not legislation, but a way of saying, as Nathan said to David at the close of the classic parable of the Old Testament, 'You are the man.' [10] It is a reminder that the parables are precisely not interesting stories of general application, but the call of the Kingdom to a specific group or individual at a particular moment.

This insistence on the parabolic character of the ethical sayings of Jesus should deliver us from the danger of taking them either as literal injunctions for any situation or as universal principles for every situation. The Sermon on the Mount does not say in advance, 'This is what in

[5] Mark 10:2-9.
[6] See especially C. H. Dodd, *Gospel and Law* (1951).
[7] Mark 10:21.
[8] Matt. 13:46.
[9] Luke 10:37.
[10] II Sam. 12:7.

any given circumstances you must do,' but, 'This is the kind of thing which at any moment, if you are open to the absolute, unconditional will of God, the Kingdom (or love) can demand of you.' It is relevant not because it provides us with an infallible guide to the moral life, but because as Martin Dibelius put it, 'we are able to be transformed by it.'

Jesus' teaching on marriage, as on everything else, is not a new law prescribing that divorce is always and in every case the greater of two evils (whereas Moses said there were some cases in which it was not). It is saying that love, utterly unconditional love, admits of no accommodation; you cannot define in advance situations in which it can be satisfied with less than complete and unreserved self-giving. It may mean selling all one possesses,[11] putting one's whole livelihood in the collection,[12] giving up one's clothes or lending one's money entirely without question,[13] cutting off one's right hand or pulling out one's eye.[14] Yet equally clearly not every situation will demand this, and Jesus' sayings make no attempt to adjudicate on conflicting claims[15] or to take into account the needs of third persons such as every real-life situation raises (e.g., who is going to maintain the widow after she has pledged her total means of support or the children of the man who has given everything to a beggar). Of course, love must consider these—and equally unreservedly. Jesus never resolves these choices for us: he is content with the knowledge that if we have the heart of the matter in us, if our eye is single, then love will find the way, its own particular way in every individual situation.

What the supranaturalist ethic does is to subordinate the actual individual relationship to some universal, whether metaphysical or moral, external to it. The decision is not reached, the judgment is not made, on the empirical realities of the particular concrete relationship between the persons concerned. Man is made for the sabbath, and not the sabbath for man. Be the individual circumstances what they will, the moral law is the same—for all men and for all times. It is imposed on the relationship from without, from above: the function of casuistry is to 'apply' it *to* the case in question.

Such an ethic is 'heteronomous,' in the sense that it derives its norm from 'out there'; and this is, of course, its strength. It stands for 'absolute,' 'objective' moral values and presents a dyke against the floods of relativism and subjectivism. And yet this heteronomy is also its profound weakness. Except to the man who believes in 'the God out there' it has no com-

11 Mark 10:21.
12 Mark 12:44.
13 Matt. 5:40, 42.
14 Matt. 5:29 f.
15 Luke 12:14.

pelling sanction or self-authenticating foundation. It cannot answer the question '*Why* is this wrong?' in terms of the intrinsic realities of the situation itself.

The revolt in the field of ethics from supranaturalism to naturalism, from heteronomy to autonomy, has been with us so long that we need not spend much time on it. It began with the magnificent grandeur of Kant's autonomous ideal, perhaps the greatest and most objective of all ethical systems. But this was really only secularized deism—and not completely secularized at that; for though Kant dispensed with the hypothesis of God to account for the source of the moral law, he brought him back, as a very crude *deus ex machina,* to ensure the eventual coincidence of virtue and happiness. Kant's moral idealism was living on religious capital. As this ran out or was rejected, it came to be replaced by every kind of ethical relativism—utilitarianism, evolutionary naturalism, existentialism. These systems, so different in themselves, have this in common: they have taken their stand, quite correctly, against any subordination of the concrete needs of the individual situation to an alien universal norm. But in the process any objective or unconditional standard has disappeared in a morass of relativism and subjectivism. Tillich sums up the situation in words that refer to culture in general but apply just as much to its ethical aspect:

> Autonomy is able to live as long as it can draw from the religious tradition of the past, from the remnants of a lost theonomy. But more and more it loses this spiritual foundation. It becomes emptier, more formalistic, or more factual and is driven towards scepticism and cynicism, towards the loss of meaning and purpose. The history of autonomous cultures is the history of a continuous waste of spiritual substance. At the end of this process autonomy turns back to the lost theonomy with impotent longing, or it looks forward to a new theonomy.[16]

What does Tillich mean by this word 'theonomy'? It corresponds with his concern to push 'beyond supranaturalism and naturalism' to a third position, in which the transcendent is nothing external or 'out there' but is encountered in, with and under the *Thou* of all finite relationships as their ultimate depth and ground and meaning. In ethics this means accepting as the basis of moral judgements the actual concrete relationship in all its particularity, refusing to subordinate it to any universal norm or to treat it merely as a case, but yet, in the depth of that unique relationship, meeting and responding to the claims of the sacred, the holy and the absolutely unconditional. For the Christian it means recognizing as the ultimate ground of our being which is thus encountered, and as the basis of

[16] *The Protestant Era,* p. 53.

every relationship and every decision, the unconditional love of Jesus Christ, 'the man for others.' This is what it means for the Christian to 'have the mind of Christ,' [17] to let his actions be governed, as Jesus enjoined, simply and solely by the love with which 'I have loved you,' [18] or, in St. Paul's words, to 'let your bearing towards one another arise out of your life in Christ Jesus.' [19] Life in Christ Jesus, in the new being, in the Spirit, means having no absolutes but his love, being totally uncommitted in every other respect but totally committed in this. And this utter openness in love to the 'other' for his own sake is equally the only absolute for the non-Christian, as the parable of the Sheep and the Goats shows. He may not recognize Christ in the 'other' but in so far as he has responded to the claim of the unconditional in love he has responded to him—for he is the 'depth' of love. The Christian ethic is not relevant merely for the Christian, still less merely for the religious. The claim of the Christ may come to others, as indeed it often comes to the Christian, incognito: but since it is the claim of home, of the personal ground of our very being, it does not come as anything foreign. It is neither heteronomous nor autonomous but theonomous.

Love alone, because, as it were, it has a built-in moral compass, enabling it to 'home' intuitively upon the deepest need of the other, can allow itself to be directed completely by the situation. It alone can afford to be utterly open to the situation, or rather to the person in the situation, uniquely and for his own sake, without losing its direction or unconditionality. It is able to embrace an ethic of radical responsiveness, meeting every situation on its own merits, with no prescriptive laws. In Tillich's words, 'Love alone can transform itself according to the concrete demands of every individual and social situation without losing its eternity and dignity and unconditional validity.' [20] For this reason it is the only ethic which offers a point of constancy in a world of flux and yet remains absolutely free for, and free over, the changing situation. It is prepared to see every moment as a fresh creation from God's hand demanding its own and perhaps wholly unprecedented response. And that is why Tillich goes on, 'Ethics in a changing world must be understood as the ethics of the *kairos*'—of the God-given moment, mediating the meeting with the eternal in the temporal. 'Love, realizing itself from *kairos* to *kairos,* creates an ethics which is beyond the alternative of absolute and relative ethics' [21]—or what he elsewhere calls supranaturalism and naturalism.

[17] I Cor. 2:16.
[18] John 13:34.
[19] Phil. 2:5 (NEB).
[20] *The Protestant Era,* p. 173.
[21] *Op. cit.,* p. 173.

NOTHING PRESCRIBED—EXCEPT LOVE

This position, foreshadowed thirty years ago in Emil Brunner's great book, *The Divine Imperative,*[22] is given its most consistent statement I know in an article by Professor Joseph Fletcher in the *Harvard Divinity Bulletin,*[23] entitled 'The New Look in Christian Ethics.' 'Christian ethics,' he says, 'is not a scheme of codified conduct. It is a purposive effort to relate love to a world of relativities through a casuistry obedient to love.' [24] It is a radical 'ethic of the situation,' with nothing prescribed—except love.

It is, like classical casuistry, case-focussed and concrete, concerned to bring Christian imperatives into practical operation. But unlike classical casuistry, this neo-casuistry repudiates the attempt to anticipate or prescribe real-life decisions in their existential particularity. There is after all no discredit to the old-fashioned casuists, nor to the Talmudists, in the old saying that they continually made rules for the breaking of rules. They were turning and twisting in their own trap to serve love as well as law, but unfortuantely the only result is a never ending tangle of legalism in any ethics which attempts to correct code law with loving kindness. The reverse of these roles is vitally necessary. It is love which is the constitutive principle—and law, at most, is only the regulative one, if it is even that.[25]

The classic illustration of this insistence in the teaching of Jesus, that the sabbath is made for man and not man for the sabbath, that compassion for *persons* overrides all law, is his shocking approbation of David's action in placing human need (even his own) above all regulations however sacrosanct:

Have you not read what David did, when he was hungry, and those who were with him: how he entered the house of God and ate the bread of the presence, which it was not lawful for him to eat nor for those who were with him, but only for the priests? [26]

It is, of course, a highly dangerous ethic and the representatives of supranaturalistic legalism will, like the Pharisees,[27] always fear it. Yet I believe it is the only ethic for 'man come of age.' To resist it in the name of religious sanctions will not stop it: it will only ensure that the form it takes will be anti-Christian. For as Fletcher says,

Torah law in this era is suffering a second eclipse, even more radical than when Jesus and St. Paul first attacked

[22] 1932, Eng. tr. 1937.
[23] October 1959, pp. 7-18.
[24] *Op. cit.*, p. 10.
[25] *Op. cit.*, p. 17.
[26] Matt. 12:3 f. See the whole context Matt. 12:1-14.
[27] Matt. 12:14.

it—because the cultural-context, the milieu controls, are more appropriate today to such an eclipse than in the apostolic and patristic period.[28]

The fact that the old land-marks are disappearing is not something simply to be deplored. If we have the courage, it is something to be welcomed—as a challenge to Christian ethics to shake itself loose from the supports of supranaturalistic legalism on which it has been content to rest too much. And this is bound to be disturbing. To quote Fletcher again,

> This contemporary shape of Christian ethics was accurately described and labelled as 'existential' or 'situational' by Pope Pius XII in an allocution on April 18, 1952.[29]
>
> He denounced it, of course, pointing out that such a non-prescriptive ethic might be used to justify a Catholic leaving the Roman Church if it seemed to bring him closer to God, or to defend the practice of birth control just because personality could be enhanced thereby! Four years later, February 2, 1956, the Supreme Sacred Congregation of the Holy Office called it 'the New Morality' and banned it from all academies and seminaries, trying to counteract its influence among Catholic moralists.[30]

But of course Protestant and Anglican reaction is equally suspicious when it becomes clear what judgements it may lead to or what rules and sanctions it appears to jeopardize.

For nothing can of itself always be labelled as 'wrong.' One cannot, for instance, start from the position 'sex relations before marriage' or 'divorce' are wrong or sinful in themselves. They may be in 99 cases or even 100 cases out of 100, but they are not intrinsically so, for the only intrinsic evil is lack of love. Continence and indissolubility may be the guiding norms of love's response; they may, and should, be hedged about by the laws and conventions of society, for these are the dykes of love in a wayward and loveless world. But, morally speaking, they must be defended, as Fletcher puts it, 'situationally, not prescriptively'—in other words, in terms of the fact that persons matter, and the deepest welfare of these particular persons in this particular situation matters, more than anything else in the world. Love's casuistry must cut deeper and must be more searching, more demanding, than anything required by the law, precisely because it goes to the heart of the individual personal situation. But we are bound in the end to say with Professor Fletcher: 'If the emotional and spiritual welfare of both parents and children in a *particular* family can be served best by a divorce, wrong and cheapjack as divorce commonly is, then love requires it.' [31]

---

[28] *Op. cit.*, p. 15.
[29] *Acta Apostolicae Sedis,* (1952), xliv, pp. 413-19.
[30] *Op. cit.*, p. 16.
[31] *Op. cit.*, p. 15.

This will once again be greeted as license to laxity and to the broadest possible living. But love's gate is strict and narrow and its requirements infinitely deeper and more penetrating. To the young man asking in his relations with a girl, 'Why shouldn't I?,' it is relatively easy to say 'Because it's wrong' or 'Because it's a sin'—and then to condemn him when he, or his whole generation, takes no notice. It makes much greater demands to ask, and to answer, the question 'Do you love her?' or '*How much* do you love her?,' and then to help him to accept *for himself* the decision that, if he doesn't, or doesn't very deeply, then his action is immoral, or, if he does, then he will respect her far too much to use her or take liberties with her. Chastity is the expression of charity—of caring, enough. And this is the criterion for every form of behaviour, inside marriage or out of it, in sexual ethics or in any other field. For *nothing else* makes a thing right or wrong.[32]

This 'new morality' is, of course, none other than the old morality, just as the new commandment is the old, yet ever fresh, commandment of love.[33] It is what St. Augustine dared to say with his *dilige et quod vis fac,*[34] which, as Fletcher rightly insists,[35] should be translated not 'love and do what you please,' but 'love and *then* what you will, do.' *What* 'love's casuistry' requires makes, of course, the most searching demands both upon the depth and integrity of one's concern for the other—whether it is really the utterly unselfregarding *agape* of Christ—and upon the calculation of what is truly the most loving thing in this situation for every person involved. Such an ethic cannot but rely, in deep humility, upon guiding rules, upon the cumulative experience of one's own and other people's obedience. It is this bank of experience which gives us our working rules of 'right' and 'wrong,' and without them we could not but flounder. And it is these, constantly re-examined, which, in order to protect personality, have to be built into our codes of law, paradoxically, 'without respect of persons.' But love is the end of law[36] precisely because it *does* respect persons—the unique, individual person—unconditionally. 'The absoluteness of love is its power to go into the concrete situation, to discover what is demanded by the predicament of the concrete to which it turns.' [37] Whatever the pointers of the law to the demands of love, there can for the Christian be no 'packaged' moral judgements—for per-

[32] See the essay on 'The Virtue of Chastity' in J. Macmurray, *Reason and Emotion* (1935), and H. A. Williams, 'Theology and Self-Awareness,' in *Soundings*, pp. 81 f.

[33] I John 2:7 f.

[34] *Ep. Joan,* vii. 5.

[35] *Op. cit.,* p. 10.

[36] Rom. 13:10.

[37] Tillich, *Systematic Theology,* vol. i, p. 169.

sons are more important even than 'standards.'

Seeking to retain his integrity in these judgements will inevitably bring the Christian into conflict with the guardians of the established morality, whether ecclesiastical or secular. He may often find himself more in sympathy with those whose standards are different from his own and yet whose rebellion deep down is motivated by the same protest on behalf of the priority of persons and personal relationships over any heteronomy, even of the supranatural. For many of these may be feeling their way through to a new theonomy to which the Christian must say 'yes,' even if the *theos* is not 'the God and Father of our Lord Jesus Christ.' D. H. Lawrence, for instance, comes very near to what we have been saying when in speaking of that which is at the heart and depth of a person, he writes:

> And then—when you find your own manhood—your womanhood . . .—then you know it is not your own, to do as you like with. You don't have it of your own will. It comes from—from the middle—from the God. Beyond me, at the middle, is the God.[38]

'God is the "beyond" in the midst of our life': Bonhoeffer's words[39] are almost identical. 'The God,' no doubt, is very different;[40] but at least there is a way through here to the transcendent in a world without religion. And on that 'way' the Christian must be found if he is to say anything to those who walk along it. In morals, as in everything else, 'the secret of our exit' from the morasses of relativism is not, I believe, a 'recall to religion,' a reassertion of the sanctions of the supranatural. It is to take our place alongside those who are deep in the search for meaning *etsi deus non daretur,* even if God is not 'there.' It is to join those on the Emmaus road who have no religion left,[41] and there, in, with and under the meeting of man with man and the breaking of our common bread, to encounter the unconditional as the Christ of our lives.

---

[38] *The Plumed Serpent* (1926), Phoenix edition, p. 70.

[39] *Op. cit.,* p. 124.

[40] For a balanced Christian assessment of Lawrence's understanding of God, cf. M. Jarrett-Kerr, *D. H. Lawrence and Human Existence* (2nd ed., 1961), pp. 129-57.

[41] Luke 24:21.

Part Three

The Practice of Christian Decision-Making

I. Human Sexuality: A Relational Approach

If the popular press, theological journals, and pulpit oratory are to be trusted, we are in the midst of a "revolution in morals." Fascination with this topic has been so prevalent that it has served not only as program material for club meetings but also as a significant campaign issue in the 1964 presidential election. The sheer contemporaneity of the proclamation suggests that the phenomenon is unique to this generation; but even superficial research will reveal that each age, in comparison with the previous one, has regarded itself as morally revolutionary.[1] One need point only to the fluctuations in hemlines and decolletage and the accompanying comments in newspapers and magazines as evidence of the fact.

There are important changes in sexual mores (which is what "revolution in morals" popularly means) occurring; of that there is little doubt. It was customary, in rural churches only a few years ago, for mothers unabashedly to nurse their babies during the morning service. This may never have been acceptable behavior in urban churches, but it is still practiced, with decreasing frequency, in some rural settings. Although this is in some rigorous sense an instance of public nudity, it is not what is usually meant when one speaks of a "revolution in morals." Instead, when reference is made to less restraint and more freedom in sexual mores, it is particularly the college and university student and collectively the younger generation that is popularly in mind.[2]

The Kinsey reports, *Playboy*, and more recently clinical experiments by physicians have tended to show, on the other hand, that the collegiate population does not have exclusive (or maybe even predominant) claim to the "revolution in morals" and, further, that "revolution" may well be an extravagant description of the recasting in mores that is actually going on. Still, there is a "new moral-

[1] Cf., for example, Frederick Lewis Allen, *Only Yesterday* (New York: Harper, 1931), Chap. 5; "The Morals Revolution on the U. S. Campus," *Newsweek*, April 6, 1964, pp. 52-59; and "The Debilitating Revolt," *Christianity Today*, July 21, 1967, pp. 24-25.

[2] This assumption, however, is not without challenge. Dr. Graham B. Blaine, Jr., a psychiatrist at the Harvard and Radcliffe Health Service, states that "many of the religious leaders who deal directly with college students are reluctant to make an emotional or spiritual appeal for adherence to the old standards for fear of being ridiculed by the more science-oriented, materialistic students who take nothing on faith but instead demand a logical reason for every rule. Actually, these students are a vocal minority that does not deserve the attention given it by those who should be more concerned with the substantial portion of the student population that is looking to religion for support for its own high standards." (*New York Times*, January 16, 1964.)

ity," and it deserves attention and critical understanding.

A few years ago one might have generated a heated exchange if pacifism were mentioned. More recently the civil rights movement was sure-fire discussion fodder. Nowadays, both of these together with almost everything else run a poor second to the new morality. *New* conjures in the popular mind a notion of reversing previous mores and substituting something entirely different for them; *morality* is seldom thought to refer to anything but sex. This, of course, is neither novel nor distinctly contemporary. In 1930 Wilbur Urban Marshall observed that "the terms moral and immoral, morality and immorality, are often identified exclusively with the special field of morals connected with the life of the sexes." [3] Our day is not exceptional in this respect: the new morality is generally understood to be a set of sexual mores very different from those of the previous generation. And since the behavioral patterns of parents are, *ipso facto,* thought to be more conservative than those of children, the style of the children's sexual conduct is in turn "liberal," and hence "revolutionary." The new morality is popularly synonymous with today's sexual revolution.

It needs to be said that this conclusion is mistaken and that the new morality, in its present mold, is technically no more preoccupied with sex than it is with politics or economics. The current new morality is simply a way of doing ethics that is competing with certain other ways. What is strange about it is not the public fascination with its application to sex but the popular attention now being given to problems of ethical method (which are usually relegated to dry and dull philosophical and theological disquisitions). It is because the new morality has come to this (perhaps questionable) distinction—and because its discussants alternately damn and exalt it, enthusiastically embrace and just as heartily repudiate it—that it is worth the effort to identify the ways in which this is a child of *our* time, and describe it more carefully and precisely than dormitory bull sessions or Sunday school classes are likely to do. When we have done this, we will illustrate the problems and possibilities in terms of a Christian understanding of human sexuality.

The phrase "new morality" often stands for any moral posture so long as it is supposed to be novel. Some who advocate it argue that there are no moral laws which bind conscience;

[3] Wilbur Urban Marshall, *Fundamentals of Ethics: An Introduction to Moral Philosophy* (New York: Henry Holt, 1930), p. 287. Two years earlier Durant Drake, then Professor of Philosophy at Vassar College, had published a book titled *The New Morality* (New York: Macmillan, 1928), in which he stated: "By 'the new morality' I mean the morality which, basing itself solidly upon observation of the *results* of conduct, consciously aims to secure the maximum of attainable happiness for mankind. . . . The dominant moral codes throughout human history have been based upon authority. . . . At last, however, a scientific, experimental attitude toward morals is becoming diffused among the more educated classes . . ." (p. v).

others say that whatever value a moral law possesses is only a relative matter and that no value or law is inexpendable and absolute. Historically the phrase gained popular currency after it was used by an agency of the Roman Catholic Church. As early as 1950 Pope Pius XII complained of certain philosophical "fictions," including existentialism, which were threatening the Church's *magisterium*.[4] Two years later, in a broadcast on "The Christian Conscience," he condemned the view that conscience cannot be commanded by laws and principles.[5]

What Pius XII found objectionable in existentialist or "nonprescriptive" ethics was its rejection of a standard of conduct which can and must be applied *ubique, semper et ab omnibus*—everywhere, always, and by all people in the same way. Instead of ideas or rules or laws to prescribe appropriate behavior, the advocates of *la morale de situation* rely, he argued, upon the existential moment for indication of fitting conduct. Roman Catholicism, of course, has not been alone among Christian bodies in opposition to this way of doing ethics. Certain Protestant groups (indeed most Protestant groups, in their formal statements) are at one with Rome in affirming that there are some acts which are enjoined everywhere, always, and for everybody alike; and other acts, correspondingly, which are prohibited. The current debate over situation ethics and the new morality rages most passionately, in fact, among Protestants.

THE "OLD" MORALITY

In the United States, the thrust of the new morality, especially as it has to do with sexual ethics, is not directed toward the absolutist ethics of Roman Catholicism so much as it is toward the absolutist ethics of a particular brand of Protestant piety, variously identified but probably best known as "fundamentalism."

Among the several articulate proponents of this point of view is the conservative theological periodical, *Christianity Today*. In an article titled "Love Without Law," the former book review editor of *Christianity Today*, James Daane, undertook to describe what he frankly called the "old morality." [6] It is first of all, according to Daane, an approach to decision-making which regards the biblical moral laws and ethical principles as "definitive of the nature and demands of *agape*." Biblical injunction is definitive, that is, binding and authoritative, because it does not in any way depend upon man's developed moral sense; in-

[4] *Acta Apostolicae Sedis,* 42 (1950), 561-77.
[5] *Ibid.*, pp. 44 (1952), 413-19.
[6] James Daane, "Love Without Law," *Christianity Today,* Oct. 8, 1965, pp. 32-34. Copyright 1965 by *Christianity Today;* selections reprinted by permission.

stead, it is a gift which places certain demands upon those who accept it. These laws and principles are not "the provisional accumulation of man's moral wisdom acquired through experience, devoid of the quality of a moral imperative, and subject to modification of further moral wisdom acquired through additional moral experience." They are simply *given* as "revelatory definitions of the nature of *agape*," and they are either accepted or rejected but never modified or changed. As definitive of the nature of God's love, biblical laws and principles have an absolute and eternal force: "They prescribe some actions as always right, and some as never right and always wrong."

It is Daane's contention that God, in his Word to man, has not been indistinct and ambiguous. Instead, he has addressed us in such a precise and unequivocal way as to specify "in advance that some things are always wrong and some always right" and therefore, because of the clarity with which God has spoken, we do have presented to us "a list of things that are always morally wrong" (and, one would infer, also a list of things that are always morally right). With direct reference to the new morality, Daane further insists that "God has not left the nature and demands of *agape* so wholly undefined that no person can know what is right or wrong until, in the changing situations of life, he himself decides."

This approach commends itself chiefly for two reasons. The first is that it takes its cue from God's speech to the world; it is the character of God's Word which is his self-revelation that establishes the authority of the biblical witness. It is its own authentication, and one cannot therefore appeal to other criteria (nor need he do so) for verification. If one is to be God's man in the world, he must submit himself to God's intentions and ordinances for the conduct of life; or, to put it into Paul's language, he must live in the world by God's power.

The second reason is that "an ethic in which love is not authoritatively defined but is left to be defined by each person within the situations of life is only one step from tyranny." A thoroughgoing doctrine of original sin, together with a realistic understanding of the ways in which it insinuates itself into even our most altruistic motives, underlies this second reason. Daane recognizes that when an individual is left wholly to himself, without any moral or legal restraint, his self-love has the capacity (some would say, inevitably) to turn him into a tyrant and his neighbor into his victim. The moral logic, according to Daane, is self-evident: One should be exceedingly cautious about relinquishing this kind of decisional responsibility to this kind of potentially dangerous self, because "after one surrenders the binding character . . . of *agape* in moral law and ethical principles, one is left to himself to define the nature and demands of *agape*." [7] This is a task for which man, as we know him, is not only ill-fitted but quite incapable.

In sum, the old morality represents a way of doing ethics which can be called absolutist. There are some acts which, because they are specifically *commanded* by Bible or church, are always and for everybody alike right; and there are other acts which, because they are specifically *forbidden* by Bible or church, are always and for everybody alike wrong. The unchanging element in God's revelation of himself is not some intention or purpose which he communicates but the *content* of a particular command. There are no exceptions to these rules. They are eternally valid and unchanged despite their participation in the relativity and flux of history. As Carl F. H. Henry, the editor of *Christianity Today,* states it:

> The Christian ethic is a specially revealed morality—not merely a religious ethics. It gains its reality in and through supernatural disclosure. Biblical behavior is not based solely on human values and ideals. Its fountainhead is the will of God. It is received in the Divine confrontation of man by commandments, statutes and laws, and face-to-face in the incarnation.[8]

We indicated in the introductory chapter of this book the major criticisms of the old morality: (1) legalistic systems easily deteriorate into codes or laws which are taken to be more important than persons; (2) no set of rules is ever complete or sensitive enough to cover the full range of human decision-making; and (3) legalistic systems call for abdication of human decision-making. To these criticisms we can now elaborate two more, one theological and the other historical.

The identification of God's will with some given command of fixed content makes God's living presence superfluous. If God has spoken so completely and definitively—whether through Bible, or church, or whatever—that he cannot (or will not) alter what men understand him to have said, then he might as well be dead! There is no further need for him to speak; indeed, the possibility of future or present speech is removed in direct proportion to the measure in which utter finality and absoluteness is at-

[7] *Ibid.* This sentiment was forcefully dramatized in Robert Bolt's play, *A Man for All Seasons* (Vintage Books; New York: Random House, 1960). The following conversation takes place between Sir Thomas More and William Roper:

Roper – So now you'd give the Devil benefit of law!

More – Yes. What would you do? Cut a great road through the law to get after the Devil?

Roper – I'd cut down every law in England to do that!

More – Oh? And when the last law was down, and the Devil turned round on you—where would you hide, Roper, the laws all being flat? This country's planted thick with laws from coast to coast—man's laws, not God's—and if you cut them down—and you're just the man to do it—d'you really think you could stand upright in the winds that would blow then? Yes, I'd give the Devil benefit of law, for my own safety's sake. (Pp. 37-38.)

[8] Carl F. H. Henry, *Christian Personal Ethics* (Grand Rapids: Eerdmans, 1957), p. 193.

tributed to past utterances. The question of whether man has heard and understood God's speech aright is yet another matter, but an impressive one for students of the Bible and theology. This is the reason that Protestant fundamentalist scholasticism, and not the "death of God" theologians, has borne most eloquent testimony to Christianity *post mortem Dei.*

The other criticism of the absolutism of the old morality is that it denies the unique and special character of different historical moments by insisting that all times be regarded and treated as morally alike. There is no provision made for responding differently to different situations, persons, needs. The radical egalitarianism of time and place and person undermines temporal, spatial, and personal uniqueness. *Ubique, semper et ab omnibus* makes personal existence virtually mechanical.

THE DIVINE COMMAND: MONOGAMY

Now what all this comes to in the matter of human sexuality is fairly straightforward and uncomplicated. The institution of monogamous marriage is taken to be the biblical expression of the nature and demands of *agape* in the celebration of human sexuality. As Georgia Harkness puts it:

> Monogamy can be viewed, on the one hand, from the standpoint of sociology and psychology. It is an aspect of human culture about which a scientific judgment can be made as to the most advantageous form of domestic relationship. On the other hand, it must be viewed by the Christian in a religious perspective, to discern what is the will of God as that will is revealed by Jesus. *From both standpoints, monogamy is the only right form of marital relation.*[9]

Carl F. H. Henry interprets the creation narratives, together with the Decalogue and the teachings of Jesus, as enforcing monogamous marriage as the divine intention for man: "The creation of a single male and from his side a female companion as his helpmeet, is to provide a permanent spiritual and moral basis for monogamous marriage. As in origin, so in life, the man and his wife are to coalesce into the unity of one being." [10]

The logic of this view concludes that since monogamous marriage was instituted by God as the appropriate context for the celebration of human sexuality, intercourse within marriage is all right and, conversely, intercourse outside marriage is all wrong. Marriage, it should be noted, is throughout assumed and understood to be a legally sanctioned institution.

On this view, one is presented with

[9] Georgia Harkness, *Christian Ethics* (Nashville: Abingdon Press, 1957), p. 129. Italics added.
[10] *Christian Personal Ethics,* p. 273.

a clear-cut distinction and an unequivocal demand: Marry, or abstain from sexual intercourse. Miss Harkness again states the point succinctly:

> To the matter of sex intercourse outside of marriage a very positive No must be spoken, not only because it is condemned repeatedly in the Bible and throughout the Christian tradition, but for the reason . . . [that] the sex relation between a man and a woman was instituted by God for marriage and for marriage alone; any other use of it is a sacrilege.[11]

This is reminiscent of the instruction many of us received as adolescents, and it would not be surprising if this also parallels what you were taught. Our considered response to it is critical not only for what it says but also for what it fails to say.

There are, for example, no biblical prescriptions for monogamy in marriage; nor is there a corresponding prohibition against polygamy.[12] The most explicit biblical statements simply commend marriage as a normal adult state. They do not, as did the Council of Trent, attach special merit to either marriage or celibacy or exalt one above the other.[13]

It is truer to both the biblical witness and cultural anthropology to conclude that God has commanded neither monogamy nor polygamy nor polyandry nor any other sexual arrangement as the normative marital state. Polygamy flourished, not because the Lord commanded it, but in a time when the position of women was frankly inferior to that of men. If there are now theological and moral sanctions against polygamy and in favor of monogamy, they are best understood and formulated in terms of an equality between men and women which is more faithful to a Christian understanding of creation and reconciliation. The danger, of course, is that by making the Western cultural institution of monogamous marriage normative, couples may indeed experience the outwardness of sexual intercourse but be deprived of its inwardness, which depends not upon legal sanctions but upon a condition of the heart or will.

What the old morality fails to say has mainly to do, we think, with questions of personal exploitation, of whether the spirit of adultery or lust may sometimes find expression within marriage, or whether any institutional

[11] *Christian Ethics,* p. 135.

[12] The most complete treatment by a Protestant scholar of what the biblical materials actually say about sex and love is found in William Graham Cole, *Sex and Love in the Bible* (New York: Association Press, 1959).

[13] In Session XXIV of the Council, Canon 10, dated November 11, 1563, the following is recorded: "If anyone says that the married state is to be preferred to the state of virginity or celibacy, and that it is not better and happier to remain in virginity or celibacy than to be united in matrimony (cf. Matt. 19:11 f.; I Cor. 7:25 f.; 28:40), let him be anathema." Henricus Denzinger, *Enchiridion Symbolorum: Definitionum et Declarationum de Rebus Fidei et Morum* (32 ed. rev.; Frieburg im Breisgau: Verlag Herder KG, 1963), p. 417.

structure can guarantee a truly agapeic relationship between persons. Questions like these are entirely and consistently subordinated in the old morality; the prior question is always whether an externally correct environment has been provided. Social or cultural convention is thus incomparably more important than persons; or, to put it differently, the institution of marriage has become determinant of the meaning of human sexuality. But this is a reversal of the biblical priorities: sex is neither based on nor in the service of marriage; it is just the other way round. We need to understand that marriage, like the sabbath, was made for man—not vice versa.

THE "NEW" MORALITY

Juxtaposed to the old morality and competing with it as a way of making Christian decisions is situation ethics or the new morality. Both these terms, like others that characterize broad movements, are so inclusive that they embrace the positions of many modern moralists, and when this happens the phrase loses its edge and force. We will therefore examine (chiefly) the work of Bishop John A. T. Robinson, who initially popularized the phrase, "the new morality." [14]

The difference between the old and the new moralities, as Robinson views them, is mainly the difference of their respective starting points. They constitute, he says, "two approaches to certain perennial polarities in Christian ethics, which are not antithetical but complementary." [15] In contrast to the old morality, the new morality does not supply an ethical code or a set of legal norms. One of the important reasons for this is that proponents of the new morality do not regard the biblical commandments, in their specific content, to be unambiguously and transparently clear expressions of God's intention. There is, in other words, an explicit principle of interpretation at stake in Bible study: God does not speak to us in propositions; we approach the biblical text with certain definite questions which themselves help to shape the answers we receive.[16]

As a consequence, the new morality offers only Jesus' proclamation of the kingdom of God, together with corollary considerations which derive from that primal fact. If the old morality begins with the "deductive, the transcendent, and the authoritative,"

[14] See John A. T. Robinson, *Honest to God* (Philadelphia: Westminster Press, 1963), esp. chap. 6.

[15] John A. T. Robinson, *Christian Morals Today* (Philadelphia: Westminster Press, 1964), p. 10.

[16] Rudolf Bultmann has greatly influenced this approach to biblical study. Especially instructive is his essay, "Is Exegesis Without Presuppositions Possible?" in Schubert M. Ogden (ed.), *Existence and Faith: Shorter Writings of Rudolf Bultmann* (Meridian Books; Cleveland: World, 1960), pp. 289-96. The philosophical theology of Paul Tillich, and especially his "method of correlation," has similarly shaped this general procedure. Cf. esp. Paul Tillich, *Systematic Theology,* I (Chicago: The University of Chicago Press, 1951), 66-8.

it is characteristic of the new morality to start with "persons rather than principles, from experienced relationships rather than revealed commandments." [17]

As Robinson understands the New Testament, Jesus calls men "to subject everything in their lives to the overriding, unconditional claim of God's utterly gracious yet utterly demanding rule of righteous love." [18]

There are, then, no specified (nor perhaps even preferred) modes of conduct which are universally applicable—*ubique, semper et ab omnibus.* Jesus asks only that his disciples be open in every circumstance, without predispositon or prejudgment, to the unconditional and absolute demand of love. Thus, instead of prescriptive codes, the most that can be claimed for this way of doing ethics is that one is offered a "direction, a cast, a style of life" which should correspond to the expression of *agape* in whatever time or place. It is openness to the unconditional obligation to love that is the constant element in the new morality. To show love is the one among the many different and distinctive responses that may be called for by diverse contexts and dissimilar situations. "Jesus never resolves these choices for us," says Robinson; "he is content with the knowledge that if we have the heart of the matter in us, if our eye is single, then love will find the way, its own particular way in every individual situation." [19]

This approach to Christian ethics commends itself for several reasons. Through its insistence that the obligation to embody God's love is the only unconditional claim placed upon us, it tends to avoid the idolatry that develops when laws are given absolute sanctity and require unequivocal obedience. It also permits each situation to speak its own need with basic integrity by maintaining an openness and freedom toward each new situation. One might argue further that this way of approaching the decision-making process is more congenial to the doctrine of justification by grace alone. Amid the relativities of historical situations, what is "good" and "right" cannot be antecedently prescribed. New occasions do teach new duties (though there is another sense in which the Christian's duty is always the same, i.e., to show love), and one is thereby thrust away from confidence in codes and pride in good works to reliance upon God's grace for justification of behavior. This means, of course, that appeal cannot be made to any legal sanction for authentication of choices and conduct. In freedom and knowledge of the situational problematics, one is entrusted with the possibility for act-

[17] *Christian Morals Today,* pp. 34-35.

[18] *Ibid.,* p. 12. The parallel statement in *Honest to God* is: "Life in Christ Jesus, in the new being, in the Spirit, means having no absolutes but his love, being totally uncommitted in every other respect but totally committed in this" (p. 114).

[19] Robinson, *Honest to God,* p. 112.

ing response-ably to incarnate God's *agape* in this place, with these people, in this situation.

If the problem with the old morality is its denial of the possibility for genuinely human responsibility and moral agency by constructing a legalistic ethics, the difficulties with the new morality are correspondent at the other end of the spectrum. Bishop Robinson concludes his little book, *Christian Morals Today,* with the observation that this approach to Christian ethics is the only one that truly "makes sense to our scientifically trained world" because it moves "from experience to authority, through the immanent to the transcendent." Then he adds:

> The Christian in treading this way with the rest of his contemporaries is not abandoning the authoritative or the transcendent. Rather, he has the double trust, born of his doctrines of Creation and of the Incarnation, that, since man is made in the image of God, a true humanism *must* lead through to the divine, and, since in the man Christ Jesus he has *the* image of the invisible God, he knows what a genuinely human existence is.[20]

The relative novelty of this approach lies not so much in its content[21] as in the extravagance of its claims and the radicality of its individualism and subjectivism. We can reiterate here the basic criticisms of all formal methods in Christian ethics: (1) the essentially corporate character of the Christian life is not adequately recognized and acknowledged; (2) the bewildering complexity of alternatives in most morally significant situations is overwhelming without the support and direction afforded by principles which are more specific than the general command to love; (3) the abandonment of law and principle tends inevitably to antinomianism and capriciousness in the decision-making process.

Beyond these, it deserves noting that the informing epistemological assumption of situation ethics is very similar to the doctrine of the inner light. All men, presumably, have the private capacity to discern the will of God in an unmediated way. No positive law or externalized, objectified revelation (not even biblical precepts) exercises comparable influence in the doing of ethics. There are no universally valid moral maxims. The result of this epistemological error corresponds in important ways to the first criticism we stated: the privatizing of revelation tends to moral anarchy.

Finally, the legalist treats history as though it were a string of beads, each

[20] *Christian Morals Today,* p. 46.

[21] Emil Brunner was eloquently arguing for an "occasionalist" ethics in the 1930's and stated in his classic treatise on Christian ethics: "God's Command does not vary in *intention,* but it varies in *content,* according to the conditions with which it deals. . . . Love . . . is free from all this predefinition, for it means being free for God. . . . Love is 'occasionalist.' She does not know the Good beforehand. . . ." *The Divine Imperative,* trans. Olive Wyon (Philadelphia: Westminster Press, 1947), p. 134.

bead having a definite place and function on the string and held together by the unifying thread. The advocate of the new morality, on the other hand, insists so much upon the uniqueness of historical moments that discontinuity (or absurdity) and not purpose characterizes human existence. He has only himself to fall back on, to give continuity to his existence. Bereft of more cogent and dependable resources, he tends to caprice and expediency in decision-making.

Robinson insists that, in emphasizing a different starting point, he does not wish to deny the validity of the old morality but to establish a complementary polarity. In practice, however, the approach of the old morality is discredited as obsolete and unbiblical, and Robinson loses the delicate balance which, at the outset, he says he seeks. In the end, existential and theological extemporism best characterizes this way of doing ethics.

THE DIVINE COMMAND: LOVE

The way in which the new morality addresses itself to the matter of human sexuality is both simple and complicated. At the level of general problems of ethics, such as human sexuality, the new morality is regularly committed to the proposition that there is only one obligation, and that is to show love. This is plain enough since, as Joseph Fletcher says, "situationism is a *method,* not a substantive ethic." [22] But when a specific problem is at issue, the effort to decide what is the loving thing to do in a world of relativities can become very complex indeed. We will not attempt analysis of an isolated instance in which human sexuality is at issue morally. Instead, and following Robinson, we will examine briefly the relationship between sex and marriage.

Robinson begins, correctly, by asserting that intercourse, just because it occurs within marriage, is not necessarily right. He acknowledges that the old morality establishes the "marriage line" as decisive, but maintains that "the decisive thing in the moral judgment is not the line itself, but the presence or absence of love at the deepest level." He grants that sexual congress outside marriage "is bound to be the expression of less than an unreserved sharing and commitment of one person to another," if for no other reason than that *full* responsibility of each for the other cannot be enjoined, i.e., there is no direct obligation for both bed and board. Nevertheless, the *risk* of premarital coition is worth running since "in the sight of God . . . persons matter

[22] Joseph Fletcher, *Situation Ethics: The New Morality* (Philadelphia: Westminster Press, 1966), p. 34.

more, imponderably more, than any principles." [23] It is owing to this primacy of the personal that Robinson rejects the dictation of moral choices by objective moral norms.

Marriage, then, may provide a useful and even desirable context for sexual intercourse; but neither it nor any other institutional or legal framework guarantees the legitimate and authentic expression of human sexuality. "Young people today," says Robinson, ". . . want a basis for morality that makes sense in terms of personal relationships. They want *honesty* in sex, as in everything else . . . having physical relationships that *truthfully express* the degree of personal commitment that is there underneath." [24]

Sexual intercourse, when it occurs in situations which conform to and incorporate these criteria, is presumably all right. Similarly, however, no moral criteria which insist upon merely the externals (e.g., legal marriage) are valid. What is critical and morally authenticating is whether love for the other person as person is intended and expressed in sexual behavior, i.e., whether the other person is exploited or served.

When this aspect of Robinson's new morality is understood, he becomes something less than a threat to the tranquility and security of monogamous marriage. In fact, Paul Ramsey has called this series of qualifying criteria Robinson's "bourgeois conception of 'the marriage line.' " [25] which is to say that Robinson's boundary for sex outside marriage is fairly conventional after all! [26]

The most revolutionary idea that can be claimed for Robinson is that he rejects the formal necessity of legal marriage as the validating criterion of human coition. But if this is revolutionary, it certainly is not new. A Christian view of marriage is never preoccupied with ceremonies and conventions. These things may exhibit the marriage publicly; but a man and a woman marry each other. They are married when they pledge themselves to each other and consent to be responsible for each other. The common law recognizes marriage of this kind; indeed, this is also the position of the church.[27] It is the couple themselves who consent together, witness the same, and pledge their fidelity to each other in wedlock; the priest, together with others present, simply witnesses.[28]

In a real sense, then, this means

[23] *Christian Morals Today,* p. 42.

[24] *Ibid.,* p. 45.

[25] Paul Ramsey, *Deeds and Rules in Christian Ethics* (New York: Scribner's, 1967), p. 41.

[26] A similar observation can be made about Joseph Fletcher's qualifications: "If people do not believe it is wrong to have sex relations outside marriage, it isn't, *unless they hurt themselves, their partners, or others."—Situation Ethics,* p. 140. Italics added.

[27] According to the *New Catholic Encyclopedia,* ed. Staff of The Catholic University of America, IX (1967), 293: Common law marriage is a "true marriage with the same rights and duties, the same laws governing separation and divorce, as in a formal marriage."

[28] Cf. *The Catholic Encyclopedia,* ed. Charles G. Herbermann *et al.,* IX (1910), 700.

that the couple is married before they make their public vows; and similarly (if Robinson's qualifications are met), they are married before sexual consummation. On the other hand, it would be erroneous to understand this covenant as a radically privatized event, since it would then be neither covenant nor event. In somewhat the same way that one does not know what he is thinking until he says it, the articulation and publication of the marital intention in a public act both ratifies and makes believable the promise-making between these two. This prompts Ramsey correctly to observe that Robinson is, then, really not talking about *premarital* sexual intercourse since,

> Beginning by asking about the limits upon pre-marital sexual relations between engaged couples, it turns out that marriage covers the whole ground of the action sought to be justified; and there remain only legal, or practical, considerations about whether public acknowledgment can or should be secured for the fact that a mutual acknowledgment of marital responsibility and the marriage relation itself has been assumed by the partners.[29]

Despite the qualifications by Robinson and other advocates of the new morality, the mistaken impact of this teaching on the popular understanding is nevertheless that it does not matter what you do so long as you show love. It is all right to lie if you do it lovingly. It is all right to fornicate if you really love each other. It is all right to steal and to kill if these are loving deeds. Because love cannot be confined to any pattern of behavior, because "time makes ancient good uncouth," it is assumed that there are no rules, no principles, no laws that represent or embody or communicate what love requires.

INCARNATION AND HUMAN SEXUALITY

Commenting on the essay by a group of Friends called, "Towards a Quaker View of Sex," Tom F. Driver observed:

> The Friends group was right to see that in our present cultural situation it is no longer sufficient to reiterate traditional standards. . . . For the problem is that the traditional standards are no longer felt by the society to be derived from a genuine authority. . . . [But] when traditional religious authority is not felt by a man to be binding upon his conscience, then it is not possible to preach to him the Law and the Gospel at the same time. Well aware of the disasters created by preaching the Law only, ministers tend to say more about the Gospel. But in the long run this has the effect of undermining the Law itself, at least in so far as the Law must be

[29] *Deeds and Rules in Christian Ethics,* p. 41.

spelled out as a specific guide to conduct.[30]

The place to begin is with the understanding that a Christian view of any subject—race, politics, or sex—is founded upon certain distinctive and characteristic presuppositions. These are of the same logically unprovable stuff as the presuppositions of any other discipline, of natural science or philosophy, for example. Natural science begins with the supposition that man is a product of nature and that he can therefore be considered and understood by reference to natural categories. Philosophy begins similarly with a basepoint, namely, that reality is sufficiently rational as to be understandable and that the human mind is adequate to the task of understanding. Christian faith also has its own initial act of faith, and this is that God is revealed in the person of Jesus Christ as the real and authentic center and source and goal of all of life. In the language of the prologue to John's Gospel, the creative principle of the universe, the *logos,* was made flesh and dwelt among us as one full of grace and truth. (John 1:14-18.)

Biblical scholars generally agree that the word "flesh" (*sarx*) is no accident in John's Gospel. Because it is intentionally employed, it signifies Christianity as the most materialistic of the world's religions (Communism to the contrary notwithstanding!). Christian faith alone among the world religions declares that its God incarnates and enfleshes himself in the conditions of human existence. John's prologue, and the use of the word "flesh," also connotes the first and most profound element in a Christian understanding of human sexuality. It means for the Christian that the whole of human nature, including the body, became the vehicle of God's self-revelation. With that role a certain dignity is imposed upon the body that gives it a very high place in considerations of human morality, and particularly human sexuality. John, far from being the spiritualizer of early Christianity, is the ardent advocate of a thoroughly incarnational theology.

Implied in this approach is the rejection of two closely allied (and erroneous) positions. The first of these is the notion of a body-spirit dualism which holds that the body is evil and ugly because it is matter, corporeality, flesh and blood. For advocates of this point of view, the goal of life is to be free from the bondage to the flesh, to escape the limitations of the body by gaining access to a nonmaterial, ultrarational mind which is crystalline in its pure reason. If matter is used at all, it is as a means to its own denial. Asceticism, the second of these positions, is just such a program and maintains that sex (because it par-

[30] Tom F. Driver, "On Taking Sex Seriously." Quoted by permission from *Christianity and Crisis,* Oct. 14, 1963, p. 176.

ticipates in and expresses itself through the body) must somehow be spiritualized (that is, disembodied and excarnated) if it is to be acceptable. Most of us do not find either of these options attractive or viable. A variety of reasons could be cited to account for this attitude, but we will concentrate on an explication of a Christian view of the place and function of sex in human experience and existence.

Because of the Incarnation the Christian who approaches the study of sex will understand the sexual organs to be parts of the whole human nature through which the Christian revelation came. This means that these organs will be treated with respect and honor and that impurity as such cannot and does not attach itself to them. Only the mis-use and ab-use of these parts of the body brings dishonor to them. This is a viable interpretation since, again, the starting point is with God and his activity in the world. Of course, God is frequently the last reality we venture to talk about when we commonly speak of sex; but to call him the Creator and Sustainer and Perfector of human existence is to recognize his purpose somehow in the entire process. We thus affirm not only that we come from God but also that we are intended to function in the fulfillment of his purpose for us. Whatever assists in the realization of his purpose for us is by definition good; and if sex can render such assistance then it can be claimed that sex is a positive good.

As the biologic occasion which makes possible the meeting of sperm and ovum, human coition is in principle bound up with procreation—and, in our society, with family life. It deserves more careful notice than it often receives that children of such a union as this are pro-created. By this prefix "pro" we mean to guard the fact that when man creates he does so on God's behalf. We also commonly use words with a "re" prefix to describe the process by which the race is perpetuated. And here again, with a word like re-produce, the prefix points backward to suggest the reoccurrence of a previous happening. There is, then, a profound sense in which the Christian maintains that man is not the creator *de novo* of his children.

But then there is another sense in which the children would not be there unless man played his part; so whether in or out of wedlock, procreation in this biologic sense takes place. Nevertheless, to act on behalf of someone is a different matter; and to procreate, to reproduce, in any authentic sense is Christianly to be aware that coitus itself is a potential means of grace—that is, human sexual intercourse can (and should) be an instrument of the intentionality for which pregnancy and birth are the practical results. Even procreation, then, one of the basic drives of human species life, is not its own rationale or explanation. Parenthood is not defined by reference to simple fecundity; and to be a mother or father signifies more than mere breeding. In a similar way, the body and sexual organs can assume a kind of sacramental character in the measure to which objective function serves and expresses an intentional relationship.

If one begins, not with an affirmation of human sexuality but with the proclamation of a sovereign, creative, active, loving Father (a word which itself has definite sexual connotations!), then one affirms at the beginning some value priorities in the unity and harmony of the created order. Sex, as every other part of reality, is not accidental but deliberately a part of the purpose and plan of God.

As a work of the Creator, sex is understood by the Christian to be good. Indeed, according to the Bible, it is in a sense sacred. Man is a psychophysical unity, and this unity is neither to be sundered nor its constituents discriminated against. The person, who is this unity, thinks it good that he is *who* he is and that he is *what* he is. There is, in neither Old nor New Testament, the notion that the body is bad and the mind is good.

In the Old Testament sex is regarded as something good, and sexual relations are considered a normal state for adult life. In the New Testament Jesus is reported to have blessed marriage and implied that it was ordained by God.[31] Throughout the Bible human sexual relationships are also employed to illustrate God's attitude toward his creation. Sometimes these examples affirm (e.g., Hosea and Gomer), and sometimes they deny (e.g., David and Bathsheeba) the relationship God desires and intends. In any case, the biblical attitude toward sex knows nothing of the separation of values maintained by sexual asceticism, and it does not grant that continence is a meritorious and better way of managing one's sexual life; neither does it, as we pointed out earlier, establish a simple identification of the person with his natural biological functions.

It is no secret, nevertheless, that sexual asceticism was advocated and practiced in the early church, and particularly among some of the sects (e.g., the Gnostics). One explanation for this change is the influence that was exerted upon early Christians by Graeco-Roman and oriental mystery religions. These religions, whatever their differences, were generally agreed that the flesh was evil and that the less one had to do with it the better. Not only were fleshly lusts aroused by sexual impulses, but also other persons (i.e., other souls captive to evil bodies) were reproduced.

Another reason for this ascetic perspective, and one more directly related to the faith and life of the early

[31] Cf. Cole, *Sex and Love in the Bible,* chaps. 1-4.

church, is put forward by Cole: "It is true that celibacy and virginity were regarded as possible vocations for the Christian, especially in times of persecution and in view of the imminence of the coming of the kingdom. But the motivation was apocalyptic and not dualistic." [32] The frequent rejoinder to this interpretation cites I Corinthians 7:1-16 and argues that Paul implicitly sanctioned a body-spirit dualism by exalting celibacy over marriage. Candor obliges one, at such an impasse as this, simply to admit the conflict and choose among the alternatives. There is no doubt that Paul's view was at variance with the traditional Jewish attitude. Genesis 2:18 states that "It is not good that the man should be alone," and a number of cultic practices (e.g., Levirate marriage) indicate the extent to which marriage was regarded as a solemn obligation. While Paul encouraged celibacy, he nevertheless did not insist upon it; neither did he regard marriage as a sin. It was, in his view, simply a concession to the weakness of passion. This is the heart of the matter; it is also occasion for regret that Paul was so preoccupied with the sexual aspects of marriage that he failed to appreciate the other dimensions of this relationship except in those infrequent instances when he spoke of marriage as paradigmatic of the relationship between Christ and the church.

On the other hand, the second letter to the Thessalonians certainly supports the notion that apocalypticism was responsible for several unconventional attitudes and practices in the early church. In this epistle, Paul chides those Christians who had become lazy adventists, who refused to work because they expected the imminent coming of the kingdom. Apart from their mistaken theology, these people were also an economic burden to the community. Of special interest in this context, however, is the observation that these idle apocalypticists had forsaken ordinary work in order to prepare and watch for the Day of the Lord. II Thessalonians and I Corinthians have, then, this much in common: both letters address themselves to an attitude of otherworldliness. Whereas I Corinthians seems to reflect Paul's expectation of the imminent Parousia, II Thessalonians indicates his pragmatic bent. In the final analysis, the evidence is not conclusive either way; but the greater weight of it seems to support Cole's judgment.

The tendency toward celibacy and virginity as a more meritorious way nevertheless continued. In the third century the great Alexandrian scholar and teacher, Origen, was so thoroughly convinced that women were the daughters of Satan that he castrated himself in an effort to avoid their temptations. By the Middle Ages St. Jerome regarded the only good accomplished by marriage to be that

[32] *Ibid.*, p. 228.

it would produce children who would themselves be celibate! And with Thomas' systematization of Catholic theology it was settled that for Roman Christians celibacy is a more commendable and praiseworthy way. As recently as 1954 Pope Pius XII, in his encyclical *Sacra Virginitas,* reaffirmed the traditional Roman position:

> It is not to be thought that such pleasure [i.e., venereal pleasure], when it arises from lawful marriage, is reprehensible in itself. . . . Nevertheless, it must be equally admitted that as a consequence of the fall of Adam the lower faculties of human nature are no longer obedient to right reason, and may involve man in dishonourable actions. . . . Virginity is preferable to marriage . . . above all else because it has a higher aim: that is to say, it is a very efficacious means for devoting oneself wholly to the service of God, while the heart of married persons will always remain more or less "divided." [33]

The sixteenth-century reformers repudiated the medieval double standard of sex ethics and argued not only that marriage is of equal worth with celibacy but that the doctrine of justification by grace alone denies the redemptive worth of acts (like celibacy) which are committed with a calculated view toward accumulating merit. Martin Luther, in fact, is reported to have exalted marriage over celibacy with the argument that virginity is an evasion of social responsibility! [34] The Protestant Reformers were on the right track in terms of both reaffirming man's basic psycho-physical unity and regaining the biblical view that sex is good and marriage a normal state.

COITION, REPRODUCTION, AND COMMUNITY

The Bible teaches that sex has a twofold function in human life. Sexuality is obviously a means for procreation; but it also (though perhaps less obviously to the casual observer) is a way to express love and establish community between persons. Love, as we described it earlier, is not a *thing* but an attitude, a disposition, an inclination to affection and goodwill and charity. When one understands this, and relates it to purposive activity, it makes sense to say that in God's action (and thus normatively for authentic human behavior) love precedes creation. Indeed, certain passages in the Bible (e.g., John 3:16) make the point explicitly: it is because God loves that he relates to the world at all. And it is because God loves in a certain way that he relates to the world as Creator, Sustainer, Judge, and Savior. The Bible, then, tells us not only who created the world but why he did it! The world is created out of God's love and desire for fel-

[33] *Acta Apostolicae Sedis,* 46 (1954), 161-92.
[34] E. Clinton Gardner, *Biblical Faith and Social Ethics* (New York: Harper, 1960), p. 216.

lowship; and it is this intention for the world that becomes the criterion by which the world is judged.

Although most of us do not take the time or trouble to develop the theological and philosophical arguments which support such a view, we do commonly acknowledge its validity in terms of our sexual behavior. In popular practice, people fall in love and then have babies. We do not normally have babies and then fall in love because, if in nothing more than an inchoate apprehension of value, we regard the baby as an expression of an antecedent affection and relationship between the parents. When this occurs within the socially acceptable context of our culture (i.e., monogamous marriage), all concerned are glad to esteem the baby as the fruit of this love.

The current "morals revolution," however, generally has little to do with thoughts like these. There are notable exceptions, but for the most part the recasting of sexual mores appears to focus on venereal pleasure, for which the entangling alliances of pregnancy and parenthood are inconveniences to be avoided.[35]

From our theological perspective, however, there is a profound sense in which fellowship and reproduction are inseparable in sexual intercourse. Each depends upon the other for meaning and purpose and value. But this "no" to distinguishing recreation from procreation is a relative "no" since there are undeniably those specific instances in coition in which one or the other role is given priority. To give priority is not, of course, to violate the connection; it is only what it claims to be, namely, the *temporary* suspension of one obligation when, for adequate reasons, both obligations cannot be accomplished simultaneously. There may, then, be those occasions when couples appropriately and deliberately make love without any *immediate* intention of making babies, just as there are, conversely, those occasions (however rare) when making babies is *immediately* decided by ovulation rather than a spontaneous, deep, and irrepressible personal need.[36] Each penultimate intention,

[35] One exception to this generalization is certainly that league of young women (more prominent in Britain than the United States) who want to be free to be mothers without the burdens of wifery. Looking toward the year 2000, Margaret Mead has suggested that the present style of family organization may appropriately give way to a "new style with an emphasis on very small families and a high toleration of childless marriage or a more encompassing social style in which parenthood would be limited to a smaller number of families whose principal function would be child rearing; the rest of the population would be free to function—for the first time in history—as individuals." Cf. Margaret Mead, "The Life Cycle and Its Variations: The Division of Roles," *Daedalus,* Summer, 1967, pp. 871-75.

[36] Paul Ramsey has argued that both the unitive and procreative purposes of sexual intercourse are "in some sense 'objective' and effectual" and that "the crucial question is not the order of preference to be assigned the procreative and the unitive purposes of sex and marriage. It is rather the question whether sexual intercourse as an act of love should ever be separated from sexual intercourse as an act of procreation." Ramsey's answer is that these purposes are both primary and equal, that is, the unitive purpose is the primary *meaning* of coition and the procreative purpose is the primary *end* of it. It therefore "makes sense to say that there are responsibilities violated, to which

however, is coimplicate of an ultimacy which embraces both. In other words, fellowship and reproduction are dialectically united as the bipolar purposes of a single activity. In those situations in which intercourse is primarily intended as a means to and enhancement of community between persons, the *willingness* to incarnate that loving relationship in another human life witnesses (at least in part) to its responsible and authentic character; and, similarly, in those instances in which intercourse is primarily intended as a means to procreating new beings like ourselves, the antecedent loving relationship testifies (at least in part) to its responsible and authentic character. Thereby we avoid two errors: the naturalism of doctrinaire Catholicism which assigns inordinate importance to reproduction,[37] and the sentimental subjectivism of popular Protestantism which tends to exalt personal freedom and venereal pleasure at the expense of public responsibility and sexual integrity.[38] A hedonistic desire for childlessness and freedom from parental responsibility would be just as morally objectionable as aborting a pregnancy for mere convenience' sake. There may be good reasons for childless marriages and for terminating pregnancies (as we believe there are), but they must be grounded in personalism rather than naturalism.

If we can begin to overcome the cultural, religious, and philosophic traditions which identify the human person in terms of some kind of substantive speculation, we may be able to understand that we do not *have* sexuality in the sense that it is a possession to be

men and women should be sensitive, when they engage in sexual relations with the intention of putting entirely asunder the act of sexual love from the procreative meaning of this very same act." The difficulty with Ramsey's argument is not his insistence that the unitive and procreative purposes should be allied; this is altogether appropriate. What is problematical is his requirement that they be simultaneously primary. While it may be arguable ontologically, it is a dubious psychological claim unless the *meaning* of coition be somehow understood as coterminous with orgasm, that is, the moment in which the meaning and the end of intercourse are given simultaneous expression. This is, however, a naturalistic logic at base and fails to take account, among other things, of the ways in which pre- and post-coitive sexual activity communicates meaning in ways which do not depend upon a not-yet reproduction for authentication. Further, one's personal inability to maintain dual purposes simultaneously primary may be less an expression of irresponsibility than of creatureliness. Cf. Paul Ramsey, "A Christian Approach to the Question of Sexual Relations Outside Marriage," *The Journal of Religion,* April, 1965, esp. pp. 103-7.

[37] On July 29, 1968, Pope Paul VI reaffirmed the traditional Roman Catholic position in his encyclical "Humanae Vitae" when he explicitly forbade direct intervention for the control of conception and enjoined "the transmission of life" as the regulative principle for human sexual intercourse.

[38] One thinks of the now voguish phrase, "between consenting adults." In context, whether in *Playboy* or theological journals, this expression signifies the legitimacy of any kind of behavior so long as it is done privately between consenting persons of adult age. Of course, murder and rape (among other kinds of behavior) would be excluded from a list of acts appropriate under this head, perhaps chiefly because of the absence of consent! But consent, as doctors and lawyers know, is an elusive category. One aphorism has it that the difference between rape and seduction is patience. But, more importantly, there may be serious questions addressed to consenting adults and having to do with those obligations which pertain to the structures and institutions which make freedom possible. The context which permits adults to consent may itself be jeopardized by what it is they are consenting to!

kept or discarded. We *are* sexuality; and sexuality is at least one of the ways in which we relate to each other at depth levels of personal experience. Sexuality is a communication between us. It is an engendering and establishing of community between us. And while it certainly employs those organs of the body commonly called "reproductive organs," they function to perform a service *for us:* what we *do* with them expresses who we *are* in relationship. It is from this perspective that marriage, rape, adultery, and fornication begin to take on human meaning: what these words signify is a certain quality (or lack of it) of relationship. What they mean is not adequate if limited to an objectification of sexual behavior under certain stereotypical or merely legal tags.

This way of talking obliges us, of course, to stop speaking of human sexuality as though it were simply a bodily metabolism or natural phenomenon. Plants and animals exercise their sexuality this way, and they reproduce other plants and animals. But there may be at least this much difference between the sexual activity of persons and that of plants and animals: persons reproduce other unique persons. Moreover, we do not normally attach special significance to the mating that goes on between plants and animals (except, in some instances, to control genetic strains); neither do we commonly regard the young seedling or animal nursling as evidence of some sort of special relationship between its parents! Sexuality as a merely natural phenomenon "throws off," as it were, an objective evidence of itself. But sexuality as personal responsibility eventuates in enfleshment of the personal and responsible act of coition —whether by public proclamation of the marriage bond or by the public evidence of a baby. In both cases, the sexual union of men and women is never a matter of simple reproduction; instead it is always an evidence, when it is genuine, of an antecedent relationship between them which expresses itself (i.e., incarnates itself) in this mode.

What all this comes to in terms of offering guidance for decision-making in sexual relationships is perhaps suggested already. In principle, the approach we have taken is less precise than the old morality but more specific than the new morality in suggesting definite types of sexual conduct which are appropriate for Christians. It is a kind of principled contextualism which simultaneously acknowledges the obligation of Christian ethics to be situationally relevant and affirms that there are some moral maxims derived from Christian faith and experience which are so commonly applicable as to be, for most practical purposes, compelling to conscience.

Christian norms for sex and marriage are thus formulated as expressions of love. As a basically attitudinal ethics, this approach has sometimes been taken to mean that anything goes so long as two people love each other.

We have argued, however, that love is a multi-dimensional relationship and that, contrary to some proponents of the new morality, its embracing character cannot be limited to what goes on between two people. There is no thought here of invading privacy; what is at stake is recognition that the sensitive person will be aware that God, self, beloved, and society are all coimplicates in any given loving action. We have argued that no merely institutional circumstance (e.g., legal marriage) can authenticate sexual congress, that intercourse is fitting conduct for Christians only within love and evil apart from love. We do not accept, however, the frequently appended argument that the full range of loving responsibility is exhausted (or at least largely accounted for) when two people decide that they love each other. An obligation to God and society still impinges upon the lovers; and their private conduct must somehow reflect their awareness of and sense of accountability toward these others as well as themselves. This means that, pragmatically in our culture and civilization, monogamous marriage now offers the best promise of achieving these positive results. There are increasing numbers of couples who are willing to confirm that this is so and that they find most happiness, contentment, excitement, and satisfaction in just this kind of sexual arrangement.

We may have come to a fairly conventional position after all, but for reasons that are somewhat unconventional. The Bible recognizes that sexual intercourse can take several forms, ranging along a spectrum from defective and false unions (e.g., rape and prostitution) to appropriate and true relationships (i.e., unions which are grounded in regard for and interest in the well-being of each for the other in the presence of God) . Only love is adequate to describe this latter form. Human sexuality thus functions normatively as the expressive instrument of an antecedent loving relationship; materially, sex expresses and signifies a certain quality of relationship between persons. This is so whether the primary intention of any given instance of coition is re-creation or pro-creation. In both cases, coition is an activity which, in its own unique and special way, seeks the well-being of an other. As this kind of activity, sexuality is a human resource which can honor our Lord's commandment to serve, and not exploit, the neighbor. Human sexuality finds its truest and most authentic expression in a relationship between persons which is rooted in mutual respect and affection; and it is upon this criterion that the moral quality of coition depends. True and authentic sexual unions are based upon a love which is responsible to God, the beloved, the larger social neighbor-hood, and self. Marriage, then, springs from love, but it is fidelity that gives stability. The phrase from Genesis is "and they became one flesh," and it is an apt summary: sexuality is the human possibility of belonging to each other. As such it both derives from and is a paradigm of the Christian's communion with God.

II. The Human Shape of Life

According to reliable estimates, about one million abortions are performed annually in the United States. Of this number, approximately 99 percent are estimated to be illegal. About 1,000 deaths annually are attributed to illegally performed abortions and, beyond these fatalities, thousands of other women suffer irreparable mutilations. The Kinsey Institute has estimated that 20-25 percent of the white female population in the United States submits to illegal abortion sometime during their lives; the figure is comparable among upper-class Negro women but significantly higher among lower-class Negro women. In Britain it is of interest that the highest instance of induced abortion occurs in urban, better-educated, higher-income groups in which contraception is most generally practiced.

It is generally well known that infanticide was employed as a population control method among the Greeks and Romans; and, more recently, Japan has resorted to feticide for similar purposes. Abortifacients, of course, have long been known and used, but these, like surgical abortion, have been strictly limited by law in their application—not as a protection to nascent life but, since death frequently resulted to the consumer, as a protection to existing adult life. In addition, therefore, to philosophical and theological questions which might be asked in their own right, we are confronted by the weight of historical and cultural experience which seems squarely to oppose (though for different reasons than those currently argued) the practice of abortion. The urgency of the matter in our own time cannot be gainsaid. It is commonly acknowledged that there is demand for abortion in circumstances exceeding the present permissions of existing law and that many people are increasingly willing to meet that demand. If the personal and social consequences of illicit practice are undesirable, we must undertake a more contemporary understanding of the problem in order either to affirm the values now expressed in law and cultural convention or to revise those values in ways which are more consistent with present understanding.

Christian social ethicists in the twentieth century, largely in reaction against pietistic moralism, have given considerable attention to problems which develop out of political, economic, and social life, but have tended generally to neglect those problems which are related to the ethics of medical care—to birth control, artificial insemination, sterilization, abortion, organ transplantation, euthanasia, and the like.

Protestant moralists, in particular, have been so preoccupied with other concerns that medical ethics has been almost singularly neglected.[1] In rather sharp contrast to the paucity of work done by Protestants, there is a long and distinguished list of studies in medical ethics by Roman Catholic theologians.[2]

Probably as striking as any other facet of medico-moral reflection is the fact that physicians and surgeons are publishing increasing numbers of articles on these problems in professional journals; and occasionally their ideas find expression in small books.[3] These works are augmented by medico-legal studies, written by lawyers, which discuss the issues in terms of both positive law and Christian morals.[4]

[1] There are certain notable exceptions to this generalization, foremost among them being Joseph Fletcher, *Morals and Medicine* (Princeton: Princeton University Press, 1954) and Willard L. Sperry, *The Ethical Basis of Medical Practice* (New York: P. B. Hoeber, 1950). Other Protestant theologians will be cited later in this chapter, but their observations on these subjects have occurred within larger contexts than medical ethics *per se.* A helpful study of religious dimensions in the vocation of medicine is James T. Stephens and Edward LeRoy Long, Jr., *The Christian as a Doctor* (New York: Association Press, 1960). See also Daniel T. Jenkins (ed.), *The Doctor's Profession* (London: SCM Press, 1949).

[2] The following are fairly representative of modern Roman Catholic teachings: Gerald Kelly, *Medico-Moral Problems* (St. Louis: The Catholic Hospital Association of the United States and Canada, 1958); Charles J. McFadden, *Medical Ethics* (5th ed. rev.; Philadelphia: F. A. Davis, 1961); E. F. Healy, *Medical Ethics* (Chicago: Loyola University Press, 1956); Thomas J. O'Donnell, *Morals in Medicine* (2nd ed. rev.; Glen Rock, N.J.: Newman Press, 1959); Jules Paquin, *Morale et Médecin* (3rd ed. rev.; Montréal: L'Imprimerie du Messager, 1960); and a pamphlet prepared as a code of medical ethics for Roman Catholic hospitals, *Ethical and Religious Directives for Catholic Hospitals* (2nd ed. rev.; St. Louis: The Catholic Hospital Association of the United States and Canada, 1957).

[3] Three such volumes are Henry K. Beecher, *Experimentation in Man* (Springfield: Charles C. Thomas, 1959); Francis D. Moore, *Give and Take: The Development of Tissue Transplantation* (Philadelphia: W. B. Saunders, 1954); and Irving Ladimer and Roger W. Newman (eds.) *Clinical Investigation in Medicine: Legal, Ethical and Moral Aspects* (Boston: Boston University Law-Medicine Research Institute, 1963). Other books describing some of the frontiers of modern medicine are being written by informed laymen, e.g., Fred Warshofsky, *The Rebuilt Man: The Story of Spare-Parts Surgery* (New York: Thomas Y. Crowell, 1965). Attempts by physicians to develop systematic statements on the ethics of medical care are quite uncommon, but one such instance is John Marshall, *The Ethics of Medical Practice* (London: Darton, Longman & Todd, 1960).

[4] Among these works, three are prominent: Glanville Williams, *The Sanctity of Life and the Criminal Law* (New York: Knopf, 1957); and two books by Normal St. John-Stevas, *Life, Death and the Law* (Bloomington: Indiana University Press, 1961) and *The Right to Life* (New York: Holt, Rinehart & Winston, 1963).

This chapter is an exercise in the application of Christian moral principles to one of these problematic areas: abortion. Medical issues most frequently emerge from actual clinical situations. We will deal, therefore, with a single case study in an attempt to work through the decision-making process in the tension between theological affirmations and existential alternatives.[5]

THE SITUATION

Mrs. Roberts is thirty-three years of age. Her husband is currently unemployed, and the family lives in what might be called marginal poverty. There are six living children, ranging in age from eighteen months to thirteen years. One child is afflicted with a congenital defect, and his life-expectancy is limited to eight to nine years. All of Mrs. Roberts' previous pregnancies have been complicated by postpartum hemorrhages and severe anemia. The last four pregnancies required caesarean section.

Mrs. Roberts is currently in the first trimester of her seventh pregnancy which, owing to her physical condition and the family's poverty, was unintended by either herself or Mr. Roberts. In the second week of pregnancy, Mrs. Roberts was exposed to Rubella (infectious German measles), and she subsequently contracted the disease. Her physician pointed out the dangers, explaining that there is a 50-50 medical risk that Rubella infection contracted in the first month of pregnancy will eventuate in either loss of the child through dangerous miscarriage or that the child will be born with one or more defects (mental retardation, blindness, heart defect, deafness, disease of the bone, or blood abnormality). He also advised her that there is additional risk that the child might be born with a combination of defects, that a total of five such defects have been detected in a single affected child. The physician recommended induced therapeutic abortion on the grounds that it is required for the health of the mother and/or to avoid the birth of a deformed fetus.

Mr. Roberts concurred with the physician's recommendation. He agreed that the medical risk in itself was too great and added that considerations for the care and preservation of the present family clinched the case for abortion.

There are already a number of factors confronting the decision-maker, in this instance Mrs. Roberts, which have not explicitly raised any theological questions: considerations of health, economics, family, and the like can be dealt with in terms of their own internalized values. But we are

[5] Names and other identifying information have been altered to protect persons. Otherwise, the case is factual.

especially concerned with a Christian ethical approach to the problem of abortion and therefore need to make theologically explicit what is otherwise only implied in the acceptance of these responsibilities.

THE BASIC ISSUE

Unless it can be claimed that man's personal freedom signifies, at least in part, his control over his existence between the terminals of birth and death, his freedom *for* self-transcendence and *from* naturalistic determinism is illusory. Whether Christian ethics, then, has anything instructive to say to this situation and others like it will depend, first of all, upon whether a naturalistic-vitalistic or personalistic philosophy of life is adopted. A second question to be settled early, and one largely derivative from the first, is whether fetal life is *vita in potentia* or *vita in situ,* that is, whether fetal life is potential or actual human life. Here the question is specifically raised whether, on theological grounds, one affirms fetal life to be personal being.

The classical Roman Catholic distinction has been drawn between *fetus animatus* and *fetus inanimatus;* but, historically, at least three different theories of the origin of the soul and the time of its joining the body have been held in the Roman Church. (1) One view, represented by Tertullian, is called Traducianism or Generationism and holds that the soul (*anima*) comes into existence with the body in and through generation by the parents, as a biological transmission from the seed of Adam.[6] This teaching prepared the way for the doctrine of inherited original sin. (2) A second view, represented by Clement of Alexandria and called Creationism, held that the soul was immediately and directly created by God at the moment of conception.[7] (3) The third position, represented by Augustine, claimed that no soul was present in fetal life until the moment of "quickening," or the moment the mother detected the stirring of life. Augustine regarded both the Traducianist and Creationist arguments as theological traps to be avoided: the Scriptures offer no conclusive proof, he contended, that the soul is directly created by God and, moreover, the stain of original sin upon the soul should make one cautious about attributing immediate and direct creation of the soul to God. On the other hand, his controversy with the Pelagians made him wary of conclud-

[6] Tertullian, "De Anima," 27. J.-P. Migne (ed.), *Patrologiae Cursus Completus,* Series Latina (Parisii: Apud Garnier Fratres, 1879), II, p. 694.

[7] Clement of Alexandria, "Stromata," IV, 6. Alexander Roberts and James Donaldson (eds.), *The Ante-Nicene Fathers* (Grand Rapids: Eerdmans, 1951), II, pp. 413-16.

ing that the soul comes by natural generation.[8]

Thomas Aquinas, probably following Aristotle more than Christian speculators, held that the soul is not generated with conception but that it is created at the same time that it is "infused" into the body.[9] This "infusion" was thought to occur about the fortieth day in the male embryo and about the eightieth day in the female embryo.[10]

The official terminus of this long and sometimes bitter debate, according to Protestant and Roman Catholic authorities alike, was Pope Innocent XI.[11] In Proposition 34 of his 1679 decree, *Errores doctrinae moralix laxionis,* the Pope "condemned and prohibited" the view that it is licit to induce abortion before animation of the fetus in order to spare a pregnant girl death or shame.[12] More directly to the point, Proposition 35 states that it is erroneous doctrine that every fetus, so long as it is in the womb, probably lacks a rational soul but "begins to have the same at the time that it is born." [13] Consequently, Innocent concluded that it is prohibited to hold "that no homicide is committed in any abortion." [14]

At best, however, this decree only condemns certain views. It does not specifically promulgate positive doctrine. The result, then, as Fr. Gerald Kelly rightly says, is that "We [i.e., Roman Catholics] have no divine revelation on this point, nor any official pronouncement of the Church which clearly condemns or approves either theory." [15] Nevertheless, there can be no question that the teaching of the Church does favor, despite its indirect expression, the view that a human person is present from the moment of conception. On this ground, the notion of fetal life as *vita in potentia* is rejected in preference for *vita in situ.* Canon 747, for example, insists that "every aborted fetus shall be baptized without any condition, if it is known with certainty that it is alive, no matter at what period of gestation it is aborted; if there is doubt that it is alive, it shall be baptized conditionally. *The obligation imposed extends to even the smallest fetus, even though*

[8] Augustine, "De Anima et ejus Origine." Philip Schaff (ed.), *A Select Library of the Nicene and Post-Nicene Fathers of the Christian Church* (Grand Rapids: Eerdmans, 1956), V, pp. 315-71. See also Augustine, "Ad. Optat." 190, al. 157. J.-P. Migne (ed.), *Patrologiae Cursus Completus,* Series Latina (Parisii: Apud Garnier Fratres, 1902), XXXIII, p. 861.

[9] Thomas Aquinas, *Summa Theologica,* trans. Fathers of the English Dominican Province (New York: Bensiger Brothers, 1947), Part I, q. 118, arts. 1-3.

[10] *De animalibus,* IX, or *De generatione animalium.* Cited in Joseph Fletcher, *Morals and Medicine* (Boston: Beacon Press, 1954), p. 90.

[11] Cf. Fletcher, *Morals and Medicine,* p. 90; Healy, *Medical Ethics,* p. 191.

[12] Henricus Denzinger, *Enchiridion Symbolorum: Definitionum et Declarationum de Rebus Fidei et Morum* (32nd. ed. rev.; Freiburg im Breisgau: Verlag Herder KG, 1963), p. 461.

[13] *Ibid.*

[14] *Ibid.*

[15] *Medico-Moral Problems,* p. 66.

it be aborted immediately after conception." [16] Pope Pius XI, in his encyclical "Casti Connubii," further demonstrates the development and acceptance of this view in papal pronouncements. And the "Ethical and Religious Directives for Catholic Hospitals" explicitly illustrates the evolution of the Church's official position by stating unequivocally, in Directive 14: "Every unborn child must be regarded as a human person, with all the rights of a human person, from the moment of conception." [17]

If Mrs. Roberts were a Roman Catholic, her question would quickly be settled by affirming the life of the fetus to be human and inviolable. And she would have no alternative, unless the law of double-effect could be employed, than to go through with the pregnancy to its natural termination.[18]

That Mrs. Roberts is a Protestant tends to complicate the matter because, while there is no canon law or other specific directive from the Church to guide her decision-making, there is a system (however unsystematic and inchoate) of values that will impinge upon her choice. It is this "hidden agenda" that we must try to make explicit. In doing so, we will of course reject the notion that abortion is an inappropriate subject for theology or Christian ethics.[19] To argue otherwise would be to acknowledge that there are some areas and dimensions of human life which are outside the scope and interest of Christian ethics and, further, that our existence can be segmented into relatively autonomous spheres. Protestants cannot accept either of these positions. Instead, it is with the wholeness and unity of human life and God's intention for it that we are concerned; and no part of our history or experience may therefore properly be excluded from our interest. A responsible and intelligent and faithful decision by Mrs. Roberts will then have to take into consideration a broad cluster of obligations and goals.

[16] John A. Abbo and Jerome D. Hannan, *The Sacred Canons* (St. Louis: B. Herder, 1952), I, 752-53. Italics added.

[17] McFadden, *Medical Ethics,* p. 411.

[18] The principle of double-effect is a formula which "supposes that an action produces two effects. One of these effects is something good which may be legitimately intended; the other is an evil that may not be intended." Further, four specific conditions must be fulfilled in order to employ the principle: (1) the action, considered by itself and independently of its effects, must not be morally evil; (2) the evil effect must not be the means of producing the good effect; (3) the evil effect is sincerely not intended, but merely tolerated; (4) there must be a proportionate reason for performing the action, in spite of its evil consequences. The principal issue at stake concerns whether fetal life is disturbed or interrupted by direct or indirect means: the former means is never licit, whereas the latter means may be sometimes permitted. Cf. Kelly, *Medico-Moral Problems,* pp. 12-14.

[19] Reuel Howe represents another point of view. He speaks approvingly, for example, of the minister's answer in the following instance: "The couple . . . asked whether the Church was against medical abortion, and the minister informed them that Protestant churches generally do not take a stand against it and hold the opinion that since it is a medical problem, it should be decided by responsible medical authorities." See Reuel L. Howe, *The Miracle of Dialogue* (New York: Seabury Press, 1963), p. 54.

MEDICAL ASPECTS OF THE CASE

The basic values of the medical profession are affirmed in the Hippocratic Oath and in "codes of ethics" which have evolved from it. None of these codes, however, defines what is meant by the phrase "human life," and thus, although physicians are obligated to "abstain from all intentional wrongdoing and harm, especially from abusing the bodies of man or woman," they have no clear instruction for making particular decisions in the face of increasingly complicated medical problems. This is especially true in a case which gives indication of the need for therapeutic abortion since there are, presumably, two lives at stake: the mother's and the fetus'.

Since Mrs. Roberts was still in the first trimester (probably the third to fifth week, since the incubation period for Rubella is from one to three weeks), it is arguable that the embryo had neither quickened nor become viable. Physicians might contend that the embryo, as a completely dependent organism, was not yet human life. Further, the medical diagnosis is plain enough: the threat posed by contraction of Rubella is a 50-50 chance of dangerous miscarriage or the birth of a seriously deformed infant. Of course, there is a corresponding 50-50 chance that all will go well; but either way 50-50 is a very poor medical risk. Apart from religious commitments, the recommendation of the doctor appears to be in keeping with the professional standards of medical practice: the risk is too great to permit nature to run its course, and consideration for the health of the mother warrants medical intervention.

LEGAL ASPECTS OF THE CASE

Mrs. Roberts' legal status is not entirely clear from the description we have given of her case. Throughout the United States there are restrictive statutes which forbid abortion, but most of the states have expressly provided for exceptions to the general rule.[20] In several states, for example, "quickening" still has legal significance; and, as an instance of this contingency, the Mississippi statute enjoins no criminal liability to the physician if the fetus is destroyed before quickening. Exceptions of this sort are subtle and often difficult to prove, and therefore somewhat impractical. Further complicating is the fact that "there is no fixed time in the gestation at which medical evidence can assert that quickening invariably takes place." [21]

Most states do provide expressly

[20] Cf. Mary S. Calderone (ed.), *Abortion in the United States* (New York: Paul B. Hoeber, 1958). Despite its publication date and the constant changing of law, this book is still one of the most authoritative and dependable on this subject.

[21] Glanville Williams, *The Sanctity of Life and the Criminal Law*, p. 158.

that if abortion is necessary to preserve or save the life of the mother it is lawful. Professor Glanville Williams, a distinguished British legal authority, has stated that while there may be significant difference between "preserving" and "saving," the former is arguably wider in its implications and that "it seems likely that the American courts, like the English, will allow the surgeon to operate in order to prevent the curtailment of the mother's life; he need not expect her death during the period of gestation or in delivery." [22]

The judicial precedent for this view was expressed in the celebrated Bourne case in England. Mr. Bourne, an obstetrical surgeon at St. Mary's Hospital, performed an operation which terminated the pregnancy of a fourteen-year-old girl who had been raped. Although he had received the consent of the parents and consulted with other doctors, he was indicted under the Offences Against the Person Act of 1861, which strictly prohibited any act intended to procure a miscarriage. Mr. Bourne's defense argued that the operation was necessary, if not to preserve her life at least to safeguard her mental and physical health. Justice McNaughten ruled, in part, that

> The law is not that the doctor has got to wait until this unfortunate woman is in peril of immediate death and then at the last moment snatch her from the jaws of death. He is not only entitled, but it is his duty, to perform the operation with the view to saving her life. . . . As I have said, I think that those words [*viz.*, 'for the purpose of preserving the life of the mother'] ought to be construed in a reasonable sense, and, if the doctor is of opinion, on reasonable grounds and with adequate knowledge, that the probable consequence of the continuance of the pregnancy will be to make the woman a physical or mental wreck, the jury are quite entitled to take the view that the doctor, who, in those circumstances, and in that honest belief, operates, is operating for the purpose of preserving the life of the woman.[23]

There is currently a trend in both legislation and judicial decisions to liberalize the conditions under which abortions may lawfully be performed. The most significant of these has been put forward by the American Law Institute in its Model Penal Code and provides for legal abortion when indicated by (1) substantial risk that continuation of the pregnancy would gravely impair the physical or mental health of the mother, or (2) substantial risk that the child would be born with grave physical or mental defects, or (3) pregnancy resulting from legally established rape or incest.[24] Four states have adopted legislation which is patterned after this Code, and

[22] *Ibid.*, pp. 164-65.

[23] *R.* v. *Bourne* (1939), 1 K. B. 472 (1938) 3 All E. R. 615; 108 L. J. K. B. 471, C. C. A. Cited and quoted at length in Calderone, *Abortion in the United States*, pp. 193-95.

[24] *Model Penal Code,* Section 230.3 (2), (3) (Proposed Official Draft, 1962).

other states annually consider revising their statutes. Most state statutes, however, continue to require necessity to preserve the life of the mother in order to avoid criminal prosecution. But this is an ambiguous requirement and reflects the great need for clarification of present statutory language together with a more carefully specified network of circumstances under which abortion may be legally performed.

Since many doctors are still reluctant to operate except in the clearest of cases, it is plain that more precision, if not liberality, is needed. The British Parliament did move, in 1966, to legalize abortions where justified on medical advice.[25] And the American Medical Association's Committee on Human Reproduction recommended, in 1965, that the AMA endorse abortion under the conditions specified in the ALI Code and urge development of uniform state laws to deal with the matter.[26] According to an article in a religious periodical, movements in this direction would certainly reflect public approval in the United States, despite different religious commitments. The National Opinion Research Center of the University of Chicago was cited as showing that among Protestants, Catholics, and Jews alike a majority favored legalizing abortion when the health of the mother is in danger. There was, however, less general agreement with respect to those situations in which there was possibility of serious defect in the baby, or the family could not bear the economic burden of additional children, or the woman was unmarried and did not intend to marry the man involved.[27]

Although legislation is continually changing to meet current situations, the sum of the matter presently appears to be that if Mrs. Roberts were resident in a state where the statutory exceptions applied in her case, the abortion could be lawfully performed. In both England and the United States most of the law now generally requires the prosecution to prove that the operation was *not* necessary, and this would seem to favor the practitioner and patient by removing from them the burden of proof. The doctor need only state why he thought the operation necessary; thereafter the persuasive burden of proof to the contrary rests upon the prosecutor.[28]

MORAL ASPECTS OF THE CASE

We pointed out earlier in this chapter that the moral dimension of this problem and others like it hinges upon certain theological commitments and the way in which they are related to the conduct of human life. Foremost

[25] Associated Press, *Durham* (N.C.) *Morning Herald,* July 23, 1966.
[26] Associated Press, *Durham* (N.C.) *Morning Herald,* November 29, 1965.
[27] "Protestants, Catholics Share Legal Abortion Views," *Christian Adovcate,* May 5, 1966, pp. 21-22.
[28] Williams, *The Sanctity of Life and the Criminal Law,* pp. 180-83.

among these is one's understanding of what constitutes human life and whether embryonic or even fetal life can be said to be distinctively human. Roman Catholic moralists have systematically answered that question in the affirmative; Protestants have generally adopted the Catholic conclusion and its rationale but without seriously relating it to other tenets of Protestant theological reflection; and the orthodox Jewish position differs from both.

It is with a Protestant view that we are mainly concerned, and it will perhaps suffice, therefore, to indicate briefly the opinions held by Roman Catholicism and Judaism. Fr. Charles J. McFadden has succinctly stated the Roman Catholic belief:

> Direct and voluntary abortion is a moral offense of the gravest nature, since it is the deliberate destruction of an innocent life. . . . *Such an action is essentially murder*. . . . The unborn child is . . . essentially a human being with all the rights of any other human person. . . . The child is a human person whether it be in the womb of its mother, in the arms of its father, or playing in the street. The direct and deliberate destruction of that life is therefore sheer murder, regardless of the excuse which anyone might ever offer to justify it. In the light of the moral law, the simplicity of the matter leaves little more to be said. Briefly, every living human fetus, regardless of its stage of development, is a human person and any act which is a deliberate and direct destruction of that innocent life is therefore an act of murder. . . . Moral law unhesitatingly brands therapeutic abortion as murder in each and every case in which so-called medical "authorities" teach its indication. . . . Briefly, no matter how readily and certainly direct abortion could preserve a mother's life or health, it is not morally permissible. . . . It is nothing more or less than the deliberate murder of an innocent life in order to preserve thereby the life or health of the mother.[29]

The unstated but undeniable premise for this view is the supposition that human values and the law of nature are coterminous. Thus, basic moral maxims are formulated in terms of what is natural so that the correct conduct of life corresponds to nature.

[29] McFadden, *Medical Ethics,* pp. 132, 135. Papal sanction for such a view may be found in the encyclical, *Casti Connubii,* issued by Pius XI, December 31, 1930, where it is stated: "As to the 'medical and therapeutic indication' to which . . . we have made reference, Venerable Brethren, however much we may pity the mother whose health and even life is gravely imperiled in the performance of *the duty allotted to her by nature,* nevertheless what could ever be a sufficient reason for excusing in any way the direct murder of the innocent? This is precisely what we are dealing with here. Whether inflicted upon the mother or upon the child, *it is against the precept of God and the law of nature:* 'Thou shalt not kill.' The life of each is equally sacred, and no one has the power, not even the public authority, to destroy it. . . . Those who hold the reins of government should not forget that it is the duty of public authority by appropriate laws and sanctions to defend the lives of the innocent, and this all the more since those whose lives are endangered and assailed cannot defend themselves. Among whom we must mention in the first place infants hidden in the mother's womb. And if the public magistrates not only do not defend them, but by their laws and ordinances betray them to death at the hands of doctors and others, let them remember that God is the Judge and Avenger of innocent blood which cries from earth to Heaven." Italics added.

By definition, any thing or any act which interferes with or alters nature or the natural course of events is thus morally objectionable. This reasoning informs the entire range of Roman Catholic moral reflection, and specifically accounts for prohibition of all direct means to induce abortion, prevent conception, or bring about sterilization.[30]

We nonetheless regard this as an impossible maxim for any existence which operates above the level of mere cause and effect; and we claim, moreover, just such an existence for distinctively human life. G. E. Moore has defined those theories of ethics which "declare the sole good to consist in some one property of things, which exists in time; and which do so because they suppose that 'good' itself can be defined by reference to such a property as *naturalistic*." [31] Whatever occurs naturally becomes *ipso facto* good, and any direct intervention is correspondingly "un-natural" and therefore *ipso facto* bad. The logical absurdity of such a position would prohibit taking aspirin for headache, to say nothing of complicated surgical and medical procedures. Moore's reasoning is much to be preferred:

> If everything natural is equally good, then certainly Ethics, as it is ordinarily understood, disappears: for nothing is more certain, from an ethical point of view, than that some things are bad and others good; the object of Ethics is, indeed, in chief part, to give you general rules whereby you may avoid the one and secure the other. What, then, does "natural" mean, in this advice to live naturally, since it obviously cannot apply to everything that is natural? [32]

Joseph Fletcher has similarly analyzed the fallacy of naturalistic ethics:

> It [i.e., naturalistic ethics] suggests that whatever situation at any time exists is good; that whatever is, is good. This is meaningless in ethics, if not in every other forum. Going by nature is anti-moral when going by nature's ways is made the norm, for to follow such a norm is to forsake the imperative mood for the indicative mood, and to convert ethics from an enterprise in value-judgments into a descriptive discipline aimed at making human actions coincide with natural, i.e., given, conditions. When nature rules, conscience is made of none effect and reduced to the amoral level of natural cause and effect, that is, *non compos mentis*.[33]

A thoroughgoing naturalism both depersonalizes and dehumanizes the decision-making process because it subordinates man's capacity for self-determination and purpose to the erratic, sometimes capricious, and always impersonal forces of his natural environment.

---

[30] Cf. Kelly, *Medico-Moral Problems,* chap. 19.
[31] G. E. Moore, *Principia Ethica* (Cambridge: Cambridge University Press, 1960), p. 41.
[32] *Ibid.,* p. 42.
[33] Fletcher, *Morals and Medicine,* p. 223.

The most authoritative work in our problem area by an orthodox Jewish scholar is *Jewish Medical Ethics,* by Rabbi Dr. Immanuel Jakobovits.[34] In this work Rabbi Jakobovits demonstrates conclusively that, according to both the Talmud and subsequent rabbinic interpretation, "The point at which human life commences to be inviolable and of equal value to that of any adult person is . . . distinctly fixed at the moment when the greater part of the body—or, according to some versions, the head—has emerged from the birth canal." [35] He cites in addition the teaching of Maimonides on the question whether the unborn child can ever be regarded as an aggressor in pursuit of the mother's life. In sum, this teaching holds that the child may indeed be sometimes regarded, and if so that it is permissible to dismember the embryo in the womb "by drug or by hand, for it is like a pursuer [intent on] killing her." The exception to this general rule is again the condition that the child's head not be presented, for "if its head was already delivered, it may not be touched, for one does not set aside one life for [the sake of] another, and that is the natural course of the world." [36]

Although there are unquestionably certain naturalistic assumptions accompanying this view, they are tempered with a recognition of and appreciation for another, more personal and relational, dimension of human life. For this reason alone, this view offers better prospect than the naked naturalism of Roman Catholic moral theory for responsible human agency in making discreet moral judgments. But of this we will say more later.

Popular Protestant notions about the inviolability of human life—indeed, about what can appropriately be described as human life—appear, for the most part, to be a confused jumble of subjectivism and naturalism. That is, how one "feels" at a certain time about certain matters is coupled with a vague notion about "how things ought to be" to give most Protestants their moral direction. This is less true of some areas (for example, politics) than others; but it seems to be particularly true about the terminals of human existence—birth and death. A recent lecture by a distinguished professor emeritus of obstetrics, who was self-consciously and vigorously pro-Protestant, only confirmed the confusion when he maintained that induced abortion is "right" when it is practical, utilitarian, and numerically advisable in order to secure the greatest good for the greatest number.[37] While all these considerations are

[34] Immanuel Jakobovits, *Jewish Medical Ethics* (New York: Bloch, 1962).

[35] *Ibid.,* p. 184.

[36] *Ibid.*

[37] Nicholson Joseph Eastman, "Induced Abortion and Contraception: A Consideration of Ethical Philosophy in Obstretrics." The First Annual Merrimon Lecture, the University of North Carolina School of Medicine, March 16, 1966. *Obstetrical & Gynecological Survey,* 22:3, 1967.

more or less appropriate to a decision on abortion, they do not in this restricted cluster approximate the range and mix of values at stake. In this instance, then, the conclusions reached together with supporting argument are valid, if at all, only in a most limited and inconclusive fashion.

A broader and more comprehensive view of abortion, and specifically of Mrs. Roberts' problem, will recognize that there is more at stake than just a decision affecting a human embryo. Naturalistic ethics commits the error of offering a simplistic answer to what it takes to be an uncomplicated question. We can agree that one of the questions, or part of the large question, certainly has to do with one's relationship to that potential human life that has begun to take shape embryonically. But we also recognize that Mrs. Roberts has a number of other responsibilities and obligations as well, just as we know that her love goes out to her husband and other children as well as to the developing life within her body. One of the decision-making tasks for Mrs. Roberts will be to choose which of these responsibilities and loves she will honor and take into consideration; and after that, she will still be faced with designating which of these has priority in this critical choice which she must make. All these factors bear upon her understanding of the meaning of human life, both her own and those with whom she has these several relationships. In a word, these considerations face Mrs. Roberts with the necessity of concrete application of the principle of neighbor-love; but in order to fulfill this obligation, she must decide who the neighbor is and, since in this case there are several competing neighbor-claims, what relative priority is to be assigned to each in relation to all the others.

Helmut Thielicke and Dietrich Bonhoeffer are two modern Protestant theologians who have commented upon the problem of abortion from the perspective of Christian ethics. Thielicke argues that the fetus, because it has a circulatory system and brain, has autonomous life. Indeed, he says, "These elementary biological facts should be sufficient to establish its status as a human being." [38] In his judgment there is not the slightest question that embryonic life is human and therefore sacrosanct and inviolable.[39]

Bonhoeffer arrives at the same conclusion but for somewhat different reasons. His position takes its cue from an assumption about the divine intentionality of nascent life which holds that the embryo itself is evidence of God's purpose to create a human being. The embryo's right to life is there-

[38] Helmut Thielicke, *The Ethics of Sex* (New York: Harper, 1964), p. 228.

[39] *Ibid.*, p. 245. He holds, moreover, that "once impregnation has taken place it is no longer a a question of whether the persons concerned have responsibility for a *possible* parenthood; they have *become* parents" (p. 227).

fore divinely bestowed, and any deliberate deprivation of that life is, in turn, "nothing but murder." [40]

Despite Bonhoeffer's introduction of a divine intention for nascent life, both he and Thielicke fall prey to a kind of naturalistic determinism as the solution to our problem. In ways that are very similar to the reasoning of natural law theory, embryonic and fetal life are designated "human" and therefore inviolable. In consequence, it has to be admitted that a moral absolute has been introduced in the measure to which nascent life exercises a tyranny over mature life. Why fetal life is more precious or sacrosanct than, for example, the mother's life is far from clear. Indeed, on these premises, God's will is merely a postulate inferred from observation of nature.[41] If the logic of this position were rigorously pursued to its absurd conclusion, we would be obliged to forego any direct and intentional interference with natural processes, even that undertaken in order to make life more distinctly human and personal. To "suffer the slings and arrows of outrageous fortune" may appear to be a noble and courageous posture, but in this instance it requires the abdication of genuine moral responsibility to a nerveless fatalism.

More congenial to the approach we prefer to take, and no less seriously aware of the problematics which preoccupy Thielicke and Bonhoeffer, are the reflections of Karl Barth on this subject. It will probably come as a surprise to most that Barth dealt with questions relating to medical ethics; yet he wrote almost five hundred pages on abortion, euthanasia, contraception, and related topics.

The genius of Barth's approach lies in his use of dialectic. Whereas Christian moralists, whether Protestant or Roman Catholic, generally tend to settle questions in favor of one or another value, Barth claims that negative answers must always be balanced by affirmative answers, and vice versa. In the same breath that one says "yes" to a value or proposition or preference, he must simultaneously modify or even negate it by saying "yes" to another. If it were not that temporal immediacy requires that we decide some things *now,* we would go on indefinitely with this dialectical procedure. But decide we must; and Barth, in recognition of this fact, therefore impresses upon us the importance of the provisional and tentative character of all human decisions and values. None can be allowed to become absolute and rigid because only God can claim the kind

[40] Dietrich Bonhoeffer, *Ethics* (New York: Macmillan, 1955), p. 131. In a note to this passage, Bonhoeffer zestfully pursues the logic of his position: "If the child has its right to life from God, and is perhaps already capable of life, then the killing of the child, as an alternative to the presumed natural death of the mother, is surely a highly questionable action. The life of the mother is in the hand of God, but the life of the child is arbitrarily extinguished. The question whether the life of the mother or the life of the child is of greater value can hardly be a matter for a human decision." (P. 131.)

[41] Cf. Albert Schweitzer, "The Ethics of Reverence for Life," *Christendom,* Winter, 1936, pp. 225-39.

of certainty we long for in our decision-making.

Barth begins his treatment of abortion with a statement that is almost identical with the position of Thielicke. The embryo, he says, is autonomous because it possesses its own brain and nervous and circulatory systems. And if its life is affected by the life of its mother-host, as surely it is, it also affects her life. For example, it may live after its mother's death and even be saved by operation on her dead body. It is this kind of relative independence that establishes the fetus as a "human being in its own right." [42] In addition, and reminiscent of the position taken by Bonhoeffer, Barth insists that "we must underline the fact that he who destroys germinating life kills a man and thus ventures the monstrous thing of decreeing concerning the life and death of a fellow-man whose life is given by God and therefore, like his own, belongs to Him." [43] Whether one can assume this kind of responsibility in performing or being party to an abortion is thus answered by Barth with a definite "no."

On the other hand, if this prohibition be established by reference to the divine will—that is, if it is God's "no" that informs the view that abortion is sin, murder, and transgression—one must entertain the possibility of forgiveness for this action.[44] And this, in turn, raises the problem of the exceptional case; or to put it dialectically, the possibility of saying "yes" to abortion. The reasoning process here is fundamental to Barth's theological method: "Human life, and therefore the life of the unborn child, is not an absolute, so that, while it can be protected by the commandment, it can be so only within the limits of the will of Him who issues it. It cannot claim to be preserved in all circumstances, whether in relation to God or to other men, i.e., in this case to the mother, father, doctor and others involved." [45] The human "no" which is inferred from the sixth commandment cannot be, nor should it be, given the last word. God can limit and even reverse what we suppose conditionally to be his will. Thus Barth is prepared to say that we must acknowledge that there are situations in which the destruction of nascent life is not prohibited but positively enjoined.[46]

At this point Barth comes to the crux of the decision-making moment as a personal and relational crisis, for he recognizes that there are situations in which, after all the arguments for inviolability are considered, abortion becomes the *ultima ratio.* These situations occur when we are faced with an unavoidable conflict between lives of the unborn child and the mother. In such situations the sacrifice

[42] Karl Barth, *Church Dogmatics* (Edinburgh: T. and T. Clark, 1961), III, Part IV, p. 416.
[43] *Ibid.*
[44] *Ibid.*, p. 419.
[45] *Ibid.*, p. 420.
[46] *Ibid.*, p. 421.

of one or the other life is inescapable if either is to be preserved. In this circumstance, he argues, "It is hard to see why . . . the life of the child should always be given absolute preference. . . . On the basis of the command, however, we can learn that when a choice has to be made between the life or health of the mother and that of the child, the destruction of the child in the mother's womb might be permitted and commanded." [47]

In order to assist one in the making of these admittedly difficult and ambiguous decisions, Barth offers four guidelines which should be observed as one calculates the risks and chooses one or another course of action. First, both lives must be respected, and neither the nascent life of the embryo or fetus nor the mature life of the mother can be regarded callously. Second, "the most scrupulous calculation" of all the factors must be undertaken so that the sorting and weighing and choosing of values is neither careless nor clouded. Third, the entire decision-making process must "take place before God and in responsibility to Him" so that no merely human reason or justification for decision supplants this primary loyalty. Finally, one must, to use Luther's words, "sin bravely"; that is, one must, in the last analysis, acknowledge that the unqualified rightness or goodness of his choice cannot be antecedently guaranteed but must go ahead with it nevertheless in the confidence of God's forgiving grace.[48]

Barth has managed in this way to maintain a healthy tension between two distinctive views of human life—one of which is basically naturalistic and the other of which is relational—while offering a methodological model for decision-making which is not paralyzed but activated by finite ambiguity and difference. In other words, both commandment and situation are permitted to assert their relative bearing upon the decision at hand.[49]

Beyond these considerations and before venturing a provisional decision in the case of Mrs. Roberts, one must begin to describe (however tentatively) what is meant by words like "personal" and "human." In very general terms we want to argue here that life is human in the measure to which it is becoming more intensely personal and self-fulfilling, more acknowledgedly relational and response-able, more self-consciously purposive and self-directed.

To be a human person is not a matter of *statically* being a certain kind of substance, but rather a matter of *becoming* personal through temporal duration. Hence, personal being and becoming is not simply an either/or matter but a matter of variable degree, which is referable to one's being less or more fully and intensely personal.

[47] *Ibid.*
[48] *Ibid.*, pp. 422-23.
[49] Cf. Introduction, *supra.*

Old friends may be more fully personal than new acquaintances; a relatively loving person will be more fully personal (at least in respect of the love dimension of personal life) than will be a relatively unloving person.

Another way of stating this principle is to claim that personal maturation is a temporal process of becoming progressively more fully and intensely personal, that personal maturity only occurs within the context of relationships. Personal life, then, is constituted not merely by becoming and living as an individual self but also by becoming and living in interpersonal relationships. And this, in turn, suggests that *acceptance*—both of oneself by oneself and of oneself by another self—is the context within which personalizing relationships mature and come to have value. In some important sense being and becoming a human person means entering into both inter- and intra-personal relationships.

In the final analysis "personhood" or "being personal" may be an empirical concept, but in the process of becoming-personal-in-time the personalizing relationships of other persons exercise continuing antecedent priority. It is these relationships which confer upon the developing organism the possibilities of becoming more and more fully personal. Nevertheless, these personalizing relationships do not rigidly determine the personal development of the individual (else the development would not be "personal"); but these networks do constitute the relational field or context within which personal becoming is possible, and they may evoke or call forth spontaneous and free response toward the personal from the developing individual.

The religiously ultimate perspective upon all human personhood sees it as a gift made possible by the personalizing relationship which God initiates with his creatures. But regarding the initiating *time* of God's personalizing relationship a considerable measure of agnosticism seems empirically wise. In the evolutionary process we cannot date God's initiating personalization of the first man (or couple, or group); nor can we specify an exact time with any individual human being. To designate such a time as conception, or forty days, or quickening, or head presentation, or completed birth, or at any other moment would be entirely arbitrary. This agnosticism regarding the time of initiation, however, does not in any way vitiate the point that it is God himself who initiates with the developing organism (at whatever stage) the ultimately personalizing relationship which confers upon a not-yet-human and not-yet-personal creature the unique and sacred dignity of becoming-personal and becoming-human.

Although we think agnosticism appropriate with regard to the time of

God's initiating relationship, agnosticism regarding a "time of cessation" would radically vitiate this understanding. The Christian conviction is that whenever God takes up a personalizing relationship with one of his creatures, he undertakes also enduringly to sustain and enable and finally to consummate this becoming-personal which he has himself begun. God's personalizing relation, once initiated, is never-to-be-ended. This, in fact, is the central conviction of Christianity regarding the nature and destiny of man: that God initiates, sustains, wills to perfect, and shall never allow to be cut off his personalizing relationship to us—a relationship by which he beckons us and graciously enables us to come into the fullness of interpersonal life, which we see perfectly opened up for us in Jesus Christ.

The fulfillment of interpersonal life is seen, then, in the Christian view to require—sooner or later—reconciliation whenever an alienating breach has separated persons. And the applicability of this understanding is both this-worldly and eschatological, i.e., both now and at the end-time. Specifically with reference to taking the life of another—however justifiably in the given context, or however unrealized the potential of that life—one can do so as a Christian only in the sobering awareness that he shall yet have to be reconciled even to this very one.

If and insofar as in a particular case of intentional killing the motivation were *entirely* and *purely* one of love and obedience to a sense of obligation either toward the one killed (as conceivable, for example, in an abortion) or toward others, there might be no individual guilt in the individual act of killing. However, since God alone could know that the motivation in the act was entirely pure, and since the corporate interconnectedness of sin precludes the possibility of a strictly "isolated" case, the killer (if he is a Christian) will appropriately pray for God's forgiveness—not for unrealistic notions of imaginary guilt, but for whatever guilt *God* may see.

In cases in which, after a careful assessment of the knowable medical facts under the guidance of a responsible concern to follow the obligations of love, a decision to perform an abortion is made, those responsible for making and/or executing that decision should recognize that (for all they know) it may be that God has already initiated his never-to-be-severed personalizing relation with this young developing creature. And if this be in reality the case, God may yet require of them (not as a punishment, but as a further service of love) some kind of eschatological responsibility through which this creature will finally become fully human and the alienation between these two reconciled.

A PROVISIONAL CONCLUSION

That Mrs. Roberts is a Protestant offers prospect of a free and responsible decision which, as we have seen, might on other grounds be unavailable to her. She must therefore make a choice, in the first instance, not about the abortion *per se* but about many prior questions and factors which impinge upon her in this decisive moment.

Certainly, considerations for her own health and well-being, both present and future, should not be carelessly rejected. In many ways her love for her husband and their six living children will be shown in the measure to which she expresses an ordinate concern for herself. The medical risk, she has been advised, is very poor indeed, should she elect to permit this pregnancy to go to its natural termination. There is, then, the obvious threat of deprivation of wife and mother to the husband and children, the hardship of the father rearing a poverty-ridden family without a mother, or the additional possibility of family complications resultant from the advent of a deformed or defective child into its midst. Moreover, the family already has responsibility for one child with serious congenital defects. The more inclusive concern for community sanctions, including possible criminal liability under the law, must be in the picture; but the statistical instance of illegal abortions in the United States would suggest that this concern will not be either definitive or determinative in her decision.

What she believes to be ultimately true about the nature of the world and man, and God's intention for them, will constitute one of the critical elements in the decision-making process. If she accepts a naturalistic-vitalistic definition of human life, her answer is effectively given her before she asks her question. If, on the other hand, she regards human life as uniquely life-in-relationship, if she understands her own authentic being as one which is referable to God and his creation, then it is her affirmation or denial of those relationships which itself is constitutive of who she is as a person. And the question confronting her, whether to abort this pregnancy, can then be answered specifically with reference to those relationships which she values, those neighbor-claims which she honors.

In the statutes defining first-degree murder, two conditions are required: premeditation and malice. Such a view as we are proposing here demonstrates the absurdity of this legal fiction which always presumes that if human life is taken intentionally and with forethought, it must correspondingly be taken with hatred and enmity. It need not be held, as though it were irreversible logic, that Mrs. Roberts hates and despises the embryo in her womb if she freely chooses to destroy it. All that is certain is that she preferred another life—perhaps her own, perhaps in a larger sense that of her husband and family—to the nascent and germinating life within her.

If her assessment of the several sets of problematics that impinge upon this decision favors the exercise of her personal freedom in ways that contravene naturalistic and vitalistic impulses, she *can* choose responsibly to terminate this pregnancy. For what is morally at stake is whether she is able to control her existence and shape her life in ways that are personally and relationally meaningful and purposive. Of course, in accomplishing this the entire cluster of values and persons involved in this decision needs to be clearly in focus.

A decision, however, even on these critical grounds is a calculated risk—the fetus could be normally formed and enjoy an entirely uneventful gestation and birth, and the mother could survive the pregnancy without complication or detriment to her health. But her choice will finally forego the possibility of this knowledge, and with it the secure knowledge of having made either a wise or a good decision. In the last analysis, Mrs. Roberts must have the capacity to live with risk—which is, at least morally, what the Protestant doctrine of justification *sola gratia,* by grace alone, is all about.

III. The Politics of Dissent

One of our biologist friends speculates that vertebrate creatures are the product of a long and sustained conflict, not only among themselves but also between themselves and their environment and themselves and other forms of life. He thinks, correspondingly, that jellyfish and their kin may be the products of withdrawal from controversy and struggle. If he is correct, and there is an impressive body of evidence to support the hypothesis, the price to be paid for backbone and spinal column is abrasion and struggle. Refusal to pay that price evolves a spineless creature!

In a certain sense this speculation is paradigmatic of human civilization since it, like biological evolution, is a process engaged in perpetual conflict. Indeed, there is no time in human history which has (so far!) been exempt from controversy, struggle, and combat. If conflict has not taken one form, it has taken another: military, economic, political, ecclesiastical, social—the list could be extended indefinitely to include all those instances of human interrelationships which signify a collision of interest and an appeal to power for the resolution, however temporary and provisional, of antagonisms. The utopian dream—whether articulated by Thomas Münzer, G. W. F. Hegel, Mother Ann Lee, John Humphrey Noyes, Karl Marx, or Woodrow Wilson—remains just that: a dream, unfulfilled and frustrated by the reality of stubborn and persistent conflict. No society has yet managed to insure immunity from the kinds of competition that threaten its dissolution. And what is true of secular communities is no less true of religious institutions: the story of both is a narrative of unrelenting struggle, either internal or external and sometimes both.

In the late 1960's there has been a curious blurring of the distinctions that usually pertain to secular and religious dissent. The Vietnam War, in particular, has provoked a special brand of protest, not paralleled even by the conjunction of political and religious sentiments in the Civil Rights movement of the 1950's and early 1960's. "Hell No, We Won't Go" and "I Don't Give a Damn for Uncle Sam; I Ain't Going to Vietnam" are slogans that express not only disenchantment with the political and military aspects of the war but also what is widely called its "immorality." Students trapped a Navy recruiter in his car and held him captive for four hours; Dow Chemical job interviewers were picketed and their interviewing stymied by sit-ins which clogged the doors; clergy poured their own blood into the selective service files in the City of Brotherly Love; and on some campuses faculty members counseled students who wished to evade the draft. Militant antiwar sentiment and specifically moral indignation were joined in a coalition which protested in the names of both God and country.

More Americans are behind prison bars today for refusing military service than in any year since 1947 when the number of Selective Service violators still reflected swollen World War II draft calls.

In 1967 the average sentence for the draft law breaker jumped to 32.1 months from 25.4 months in 1966 and 13.4 months in 1950. It compares with the World War II year of 1944 when the average sentence was 33.4 months, the longest on record.[1]

FREEDOM AND ORDER

A moral analysis of behavior of this sort must come to some conclusions about the appropriateness of action; but it must also sort out the complex

[1] *New York Post*, May 27, 1968.

of factors which contribute to such conduct. One of the useful ways to describe conflict is to point to some of the perennial polarities that characterize the human condition and those institutions which reflect and embody its values. Robert E. Fitch, with telling and direct simplicity, has indicated the tensions in the major branches of Christendom: "There is a Catholic strength, and its name is order. There is a Catholic sickness, and its name is tyranny. There is a Protestant strength, and its name is liberty. There is a Protestant sickness, and its name is anarchy." [2] There is surely the danger of caricaturing when one paints with such broad strokes; nevertheless, Dean Fitch has identified the classical motifs of Catholicism and Protestantism in a way that is faithful to the stated values of each, whatever an analysis of the actual conduct of their respective affairs might reveal.

One can reasonably infer from this observation that order and liberty are not mutually exclusive values and that, indeed, they ought normatively to complement each other in ways that would strengthen their joint participation in the structures of institutional Christianity. The danger consists in failure to appreciate how order and liberty are interdependent. In any institution that takes account of the human condition, the presence of both is imperative.

The importance of order in Catholic Christianity has typically been expressed in Cyprian's maxim, *salus extra ecclesiam non est* (sometimes rendered *extra ecclesiam nulla salus*)—there is no salvation outside the Church. And at the other pole in the Christian tradition, although not precisely parallel, is the Protestant slogan, *ecclesia semper reformanda*—the Church is always (and ought to be) engaged in reformation. That these epigrams have tended to characterize the fundamental differences between Catholicism and Protestantism demonstrates how conveniently conflict can be dissolved in favor of a clever but false and inadequate option. Karl Barth once employed the analogy of a tight-wire walker to describe the process of living within tension: constant motion on the wire between the poles must be maintained if one wants to avoid losing balance and falling off. Something like this applies also to institutional forms: the ability to live in the tension between freedom and authority is preconditional for a viable structure. The sacrifice of either pole for the other offers the grim prospect of tyranny, on the one hand, or anarchy, on the other.

There are many incidents in our national history which would aptly illustrate this point; but since this is a study in Protestant Christian ethics, it may be appropriate to choose an example from a Protestant institution which is also, in rather remarkable

[2] Robert E. Fitch, "The Protestant Sickness," *Religion in Life*, Fall, 1966, pp. 498-505.

ways, indigenous to this country. Methodists were originally a religious society within the Church of England; indeed its founder, John Wesley, was an Anglican priest and remained so throughout his lifetime. Wesley was also a reformer and critic—a dissenter,[3] though not in the usual ecclesiastical sense—but not a separatist. He vigorously protested what he took to be the failure of the Established Church to fulfill its mission and ministry to the people and undertook to remedy the situation by organizing a network of religious societies and encouraging laymen to preach; but simultaneously he honored the faith and sacraments of Anglicanism and made no move to revolt from or destroy the established ecclesiastical structures. In fact, twenty-six years before the American Methodist societies constituted themselves as a Church, Wesley wrote an essay on "Reasons Against a Separation from the Church of England." [4]

Wesley's arguments, however, did not convince the members of the American societies, and in 1784, at the now celebrated "Christmas Conference," Thomas Coke and Francis Asbury were designated superintendents, and what had formerly been a religious society became the Methodist Episcopal Church. From this initial rupture of the tension between Methodist liberty and Anglican order a long series of divisions subsequently beset the American Methodists. In the 1790's, James O'Kelley led the Republican Methodists to form a new sect, and in the 1830's the Methodist Protestant Church was founded. Between 1813 and 1817 independent churches were formed by Negro Methodists, and in 1844 the Methodist Episcopal Church divided North and South.

The revolutionary spirit of the eighteenth century doubtless played an important role in the history of American Methodism, as did the independent spirit of the frontier and the issue of slavery. It has sometimes been said that Methodism is uniquely the religious expression of a distinctly American consciousness. One Methodist, who became a bishop, has written:

> Our church is suited to the American temperament, which it has always expressed and embodied in all its actions and viewpoints. . . . The big . . . faults [of our church]—and we have them, let us confess—are the big American faults; and the big . . . virtues [of our church]—and thank God, we have them too—are the big American virtues. . . . When Theodore Roosevelt was president, he once privately remarked to the chaplain of the United States Senate, who was [of

[3] "A term signifying disagreement in respect of opinion or practice; in England practically synonymous with separation from the Established Church." Cf. Peter G. Mode, "Dissent and Dissenters," *A Dictionary of Religion and Ethics,* ed. Shailer Mathews and Gerald Birney Smith (New York: Macmillan, 1923), p. 133.

[4] *Works,* XIII, 225-32.

our church], "Your church is the church of America." [5]

Freedom, independence, dissent, and separation have now produced twenty-three distinct Methodist bodies in the United States.[6] Three of the larger Methodist churches united in 1939, and union between The Methodist Church and the Evangelical United Brethren was effected in 1968. There is good reason to think, in this ecumenical age, that unrestrained proliferation may be nearing its end; certainly a moratorium of sorts is being enacted.

It is historically true that religious societies and sectarian groups have had their initiating impulse in a reforming desire for emancipation from unyielding and ossified institutional structures; and this is so in both the Catholic and Protestant traditions, as it is also in Judaism (which now consists of three major bodies). In the Christian tradition it is the freedom to follow Christ—beyond the restricted boundaries of the organization against which protest is directed—that has been the implied if not always articulated motivation underlying every dissenting movement and all authentic reform. It has been the restraint of Christian liberty, imposed by creeds or dogmas or structures, that has led to the open rupture of established churches. Roman Catholicism has been remarkably successful, through a complex maze of orders and societies, in accommodating the encompassing institution to personal disciplinary, devotional, and vocational preferences; but its inability to accomplish this at every point is witnessed to by Eastern Orthodoxy and Protestantism. Of these latter two, Protestantism has proliferated to the extent that, as one of our professors used to say wryly, "There are now more sects than insects!" But it has all been undertaken as an expression of dissent, as a yearning for liberty to be open and responsive to God and obedient to his Spirit.

In order now to assess the morality of dissent, we must look at its purposes and methods and consequences in more careful detail and consider whether dissent, together with some of its forms (for example, violence), still provides a Christianly viable mode of behavior. The question here is not whether this or that economic or political or social program is simply a practical extension of the Christian gospel and thus binding upon the collective conscience of Christians; this was the simplistic error of many popularizers of the Social Gospel. Instead, what is at stake is a critical analysis of certain behavioral modes which, in contextual perspective, may be said to be more or less appropriate for Christians.

[5] Nolan B. Harmon, *Understanding The Methodist Church* (Nashville: The Methodist Publishing House, 1955), 21-22.

[6] Cf. Frank S. Mead, *Handbook of Denominations* (4th ed.; Nashville: Abingdon Press, 1965), pp. 147-58.

PURPOSES AND MODES OF DISSENT

At a rudimentary level, the purposes of dissent are (1) protest, for the sake of conscience, against a predominating power structure or value system, (2) restraint and/or modification of unbridled political power, and (3) active participation in direct and specific action to effect systemic alteration in the patterns of prevailing mores. In both the Christian tradition and Western democratic political theory these purposes are held to be more or less inalienable human rights which function to respect individual conscience and to protect society from the tyrannizing tendencies of unchallenged political power.

As conscientious protest, dissent expresses itself in its most benign form; that is, it provides mainly for achieving moral identity and the self-satisfaction gained from having expressed opinion on some controversial subject in ways that are consistent with one's basic commitments and beliefs. A "protest march" or a "picket line" or letters to the editor of the local newspaper are contemporary instances of this form of dissent. At this level the protesting action is (1) *generally directed* toward (2) some *vaguely perceived structure or system*. This is not to say, of course, that the action is misdirected or that there is not a bill of particulars toward which the action is directed. On the other hand, it is arguable that this kind of action is more a witness to the values of the actor than it is a concerted effort calculated to achieve specific and effective alteration of structural deficiencies. Protest and dissent, at the level of conscientious objection, are chiefly opportunities for the expression of personal and private moral discontent or outrage; and the power which this form of dissent wields is largely limited to persuasion by means of exhortation and inducement. Action of this sort is fundamentally an appeal to the moral sensibilities of those toward whom the protest is directed, in which case the participation of the dissenters in actual change (which occurs or might occur in consequence of this action) is largely oblique and indirect. Further, there is the frequent possibility that protest of this sort—by entrenching latent resistance, or by identifying the dissenter with a panty-raid mentality and thus diminishing the power of his personal influence, or by some similar mechanism—may actually foreclose opportunities for real change and thereby become dysfunctional. If one expends his energies tilting against windmills, he is likely not to be taken seriously when he hunts for real beasts of prey. Misunderstanding, alienation, and overt hostility are frequently the social and political by-products of dissent for conscience's sake.

By definition, this form of protest is orderly and nonviolent; it attempts to employ established methods for altering mores; it is usually willing to be patient and allow change to take place more or less gradually; and it retains identity with the larger social whole by refusing to draw the lines of difference hard and fast, on the assumption that the superordinate powers are malleable and admit of redirection and alteration of the existing systems and structures. This approach was particularly evident in the civil rights movement of the 1950's and early 1960's; and the strategy of direct nonviolent action was devised with reference to these basic assumptions. The measured success of efforts to alter patterns of racial discrimination in the nation depended upon the capacity of the superordinate powers to be persuaded and to effect the appropriate changes, first through legal conventions and then through social customs. That this form of dissent is now being increasingly challenged by a more militant protest is attributable to a number of factors—the painfully slow progress of reform; the national awareness of poverty, reaction and backlash; internal conflict over the Vietnam War; and many others—but it is only the focus and form of dissent that is being recast, this time in revolutionary ways against the superordinate power itself; and this brings us to the second and third purposes of this kind of behavior.

In its more direct and specific modes, dissent is undertaken to effect restraint or fundamental changes in the prevailing system which informs and governs society. The means to this end are either modification of the in-power authority or structural alteration of the authority system itself. At this level of involvement the concern for moral identity may be assumed, and narrow personal and private self-satisfactions become somewhat immaterial except in the measure to which individual action functions to achieve direct political consequences. If action is calculated to express *intentions* in the conscientious protest mode of dissent, it is here calculated and measured by its capacity to *effect intentions* in *actual consequence.* Dissent in this form only succeeds when political or social or economic change occurs in ways that are commensurate with announced objectives and developed strategies. Whatever means are employed at this level, the critical assessment of means is always calculated to the achievement of stated goals. Strategy thus becomes a crucial determinant.

It is important to understand, at this juncture, that action may take several forms and serve many goals, and that the success or failure of a given action is assessed by the extent to which its consequences agree or disagree with its intentions. If anything sanctions means it is ends, since methods are useless if they fail to accomplish the desired goal. This is why, again, ethics is logically prior to morals: *ethics* is concerned with discriminating among competing goals and obligations; *morals* is concerned with the determination and development of appropriate tactics of human action, that is, with tactics which are calculated to achieve the stated goal. "Where do I look to learn what I may or should do?" is the ethical question which precedes the moral query, "What will I do, and how will I do it?"

Dissent which seeks to restrain power or reshape superordinate authority must consider both of these questions. When a goal or obligation is affirmed, it is not well served by an action which fails to effect the change needed to achieve that goal or obligation. The polar complementaries might be stated as follows: action requires articulation of objectives for understanding and purpose just as, correspondingly, articulation requires action for effecting change and achieving goals. In a profound sense, then, the form of action (when it is appropriately chosen) is fitted to acceptance or resistance to change as this is perceived in the authority which is the object of change. There was a time, for example, when black citizens in this country were content with benevolent white paternalism; more recently, black citizens employed the conventional mechanisms of our society to gain limited access to full participation in the mainstream of American life; it is now increasingly evident that large numbers of black Americans have redefined their goals in such a way as to challenge the system, the "American way of life," itself. With each redefinition of goal there has developed a tactic more appropriate and promising to the achievement of that goal. Now, somewhat in retrospect, one ought to appreciate that there is a great distance *strategically* between being a "good nigger" who is glad for whatever he gets from the big house and a black power advocate who demands that he get what he wants from the White House. One employs the method of ingratiating subservience; the other uses the tactics of militancy, which may include violence.

THE RISK OF VIOLENCE

Violence, of course, is not a "given" nor the only means by which dissent can challenge the structures of authority and power; but neither is it irreversibly ruled out as a viable means to effect change. There is always the *risk* of violence attached to every movement which has as its goal the transformation of existing systems. In the long run, it may well be within the power of the system under attack to prevent or to precipitate the rage and fury of forcible change. The system's capacity for resiliency and change defines the limits of violent countervailing power. Violence becomes an alternative for effecting change when the superordinate power resists change and persists in the *status quo ante.* Like irreformable authority, however, violence tends to irrational conduct and inevitably strikes out not only at the vested authority itself but at relatively innocent parties as well.

The political viability of dissent which intends to restrain power or reshape authority is a function of (1) the power vested in the dissenters and (2) the transigency or intransigency of those who are currently in control of the system. Power is simply the capacity to effect change or, conversely, to maintain the *status quo ante.* But naked power is not alone an adequate or appropriate human political value; indeed, power *per se* is morally neutral, and no judgment can be made about its goodness or badness until it expresses itself concretely toward the achievement of some specified goal. Power, to be moral or immoral, must be employed purposively, and it is the use to which power is put that measures its value or disvalue. Commonly, in judicial proceedings, police are permitted to use that power or force which is necessary to apprehend or subdue a criminal. It is the employment of inordinate force that occasions charges of police brutality. When power is used indiscriminately and recklessly for its own sake it becomes functionally immoral.

Similarly, the power of dissent demoralizes and dehumanizes both the dissenter and the object of protest when that power is purposeless or indiscriminately applied. That frustration and anger may provoke one to strike out blindly at whatever is near at hand, as in the riots of the late 1960's, may be entirely understandable as the spontaneous response of a deprived humanity; but this animal instinct serves little if any constructive purpose, transvaluing intention, structural restraint, or reshaping that would correct and change the conditions which provoked this action. Responsible power is both purposive in the goals it seeks and discriminating in the objects to which it is addressed. Otherwise, it is nihilistic.

But this is a judgment applicable to the superordinate power as much as it is to those who dissent from it. If the dissenter confronts the dangerous possibility of anarchy, it must correspondingly be noted that the in-power authority (perhaps the state, or the police) is continually *tempted* by its power to tyranny and totalitarianism. Much is said, and most of it appropriately, about the obligation of individuals to the nation and about the infeasibility of permitting persons the absolute and unrestrained right to dissent with impunity from any and every national circumstance which is morally offensive, or personally discomfiting, or whatever else, to themselves. The common rubric is "law and order." It needs also to be emphasized, however, that no more than an individual can exercise absolute dominion over the state can the state coercively shackle the individual. In the Christian tradition, both state and individual are subordinate to God, who alone exercises sovereignty and dominion over his subjects; and this suggests that there is a becoming modesty, therefore, in the claims to sovereignty which any creature or group of creatures presumes to make.

There is in this country a long and distinguished tradition which acknowledges respect for individual conscience; and the ground for this respect is not only in the notion that conscience is inviolable (*conscientia est semper consequentia*) but also in the awareness that the national interest is best served by the guaranty of this freedom. Dissent, then, for conscience' sake—even when such dissent challenges the very system which guarantees it this right—must be respected; indeed, sometimes dissent of this sort may even be commanded. The Nuremburg Trials employed precisely this reasoning to convict Nazi defendants of crimes against humanity: they were not allowed to abdicate their obligation to dissent by appealing to the legality of their actions or their duty to the vested authority. With what may have been proleptic awareness of the Nazi menace, Karl Barth wrote in 1938:

> It could well be that we could obey specific rulers only by being disobedient to God, and by being thus in fact disobedient to the political order ordained of God as well. It could well be that we had to do with a Government of liars, murderers and incendiaries, with a Government which wished to usurp the place of God, to fetter the conscience, to suppress the church and become itself the Church of Antichrist. It would be clear in such a case that we could only choose either to obey this Government by disobeying God or to obey God by disobeying this Government.[7]

Peter's answer to the Jerusalem high priest was similarly direct: "We must obey God rather than men." [8]

Decisions of this sort, however, always carry with them a significant and irreducible element of risk.[9] No Christian will quarrel with the assertion that "we must obey God rather than men"; but we also know that God uses men and the institutions of men as servants of his will. It is sometimes very difficult indeed to discriminate between those men and institutions which are in the service of God and those which are not. In fact, under the sovereignty of God historical structures change. We are, as Augustine perceived, citizens of two cities; and this is simultaneously both the splendor and the tragedy of our hu-

[7] Karl Barth, *The Knowledge of God and the Service of God According to the Teaching of the Reformation,* trans. J. L. N. Haire and Ian Henderson (London: Hodder & Stoughton, 1938), p. 230.

[8] Acts 5:29 (RSV). Socrates, in Plato's *Apology* (sec. 29, D), affirms a similar principle.

[9] For a fuller explication of the risk factor in decision-making, see Harmon L. Smith, "When Love Becomes Excarnate," *Storm Over Ethics,* John C. Bennett *et al.* (Philadelphia: United Church Press, 1967), pp. 88-111.

manity. We have neither an infallible moral intuition that our choices are right nor antecedent certainty that the consequences of our action will be appropriate to the situation. It is important, therefore, to pool the decision-making resources available to us—moral intuition, rational reflection, situational analysis, and anticipated consequences—in order to assist us in making responsible choices among alternative courses and competing claims, and in order to dissent *from* penultimate *for* more ultimate goals and obligations.

VARIABLES IN THE MORAL CALCULUS

We can begin to get at this by examining those facts which correlate positively and negatively with dissenting action, in the light of which the relative morality of a given action may be provisionally assessed.[10] This series of variables is not exhaustive but it is indicative of those kinds of factors which, when weighed and balanced against each other, can provide strategic analysis of dissenting action.

(1) Determination of the gravity and magnitude of the wrong to which action responds is fundamentally important. This is not to say that evil must attain epidemic and national proportions before something is done about it, but it is to caution against expending energy on grievances which are trivial and of relative unimportance. The relative morality of an action will, in part, positively correlate with the seriousness and extent of the wrong and negatively correlate with its frivolity and indifference.

(2) In a democratic society it is appropriate, particularly when considering dissenting action which may be civilly disobedient, that prior political and judicial processes be either exhausted or demonstrably incompetent. Dissenting acts are politically vitiated if there is suitable recourse to legal alternatives. In addition, the possibility of cultivating the destruction of democratic institutions should not be entertained except under the most extenuating circumstances; and even then a viable option to extant institutions needs to be more or less plainly envisioned in order to avoid a chaotic nihilism. The relative morality of a dissenting action will, in part, be positively correlated with the prior exhaustion of conventional political and judicial procedures and negatively correlated with the availability of legal alternatives and the threat to social order.

(3) In the Christian tradition

[10] Professor William W. Van Alstyne, of the Duke University Law School, suggested several of the variables in the moral calculus which will be employed here. He is not responsible, of course, for the ways in which we have chosen to apply them.

peaceful means have typically been preferred to coercive techniques. This is not to say, of course, that Christians repudiate power; it is only to claim, for example, that the power of persuasion is morally preferable to compulsion. To argue this way is not to rule out absolutely the use of force. It is simply to hold that peace is better than war, that reason is better than hysteria, that gentleness is better than *brute* force. An action is positively correlated with its noncoercive character and negatively correlated with its propensity to violence.

(4) The willingness or unwillingness of the actor to endure the consequences of dissenting action constitutes still another factor in the moral calculus. It has been one of the impressive traits of those adherents to the philosophy of direct but nonviolent action in the civil rights movement that they willingly suffer the penalties of civil disobedience. This has the double effect of impressing one and all with the seriousness of dissent and of expressing confidence in the democratic processes to right the wrongs of racial injustice and oppression. Willingness to share fully in the uncomfortable consequences of an action helps to measure the relative morality of that action.

(5) Intrigue and concealment are usually sufficient cause for questioning motivation and intention, and acts which appear to be plots or conspiracies are thus generally self-defeating. Openness, on the other hand, is taken to be a sign of honesty and integrity of plan and purpose. The relative morality of an act is positively correlated with the measure to which it is "above board" and, correspondingly, it is negatively correlated with the extent to which it is "under the table."

(6) H. Richard Niebuhr, more than any other American ethicist, talked of the appropriateness of action as a mark of its relative moral worth.[11] Actions are not to be assessed for their rightness or wrongness apart from the relation they bear to a particular set of circumstances, both existential and theological. The relative morality of a given act depends, at least in part, upon the way it fits one's understanding of his obligation to God and the needs of the situation. An act is positively correlated with the close relation of the act to the wrong, that is with the appropriateness of the act to the wrong; it is negatively correlated with the distance between the act and the wrong, and the lack or absence of fit of the act to the wrong.

(7) Sometimes, for lack of strategic precision and adequate problem definition, acts fail to accomplish their desired purpose. Effective political

[11] Cf. H. Richard Niebuhr, *The Responsible Self* (New York: Harper, 1963). One will also find particularly instructive, on this point, Niebuhr's essay, "The Center of Value," originally published in *Moral Principles of Action,* ed. Ruth Nanda Anshen (Harper, 1952). We have included this essay in Part II above.

change is greatly dependent upon the clarity of the act in the appeal which it makes, both to those toward whom it is directed and to those who observe conflict as spectators. Whether, then, action is direct or oblique, common understanding of its rationale is a high priority. The relative morality of a given act is, in part, calculated by reference to the clarity or obscurity of the appeal which the act undertakes to elicit from both "target" and "observer" audiences.

(8) Finally, unless one wishes to jeopardize or destroy the foundations of national life, action deserves to be formulated in consideration of the ways in which it either engenders or alienates democratic support. Fascistic means, for example, are inconsistent with democratic means; but what may be even more noteworthy is that fascistic means contradict democratic goals. Some methods are simply incompatible with some ends. Given the political philosophy of the United States and the national ethos, an act is positively correlated with its probability for engendering democratic support, and it is negatively correlated with its probability for estranging that support.

Perhaps it should be reiterated that these variables are supposed to be not exhaustive but illustrative of the factors in this kind of decision-making process. They provide useful clues for strategic planning; and while no one of them serves to qualify or disqualify a particular action, the greater weight of their combined *fit* and the relative order of importance assigned to each of them does function to indicate preferred behavioral alternatives.

THE CHURCH IN POLITICS

The phenomena of dissent and protest, and even violence, are not new in American life. Their roots are as old as the republic; their seeds were sown in the colonizing of this land by European settlers and African slaves. According to the *Report of the National Advisory Commission on Civil Disorders,* "Racial violence was present almost from the beginning of the American experience." [12] It may be that we are just now witnessing the awful consequences of 450 years of slavery and indentured servitude; our predominating domestic problems are racism and poverty. The significant political difference is that the sporadic and localized rebellions of Denmark Vesey and Nat Turner have been superceded by highly organized and skillful assaults upon the systemic hypocrisies of American life itself. Moreover, the moral gap between creed and deed, of which Gunnar

[12] *Report of the National Advisory Commission on Civil Disorders* (New York: Bantam Books, 1968), p. 208.

Myrdal spoke so persuasively,[13] is slowly and painfully being bridged; and the force of changing law is being employed to guarantee that the language of the Declaration of Independence is no longer an idealized fiction but an expanding fact.

From its earliest times, Christians have attempted to formulate a theological understanding of the state and political processes. Sometimes these statements have tended to identify church and state as discrete components of a single *corpus Christianum;* at other times political authority has been regarded as demonic, and complete separation between church and state has been called for. To consider, as we have in this chapter, questions of Christian social policy tacitly acknowledges that some communication is appropriate between church and state, churchman and citizen. We need now to explicate some of those basic assumptions.

It is not necessary here to undertake a full exposition of the doctrine of the church,[14] but only to point to those theological and sociological dimensions of the church which are co-implicants and hence contributory to the church's role in society. The church, in other words, is "in the world, but not of the world."

Two presuppositions, especially, condition the church's being in the world. The first of these is that the church claims to be the recipient of a revelation which is at once final, unique, and universal; a revelation which simultaneously establishes the church's reason for being and the limits for the realization of that "being" in the world. Jesus came proclaiming the kingdom of God, but that goal is not fully realized in human history, and the church's task is to be a herald and foretaste of God's kingly rule in the hearts and lives of men. The church will thus be a perennial source of criticism and correction to any culture and national state.

The second presupposition of the church's being in the world is that Christian faith is not concerned solely with the spiritual life of individuals. The church is attentive to persons, and thus it is alert to those influences which mold character. In the measure to which society is instrumental in shaping personal development, the church is deeply concerned with society. If the church's task is to proclaim the center of value, it cannot ignore public life; for the church is not merely a spiritual society but a community of faith concerned with persons and their values and all those influences, from whatever quarter, which shape the formation of personal and social existence.

The supreme treasures of the church might, therefore, be described as holiness and catholicity, in view of

[13] Gunnar Myrdal, *An American Dilemma: The Negro Problem and Modern Democracy* (New York: Harper, 1944), 2 Vols.

[14] Cf. Part I, *supra.*

which a twofold mission derives. The church's role is not to advocate general maxims of political or social or economic science but to enunciate Christian moral principles, derived from its commitment to God, in order to elicit from citizens their appropriate responses *in* these areas of human life. The church's negative task, on the other hand, is to counteract the tendency and difficulty of all government to treat persons as cases or things; between the lines of state action, there is felt need for the recovery of the personal equation.

Unlike the church, the state lays no claim to a specific revelation from God as the condition for its being. Some have argued that the state emerged through a kind of actual or implied contract or compact; others maintain that human beings are naturally social and gregarious creatures and that some form of government is a natural consequence of this fact. There is doubtless truth in both views. What is functionally relevant is that political progress has not come by fashioning unity out of multiplicity but by the creation of and provision for liberty for the several component groups (from families to political parties) within the social unity. Plato regarded the ethical problem to be "out of many to become one"; the political problem is to make a place for multiplicity within a given unity. At least in its internal affairs, then, the state's primary obligation is to the several relationships among the subordinate groups of which it is comprised. It exists as a *communitas communitatum*, a community of communities, and as such performs a dual role.

The state's primary function is to make and enforce law for the governance of the several departments or groups of life which constitute the society of which the state is the organ of unity. But order, even of this sort, subserves a more indispensable good in the life of the community, and that higher good toward which all else points is nothing less than the effective freedom of persons and groups which enables them to be self-determinative of responsible choice and action. The supreme role of the state, Christianly understood, is to secure and to guarantee freedom. Law, as the servant of justice, communicates that role by describing the limits of freedom; that is, law restrains the sin of irresponsible freedom and aims at converting the evil will responsible for such acts by representing the judgment of society on the evil-doer. But force, even when appropriately applied by law to immature character, is largely negative; at best it is only preparatory to the rebuilding and remolding of character which love alone can accomplish. Law, then, is finally inadequate to insure the fulfillment of justice in human social relations because its method is not entirely conducive to an authentic conversion of will.

The second factor of the state's function is the other side of this coin: the state does not violate its citizens when it enforces the law but thereby binds them to conduct which is expressive of their own best character. Few (if any!) citizens are so well established in morality as to be able to dispense with the law and its sanctions without moral deterioration. The law is then a schoolmaster which leads us to our true virtue.

It is perhaps unavoidable that the state and the church clash on occasion; this would be expected if only because the state embraces all persons and communities within its boundaries. But the encounter between church and state is not unique, nor is it fundamentally different from the conflicts which the state will have with other groups. As the Christian's duty is to maintain and interpret the faith of Christ, so the scientist's duty is to seek and promulgate scientific truth; but neither is amenable to control by universal regulations which may be at the disposal of the state. The duty of service to its constituent parts is the state's true dignity. William Temple stated the matter like this:

> To obey is as noble as to command, to command as noble as to obey, if each is done as an act of service in the allotted sphere; otherwise there is no dignity in either. The Christian can be as true a patriot as any other; he can desire for his country the foremost place with an equal zeal. The difference is in the standard or scale of values. The foremost place that he will desire for his country is the place of foremost service to God and to His Kingdom. The State is concerned with Law; it cannot be, as the Church ought to be, a spiritual pioneer; its function is to consolidate the moral gains already won and save us from falling below the normal level of our own achievement. Hence it must be firm and even stern in its action. Its way of manifesting love is to be just, and there are other and higher ways. But the State which has learnt its true function has, none the less, the highest of earthly dignities; it is an indispensable servant of the common life of men. Its form of service is to rule; but it should rule only that it may serve.[15]

The critical point at which the practical dimensions of the relations between church and state occur is, of course, in the Christian's responsibility for and participation in his role as citizen. It is here that church and state are understood not as monolithic institutions competing with each other but as a single person acting out his obligations as churchman and citizen. The heart of the matter, then, is not a question of the organization of church and state; it is, instead, the internal tension which is created within the Christian citizen who knows himself to be a member of two societies, functioning under somewhat different principles in order to serve the kingdom of God. In this awareness he may sometimes perceive it as his duty to dissent, as occasion may indicate, from

[15] William Temple, *Christianity and the State* (London: Macmillan, 1929), p. 185.

the state or from the church—and in rare instances, he may interpret it as his obligation, as a faithful Christian, to dissent from both.

The contrast between church and state is therefore not between something good and something evil; it is rather the contrast between two complementary and sometimes conflicting stages in the work which God is accomplishing in history. Neither church nor state is to be confused with the kingdom of God; yet each plays its own part in building and preparing for it. And the person who embraces in himself the polar complementarities of citizen and churchmen cannot then withdraw from either; instead he functions as a whole person within both spheres, anticipating the transformation of both into that kingdom in which justice and mercy will coalesce in perfect love. Church and state, religion and citizenship, have the same sphere—the life of man—although they act upon that sphere in different functional relationships.

Paul admonished the Roman Christians to be a transforming influence in the world. Politically understood, this means that the Christian's responsibility is couched in the realistic language of justice, for the establishment of justice is the first achievement of love. This does not exhaust the meaning of love, to be sure; but the demands of love—too severe to be fully accepted by the state and the social order—must not discourage Christian people from seeking its fulfillment in their own lives or prevent them from using it as the normative criterion by which to judge the morality of the state. There will likely continue to be a healthy tension between the actual justice achieved by the state and the plenitude of justice proclaimed by the church's gospel of love. But such a gospel not only serves the Christian citizen as the transcendent norm by which he criticizes the secular community; it is also the informing principle of his social action which makes possible and promising and hopeful the transformation of social morality and the structures of justice in the political order.

IV. Poverty and the American Ethic

Among the things which should be increasingly clear is that there is no such thing as a purely economic problem, a purely racial problem, a purely sexual problem. The identification of such problems reflects more the departmental schizophrenia of contemporary academe than the actual human situation. We have seen, for example, that the "political" problem of dissent in a democracy finally is a problem because of the need of human beings for nonpolitical as well as political satisfactions. If dissent is politically denied, one consequence is intellectual stagnation, which manifests itself not merely in political institutions but also in economic, sexual, and ecclesiastical institutions. This fact points to one of the supreme ironies of contemporary life with its various specializations: the economist seeking to solve economic problems discovers that noneconomic factors impinge upon his deliberations; the political scientist discovers that factors not susceptible to political analysis must be weighed in any socially relevant political theory; the psychologist who would understand processes of the mind discovers that many nonpsychic factors (like body chemistry, social training, commitments) complicate the picture. In the final analysis economic, political, and psychic problems do not exist independently; rather they constitute more or less definable dimensions of the larger problem, the human problem or the problem of becoming and being human.

It is in this context that professional ethicists must understand their role. The ethicist is concerned with the human problem as a whole and in all its dimensions. Herein lies both the importance and the limitations of all systems of ethics, including the Christian ethic. The importance of ethics is that it can provide the larger perspective which will enable us to see particular problems in their human context. The limit of ethics is that *in itself* it cannot provide policies and programs for dealing with the human problem in its particular political, economic, or social contexts since this requires special knowledge of systems.

The assumption of the present chapter is that Christian faith can provide the larger perspective in which to view economic problems, including the primary problem of poverty. Economic policies do play their part in making human life human or inhuman. Thus all economic policies must be, for the Christian, evaluated in terms of their capacity to increase the humanization of life, not in terms merely of their capacity to increase the GNP, to produce goods and services, or to operate with little friction. This is true in spite of the additional observation that no unproductive economy or one which does not operate smoothly can measurably increase the humanization of life. While it may be true to claim that without production human needs cannot be met, it cannot follow from that claim that production is the primary goal. No economic system or policy can be Christianly evaluated entirely in terms of its capacity to increase production. The use of production as the chief criterion constitutes the major moral error of both the doctrinaire Marxist and the *laissez-faire* capitalist.

What, then, is the place of the Christian theologian-ethicist in the economic dimension of the human problem? Clearly it is not his place to provide a comprehensive economic plan which would, because it came from a Christian, be regarded as the Christian economic system. There simply is no Christian system in economics. There may be economists who are Christian and there may be economic systems which better than other systems enable the attainment of Christian goals for human life, but there can be no Christian system. Christianity, and consequently Christian ethical concern, transcends all systems.[1] Some believing Christians have, of course, identified this or that system as the Christian way. Hence both the *laissez-faire* American way and the way of "Christian" socialism have been marked as the Christian way.

So it is that the place of the Christian theologian-ethicist, here as in other realms of social concern, is the identification of guiding principles which in particular historical contexts may increase the humanization of men. We have chosen the problem of poverty amid affluence as the concrete area of inquiry in which to demonstrate the process by which Christians might deal with problems in the economic dimension of human life.

THE FACE OF POVERTY

It is clear that poverty is a relative concept. It has to do with the gap between the wealthy and the poor, between the "haves" and the "have nots." This gap obviously is wider in some nations than in others. Taken on a world scale even whole nations must be regarded as poor in comparison to other nations. Compared to the average level of living in most of the world, the poor in the United States appear economically secure.

In view of the relativities with which one must deal, the search has been made for firm figures which can give us some idea of the extent of poverty within the United States. Such figures are difficult to establish; and even when they are established for the nation as a whole, regional and occupational variations must be taken into account. A fixed monetary figure on annual income, for example, means one thing if it relates to a farm family in rural Arkansas and quite another if it relates to a Negro family in the heart of Harlem. Precise measurement of relative poverty is impossible.

[1] This is the ethical relevance of the principle Paul Tillich has enunciated as the "Protestant Principle." Tillich's Protestant Principle, applied by him to all theological systems, is that man's ultimate commitment must never be toward the finite. All human systems are imperfect; in consequence they become demonic when they are given ultimate commitment.

Though precision escapes us in identifying poverty some rough guidelines have come into rather wide use, especially in connection with federal programs and the "War on Poverty." In 1964 Walter W. Heller, then Chairman of the President's Council of Economic Advisers, used before a House Committee the figure of $3,000 annual family income as the statistical dividing line which sets off the poor in America.[2] Heller claimed only that this is a reasonable base figure which he liked to call a "benchmark." Good arguments can be and have been made for raising or lowering the figure,[3] and regional variations have been widely employed.

Using the figure of $3,000 to mark the poverty line for a family of four and adding or deducting $500 per person for larger or smaller family units, one finds that approximately one-fifth of our population falls below the poverty mark. That percentage represents some 40 million people, or more than 9 million families. Of those, over 4.5 million families have annual money income below $1,800, and 7.5 million fall below $2,500. This is something of the statistical extent of poverty in this nation.

But the real face of poverty is not adequately reflected in statistics. Statistics do not show the human dimension of poverty in the form of sheer hunger, inadequate shelter and clothing, and the demoralizing effect on the human psyche. The crucial dimension of poverty is seen only in its ego-effects. A society which ascribes status largely in terms of what one "has" cultivates among those who do not "have" major problems of self-respect, personal dignity, and loss of hope. The young who live on the diet of the poor are damaged for life, not only in physical health but also in mental capacity. Unaccustomed to playing a noteworthy role in the community and unable for a variety of reasons to work regularly, the poor find little in life to produce a sense of self-respect and human dignity. Ego-compensations are sought in drinking, brawling, and the possession of color television sets. These activities among the poor are thought by those Americans who "have" to justify their inaction on behalf of the poor. The actions of the poor in their search for ego-strength are in turn used by the non-poor who argue that "if you do things for them they just spend their money on TV and liquor." Underlying American thinking on the matter is the American ethic which teaches that those who deserve better things

---

[2] *Economic Opportunity Act of 1964,* Hearings before Subcommittee on the War on Poverty Program, Committee on Education and Labor, House of Representatives, 88th Congress, 2nd Session (Washington, D.C.: Government Printing Office, 1964), Part 1, pp. 27-28.

[3] See, for example, *Economic Opportunity Act of 1964,* Hearings before Select Committee on Labor and Public Welfare, U.S. Senate, 88th Congress, 2nd Session (Washington, D.C.: Government Printing Office, 1964). The statement by Margaret G. Reid, Professor Emeritus of Economics, University of Chicago, is especially critical of Heller's benchmark.

have them. But more on this later. The main lines of the psychology of poverty are clear, though much research is yet to be done on the depth and scope of the psychological effects of poverty. It is apparent to those who know the poor that poverty strikes not only at the body but also at the spirit. Poverty is not only a way of eating; it is also a way of *being*.

THE VICIOUS CIRCLE OF POVERTY

The roots of poverty are deeply embedded in the soil of our economic development. The gap between the affluent and the poor stems initially from the vast industrial and technological revolution of the last one-hundred years. In the early stages of this revolution the segment of our population with the lowest income was partially protected from severe want by such enterprises as collective bargaining, Social Security, Unemployment Compensation, and similar measures of public welfare and relief. But as sweeping technological change altogether eliminated many of the jobs open to this segment of the population, programs which had staved off poverty during early industrialization proved inadequate. Even these programs have not been pursued vigorously by the federal government, and state and local governments have involved themselves in the relief of poverty in a less than halfhearted manner. We have not yet devised adequate means of dealing with the social effects of new methods and machines which have so increased American productivity in the period since World War II.

Many workers, for one reason or another, simply were unable to keep pace with rapid change. Some lacked the essential educational skills which would equip them to understand and operate increasingly complex machinery. Many were not equipped to pull up roots in the community of their youth and move to places where their skills could have been developed and employed. Programs of job retraining were inadequate to enable many to keep pace. In this shuffle Negroes were at a double disadvantage because of inferior schools and experience. When they moved from the farm to the industrial centers they were commonly herded into ghettos where conditions of life were such as to aggravate the already pressing economic and social problems. The black man was, and is, the "last hired and the first fired." Other groups were disadvantaged for other reasons. Members of broken families where there is no male breadwinner found adjustment to economic change more difficult because of the lack of jobs open to females and because of the widespread practice of paying females less than males for the same work. The elderly, being thought less able to change, were passed over in favor of employing younger people. As the technological revolution struck the farm, leaving in its wake larger farms, bigger machines, and fewer jobs, the hope of the small "one horse" operator grew ever more dim. Thus, as revolutionary change has proceeded apace, one fifth of our population has lagged farther and farther behind the majority in the ability to improve their socio-economic standing. The consequence is poverty amid affluence.

But the roots of poverty are not limited to economic and technological change. There is a sense in which poverty roots in poverty. In his testimony before the House Subcommittee on the War on Poverty Program in 1964 Walter Heller cited evidence that over 40 percent of the parents who received aid for their dependent children were themselves raised in families which had received public assistance.[4] Heller also cited a study conducted in 1959 by the Survey Research Center at the University of Michigan which showed that the poor had a history of poverty. Some 60 percent of families with disposable incomes below $3,000 had never enjoyed higher income. Among the aged poor almost 80 percent had never earned $3,000.[5]

One of the most disastrous effects of poverty is the attitudinal disposition of the poor which itself becomes a cause of further poverty. As the door of economic opportunity closes, dispositions of hopelessness on the part of the poor add the lock to the closed door making unaided escape impossible. Confronting what appears to be, and commonly is, the impossible task of opening the door of opportunity the poor characteristically lose all hope. Caught in a web which they do not understand, and subjected to ever larger economic forces beyond their power, the poor are victimized and defeated. "They tended to become discouraged and demoralized," notes one commentator, "they lost the hope which had made low living standards more bearable for their forefathers. Without hope, many were unable to take the first difficult steps of self-improvement that led out of their particular poverty pocket." [6] So it is that the poor until recent years made little noise over their plight; and for the majority of Americans, they passed unnoticed while the nation itself was caught up in a vast period of economic expansion and revolution. The result of the loss of hope was further poverty, which in turn led to greater hopelessness and even deeper poverty.

Moreover, this cycle reproduces itself in the young born into poor households and living under the conditions of poverty. Seeing little opportunity for a life other than they have known from earliest childhood—the life of the ghetto or the tenant farmhouse—

[4] *Hearings,* House Subcommittee, pp. 27-28.

[5] *Ibid.,* p. 28.

[6] Federal Reserve Bank of Philadelphia, *The New Poverty,* Series for Economic Education, 1964, p. 8.

the young of the poor tend to choose courses of action that insure their continued incapacity to overcome the forces of poverty. At a rate more than two and one-half times as great as the rate for all children the offspring of the poor drop out of school at the eighth-grade level. Some 34 percent of the children of the poor do not go beyond the eighth grade as compared with only 14 percent of all children. Under one-half of the children of the poor graduate from high school, whereas almost two-thirds of all children in the nation complete high school.[7]

So it is that the operation of this vicious circle reveals the depth of the problem. The problem of poverty is not merely that many people in the United States do not have enough to eat and to wear. It is that human beings are deprived of the very hope which sustains human life itself. The scandal of economic need in a country of affluence thus leads to depersonalization of human beings, the final denial of that which makes for human life itself. The end result of poverty, then, is the loss of humanity itself. We have not yet devoted ourselves as a nation to interrupting the operation of the vicious circle which leads from economic deprivation to hopelessness to further deprivation and more abysmal hopelessness.

POVERTY AND THE AMERICAN ETHIC

Even so brief a sketch as this of the anatomy of poverty leads inexorably to the question: why has the American majority done so little to deal with the problem? How does one account for the fact that the nation with greater wealth than any other nation of the world has lagged behind the achievement of most European countries in dealing with poverty? We have the human resources, the material power and the economic techniques for eliminating poverty. Why have these vast resources not been used effectively?

The answers commonly given bear an increasingly hollow sound, especially the answers that it costs too much to solve the problem of poverty and that the poor should go to work to earn their livelihood. Concern over the economic costs of eliminating poverty cannot be taken seriously when we observe the greater cost of perpetuating poverty. Economically speaking, the loss of human resources to poverty is greater in simple dollars than the money cost of erasing poverty. Humanely speaking this argument reverses a principle to which we have always given lip service, the idea that economic institutions are designed to

[7] These data from the Survey Research Center at the University of Michigan are quoted in *Hearings*, House Subcommittee, p. 28.

serve men, not that men are to be sacrificed to serve economic institutions. Cost-accounting of poverty is unimpressive also when we consider the vast public cost of such measures as oil depletion allowances and farm subsidies. When we deal with the poor rather than with the oil industry or the Grange, terms like "allowance" and "subsidy" strangely are replaced by terms like "welfare" and "handout." It is not the cost of eradicating poverty that prompts Congressional inaction; it is rather the fact that the poor cannot afford the lobby required to press for action.

Perhaps the most popular reaction to the problems of the poor is the advice that the poor get jobs and go to work. This we hear not only on the street but find on posters reading "FIGHT POVERTY: GO TO WORK." The roots of this point of view grew in the soil of the early American republic and the basic American ethic of work. There remains in the American mind, especially in those who "have," the idea that nothing should be done for the poor because they will not help themselves. Americans tend to feel viscerally, if not to conclude rationally, that the poor are poor simply because they are lazy and will not work. This attitude is coupled with the assumption that if a man but tries hard, is frugal in spending, and remains diligent he will succeed and prosper.

At one point in the history of this country there was more than a grain of truth in this mind-set. In the days of the republic any able-bodied person with a modicum of common sense and some effort could carve out for himself a worthy name and a good fortune. If he failed in the settled East he could move to the vast Western frontier where an ax, hard work, and a government handout under the Homestead Act would produce landholdings, economic well-being, and self-respect. This fact of life served to reinforce the notion, widespread among Protestants, that God would reward the deserving with riches and success while he would bring poverty as punishment to those of less merit. This same idea was articulated in many of the proverbs of Benjamin Franklin, like "Early to bed and early to rise makes a man healthy, wealthy, and wise." The rags-to-riches-through-hard-work principle later provided the single theme of the writings of Horatio Alger, whose *Alger Books* for boys were read by more than one generation of Americans. The companion ideas were (and they are still appealing) that anyone who tries is guaranteed success, and that the poor are stricken because they did not try hard. Poverty is the doing purely and simply of the poor. They do not have wealth because they are not deserving. (The implication of this claim is even more attractive to those who are not poor: we have wealth because we *are* deserving!)

This set of ideas, then, hammered

out on the anvil of a bygone era, continues to give solace and support to the affluent and to frustrate public efforts on behalf of the poor. So it is that a major intellectual ingredient in the problem of poverty in America is our accustomed pattern of thought toward work and the poor. These ideas constitute the American ethic. The fact that ideas which once had some validity no longer fit the economic realities has not been adequately impressed upon the American consciousness.

ECONOMICS AND THE INCARNATION

The descriptive analysis of poverty and its attendant attitudes leads to the further question of the intellectual-theological framework within which one is to understand and deal with the problem. In this and the next three sections we turn to the ideological underpinnings of a Christian concern with poverty. Among the most vital ideological foundations of Christian involvement with poverty is the set of tenets traditionally referred to as the doctrine of Incarnation.

The theology of Incarnation contrasts sharply with both Greek dualism and Protestant pietism, which are the theological bases of most American thinking on economic problems. Incarnational theology (*carnos*—flesh, hence in-carnos—in flesh) claims that it is precisely in this world—a world of rocks, corpuscles, and turnips—that human life is to find fulfillment. Jesus as the Christ lived in the world of political and economic forces, and exactly there did he live authentically as a human being. Hence he does not call men out of the present world but to new being *in* the world *through* economic, political, and social institutions in all their imperfection. Jesus hallows the life around us and wipes out the common separation of the sacred and the secular. This is a way of saying that because human life has an economic dimension "salvation" must also be in some sense economic. Herein lies the ground of Christian theological concern with that facet of life we commonly call economic.

It is true, of course, that many Christians object to the work of ethicists who "meddle" with the marketplace rather than concentrating on the job of "saving souls." The implications of incarnational theology have escaped many sincere Christians. But behind their objection there lie some very important assumptions, especially in the word "souls"—assumptions which we reject if we read the Incarnation correctly. The term "soul" (*psuche*) from the New Testament has been given essentially Greek overtones quite unlike its meaning in the New Testament. If one divides the human being into body (the dark, evil, material) and soul (the light, good, divine) as the Greeks were accustomed, it follows that divine concern is with soul. From that it follows that the ethicist must also concern himself only with the divine, the soul. But if one understands man in a biblical fashion he sees man as a multidimensional unity, not a composite entity. He sees that the redemption of man involves all of human life, including the bodily dimension. The need for food, for example, is but one dimension of the overall human need. It is a need implanted by the Creator and hallowed by the Incarnate Christ. Incarnational theology, therefore, prevents the splitting of man into segments—the economic, the political, the social—and recognizes the indivisibility of the human person.

The implications of this kind of thinking for understanding and dealing with poverty are enormous. Perhaps the most important implication is the imperative that serious Christians seek the well-being of the whole man, including his material needs which are so totally wrapped up in his needs as a person. Far from driving one to preoccupied concern with heaven, Christian theology forces one into the marketplace as one essential place for expressing concern for neighbor. For the Christian to work toward the elimination of poverty using any means, including economic ones, is for him to participate in the work of continuing creation and redemption. If the Christian is "in Christ," to use Paul's term, he is to carry on in the real world the redemptive work of God in making human life whole. Not only does Christian theology allow concern for poverty, it inevitably demands it.

It should be clear, however, that the idea of the sacredness of the material world does *not* mean that the systems within which sacred material ends are pursued are themselves sacred. One must not move from the holiness of man's economic being to an identification of God's plan with any particular economic system. This identification is of course made, some identifying God's way with the American way and others identifying God's way with the socialist way. Rather than being identified with any system incarnational theology stands in judgment over all systems. Consequently there is no such thing as "Christian economics," as we have already noted in the introduction.

The Christian, then, finds in the incarnation not only the possibility for concern with economic problems but the very necessity for that concern. Economics and the incarnation are related in other vital ways, as we shall see. For now we must turn to yet another segment of the intellectual-theological framework within which the Christian approaches the problem of poverty.

SIN AND THE ECONOMIC LIFE

Just as the doctrine of the Incarnation drives the Christian to concern with economic systems, the doctrine of sin sheds light on the actual operation of those systems. Sin, conceived as alienation of man from God, from neighbor, and from self refers initially not to social systems but to the personal dynamics which underlie all social systems. Men in a state of alienation, cut off from their moorings, build institutions which reflect that alienation. This is the meaning of the term "corporate sin" or "corporate guilt." Indeed when sin expresses itself in alienated institutions it reaches its most demonic depths and perpetuates itself through those institutions. So it is that men become the servants, and sometimes the victims, not only of other men but of institutions. Institutions created to serve human need develop a kind of autonomy which enslaves men. Such is the case of the poor in contemporary economic institutions. Of course, institutions enslave not only the poor but also those who create and maintain them, as William H. Whyte has indicated in *The Organization Man,* and as John K. Galbraith has more recently observed in *The New Industrial State.* In some such fashion one who would understand the roots of poverty must employ more than the tools of economic science. He must explore the personal roots of this economic ill.

The poor are the victims of the failure of ideas and institutions to keep pace with the economic realities of the age. Ideas and institutions characteristically lag behind the larger forces of which they are expressions. Thus the *laissez-faire* ideology concerning the poor befits the nineteenth century and the frontier republic but not burgeoning technological change, urbanization, and industrialization. How, then, are we to understand the fact that priests of the economic cultus so carefully protect the frontier mentality? The answer lies in the fact that there is much more at stake than scientific economics. Economic institutions and ideas lag behind economic developments because of vested interests of those who have power to control institutions and to disseminate ideas. Alienated from God, men enthrone as a god-substitute their own systems in an attempt to find "salvation." The problem of poverty has arisen and remained unsolved not because of cultural lag but because of idolatry. Were it not for idolatrous worship of existing institutions nothing could stand in the way of new ideas and institutions in and through which poverty could be eradicated. Ultimately, then, poverty comes into being because men produce idols from among their own economic creations.

The necessity for idol-building is a product of the loss of Eden. Man's separation from God, his alienation, underlies all his social institutions.

Not at home in the world as it really is—with men economically interdependent, possessing nothing finally—men seek to build a world to their own liking. The result is, economically speaking, a world of distorted perspectives on private property, on the place of work, on the use of wealth, and on the relative value of men and machines. Separated from God, men find themselves alone and threatened. They seek security, solace, and support from other sources than God. Racism, for example, results from men's attempt to find life and strength through a biological fiction. Nationalism represents the search for salvation through political systems. Colonialism and imperialism are economic manifestations of the same desire for security and strength. The attempt to preserve institutions beyond their usefulness represents an effort to cling to old and comfortable idols. In the final analysis it is not intellectual stagnation nor economic incapacity but idolatry which creates and maintains poverty amid affluence. Those who seek change in the economic system toward the elimination of poverty are dealing primarily not with an economic problem but with a false worship. To change is to dethrone this deity, and deities give up the throne only reluctantly.

The chief evidence of the idolatrous and deep-seated character of the problem of economic adjustment lies in the public failure to acknowledge the sources of poverty. When the poor reach the state of desperation which prompts public demonstration by a march on Washington, the popular reaction is that they are disobeying laws, slowing traffic, and constituting a public nuisance. It is widely thought that if the marchers would stay at home to work they could do something about their poverty. The failure of educational systems, the losses to bigotry, the changing character of the whole economy are overlooked, and the poor are given full credit for their own plight. Blindness of this magnitude cannot be explained simply in terms of stupidity or, more politely, cultural lag. It is a functional blindness which serves to protect privileged position and vested interest. It is not unlike the confusion of symptom and cause reflected in our attempt to deal with urban riots by securing heavier armaments for law enforcement agencies.

Sin, conceived as alienation, not only evokes idolatrous god-substitutes but has other consequences as well. Another fruit of alienation from God is alienation of man from neighbor. Economically this second dimension manifests itself in an unwillingness to acknowledge the corporate character of economic life. One who is alienated from God and who as a result has lost security is unwilling to recognize the basic fact of life, man's dependence on and responsibility for other men. The radical individualism of the Western world is the consequence. The public nature of all wealth is ignored as the affluent move to the suburbs, leaving and forgetting the poor in the inner ghettos. The alienation of man from man is symbolized by the proximity of and yet the distance between those who speed past the poor living adjacent to the superhighway. Thus, by blocking expressways the poor can get attention, albeit the attention paid a menace and not people. It remains that America is more concerned with the health of the economy than with the health of the poor. Man is alienated from man; the affluent are separated from the poor, sometimes geographically and almost always sympathetically. Not only has America failed to eliminate poverty; it has failed to become conscious of the poor.

A major characteristic of modern economic life, and perhaps of earlier ages as well, is the fundamental distortion of value systems by which the primary economic goal is to gain wealth and power rather than to meet human need. Wealth is valued over persons. Many of the "goods" of the age are deliberately constructed to cease functioning after a predetermined length of time. The auto industry, for example, not only employs the practice of planned obsolescence but also creates machines with minimal safeguards for occupants. Inadequately tested products, like thalidomide, are marketed without due regard for the user. Artificially created wants are generated in order to sell products, while real needs go unmet because they are less profitable. Advertisers employ schemes of marketing which are patently and deliberately misleading. One sells, for example, not only the shaving preparation but also the sultry-voiced female inviting the consumer to "take it off; take it *all* off." In these and other ways our economic practice puts profit above people. Rarely are we made aware that economic systems are devised to meet human need. The poor are one scandalous result. Men are alienated from men and caught up in economic practices which ignore men as men and look only to men as markets. These inverted values show the extent of man's axiological alienation from man.

If suddenly we were to change all this and to begin manufacturing and marketing with the end in view of meeting the real needs of all the population, some of the economic consequences are clear. Sales and profits would slip, and the economic machinery would grind to a halt. Our economic system is built on the assumption of man's alienation. This merely reveals the depth of the problems of the poor: the economy is not geared to meeting their needs. Since the poor do not have an economic voice, being consumers of very little, their recourse is to the political order. Since it is unlikely that in our time we will overcome the alienations on which the economy is based we can only seek to modify the operation of that economy by politico-economic power. In the final analysis the poor are no accident. Their situation in life is the result of the deliberate actions of men—i.e., men whose action has been largely to ignore them—and in consequence their plight can be remedied only by other deliberate actions.

Yet a third dimension of sin merits mention here, *viz.*, alienation of man from himself. In the sphere of economics, as in many other realms including especially race, a man's alienation from himself expresses itself in defensive reactions to change. Thus the affluent tend to lay the blame for poverty solely at the feet of the poor and to find plenty of "reasons" for doing so. Whole ideologies are born and sustained this way, including the American ethic. The poor also tend to look outside themselves for the cause of their plight and to overlook the fact that they have not seized as fully as they might the opportunities afforded them by the economic system into which they are born. This "finger pointing" scheme is part of the elaborate mechanism we employ in bolstering a weak ego and in covering our own guilt.

A more complete analysis of the personal dynamics of this defense mechanism will be treated in the chapter on racial prejudice, but a brief word is nevertheless appropriate here. The human being is alienated from himself in that he needs to appear righteous to himself while inwardly suspecting his unrighteousness. He buries awareness of his unrighteousness in the soil of the subconscious. This leaves him almost free at the level of his conscious self to think those thoughts which give him ego-support and to blind himself to threatening thoughts. So it is that those who tell the poor to get jobs as the solution to their problem are frequently quite sincere people, maybe even people of considerable goodwill. But the weakened self is incapable of objectivity in these matters because he cannot simultaneously see things as they really are and preserve the fiction of his own innocence. He must think only those thoughts which make him "look good." He must give himself credit for his own achievement, especially if his inherited station in life has afforded him advantages over others. Thus, for example, many descendants of those who received handouts of public land under the Homestead Acts are frequently the most vocal in opposing subsidies to the poor.

The major consequence of our employment of this defense mechanism is harmful social structures. The weak ego, the ego divided against itself, must find strength from such sources as economic gain and power. Too weak to accept blame and credit where actually appropriate, a man must lay blame at the feet of others. The result is social paralysis. Busy assessing blame, we do not have the will to take action to eliminate social problems, whether racism, poverty, or war. The defensive, alienated personality is so preoccupied with hiding guilt and bolstering a weak ego that he is unable to correct that action through which he incurs guilt. Here we have the vicious circle of alienation manifesting itself in public policy. Separated from himself and thus weakened, man must cover guilt, not confess it and thereby gain the perspective which enables overcoming it. The continuance of poverty is but one result.

So it is, then, that American inaction on the problem of poverty cannot be adequately understood in terms of cultural lag or inadequate economic policies. Economic systems are built by men alienated from God, neighbor, and self, and that alienation with its resultant mechanisms of defense paralyzes the mind and galvanizes it against economic change. To the alienated personality, change in any form is threatening. In this fashion the theologian understands the *personal* grounds of economic structures in which poverty will arise. The implications of this kind of analysis for economic policy are extensive, but at the minimum there are two crucial indices for those who would work to eliminate poverty.

First, this means that no purely economic change can do the job. It is human personalities, not just differences between family incomes, that is at stake. Poverty is finally a human problem, not merely an economic problem. Changes in economic policy alone may deal with the symptoms of poverty but not with the underlying human causes. Poverty is not only economic but political, educational, and attitudinal; and all these have one common base—man's alienation. To cure the *causes* of poverty we must work toward the reconciliation of men in all areas of their alienation. "Community" must replace alienation.

A second implication of this analysis for social action on poverty is that we must not expect too little from wisely chosen economic policies. Changes in policy can have effect because of the relationship between individual thinking and public policy. Not only does poverty grow out of human alienation, but also human alienation is deepened by economic systems.

If we establish an economic policy which lessens human suffering and poverty there is less guilt to be rationalized. If meaningful economic action is taken the situation of men in the society is improved, human needs are more adequately met, and we have fewer failures to justify or to bury into the subconscious. If alienation is to be finally overcome it must be by divine act, but specific economic results of particular economic policies may be changed by human acts. This is the Christian imperative for humanizing economic policies.

One final observation on sin and the economic life is that judgment for sin, i.e., the consequences of alienated action, is reaped by the society as a whole. Among the results of economic sin which builds poverty are increased crime, destruction through riot, wasted human resources, and the cost of maintaining the idle poor who are consumers but not producers of wealth. In the corrective thrust of these consequences the Christian detects signs of God's continued lordship over history.

PRIVATE PROPERTY AND DIVINE RIGHT

A third ideological matter of direct relevance to the problem of poverty is the Christian idea of Creation. The bearing of this doctrine on poverty comes chiefly on the question of property rights. Interestingly, many opponents of programs to increase economic opportunity for the poor claim, among other things, that a man's private wealth should not be taken in order to benefit those who have not gained wealth. This claim is in turn based on a presupposition which has proved pivotal for American thinking, *viz.*, that of the right to gain and hold private property.

In the seventeenth century the rising middle class found its ideological justification for growing wealth in the philosophy of John Locke. Locke's position was essentially that a man has a "natural right" to the products of his labor.[8] Though Locke does not add it, the correlative principle—that no one has a right to that for which he does not work—was added to protect the property being accumulated. With the vast growth of capital holdings, Locke's principle was further modified to include not merely one's right to that on which he had worked but also that which he gained by use of capital holdings.

While not many Americans wish to explore philosophically the concept of "natural right" in its economic application, one of the most holy of sacred cows in our stable of economic principles is that one's private property is his by right, whether "divine" or "natural." With this one goes the further principle that to give a person something for which he has not invested his labor is morally wrong and works to the detriment of the receiver's will to help himself. Welfare programs, and now the war on poverty, have long been opposed on the basis of such reasoning as this. The irony is that quite frequently those who insist most strongly that the poor must raise themselves by hard work are those whose position in society has been determined by wealth or status they inherited and for which they did not work! If their principle is serious we should declare a one-hundred percent inheritance tax and with it pay off the national debt! This in turn would do the affluent a

[8] See Locke's *Second Treatise on Civil Government,* esp. Chap. V.

favor in shielding him against indolence.

Christians have from time to time adopted the essentials of the principle of private property, claiming divine right or gift of God in place of natural right. Once Christians came to be among the upper socioeconomic classes the vast majority insisted on the right given by God to hold private wealth. The amount of property one could hold by divine right has commonly not been thought to have an upper limit, though many principles have been articulated on proper methods of gaining wealth. While the right to private property has a long history and some distinguished modern advocates,[9] there is no way of moving logically from the Christian doctrine of creation to that principle. Since so much depends upon our assessment of this basic principle, and since any program for action on poverty must presuppose something of property rights, it is essential that we reexamine the theology of property. Hopefully a clearer theology of property will provide the conceptual basis on which anti-poverty programs might rest.

Theologically speaking all things finally "belong" to God alone. No man "owns" anything in an absolute sense. This is the truth in the popular saying, "you can't take it with you when you die." Ownership, practically speaking, means power to control the use of wealth. This power is given by society, not by God. Some societies place more control of wealth in private hands than do others, but in all cases rules of ownership, or power to control the disposition of wealth, are humanly and not divinely established. When those who establish the rules for particular societies are Christian they may or may not inaugurate widespread private control. Indeed, Christian Socialist parties in Europe claim a Christian basis for socialism, just as many capitalists claim Christian sanction for a so-called free-market economy. Moreover, Christians have found it possible to be obedient to God under a variety of economic systems, this being the point of Karl Barth in his exchange with Reinhold Niebuhr.[10]

What, then, does a Christian theology of property entail? In the first place, it is apparent under the doctrine of creation that all things—the world, wealth, and human life itself—belong to God. *No man owns anything* in a final way. In the second place, it is clear that God entrusts the world to men for their control and use. This theme is expressed biblically in God's giving Adam "dominion"

---

[9] See George F. Thomas, *Christian Ethics and Moral Philosophy* (New York: Scribner's, 1955), pp. 311 ff.

[10] Rose Marie Oswald Barth, "Karl Barth's Own Words," *Christian Century*, March 25, 1959, pp. 352-55. Reinhold Niebuhr, "Barth's East German Letter," in *ibid.*, Feb. 11, 1959, pp. 167-68. See also two related articles: Reinhold Niebuhr, "The Test of the Christian Faith Today," in *ibid.*, Oct. 28, 1959, pp. 1239-43; and Karl Barth, "Recapitulation Number Three," in *ibid.*, Jan. 20, 1960, pp. 72-76.

over the world's contents (Gen. 1:28-30). In the third place, we note God's purpose—that men might have life—in entrusting the world to human care. It is for the purpose of making men human, for instance, that God enters the Covenant with Moses and that he establishes the New Covenant in Jesus.

From these three principles we gain a Christian theology of property. Note first that human "ownership" is tenuous at best. The property in our possession is not ours—we are "trustees," not "owners." Possessiveness, therefore, is inappropriate. Note secondly that the purpose for which property is entrusted by God is that men should have life. The use to which property is to be put is thus specified: it is to be used for the enrichment of *human* life, not just the life of the trustee. Note thirdly that no specific methods of gaining that end—the enrichment of human life—are enjoined. That is, the scheme for control and distribution is not specified. In light of this analysis, therefore, neither capitalism nor socialism nor any other economic system can claim special Christian sanction. Theology thus establishes the goal toward which men must exercise their trust, but it does not fabricate the systems through which men must seek that goal.

The Christian imperative, then, is clear. Men are obliged under God to establish that system of ownership and distribution which for their time and place most effectively guarantees life to all men. If a system of private ownership can for a given era serve that end more effectively, then there is a conditional imperative for private ownership ("conditional" here meaning so long as that condition prevails). If under other conditions public ownership more completely assures life to all men, there then prevails a conditional imperative for public control.

The point of this is not to argue that in our time and place increased public control is demanded, though this possibility must not be ignored. The point is rather to indicate that private control is a *conditional* principle subject finally to the divine imperative that all men should have life. It is therefore not Christianly possible to claim private control, i.e., ownership, as a divine right.

There is yet a second point which is relevant specifically in a society which leaves considerable power of control in private hands. If private ownership is the established means of securing life, private owners are obliged—if they would be responsible or responsive to God—to control wealth so as to guarantee life to all those in society. Private ownership is legitimate under God only when it serves this end. Herein lies the burden of private control. Responsibility is placed diffusely in the society. Under a system of public ownership responsibility is centrally located in the hands of a few in authority. Whether private or public control is the superior way cannot finally be judged theologically. Both systems and their variants are to be judged in terms of their effectiveness in guaranteeing life to men. The burden of both systems is that men, alienated as they are, tend to make private use of whatever wealth is placed in their hands. Men tend to be so impressed with the ego-strength they derive from possessions as to ignore the fact that all property finally belongs to God and is by him entrusted for the well-being of all men. This latter awareness is essential in principle for any Christian conception of property rights. In any case, the *right* to control wealth, whether public or private, is a *conditional* right. The condition is that wealth must be controlled in response to human need, i.e., "responsibly."

So it is that the Christian imperative concerns not the issue of *who* controls wealth but the ends sought by wealth. As regards the present situation of poverty in America, this seems to mean that we have in fact deprived the poor of their divine birthright. Those into whose hands wealth has been placed in trust have in fact denied a segment of the population the possibility of material possession and with that the right to life itself. The divine imperative is that ways must be found by which the poor may share in the life given all men by God.

This theological principle does not contain in itself prescriptions for concrete programs which would enable its own implementation. The drawing of programs is finally a task for economists and others who can anticipate the effects of this or that program on the entire economy and especially on the economic well-being of the poor. Christian ethicists are rarely, if ever, competent to judge the *economics* of any particular plan. They need to rely on specialists. But it is equally true that the *goals* to be sought are by their very nature moral and cannot be arrived at through economic science or expertise. The goal is to see to it that every citizen in our society, and ultimately the world, receives that which sustains life of a *human* sort.[11] This must, for the Christian, be the overriding aim of economic policy and practice. Fortunately there are economists, some of them Christian and some not, who for a variety of reasons have accepted that goal. The problem remains to find and implement the policy which will most adequately allow the achievement of that goal.

THE RIGHT TO WORK AND THE RIGHT TO BE

The major symptom (and to an extent the cause) of the plight of the poor is that they do not have jobs. In a society which has traditionally re-

[11] For a note on the nature of human life see Part III, Chap. II.

garded the doing of a job as the means of gaining property, and has not yet provided other means toward that end, the lack of a job proves disastrous. Our civilization continues to operate largely under the principle—with ever so slight a twist of Locke—that *only* through the doing of a job is one entitled to receive the goods and services required for life. In theory at least we reward those who produce with wages and thereby meet their needs as consumers. Thus, not to have a job means initially to suffer as a consumer. More importantly, however, the jobless suffer as persons. In a society where such high value is placed on production it is inevitable that the rewards of production function to meet not merely the consumptive needs of the producer but the ego-needs as well. From his job a man derives not merely a paycheck but also a sense of fulfillment and self-esteem. Thus to deny a person the possibility of participating in production is, in our society, at least, to deny him part of his noneconomic humanity. For this reason, incidentally, no welfare payment in any amount can replace work as productive activity.

The problems of our civilization in this regard are enormous, but two chief difficulties loom largest on the horizon. One is the short-term problem of jobs, and the other is the longer-range question of work itself. The word "job," as distinct from the broader term "work," denotes a contractual arrangement between human beings. Appropriate conditions being established, an employer agrees to pay for the services of an employee. The term "work," on the other hand, denotes a kind of creative human activity through which man's environment is made more livable. Obviously, some work expresses itself in the formation of jobs (for production of goods and services), whereas other work is done non-contractually (e.g., volunteer services like beautification projects by the local garden club). In turn there are jobs which would not qualify under the definition of work (e.g., the "job" of the underworld assassin). So it is that the poor suffer from a lack of jobs, not of work.

We may expect that jobs will be in increasingly short supply if present trends continue. In the modern industrial state automatic machinery takes over many of the more mechanical tasks and thereby makes for the possession of more "goods" with less effort. But machines also make for fewer jobs, especially among the more poorly trained segment of the population, those who have commonly performed the more menial and mechanical tasks. The process begun by automation in the nineteenth century has in the twentieth reached new dimensions through the development of electronic "brains" capable of controlling the automatic machines. Thus even more jobs are being removed from human hands, and again it is the lower income segment of the population that is hardest hit. The jobs which remain require more and more intensive training and more highly developed skills as well as greater geographic mobility on the part of workers. The poor are neither highly trained nor mobile.

The difficulty of completing contracts for jobs is increased since we lack not only employers but also employees. There are people who might be employed, but for a variety of reasons they are not. They often live not where the jobs are but in inner cities where major industry has not located. They often do not have the basic education or the job-training to equip them to contract for jobs. Many have never developed the habits of personal discipline which would enable them to be at particular places at specified times. Our society has, in other words, not only the unemployed but also those thought to be unemployable.

Though we have assumed that many of our citizens are unemployable, evidence is being gathered to the contrary. Experimental programs now underway suggest that those formerly thought unemployable can in fact be trained and usefully employed. The final report is not out at this writing, but a preliminary look at the experience of Lockheed Aircraft in an experimental project of training the "untrainable" suggests not only that the hard-core poor can be employed but that they become as satisfactory and productive as those hired through normal channels.[12] The potential effect on the problem of poverty is enormous. It is increasingly apparent that even the hard-core poor can be placed in the economic system. The fiscal cost, however, is great. We have not devised the programs nor given financial support for the extensive and expensive training required, but there is a growing awareness that it can be done.

Our failure to employ the educational and economic tools at our disposal to solve the problem of jobs suggests that the problem is deeper than either education or economics. The traditional American ethic does not include an adequate philosophy of work or an understanding of the human rights and obligations which must be exercised through the economy. The crucial and root problem is finally philosophical or theological in character. Our attention, therefore, must turn to a Christian theology of work.

Theologically work is understood in the context of divine love and providence. The Christian claim is that God gives men life and whatever appertains thereto. Among those gifts God provides work as a means of seizing, sustaining, and fulfilling life. As such, then, work is to be understood as part of the created order of things, not the product of man's sin and divine displeasure. Genesis notes ap-

[12] For a news report on this program see *U.S. News and World Report,* "Training the Unemployables" (July 1, 1968).

propriately that God put Adam in the garden that he might "till it and keep it," this fact being antecedent to Adam's disobedience. So it is that Genesis reflects awareness of the fact that if we strip away all the social conventions in man's relationship to his environment we find that work remains in the picture. Man and man's world are incomplete, but the possibilities of completion are provided as part of God's intention that man should be in his image. This is simply to say that man must participate in the creative process itself. Only so can he complete provision for his material wants, and only so can he participate in truly creative activity which nourishes him in the image of the creative God.

The ethical implications of this view are clear. Any man or any society who would seek to be responsive to the divine will and to participate in the divine plan must look upon work as both a right and a duty. Looked at as a gift of God to men, work belongs to all men and is not to be denied to any man by social conventions or economic institutions. Thus a society which seeks to be responsive to God will guarantee the free exercise of God's free gift as a socially established *right*. Looked at as a part of the divine plan for the completion of human being, for nourishing man in the image of God and for establishing a humane environment, work is an obligation or duty from which society can exempt no man. Since the well-being of all men is dependent on work, societies of men will justly demand that citizens discharge their *obligation* to work.

In this context, in which work is viewed as a right and as a duty, the necessities impinging on every society become clear. Men must work, if they are to be men, and not every man can do the same work. Since men are dependent on the work of other men, i.e., since every man is part of the larger body (the corporate whole), men in society are obliged to organize creative activity for the common good. (This organizational role, incidentally, becomes the creative work for some, for those who govern.) It is this process, this organization of work, that produces jobs. Jobs are not themselves part of the divine creation but are rather human devices born in response to it.

So it is that social systems are obliged to organize work in such a way as to enable participation by all men. How they organize, i.e., form contractual relationships, is not specified by a theology of work so long as the chosen method is inclusive of all men. But it remains abundantly clear that if Christians are to be obedient they must guarantee participation in work for all men. Christians must seek to organize society in such a fashion as to fulfill or complete the created order. In translation this means minimally that Christians must build economic systems which will provide jobs. It is that obligation that our present system is failing to meet. Herein lies both the Christian imperative for change and the gauge by which that change is to be judged. The divinely given right to be does include the right to work at a livable wage and toward the end of making the "garden" more humane.

The immediate task of establishing jobs, however, introduces a wide spectrum of problems. A job exists only with the confluence of three factors: definable work to be done, a person willing and able to do it, and an employer willing and able to oversee and to pay. The first two conditions are already met. That there is definable work to be done no one can seriously question. Our streets, parks, forests, and recreational facilities are littered and poorly kept. Our buildings are functional, but sterile and in need of artful attention by skilled architects and workmen. Our streams are polluted, and our air is heavy with industrial and automotive contaminants. Our population is vastly undereducated not merely in job skills but more importantly in those things which deepen one's awareness of himself and his environment. There is plenty of "tilling" left in the garden. It is equally true that there are people who do not have jobs; and some of them, moreover, are quite willing and able to perform needed tasks. Others need training not merely in general education but in job skills. We have the technical means and the wealth to undertake vast programs of training even where there is a shortage of people able to perform jobs. The key to the problem, then, seems to lie in finding the third essential, the employer able to oversee and pay.

Who, then, could and should employ those who need employment to do jobs essential to human survival? The machinery for control of such a task force already exists both in private industry and in governmental agency. Private corporations, operating as they do in enslavement to cost accounting, are not likely employers of people in work not directly essential to the corporation itself. Since the tasks to be done would benefit all the society and not just the industrial system, it is not just that private capital should be expected to establish the needed jobs. If it is the public as a whole which would reap the rewards from the work of the poor in newly created jobs, the public finally should pay. Whether we can or even should find nongovernmental methods of establishing jobs need hardly be debated here, but it remains that the administrative machinery already exists in government for seeing the job done.[13] Indeed, in such abandoned programs as the Civilian Conservation Corps and the Work Projects Ad-

[13] John Kenneth Galbraith has argued cogently that some things essential to the humane life are unneeded by the industrial system. It falls to the state to provide these things. See esp. Chap. 30 in *The New Industrial State* (Boston: Houghton Mifflin, 1967).

ministration we have political precedent and experience.

If by these or by other means we can establish jobs we will succeed in the first step to eliminate poverty. Under a Christian ethic of work we are obliged to assure men the opportunity to "till the garden," i.e., to have jobs. It is imperative that we discharge our duty in claiming for all men the right to be through the right to work.

SOME GUIDING PRINCIPLES

In keeping with the ethical method advanced in the introduction it is appropriate here that some tentative intermediate principles be suggested. It is not adequate for the ethicist to say that we desire the economic structures which effect the greatest humanity in men. It is not possible for the ethicist to spell out programs of specific nature since the creation of programs requires competence in the daily functioning of economic forces. The following, then, are offered as principles which stand between final economic goals and concrete economic policy.

1. Because of the dehumanizing effects of poverty and because poverty is a corporate and not merely an individual product, we are obliged by the humanizing thrust of *agape* to strive corporately to *eliminate* poverty as an economic and a human reality. The wealth of the nation is sufficient to enable the eradication of poverty. The means can be found among those already suggested by economists and others.

2. Since men have the right, given by God, to life and to those things which sustain it, and since we continue to employ the possession of private property as a chief means toward that end, we are morally obliged to make it possible for all citizens to obtain private property sufficient to enable humane life.

3. Since creative activity in work is essential not only for making man's environment humane but also for creating a sense of identity, achievement, and worth in persons, we are morally obliged to make it possible for all citizens to work. The principle entails necessarily two sub-principles: that we see to it that jobs are established and defined, and that we implement programs for the training and relocating of workers.

4. Since education serves not merely to provide job competence but also to enrich one's sensitivities to himself, to others, and to his natural environment, both general education and specific job training for all citizens are basic human rights which must be guaranteed by society. In this context means must be found to attract the poor into educational pro-

grams designed to meet their specific needs.

5. Since physical environment plays a central role in determining a person's perspective on life and his sense of individual well-being, the physical conditions under which the poor live must be improved to provide sound housing and a measure of familial integrity and privacy. Overcrowded, unclean, and drab living conditions are not merely symptoms and results of poverty but an active cause of the attitudes and dispositions which breed and perpetuate poverty. No significant steps can be made toward regeneration of the poor until the conditions of deprivation and want which prevail in our cities and towns are eliminated.

6. Because poverty is not merely an economic fact but a disease which infects persons at every level of their existence, it cannot be eliminated unless it is attacked simultaneously at every level. Education, jobs, housing, monetary income, and involvement in community with other persons are but segments of the single human need, the need to be human.

A POSTSCRIPT ON PROGRAMS

Among the unresolved issues confronting those who would seek action on the problem of poverty is the question: through what channel is action to be directed? Some citizens would insist on an expansion of government activity, while others would argue for a reduced role of government. Some would insist upon decreased federal action, leaving more power and responsibility in the hands of states, while others would argue that states have been singularly unresponsive to needs of the poor, a fact which demands federal action. Private business, most notably some of the larger insurance companies, has given some indication of a desire to enter the war on poverty, and support has not been entirely lacking from national foundations.

It remains, however, that most programs of major significance to the poor have been federally initiated and administered. One has the impression, moreover, that the federal government has been both more active and more wise than the various state governments. The reasons are clear. Some of the states lack resources for major programs, and still others lack the will to establish such programs as are economically feasible. Moreover, this nation is increasingly one interdependent network of economic, political, and social forces—a fact better recognized in Washington than in the various regions and states. Since poverty knows no regional or political boundaries it is a national problem which only concerted action can resolve. The federal government remains as the cohesive and comprehensive institution of national life. It is the institution to which we turned successfully in the economic crises of the thirties. It is not surprising, therefore, that Washington has in general been more responsive to the problems of poverty than have Hartford, Tallahassee, Austin, and Sacramento. What is more, the stabilizing role of big government has been accepted by and large, though often reluctantly, since the Great Depression. Graduated income tax, Social Security, legislation on fair employment practices and the like are well-established realities. Just as the problems which produced these stabilizers were too big for states to handle individually, so the problem of poverty seems too great. At the moment, therefore, it would appear not only that poverty can be adequately dealt with only by federal action but also that the will to act is located primarily in Washington.

But more important even than the issue over where the action must originate and who will act is the issue of the kind of action demanded by the present situation. What sort of program will turn the tide of poverty? Traditionally we have turned to welfare and charitable agencies, some public and others private. In the early days of the republic ecclesiastical bodies carried on much of the immediate relief work, but during the depression of the thirties public assistance was increased. Departments of Public Welfare have long rendered service of a crisis nature giving food, clothing, and financial assistance to hard-core cases of poverty. The importance of these agencies is not to be underestimated, though they have traditionally been understaffed and inadequately financed to deal effectively with the problems at hand. Moreover, we are beginning to realize that public relief deals only with the symptoms of poverty, not its causes, and that such programs succeed primarily in reducing starvation, not poverty with its several dimensions. For a long while to come emergency relief of hardship cases must be continued and even expanded, but this is admittedly a stopgap and not a solution.

Noises are being made from time to time of a guaranteed annual income, perhaps through the instrumentality of a negative income tax. The thought here is that direct subsidies would be made to all those with sub-subsistence income in order to raise the standard of living to a higher minimum. Guaranteed annual income would doubtless produce good along with some bad effects, but such a program standing alone would do little to remove the underlying causes of poverty and to restructure the attitudes which accompany it. Cast in the same ideological mold as public relief, guaranteed annual income would finally be merely an expanded charity and would do little to help people escape poverty as a way of living and thinking. Much is to be said, however, for guaranteed income as an interim measure. It could and largely would eliminate the scandal of malnourishment and literal starvation like that found among many Americans of Indian descent. Coupled with other more basic programs guaranteed annual income holds great promise.

Another kind of effort against poverty is represented by the federal Office of Economic Opportunity, the chief arm of the so-called war on poverty. OEO has traveled a rocky road in its dealings with a penurious Congress and in its efforts to avoid administrative missteps. Admittedly experimental, the program has moved haltingly and uncertainly, but behind the programs themselves there lies evidence that we are coming to recognize the many-sided character of poverty. Assuming that the problems of the poor have to do first and foremost with the lack of personal identity, little sense of achievement and self-respect, and intense frustration, OEO has sent workers into homes to listen to the poor themselves. Their aim has been to help focus the problems faced in poverty areas and to suggest lines of action which might be taken to solve the problems. In many localities, for example, it was discovered that work was available for women who could not take certain jobs because of small children in the home. In response "Mother's Clubs" have been formed by the poor themselves to care for children during the day, with each mother paying part of the cost. Night classes in secretarial skills, carpentry, auto mechanics, and the like have been organized as a result of OEO's neighborhood development efforts. Organizations of the poor have been established to secure services from local governments, to conduct voter registration drives, to clean up neighborhoods, to provide information on jobs. Though such programs have been very effective in some localities, they have been experimental in nature and regional in scope. Programs like those of OEO promise, nevertheless, to be more effective than public welfare in getting at the roots of poverty precisely because they involve the poor themselves. Since the aim is the rebuilding of persons and communities, not just filling the larder, the poor must finally be enlisted as active participants in the struggle and not merely as recipients of paternalistic favor.

In the final analysis the continued and growing existence of poverty in the United States is the product neither of the lack of reasonable programs nor of the shortage of wealth to implement them. Poverty exists finally because of a lack of determination to eliminate it. It bears repeating that in our time poverty is not primarily an economic problem but a problem in economics which stems from our failure to adjust philosophy and outlook to the demands of God for a new industrial state. The successful completion of attitudinal adjustment provides the sole cure for laggard motivation on the part of the American public.

V. Racism: A Contemporary Idolatry

No problem in American society has received more detailed attention than the problem of relations among racial and ethnic groups. Psychologists, sociologists, economists, psychiatrists, ethicists, philosophers, theologians, and innumerable prophets from every imaginable perspective have analyzed, diagnosed, prescribed, and pled their cases. This is entirely fitting and proper. No other fact of American life has so determined the character of our civilization as the patterns of thought and modes of treatment of men across racial or ethnic lines. The earliest settlers regarded aboriginal Americans both as a plague and as children of God, and they dealt with the Indian sometimes as a disease to be eliminated and sometimes as a man to be ministered to. Before the colonial period ended, chattel slavery was an accepted fact in American life, and with it our peculiar ideas and institutions were being formed. The greatest crisis the nation ever faced had to do centrally, if not exclusively, with the respective status of groups of men. Since the Civil War more energies have been spent and more ink has been spilled on race than on any comparable subject. All Americans are involved whether they wish to be or not. From the highest tribunals of justice to the most unwashed street corner, to the most remote bayou, problems of civil rights occupy our attention.

Central in the concern has been the Negro. In the minds of many Americans the problem of civil rights has to do with the question: what is the place of the Negro in American life? This fact in itself adds yet another dimension to the "American dilemma" in that justice toward other biologically or ethnically distinguishable groups is postponed. Little is heard or said, for instance, of the consistent denial of basic human rights to Indian Americans. Even in what is likely the most important single study of intergroup relations in American society, Gunnar Myrdal's *An American Dilemma,* the fate of the Negro receives the lion's share of attention. In the long run our preoccupation with the rights of Negro Americans has served to the further disadvantage of other disadvantaged groups.

In the present chapter we are concerned with all divisions of minority groups from the majority. It is not the intent, however, to deal with the distinctive problems, historical and psychological, of any group. Moreover, in illustrations and general format the Negro looms largest. The decision to allot the primary place to the Negro once again is made with some pangs of conscience, but the purpose of this book seems best served in that way. Since our goal is to illustrate how Christian faith and life bear on social realities it has appeared necessary to choose the concrete examples most widely experienced and recognized by readers. It is far more likely that the reader has known Negroes than that he has known Indians or Americans of any other distinguishable minority. Even so, the basic principles of Christian relationships are the same. The same social and civil goals must be pursued for all Americans, whether Negro, Indian, Mexican, European, or Oriental in biological or cultural ancestry. Thus when we talk of stereotypes of the Negro, for example, it is assumed that *functional* parallels can be found for each minority. Specific beliefs about and histories of each minority are different, but the same psychological and social dynamics operate for every group.

RACISM, AN IDEOLOGY AND A PRACTICE

Americans have been both intrigued and paralyzed by a set of ideas imported from Europe and modified to fit American life. Those ideas about human destiny and their related imperatives about human conduct merge to form a phenomenon best labeled "racism." Racism as an ideology contains centrally the following conviction: that certain biological subspecies of *homo sapiens* are genetically endowed with traits inferior to other subspecies. Coupled with this doctrine is the moral imperative that inferior and superior subspecies are to be dealt with according to different maxims of conduct. This set of ideas, whether consciously espoused or subconsciously presupposed, stands among the most widespread and influential ideological forces in this country.

Contrary to popular opinion, racist ideology is relatively new. Racism developed under the combined influence of two main developments in the eighteenth century—biological classification and the institution of slavery. In biology classification of living things was underway. Once schemes of classification were available racist ideology was *possible.* A felt need to justify enslavement of the Negro made that ideology seem *desirable.*[1] Proslavery forces in the seventeenth century employed biblical and theological bases for their doctrines, taking their cue from several key sources, especially the story of Noah and his

[1] This position is developed in greater detail by Gunnar Myrdal in *An American Dilemma* (New York: Harper, 1944), pp. 83-112. In an otherwise very useful volume on race, Thomas F. Gossett's *Race, the History of an Idea in America* (Dallas: Southern Methodist University Press, 1963), some confusion prevails about the origins of racism. Gossett finds racism in ancient history but admits that "it had no biology or anthropology behind it." This claim is possible only because Gossett does not give an adequately precise definition of "racism." See especially his Chapter 1, "Early Race Theories," pp. 3-16.

sons. The claim was that the races of men descended from the sons of Noah (Gen. 9:18-19). The sons of Ham, one of Noah's sons, were thought to have given rise to the Negro tribes of Africa, who still live under the curse allegedly performed by God (Gen. 9:20-27). (The curse was actually uttered by Noah, not God, and he was at the time just up from the sleep of a big drunk!) Proslavery arguments were also derived from the "tower" epic as well as from the marital prohibitions of Ezra and Nehemiah.[2] At the turn of the nineteenth century, however, the shift was being made from biblical to biological argument. The most sophisticated form of racist ideology was to emerge in the latter half of the nineteenth century in the famous work of Count Arthur Joseph deGobineau, *Essay on the Inequality of Races* (1855). DeGobineau's essay was adequately authoritative in tone to elicit approbation, especially from those who wanted justification for their treatment of minorities. It was deGobineau's writing that first provided the convenient three-race division later to become popular. Modern expressions of racism, like that of Carleton Putnam's *Race and Reason*,[3] show greater indebtedness to the noted Frenchman than to any other single authority.

The attractiveness of racism as a social philosophy roots in part in its appeal to science. The doctrine of genetic inequality seems so incontrovertible. Genetic understanding of human behavior implies that behavior is beyond deliberate change, or so racists assume. The claim that "it is in the blood" has about it a wonderfully compelling finality conveniently joined to utter simplicity. Moreover, such a doctrine is almost universally applicable in justifying the social status quo. It had special appeal in the South where every foreseeable social change threatened the precarious white planter hegemony. In the South, too, it just as readily "explains" the political dominance of key aristocratic families as it demonstrates the inevitability of outcast status for the Negro or the Oriental. Initially employed to defend slavery, racism was easily transferred to fit the new situation which followed the Civil War. It continues to provide a pseudoscientific and reassuring certainty for segregationists.

However compelling and final genetic theories of human behavior may be, the concept "race" soon encountered real difficulty. The basic problem was the apparent impossibility of precision in identifying "racial" subtypes. Search was undertaken to find the key genetic factors in "races." Elaborate measurements were made to establish a "cephalic index" by which races and individuals might be

[2] For an excellent treatment of this subject see Everett Tilson, *Segregation and the Bible* (Nashville: Abingdon Press, 1958), pp. 18-28.

[3] (Washington: Public Affairs Press, 1961.)

judged or identified, but the results were more humorous than helpful. Color charts for measuring pigmentation of skin became so complex as to be useless. Study was made of cranial capacity in racial groups on the theory that larger brains would explain "higher" intelligence. It was learned that the average cranial capacity in Negroes was about 50 cc. less than that in whites, but that Parisians boast some 200 cc. larger capacity than Americans. Neanderthal man was found to have had even more room for a brain than contemporary man. Some investigators turned from brain-size to convolutions of the cerebral surface, but no firm connection has been established racially between intelligence and the size or shape of the brain. Investigations of the endocrine glands have produced no better results in explaining behavioral patterns of racial or ethnic groups. Special attention was paid the thyroid glands to determine specifically whether the slow-moving characteristics of the Southern Negro were attributable to low thyroid output.[4] The conclusion was that no connection could be demonstrated. The chief result of such investigations so far is that genetic explanations of racial/ethnic behavior patterns are now largely discarded by anthropologists.[5]

Racist doctrine thus appears to be scientifically insecure, if not defective. But its moral defects are greater. Even if it could be demonstrated that some identifiable groups of *homo sapiens* are genetically superior to other groups the racist conclusions could not be squared with a Christian ethic, or for that matter with secular humanism. The moral defect in racist ideology lies in its presupposition that the worth of, and hence the duty toward, a human being is a function of genetic endowment. The Christian presupposition of the equality of worth in men roots not in equality of genetic endowment but in God's active concern for all men, whatever their genetic traits. The Christian doctrine of human equality thus would not be affected even by demonstrable proof of genetically based inequality of ability. One's duty to his fellowman under *agape* is never modified by the merit or ability of the one loved. What interests the theologian, therefore, is not so much the ethical relevance of genetic endowment but the readiness of men to assume that relevance. The ethicist's concern is never properly with racism's scientific validity but with the fact that men seem so ready to assume its validity in order to justify their racist conduct. The crucial question for our purposes,

[4] See M. F. Ashley-Montagu, *Race: Man's Most Dangerous Myth* (New York: Columbia University Press, 1942).

[5] A guarded statement of the matter may be found in *The UNESCO Courier* (April, 1965), available from The United Nations Educational, Social, and Cultural Organization, 801 Third Avenue, New York, N.Y. 10022.

then, is why does racism survive? For an answer to that we must turn to the nature and function of racial/ethnic prejudice.

PREJUDICE, THE INNER GROUND OF RACISM

A great variety of interpretative schemes has emerged from attempts to understand racism. Some interpreters view racism as a proper product of the victimized group, i.e., that the group is as it is thought to be. This "deserved reputation" theory is currently regarded more as a mark of prejudice itself than as a serious attempt to understand racism. Others interpret racism simply as a product of the peculiar histories of groups and their interrelations.[6] Such interpretations tend to be mere descriptions of events rather than analyses of racism as a phenomenon. Still others see racism as a manifestation of an innate "consciousness of kind," a selective gregarious instinct, or apprehension over the unfamiliar.[7]

Another approach identifies racism as one result of certain psychodynamic processes in the developing personality. Psychodynamic theories of racism are among the most widespread—and in our opinion the most productive—approaches to the phenomenon as a whole. In what follows in this section and the next we draw heavily upon the results of scholarship undertaken within a basically psychodynamic approach. Of utmost importance in this connection are the writings of the late Gordon W. Allport.[8]

Allport defines ethnic prejudice as "an antipathy based upon a faulty and inflexible generalization. It may be felt or expressed. It may be directed toward a group as a whole, or toward an individual because he is a member of that group."[9] In this view prejudice contains two essential ingredients, *belief* and *attitude.* The cognitive element, belief about the object of prejudice, must be both overgeneralized—i.e., faulty—and re-

[6] Oscar Handlin, for instance, demonstrates this view in his essay "Prejudice and Capitalist Exploitation," *Commentary,* July, 1948, pp. 79-85.

[7] See Robert E. Park, *Race and Culture* (New York: The Free Press, 1950), pp. 236 ff. Park rejects a blatant geneticism but replaces it with a theory heavily dependent on the idea that men have misgivings toward the strange or unfamiliar. His essay may be found also in *The Annals of the American Academy of Political and Social Science,* Nov., 1928.

[8] His most comprehensive work is *The Nature of Prejudice,* 1954. This book has been slightly revised and republished in paperback under the same title (Anchor Books; Garden City, N.Y.: Doubleday, 1958). Quotations from this work are reprinted by permission of Addison-Wesley, Reading, Mass. Allport's theory of human personality establishes the framework for his studies of prejudice and may be found in his *Personality: A Psychological Interpretation* (New York: Henry Holt and Company, 1937). Two of his articles are of special interest for our purposes: with Bernard M. Kramer, "Some Roots of Prejudice," *Journal of Psychology,* July, 1946, pp. 9-39; and "Prejudice: Is It Societal or Personal?" *Pastoral Psychology,* May, 1963, pp. 33-45.

[9] *The Nature of Prejudice,* p. 9.

sistant to change. Overgeneralized beliefs give rise to "stereotypes" about the outgroup. Through stereotypes all members of the outgroup are indiscriminately cast in the same mold. Stereotyping is thus crucial to prejudice and may take two forms. On the one hand the characteristics ascribed to a given ethnic group are conceived in exaggerated form, and on the other hand each representative of the group is thought to possess these characteristics simply because he is a member of that group. The volitional element of prejudice—in Allport's terms, the "antipathy"—may take any of several forms, some so mild as quiet, inner hostility and some so overt as intent to lynch.

It is clear that in order for a person properly to be considered prejudiced his relationship to a group must contain elements of both faulty belief and hostile attitude. One may, for example, employ the category "Yankee" as a kind of generalized impression of Americans without having hostility to all those regarded as Yanks. As part of our mental calculus we of necessity build categories exact enough to be useful but too general to stand up under careful analysis. Just as overgeneralized beliefs may exist without antipathy, so antipathy may exist without overgeneralized belief. For example, one may harbor hostile attitudes toward the Ku Klux Klan and each of its members without overgeneralizing the personal qualities of each member. In this instance one has antipathy toward these men because of their espoused goals. Thus, neither overgeneralized belief nor hostile attitude standing alone can properly be regarded as prejudicial.

In the prejudiced personality, however, the two ingredients are mutually reinforcing. The beliefs seem to justify, indeed to demand, hostile or rejecting attitudes since, for example, one would not appreciate a group of people who "smell bad, carry razors, are over-sexed and prone to violence." At the same time hostile attitudes serve as a filter for information which might modify the stereotype. Hostility affects perception by screening data which would seriously jeopardize the stereotype. The following dialogue illustrates beautifully:

Mr. X: The trouble with the Jews is that they only take care of their own group.

Mr. Y: But the record of the Community Chest campaign shows that they give more generously, in proportion to their numbers, to the general charities of the community, than do non-Jews.

Mr. X: That shows they are always trying to buy favor and intrude into Christian affairs. They think of nothing but money; that is why there are so many Jewish bankers.

Mr. Y: But a recent study shows that the percentage of Jews in the banking business is negligible, far smaller than the percentage of non-Jews.

Mr. X: That's just it; they don't go in for respectable business; they

> are only in the movie business or run night clubs.[10]

In this protective fashion the hostile attitude reinforces the structure of belief, which in turn supports the hostile attitude.

Ethnic prejudice, then, consists of a cognitive and a volitional ingredient, each reinforcing and giving justification to the other. Given this definition of what prejudice is we must raise the further question as to why prejudice exists. What are the roots of prejudice? How does one become prejudiced? By what dynamics is prejudice generated and spread?

In answer to these questions no single theory is adequate. It is well known that some prejudiced people change their ways of thinking about groups once they live in a nonprejudiced environment, but other people under all conditions resist modification in their thinking toward outgroups. These observations, among others, suggest that people may be prejudiced in more than one way. While all prejudiced people share the same kind of beliefs and hostilities, some seem to hold more firmly to their prejudices than do others. Why is it that prejudice is more vital to some than to others? There is evidence that the answer lies in the psychodynamics of personality. Investigations show that though some people simply "adopt" prejudice, others "develop" it. For the latter, those who generate prejudice to meet their own need, it is more vital.[11]

In discussing "adopted" and "developed" prejudice it must be stressed that they are distinguishable not in terms of the behavior of the prejudiced person, nor in terms of the intensity of his prejudice, but in terms of the role prejudice plays in the total adjustment of that personality. For some people prejudice is functional, i.e., it plays a vital role in that person's adjustment to himself and to his social environment. For others, however, prejudice is nonfunctional and has the characteristics of other learned behavior. We shall describe in turn prejudice which is adopted (nonfunctional) and that which is developed (functional).

In the nonfunctional type the underlying motive is the common human need to conform to the ways of one's society. Each individual who grows up in a society wherein racial/ethnic prejudice and discrimination are common is subject to many pressures which make for conformity to those patterns of social behavior. In a very homogeneous social environment the infant personality knows virtually no alternative to prejudicial behavior. Moreover, even if the child does encounter non-prejudiced opinions and attitudes he is not easily able to overcome the primary influence of the home. He is driven by

[10] *Ibid.*, pp. 13-14.

[11] See *The Nature of Prejudice*, pp. 297-98.

real inner needs, especially the need for status, the need to belong, and the need for a measure of security. Furthermore, *social* existence presupposes some measure of conformity, the alternative being social chaos. The child thus is pressured to absorb prejudice, i.e., "adopt" it. One learns prejudicial modes of behavior in much the same way that he learns to eat peas with a fork and not a spoon (however much more efficient the spoon might be!). He is expected to live and do like the rest of his social group live and do. When prejudicial discrimination is part of that accustomed life the child is "socialized" to live and do prejudicially.

Indeed, there is a sense in which the child growing up in some social environments cannot escape prejudice. By adopting prejudice he is meeting his needs. But it must be carefully noted in this connection that prejudice acquired in this way is not functional. In this case it is the conformity and not the prejudice which is essential or functional. One might conform to nonprejudicial modes of behavior with equally functional results. So it is that adopted prejudice is not deeply ingrained in the personality, and as a rule it offers only mild resistance to change. This is not true, of course, when the desire to conform becomes neurotic. Neurotic conformity may result in the severest form of bigotry. Even then, however, it is the conformity, not the prejudice, which functions for the neurotic personality. It is as though the neurotic person wishes to say "See! I hold the same ideas you do about this, and I hold them even more dearly."

Thus the distinction between adopted and developed prejudice has to do not primarily with its intensity but with its psychic grounds. "Adopted" prejudice may be regarded as the likely, though not always necessary, result of ego-essential conformity in a society where prejudicial behavior is socially acceptable.

"Developed" or functional prejudice, on the other hand, is one aspect of the adjustment of the structurally disintegrated personality to its threatening world. It is knit into the very fabric of personality. Its chief impetus is not the social milieu but rather the life-history and personality structure of the individual. It stems from one's attempt to meet basic psychic needs. Thus to understand prejudice of the functional variety one must examine the psychodynamics of the personality in which it occurs.[12]

Jean-Paul Sartre has given a nonanalytic but helpful description of the personality in which prejudice is functional:

The Antisemite is a man who is afraid. Not of the Jews of course, but of himself, of his conscience, his freedom, of his instincts, of his responsibilities, of

[12] The most complete study of this type of personality to date is that of T. W. Adorno, *et al., The Authoritarian Personality* (New York: Harper, 1950).

solitude, of change, of society and the world; of everything except the Jews.[13]

Another writer describes the personality this way:

The individual cannot face the world unflinchingly and in a forthright manner. He seems fearful of himself, of his own instincts, of his own consciousness, of change, and of his social environment. Since he can live in comfort neither with himself nor with others, he is forced to organize his whole style of living, including his social attitudes, to fit his crippled condition. It is not his specific social attitudes that are malformed to start with; it is rather his own ego that is crippled. . . . Prejudice . . . develops as an important incident in the total protective adjustment.[14]

Psychologists trace threat orientation of this sort to early childhood and the home (still chronologically the first and psychologically the most important institution in directing the development of personality). When the need to be loved is fulfilled the child is enabled to respond acceptingly to himself, to develop self-respect because he is respected. But when the need is frustrated by the conditional (or perhaps total) withdrawal of love the child is put on guard lest he fail to meet the conditions upon which parental affection is proffered. He fears the withdrawal of love and concomitantly the loss of his last hope for security. He fears his own power to fulfill the necessary conditions, and he fears the presence within himself of many contrary impulses. These displeasing impulses must be immediately repressed, eventually projected onto others, and always feared. When he cannot be assured of unconditional love and acceptance he must seek to meet whatever conditions are required, for without love he cannot exist as a person. The child is threatened at the very root of his existence.[15] Prejudice is generated in the attempt to deal with this threat. Thus the initial problem is one not of relating to outgroups but of adjusting to oneself, one's failures, fears, inner contradictions, and impulses.

The psychic process by which threat is translated into prejudice is a complex one indeed, but in summary form it is as follows. The insecure individual fears his own inner impulses and inadequacies. He also comes to be threatened by fear itself since that fear is unfocused; i.e., he has nothing visible of which he can be consciously afraid. In order to escape this "vicious

[13] "Portrait of the Antisemite," *Partisan Review*, Spring, 1946, p. 177.

[14] *The Nature of Prejudice*, p. 396.

[15] Further investigation on this point may be pursued in Allport, *The Nature of Prejudice*, pp. 297-311; D. B. Harris, *et al.*, "Children's Ethnic Attitudes: II. Relationship to Parental Beliefs Concerning Child Training," *Child Development*, Sept., 1950, pp. 169-81; Else Frenkel-Brunswik, "Patterns of Social and Cognitive Outlook in Children and Parents," *American Journal of Orthopsychiatry*, July, 1951, pp. 543-58; David P. Ausubel, *Ego Development and the Personality Disorders* (New York: Grune and Stratton, 1952), pp. 262 ff.

circle" of fear he represses his inner conflicts and buries them in the unconscious. A sharp cleavage henceforth develops, separating the conscious from the unconscious. In this alienated state the surface personality, that which the ordinary observer encounters, is radically different from the deeper personality, that which is known only through depth probing (with projective tests or psychoanalytic interviews). The individual must constantly hide from himself since he lacks the inner strength to resolve his alienation. In the process of covering his alienation he employs projective mechanisms through which his own fears and unwanted impulses are cast onto others. (The stereotype of the Negro as oversexed, for example, stems from the failure of the prejudiced person to accept his own sexual drives.) He is exonerated. He can now see the trouble, the threat, as coming from others, i.e., any identifiable and available racial or ethnic outgroup. Thus the social outgroup provides the threatened individual with *something* to fear. Prejudice toward the outgroup develops in the attempt to escape unfocused fear by localizing it. Moreover, one can more easily hide from his own inner impulses if he can perceive them not in himself but in others.

In addition to giving him *something* to fear, however, prejudice plays another role. The threatened personality needs not only to localize or focus his fears; he needs a believable receptacle for his own unacceptable impulses. Since he cannot project personal impulses onto impersonal objects (though animals, especially the dog or snake, sometimes serve) he needs *people* whom he can safely fear and onto whom he can cast his inner fears. Nothing but people will suffice. He has to have a human outgroup, since only persons can be believable culprits. For this reason, among others, no change in the social milieu will remove his basic prejudice. A change in milieu may, of course, require him to change outgroups. If he moves from Mississippi to New York he may abandon fear of the Negro and develop fear of migrants from Puerto Rico. But it continues to be necessary that he have some outgroup which will give focus to his fears and provide a receptacle for his projections.

In all this, it must be remembered, ethnic prejudice is a function of the individual's attempt to adjust to himself and his threatening environment. He "develops" it in response to his own maladjustment. For this reason prejudice rooting in these psychic forces is commonly most intense and impervious to change. In order for it to change, a whole new personality, a new way of life, must be constructed.

But does this process work? Just how effective is prejudice as a chief ingredient in the adjustment of personality? There is evidence that it is helpful in relieving psychic "pain" but not in curing the disease. Clearly, if there were no ego-benefits the alienated personality would not employ projective techniques leading to prejudice. Specifically, prejudice helps the threatened individual by giving him something to fear and an object against which he can take action. He can develop a coherent, even if demonic, view of his world, but it is a view in which the rejected outgroup provides the focal point. (For this reason, incidentally, the problem of race is injected into virtually every conversation by the functionally prejudiced person.) If he can find a social system which gives his beliefs and attitudes a measure of support and reinforcement the prejudiced personality can function in society as a partially productive citizen. In his former more threatened state, of course, he cannot function.

When the prejudicial adjustment is compared to the threat-oriented personality, then, it is clear that prejudice "works" toward making life more livable for the alienated individual. Even so the adjustment is never complete. The prejudiced person finds that he must establish defenses against those who would prevent him from giving expression to his prejudices. A clear example lies in current antipathy toward the federal government, especially in the South—traditionally a region of intense loyalties to country. Inner conflicts arise when the prejudiced personality must include his own government among his list of threatening forces. Even more intense conflict ensues when members of his own family do not share his prejudices.

Not only does the prejudiced personality have to establish additional defenses to protect his prejudice—itself a defense against fear—but also he must find means of covering the guilt and insecurity which result from prejudice. The projection of fears onto others does not remove the unwanted inner impulses which initially gave rise to threat. Prejudice aids only in repressing consciousness of threatening impulses, not in controlling them and modifying their threatening character. One's unassimilated and antisocial sexual drives, his suicidal and homicidal impulses, remain in the subconscious. There they continue to affect behavior and to produce the psychic grounds for guilt over being prejudiced.[16] Speaking of projection as a neurotic device Allport writes:

> It is essentially a neurotic device, and does not fundamentally relieve the sufferers' sense of guilt or establish a lasting self-respect. The hated scapegoat is merely a disguise for persistent and unrecognized self-hatred. A vicious circle is

[16] We cannot here deal adequately with the production of guilt. It comes into being when one's behavior is out of step with his society's ideals. Thus the central theme of Gunnar Myrdal's monumental study, *An American Dilemma,* is the conflict between American democratic ideals and racist practice. The nature and role of guilt is examined also in Waldo Beach, "A Theological Analysis of Race Relations," in Paul Ramsey, ed., *Faith and Ethics* (New York: Harper, 1957), pp. 205-21. See *The Nature of Prejudice,* Chap. 23, "Anxiety, Sex, Guilt," pp. 367-81.

established. The more the sufferer hates himself, the more he hates the scapegoat. But the more he hates the scapegoat, the less sure he is of his logic and his innocence; hence the more guilt he has to project.[17]

Thus, no matter how hard he tries to escape himself through prejudice the threatened individual is unable to hide. Like Adam hiding in the Garden, he knows he is being "found out."

As a method of dealing with threat prejudice leaves the personality with further tensions. While in some respects it aids adjustment, in others it blocks the more complete adjustment. If its effects are to be meaningfully reduced, threat must be dealt with in other ways, ways which will be mentioned in brief at the end of this chapter.

DISCRIMINATION AND ITS EFFECTS

Whatever may be the psychological impact of racial/ethnic prejudice, the social results are numerous. Prejudice, however mild, always expresses itself outwardly. The outward manifestation may be socially inconsequential —as in purely verbal expression—but it may take disastrous and inhuman forms—like efforts to exterminate the outgroup, genocide. Between these extremes there lie many forms of action: paternalism, spatial separation, physical attack, rioting, and lynching.

Though it lies beyond the scope of this chapter to write at length on types of discrimination, "paternalism" is so deceptive and destructive as to demand attention. This term refers to a disposition toward the Negro in which he is patronizingly seen as a ward to be protected, controlled, cared for, much as one would treat a child. Paternalism is perhaps best exemplified in the white attitudes in *Gone with the Wind*. Behaviorally it consists of doing for the "darkey" kind and helpful things, giving him clothes, medicine, or food without charge (though usually in return for some small favor). It includes the willingness to overlook many of his faults, to excuse them. It contains warm sentiments of affection and is usually accompanied by some personal sacrifice on the part of the patron.

Paternalism is among the most inhuman forms of discrimination in that through genuine but conditional affection it would deny full humanity to the Negro. The kindness is offered only when the Negro is willing to remain an "Uncle Tom" and show loyal and dutiful respect—like a child to an adult. Thus as discrimination it denies the humanity of the Negro by removing from his shoulders the burden of adult responsibility. Thereby it denies him the right to mature.

[17] *The Nature of Prejudice,* p. 389.

As an attitude paternalism seems to justify denial of equal opportunity since obviously "Tom" cannot be expected to work at more complex tasks, learn well in school, or know how to vote. As an expression of prejudice paternalism is fundamentally a form of hostility—not on the surface, of course, nor to the Negro in person, but hostility to the Negro as a mature person. As a cover for guilt it is especially effective because the willingness to overlook "Tom's" faults appears to be real love for him. The patron "feels good" for having his "kind" dispositions.

Along with many other forms of prejudicial discrimination paternalism is now fading. When in the wake of the civil rights movement the "child" refuses any longer to be treated as a child the conditional and limited character of the "affection" manifests itself. When rejected, conditional love turns to hate—rather the hatred for the Negro's full humanity bursts through the facade of affection. This fact leads many to observe that relations between the races have deteriorated. In reality, of course, the decay of paternalism is but one more upward step toward greater humanity for the Negro. The "child" is coming of age, and the "parent" is distressed!

Many other devices may be employed in assuring discriminatory treatment of the minority. Common practice in some states at one time allowed use of legislation and the courts to establish patterns of separation. Racially restrictive housing covenants, for example, were enforceable in the courts until 1947 when the U.S. Supreme Court declared them unenforceable.[18] What was formerly done through the courts to segregate is now widely accomplished through "gentlemen's agreement." The Ku Klux Klan devised its own methods of discrimination just as the "black power" advocates are establishing theirs. Whatever the devices, taken together they serve to be mutually reinforcing. Housing covenants produce and sustain ghettos, which produce diminished political voice, which produces educational and environmental disadvantage, which reinforce economic disadvantages. When any particular device of discrimination is coupled with others its net effect is increased.

It cannot be our purpose here to catalog the various types of discriminatory behavior practiced even in a small part of the United States. The facts are being collected and are available elsewhere.[19] It must suffice here simply to note that racial/ethnic discrimination has taken innumerable

[18] *Shelley* v. *Kraemer,* 334 U. S. 1.

[19] Among the best sources are the various publications of the U.S. Commission on Civil Rights with its subsidiary agencies in the states. Though Myrdal is somewhat out of date his work continues to be profitable reading; see *An American Dilemma.* The recent *Report of the National Advisory Commission on Civil Disorders* (U.S. Government Printing Office, 1968) has important data on conditions in urban ghettos.

forms. We must turn to what for our purposes is the more crucial issue, the effects of prejudicial discrimination on the outgroup. In so doing we will use Negro Americans as the primary illustration.

When speaking of the effects of prejudicial discrimination on the Negro one can collect long lists to cover the economic, political, social, familial, educational, and personal dimensions of his existence. But the most telling effects can be known only by enduring the insecurities, the hostilities, and the limitations faced daily by virtually every black man. For that reason the white reader must turn to writers who have faced prejudice and discrimination on the receiving end.[20] Foremost among the losses to prejudice is the effect of racist practice on the person of the victim. Prejudice's first casualty is the very self of the Negro. He is a marked man. He is trapped in a situation not of his own making. He reads signs on gas station doors: "Men," "Women," "Colored." He is threatened by economic, political, and social sanctions as well as by loss of life to midnight visitors. He cannot get certain jobs, not because he is unqualified but because he *is* what he is, a "Negro." Thus it is his very being as a person that is rejected, not just his talents, his ambitions, his job.

It is in this connection that we are to understand the presuppositions of the incalculably important decision of the U.S. Supreme Court in *Brown* v. *Board of Education of Topeka* (347 U.S. 483). The Court declared:

> Segregation of white and Negro children in the public schools of a State solely on the basis of race, pursuant to state laws permitting or requiring such segregation, denies the Negro children the equal protection of the laws guaranteed by the Fourteenth Amendment—even though the physical facilities and other "tangible" factors of white and Negro schools may be equal.

Declaring that the "separate but equal" doctrine adopted in *Plessy* v. *Ferguson* (163 U.S. 537) has no place in the field of public education, the Court continues:

> To separate them [Negro children] from others of similar age and qualifications solely because of their race generates a feeling of inferiority as to their status in the community that may affect their hearts and minds in a way unlikely ever to be undone. . . . Separate educational facilities are inherently unequal.

The Court acknowledges that "education" involves more than physical facilities and other "tangible" factors. It is the individual's own self-estimate, his sense of his own worth as a person, that is involved. Thus the Court im-

[20] For a look at the nonstatistical, human side of discrimination see Richard Wright, *Black Boy* (New York: Harper, 1945), and *Native Son* (Harper, 1940); Claude Brown, *Manchild in the Promised Land* (New York: Macmillan, 1965); James Baldwin, *Nobody Knows My Name* (New York: Dial Press, 1961), and *The Fire Next Time* (Dial Press, 1963).

plicitly recognizes in this decision a fundamental fact of discrimination: its first and most significant casualty is the very person of the victim.

Economic disadvantage, coupled as it is with educational and ego deprivations, ranks a close second in order of importance among the effects of prejudicial discrimination. From the ghettos of the cities to the most remote rural shack the Negro in America is poorer on the average than the white. In consequence he is less able to secure the advanced education which could lead to relief from economic privation. His problem is not merely the lack of jobs. It is that the jobs he can hold tend to be those with lower pay. Facing for life the closed doors of employment in the jobs which require greater education and skill the Negro is short not only on jobs but on the motivation to educate and prepare himself to hold jobs closed to him by racism. A vicious circle operates: on the average the black man has less education than the white; because he is deficient in education fewer jobs are open to him; with fewer jobs open to him he has no strong motive to educate himself. There is evidence now that this circle is being slowed, if not yet reversed, as a result of new opportunity for employment as well as a new chance at higher education. The history of the Negro's economic past remains with us, however, and the biblical adage remains poignantly relevant: "The fathers have eaten sour grapes, and the children's teeth are set on edge" (Jer. 31:29 RSV). This history is being sharply changed since the second World War, thanks largely to increased pressure from the Federal Government and from the Negro community itself. The pressures to desegregate economic opportunity have not been welcomed generally but they are increasingly being accepted as a fact of life. It is interesting to note that those who have long "interfered with" the Negro's economic freedom through segregation now appeal to the philosophy of *laissez faire* (noninterference) in protesting Government action on behalf of the Negro. Paradoxically, the heavy hand of Washington on wages and employment is producing a net increase in economic freedom for the Negro. The black man is less and less being "interfered with."

In addition to the effects of prejudicial discrimination on the ego and on the economic activity of the Negro, a third crucially significant effect is on the Negro family. It is an established fact that Negro families are on the average more unstable than white families and that this fact results in deterioration of the fabric of Negro society. A higher percentage of Negro marriages than white end in divorce or separation, leaving the percentage of Negro women with husbands "absent" more than twice that for white women. Illegitimacy among Negroes (in 1963) was 23.6 percent, while that among whites was 3.07 percent. Almost one fourth of Negro families are headed by females.[21] These are some of the factors which have merged to produce a largely matriarchal family structure within a larger society where patriarchy is the accepted norm. The psychological consequences of this condition, especially for the male child, are severely damaging. More than anywhere else, the roots of these conditions lie in the restricted economic activity of the Negro male. Again, the entire pattern of discrimination produces conditions which perpetuate themselves and lead to further prejudice and discrimination.

THE MORALITY OF PREJUDICIAL DISCRIMINATION

Thus far we have covered, albeit in barest outline, the factual dimensions of racial/ethnic prejudice and discrimination. Our sources have been largely those of the "social sciences." In and of itself scientific social analysis cannot provide the basis for decision-making. Some judgments of value, some commitment to goals, must be added for the development of an ethic. For the Christian the valuational dimension of decisions is provided by theology. Thus it is imperative that we now concern ourselves with the theological morality of racism, prejudice, and discrimination. This theological analysis will then serve in the final section as the basis for a Christian approach to social action in the area of race relations.

A theological interpretation stands on the same level as alternative analytical schemes. It is one among several ways of viewing the facts of prejudicial behavior. Employing the categories of the clinician the psychologist interprets racism as a psychological abnormality born of the subject's failures to adjust to himself and others. Similarly sociologists, like Gunnar Myrdal, understand prejudicial discrimination in another theoretical frame of reference. A Marxist philosopher interprets the racist phenomenon as a manifestation of economic class competition. Rationalists seek to understand racism as a product of men's failure to gain accurate information. In each case those who interpret the facts concerning racial/ethnic attitudes and practices bring to the facts their own theoretical framework. Since these frameworks are never entirely compatible with one another, the diagnoses of the malady differ. Consequently, as diagnosticians they differ on their recommendations for treatment. Even more important are the differences among the analysts concerning their ideological reasons for dealing with racism. We will approach racism as a problem from a Christian theological frame of reference. Insofar as there is conflict

[21] For a comprehensive report on the Negro family see *The Negro Family* (Office of Policy Planning and Research, U.S. Department of Labor, 1965). This is the controversial "Moynihan Report."

between a Christian analysis and a rationalist, psychological, or Marxist analysis, that conflict is a conflict in world view, in perspective on the nature of man and his world.

From the Christian standpoint none of the alternative interpretations is adequate. Several observations lead, for instance, to the conclusion that the rationalist position is inadequate. For one thing, it is apparent that correct information about racial/ethnic characteristitcs fails to erase prejudicial behavior. Men "know better but do worse." Nor is prejudice significantly reduced when the prejudiced person is given new information about prejudice itself. He may be well informed about the nature and grounds of prejudice as well as about outgroups and still retain his prejudicial attitudes. Indeed, part of the difficulty of getting at prejudice through the imparting of information is that the prejudiced mind builds mental barriers around itself, barriers which valid information cannot scale. Information which does enter the mind is twisted, often unconsciously, by the prejudiced personality to serve his own purposes. These observations, then, suggest that while deficient information is involved in racism, it has the character of a symptom rather than a cause.

Similar problems inhere in sociological, Marxist, and psychological frames of reference. But the crucial defect, from the theological standpoint, is that none of them includes the "vertical" dimension of human life. It is inescapable for the theologian that no aspect of human life can be understood purely in terms of men's relations with other men or themselves. To this "horizontal" dimension the theologian adds the "vertical," man's relation to God as the very ground of his existence. Indeed, for the Christian it is man's relation to God which alone provides a final frame of reference for comprehending man's relation with man. The vertical and the horizontal are understood to be complementary. Men's relations with men are viewed always as expressions not merely of their ideas, nor of their economic interests, nor of their psyche, but of their commitment. In the Christian view men's actions are the product of their devotions, of that to which men "give" themselves. Racism, therefore, is interpreted in light of God.

The Christian could readily agree with Allport when he theorizes that "love-prejudice is far more basic to human life than its opposite, hate-prejudice." His claim is that "one must first overestimate the things one loves before one can underestimate their contraries."[22] Racial/ethnic prejudice does precisely that in loving too much oneself, one's own characteristics, and those persons thought to be like oneself. The thing loved too little is the outgroup, those thought to be

[22] *The Nature of Prejudice,* p. 25.

different from oneself. The presupposition Allport is making here is that love is in some sense a key to understanding prejudice. With that judgment we heartily agree. But to that judgment the Christian adds the further proposition that the *basis* of man's inordinate love of himself is to be found in his failure to love God. It is man's alienation from God that results in his other wrong perspectives. Having rejected the very ground of his being, man is inevitably insecure and must find a god-substitute. Thus in the place of God he establishes himself and those he regards as like himself. In the final analysis, then, for the theologian prejudice is ultimately not merely a moral lapse, a cultural lag, or a psychological abnormality. Racial/ethnic prejudice is an idolatry. Racism is ultimately a judgment of faith, a commitment, a trust in something. Functionally it is a way of "salvation," and as such it is vital. That is to say, racist ideology is affirmed always as a way to make life whole, sensible, or meaningful. Under these conditions race has the function of a god.

In biblical fashion the Christian theologian finds the key to understanding racism, prejudice, and discrimination in the concept of sin. The fundamental fact of human existence is that men live in a state of separation from God, the humanizing ground of life, the source of meaning in existence, and the fountain from which flows the grace which alone leads to true human fulfillment. This claim presupposes the Christian's commitment to God, not to orderly social and psychological process, as the ultimately real. Life is complete only when man stands in acknowledged union with God. In disunion—i.e., sin—man is cut off, his life is groundless. Consequently he is insecure. He must find some kind of meaning, purpose, or foundation. He thus seeks out a new ground, an ultimate in which he can put his trust and from which he can derive security, solace, and support. That is to say that he looks for a "deity" to which he can give himself, i.e., in which he can have faith.[23] Sometimes he enthrones his nation, sometimes his region, his smaller in-groups, his ideologies. The racist is one who enthrones his racial/ethnic group. It is thus from his racial/ethnic group that he derives, functionally speaking, the security, purpose, and sense of self-righteousness which otherwise might have come as gifts of God. It is not surprising, therefore, that he holds to racism with a tenacity and intensity of devotion approaching, and sometimes surpassing, religious fanaticism.

Yet in all this the racist never escapes God entirely. Instead he enthrones a part of God's created order. But by deifying a part of the good creation, by giving a segment of God's work the loyalty due properly only to

[23] Here one might refer to Part One, the selection by Reinhold Niebuhr, "Man as Sinner."

God himself, he corrupts and defiles the creation. So it is that the racist never fully appreciates racial differences and cannot have genuine racial pride. (This is the flaw inherent not merely in lily-white purism but also in black nationalism!) He destroys the possibility of a humanizing and enriching appreciation of his racial membership by making it the be-all and end-all of his existence. A value overvalued loses its real value, since an overvaluation is as false to reality as an undervaluation. Thus the racist can never truly value his own racial/ethnic characteristics. By overvaluing a part of the good creation he thus corrupts its goodness.

The racist, then, is one who in idolatrous fashion transforms racial pride into rac*ism*. It is by the same process in other men that regional pride is lost when converted to region-al*ism*. The same consequence attends the corruption of loyalty to nation into national*ism*, of scientific inquiry into scient*ism*, of corporate living into commun*ism*, of individuality into individual*ism*. In each case a healthy awareness and appreciation of differences, differences inherent in God's plan, becomes infected by the sick elevation of differences into superiorities.

The person in whom these diseases are found is, of course, one who has a weakened sense of his own person, his own identity. Being alienated from his Creator, and hence losing his true potential as a person, he requires inordinate assurance of his own worth. He cannot be a true patriot who recognizes the distinctiveness of his own nation in the community of distinctive nations; his weak personality demands that he see his as exclusively the best nation. Thus, the key quality is that he is an exclusivist. His world cannot be a both-and world; it has to be an either-or world. His morality cannot be an I-thou morality; it has to be an I-it morality since he has by devaluing his neighbor depersonalized him. He divides human beings into warring factions: either they or we must *win*. Life is a war to be fought, not a peace to be enjoyed.

Racism fits into this scheme of things. For the personality alienated from God racism functions as a means of "salvation" in at least the following ways:

(1) It identifies "Satan" and the source of all the trouble in the world. In the outgroup he can find all evil lurking.

(2) It provides for him a sense of purpose, *viz.*, to fight the *battle* of life on the side of purity and goodness. His "cause" is to protect the sacred ingroup against the inroads of the demonic outgroup.

(3) It provides a sense of his own righteousness and personal worth. "Look at me," he says in effect. "I am fighting a holy war on the side of God." (In this context it is not surprising to find overtly religious and liturgical ingredients in such organi-

zations as the Klan or the Black Muslims.)

(4) It provides for comradeship, a sense of participating in a larger community of interest. "I am not alone in the struggle. I can count on the continued support of my comrades who are in this movement with me."

(5) It provides heroes ("saints") for his emulation. Racist leaders give fleshly expression to ideals. (Doubtless this has played an important role in the political success of certain Southern demagogues!)

(6) It provides an all-encompassing world view which generates a kind of cosmic order out of his chaotic world. All world problems and issues can be placed in perspective through the use of the single lens of racism.

(7) It provides the opportunity for self-sacrifice. The racist can give himself up to the cause and thus find an expression for his self-rejecting (suicidal) tendencies.

In these and other ways racism as a faith, albeit an idolatrous faith, serves its devotee. It is for him a way of "salvation" since it saves him from purposelessness, worthlessness, and unrighteousness. He might find his salvation by some other devotion. Some men similarly are "saved" by communism, and others are saved by capitalism. Still others enthrone such things as absolute codes of conduct (religious fundamentalism and Moral Re-Armament, for example), conservative or liberal political philosophies, or systems of economic production and distribution. Whatever the deity, it is drawn from the finite world of men's minds and always constitutes a violation of what Tillich has called the "Protestant Principle."

In every phase of such an analysis the theologian presupposes that authentic life and faith are to be found in God alone. This presupposition, which we wish here not to justify but to acknowledge, is the basis for all Christian ethics. As a preface to all Christian ethical thought there stands Augustine's famous dictum: "Thou hast made us for Thyself, and our heart is restless until it repose in Thee." [24]

In the perspective of Christian faith, then, racism is to be understood as one among many demonic and socially destructive manifestations of a deeper problem—man's alienation from God, the very ground in which man's life must be planted and by whose grace that life can be made whole. So understood, racism is an inauthentic way of life, an ultimate faith not in God but in a quality of personal existence. As such it stands always and without exception contrary to the will and purpose of God. Racism is thus evil in principle, in its own right, and without regard to its social consequences.[25] This is not to deny that its

[24] *Confessions,* Bk. I.

[25] A brief methodological note: In the "situation ethic" of Joseph Fletcher no such claim would be possible. His approach leaves him with a purely "consequential" ethic in which nothing (save "love-

consequences are evil in themselves, as we hope to demonstrate shortly. It is simply to leave no doubt that racism as a way of life and love is inimical to God's design for man and thus constitutes an evil to be eradicated. It means further that racial/ethnic prejudice and discrimination, the handmaidens of racism, are in like manner contrary to the will of God and are similarly to be eradicated. It is in these convictions that there lies the primary imperative for Christian social action in the area of relations between racial/ethnic groups.

Regardless of the firmness of that imperative, however, the human results of racism, those human sufferings attendant upon every expression of racist devotion, also demand loving action of the Christian. The ill-effects of racism on the victim of prejudice have been amply described by the various reports and scholarly studies already mentioned. These effects may be summed up as the denial to the outgroup of their equal right to be.[26] Whatever specific form discrimination may take, it deprives the outgroup of opportunities for education, political participation, and economic activity, as well as all the opportunities for personal growth afforded by "first class" citizenship. The American Indian herded onto reservations or harrassed in Carolina by the Klan, or the Negro squeezed into ghettos or beaten into unconsciousness by Mississippi "lawmen," or the Japanese incarcerated in concentration camps in World War II—whatever the group or the mode of discrimination—is denied opportunities which are both constitutionally and morally his. He is the victim of an unjust social system and as such constitutes a "neighbor" to whom the Christian has specific obligation.

The Christian's obligation is to take action toward repairing, and finally eliminating, the very social institutions which deny the neighbor the opportunity to become more completely a person. *Every Christian is thus obliged to work toward the total elimination of racial/ethnic segregation and the racist ideology which underlies that social system.* If he does not he is disobedient to God's command of love.

Special attention should be paid to the phrase "total elimination of racial/ethnic segregation." This is to say that for the Christian a person's

lessness") can be in and of itself, i.e., in principle, wrong. Our method, which we have called "principled contextualism," makes the assumption that whatever stands contrary to the divine purpose as seen in Jesus as the Christ is evil regardless of its consequences. If good grows from an evil act the good result does not make the act good, nor does it credit the actor. If an evil act produces good results it serves only to manifest God's goodness and lordship in bringing good out of evil. Racism as intrinsically evil *also* has social consequences which participate in the evil of racism itself. Our point methodologically is that it is not *merely* the consequences of acts which make them evil.

[26] This is the claim also of Kyle Haselden, *The Racial Problem in Christian Perspective* (New York: Harper, 1959), p. 143.

race is irrelevant in all circumstances whether for employment, voting, the country club, or marriage. Since marriage between whites and blacks is usually regarded as the final hurdle in desegregation, we can clarify the Christian norm by using racial intermarriage as the illustration. It must be clearly stated that there can be no theological or Christian basis for disallowing marriage between two people simply because one is white and the other black. Indeed, to object to marriage between the races is the ultimate in denying humanity to the outgroup. It presupposes him to be of a lower order of life. By the same token, to marry a person *because* he is white or black is to deny his humanity or personhood and make of him a "thing," a white or a black. Theologically it is clear that to object in principle to marriage between white and black is to assume that one's racial membership is more important than one's sonship to God. For the Christian standing under God's equal love for all human beings, then, distinctions of racial or ethnic sorts are irrelevant in *all* affairs of life.[27]

Racism as an ideology and practice in whatever form violates the "first and great commandment": "Thou shalt love the Lord with all thy heart" (Matt. 22:37-9). Racism relegates some neighbors to inferior status and as such constitutes a refusal to love as equal that which God loves equally. One who loves God with "all his heart" cannot but love that which God loves. One who loves God finds God's love for men reproducing itself in him. (And that claim is not a doctrinaire judgment of theory but a report on the experience of Christians!) So it is that God's concern that men should have life and have it abundantly becomes the concern of men who love God. This fact leads to the imperative for all those who call themselves Christian. God's grace (loving concern for human beings) produces love (*agape*) in the man of faith.

It must be recalled from Part One that the love of the Christian for men is not permissive but imperative in tone. Ethically speaking, God's love is received as command. The content of *agape* is not to be confused with a romantic sentiment, an inner feeling of good wishes. Racial paternalism, long sincerely practiced in the South, is but one result of this confusion of *agape* with romance. But romantic sentiment, no matter how deeply felt, cannot properly be interpreted as the primary thrust of *agape*. *Agape,* rather, demands that the Christian *serve* the neighbor no matter what may be his sentimental or fraternal likes or dislikes. Christian love, then, is a positive disposition of will; it is

[27] We are well aware of the alleged biblical objection to interracial marriage. This objection is based on a misreading of Ezra and Nehemiah, who forbade cross-cultural marriages in order to preserve the decaying Hebrew culture. See Everett Tilson, *Segregation and the Bible,* pp. 29-40.

the determination to see the neighbor's needs met.

In race relations, therefore, *agape* demands action appropriate to securing the rights of the racial/ethnic outgroup to full participation in society. *Agape* demands that the Christian seek to eliminate racial/ethnic discrimination in every form. This demand constitutes, in the "context" of racial/ethnic discrimination, one of the "principles" which must inform Christian action. Though particular approaches, programs, or methods of attack cannot be specified without further recourse to concrete facts of particular situations, the duty under *agape* to end discrimination cannot be gainsaid.

Thus racism, prejudice, and discrimination are violations of the will of God. Racism is inherently evil because it is a form of idolatry. Prejudice and discrimination are evil because they deny men the equal opportunity to be full persons. Acting out of the imperative demands of God's will, then, the Christian must find fitting ways to act, programs and policies which "fit" the situation in which he seeks to be obedient. In the final section we present a brief note on methods of acting to end prejudicial discrimination.

SOCIAL ACTION AND RACISM

Among the first principles for the Christian engaging in acts designed to change the social structure is that his concern is broader than the perspective which may be required of others engaging in similar activity. Whatever program he may undertake, the Christian must act responsibly to all men, i.e., in response to his duty toward the racist as well as toward the victim of racism. This apparent contradiction in duty does not commonly plague black nationalist groups or the Klan. Moreover, while the universal responsibility of the Christian may appear to be contradictory it is never in fact so if love is properly understood. Note, for example, that the segregationist, like the Negro victim, is dehumanized by racist practice. The segregationist, by denying full humanity to some men to that extent denies his own humanity. He is rendered less capable of the mutual relationships which make for "community" and hence for the fulfillment of life in society. Moreover, the dual facilities demanded by segregation are costly in dollars and cents. The underdeveloped human resources of the outgroup deprive any region of its most important key to social, political, educational, and economic progress. In the final analysis, then, the real and long-term needs of the segregationist are the same as the real needs of the victim: an open social system in which both may become human.

Though the real and long-term *needs* are the same, the espoused *interests* and *aims* of the segregationist conflict with the interests and aims of the victim. The victim is interested in increased opportunity and a better life. The segregationist is interested in preserving the status quo in discrimination. From this it follows that among the Christian's initial responsibilities is that of demonstrating the common human needs in order that they may become common interests. But even when he fails in this—as most of the time he does—his obligation is always to the real needs, not the felt needs, of all concerned. The object of policy is the establishment of an open and humane social system. In this fashion the Christian's obligation is universal. But in some situations it becomes necessary for the relevant actor to "take sides" and to act in ways which will be interpreted by detractors as partial and exclusive. If, for example, a public demonstration at a segregated business is chosen as the fitting act it will appear that the Christian protester is "against" the racist businessman. In fact, of course, his protest is against the segregationist policy of that businessman, a policy which is finally detrimental both to the business and to the excluded victim. Whatever interpretation may be given his actions, the Christian must seek to change the action of those who discriminate against racial/ethnic minorities. In so doing his effort constitutes a judgment on the sin of the discriminator as well as a redemptive force for justice to the victim.

Care must be taken here, however, to avoid the erroneous assumption that in concrete situations the decisions are easy. Most concrete decisions call for the exercise of preferential love by which one must "prefer" one neighbor over others. The real needs of the businessman for economic well-being, for example, may have to be temporarily sacrificed in order that greater justice may be achieved for the Negro. Christians can never make these hard choices with an easy conscience. We are finally dependent upon divine grace when it appears necessary that we violate the immediate needs of one neighbor in favor of the immediate needs of another. The claims in the preceding paragraphs do not remove the burden of hard choice: they remind us that we have duty even to the unjust, the bigot, the segregationist. Thus it is the very fact of universal obligation which creates the necessity for preferential love. Preferential love obligates the Christian to do the relatively better, not the perfectly good. In the real world of nuts and bolts the perfectly good act is never open to creatures.

In social action, then, the Christian's obligation is universal. But by what method does the Christian engage in social action? What concrete forms may his action take? The answer is: any "fitting" form. Protest marches, for example, may be required to change some racist practice. Demonstrations have as their primary aim to call public attention to discrimination. Their force is the force of conscience, and their effectiveness is limited to those social systems in which humane consciences have been formed to which appeal might be made. Unfortunately, in some sections of the United States consciences have been formed in such fashion as to make *de*segregation unconscionable. Under these circumstances demonstration is of little effect save on citizens in other parts of the land and via the news media.

When economic sanctions, in the form of boycott or selective buying, are added to demonstrations another kind of force is applied. Whereas simple demonstrations have their appeal to conscience, selective buying makes appeal to the profit motive. As such it is inherently more overt. Political action is similarly overt. Registration of voters and efforts to secure their direct and full participation in the democratic process, as well as suits in the courts, make appeal to the systems of government and their overt force. Conscience and economic sanctions are present, but in political action they are secondary to another kind of power. Some conditions demand still more forceful action, including violence and revolution. The Civil War is one instance in which no other means than armed might was capable of effecting justice.

It has been claimed by a sizable minority of Christians over the centuries that only nonviolent means are appropriate instruments for Christian action. In race relations Dr. Martin Luther King, through the Southern Christian Leadership Conference, applied that principle to social action. While it is not entirely clear in Dr. King's writings just how absolutely he framed the principle of nonviolence, we cannot divorce nonviolence as a method from the situation in which it is to be employed. Where nonviolence is appealing to a society and where it "works," i.e., where it is effective in achieving the desired social change, it is a more fitting tactic than violence. But in situations where it cannot be effective in achieving greater justice it clearly cannot be the basis for a Christian social policy. To use nonviolence as a method in situations where it will not apply is to assume nonviolence to be in *principle* right. Since justice to men is more important that the principle of nonviolence Christians in some situations may be required to engage in violent action.[28] Thus nonviolence has the status of a conditionally superior

[28] Just for an example, consider the duty of a Christian who arrives at the scene of a would-be bombing just in time to prevent it, *if* he is willing to resort to violent means. If he can prevent injury or death to the would-be victim only by physical attack upon the person with the bomb, *only* violence is the fitting response.

tactic, not a binding principle of action.[29]

It is apparent, then, that the specific duty of the Christian, the peculiar form which action must take in a given situation, cannot be spelled out in advance; but in response to the divine command to love (serve), no action, including violence and killing, can be ruled out in principle. Similarly no *action* can be selected in advance. This is the Christian truth vitally present in that ethical method now commonly called "situation ethics." [30] Thus with the duty to end racism and with an open society as his immediate goal already established, the Christian must find a tactic which is effective or "fitting." [31]

A POSTSCRIPT

Social action by the Christian may lead to success or to failure in the cause of greater justice. When he succeeds he is open to the temptation of pride over his own accomplishment. When he fails he is open to despair. When he both succeeds and fails, as he ordinarily does, he endures a kind of perpetual inner torment and uncertainty. Under such conditions the active Christian rediscovers the truth of the doctrine of *sola gratia* (by grace alone). When he is honest he knows that his success is built on his having received from God a liberating grace. When he fails he knows that the same liberating grace operates, saving him from paralyzing despair. Thus the Christian's final obligation is not to succeed but to be obedient. Though he is obliged to make every effort toward effective social change his life is not dependent upon his success in pursuing that goal. Christian experience of "justification by grace" is thus both the beginning and the end of moral action. It is grace which frees him to act and grace which sustains him in and through his action. His final claim is not that "we shall overcome," but that "God in his grace will remake men."

---

[29] For further development of this theme see Louis W. Hodges, "Christian Ethics and Non-Violence," *Religion in Life,* Spring, 1962.

[30] Perhaps a note here will avoid confusion. We have claimed above (p. 317) that racism, along with its attendant prejudice and discrimination, is in principle a violation of the divine command. Here we are claiming that no *action* can be said to be intrinsically or in principle right. In the former case reference is made to a way of being, i.e., idolatry; in the latter case we are talking of concrete acts in particular situations. We are claiming, then, that *under the principle of duty to end racism*—itself right intrinsically—no form of action commensurate with that principle can be ruled out (or in). An act might be ruled out because it is ineffective toward reaching the goal of a humane society, but never because it violates some absolutized biblical or ecclesiastical injunction.

[31] Reference here might be made to some criteria listed above (pp. 262-64) in the chapter on "Dissent."

Index

Page numbers in italics indicate that the reference is to a footnote.